CORE

LEGO® MINDSTORMS™
Programming

BRIAN BAGNALL

ISBN 0-13-009364-5

Prentice Hall PTR,
Upper Saddle River, NJ 07458
www.phptr.com

A CIP catalog record for this book can be obtained from the Library of Congress.

Editorial/Production Supervision: *MetroVoice Publishing Services*
Executive Editor: *Greg Doench*
Editorial Assistant: *Brandt Kenna*
Marketing Manager: *Debby VanDijk*
Manufacturing Manager: *Alexis Heydt-Long*
Cover Design: *Talar Agasyan-Boorujy*
Cover Design Direction: *Jerry Votta*
Art Director: *Gail Cocker-Bogusz*
Series Design: *Meg VanArsdale*

 © 2002 Prentice Hall PTR
A division of Pearson Education, Inc.
Upper Saddle River, NJ 07458

Prentice Hall books are widely used by corporations and government agencies for training, marketing, and resale.

The publisher offers discounts on this book when ordered in bulk quantities.
For more information, contact: Corporate Sales Department, Phone: 800-382-3419;
Fax: 201-236-7141; Email: corpsales@prenhall.com; or write: Prentice Hall PTR,
Corp. Sales Dept., One Lake Street, Upper Saddle River, NJ 07458.

Printed in the United States of America

10 9 8 7 6 5 4 3 2 1

ISBN 0-13-009364-5

Pearson Education Ltd.
Pearson Education Australia PTY Ltd.
Pearson Education Singapore, Pte. Ltd.
Pearson Education North Asia Ltd.
Pearson Education Canada, Ltd.
Pearson Educación de Mexico, S.A. de C.V.
Pearson Education—Japan
Pearson Education Malaysia, Pte. Ltd.

Contents

2   GETTING STARTED WITH LEJOS 46

Preface

There are 718 LEGO pieces in the latest version of the Robotics Invention System. Depending on how you look at it, 718 can either seem like a large number or a small number. In the grand scheme of things, 718 seems like a small number to me. Of those pieces, 129 are unique LEGO parts (not including color differences). Looking around me, I'd say the Robotics Invention System can build a decent representation of just about everything in this room. It can build a desk, a chair, a primitive speaker, a spinning globe, a blender, a clock (digital or analog), or probably even a simulation of a CD player. Outside my domain, the kit could produce models of automobiles, subway cars, boats, or almost any man-made machine. Looking to nature, it could create simulations of spiders, ants, scorpions, dogs, cats, and whales. True, the kit by itself can't reproduce everything in the world. It can't reproduce the envelope of a helium balloon or a complete BMW assembly line, but the things it can't do are far outweighed by the things it can. And there are probably things it can build that no one has ever thought of! I'm going to go out on a limb and estimate that 718 pieces can create an infinite number of models. From this logic, it's easy to see that 718 equals infinity.

It's no exaggeration to say that LEGO MINDSTORMS has done for robots what Henry Ford did for automobiles. LEGO has managed to put robots in the hands of ordinary people. The standardized parts and common languages means sharing of ideas in robotics is happening on a scale that has never occurred before. A brief search of the web to shows just how much MINDSTORMS has permeated through cyberspace.

If you already own the Robotics Invention System, congratulations! You have almost everything you need to create some amazing robots. The only remaining tool you need is a truly powerful programming language, and that is what this book will present to you. The language is Java, one of the most universally accepted programming languages in computers today, and this book will show how to use Java to push MINDSTORMS to the limit.

This book is not a compilation of projects, (of which there are several good ones on the market). The aim of this book it to give you the knowledge and tools you need to turn your ideas into reality, not someone elses. All the projects in this book are presented because they have some sort of lasting value. If this book has done its job, hopefully you will be surprised by what you didn't know MINDSTORMS could do.

This book will also solve the greatest mystery of the MINDSTORMS kit— what the grey foot-pedal looking part is for (see Figure below). To my knowledge, no one has yet discovered what this part does or how it is used. Not even the actual LEGO MINDSTORMS engineers who designed the part understand what it is for. Chapter 5 will answer this age old mystery.

About this Book

Chapter 1 is an introduction to the Robotics Invention System. This chapter covers just the main components of the kit, including software, the RCX brick, and the IR tower. It also introduces other kits and products that can expand your MINDSTORMS universe.

Chapter 2 is a basic introduction to leJOS, the Java platform for the RCX brick. It covers a bit of background on leJOS, the basic features that distinguish it from other RCX development tools, and instructions on how to install leJOS as well as a powerful IDE.

Figure 1   The mystery part.

Chapter 3 is a high-speed introduction to Java. Those who are familiar with Java may opt to just skim the Notes and Warnings, which point out differences between leJOS Java and Sun's Java.

Chapter 4 demonstrates, through code examples, how to access motors, sensors, and other components of the RCX brick using Java.

Chapter 5 is an encyclopedia of the Robotics Invention System parts. It goes through each of the 129 unique parts of the kit so you can put a name to the part and identify all the uses. If you ever wondered what the other versions of the kit contained, this is where you can find out. There is also a section on common LEGO structures that will help you to rapidly build key structures.

Chapter 6 introduces the concept of Behavior Control programming, a technique of programming insect level, behavior based intelligence. The leJOS API contains several classes for programming your own behavior control, making this an easy and powerful addition to robotics programming.

Chapter 7 begins the concept of navigation. The first part of the chapter lays out the fundamental concepts of navigation and tries to impress upon the reader a true understanding of just what it is about navigation that makes it so difficult for robots. It then moves on to real world examples of navigation programming using leJOS.

Chapter 8 continues the topic of navigation, but this time using a pair of rotation sensors to achieve even more accurate navigation than possible with timing methods.

Chapter 9 presents unique ways of detecting objects before the robot collides with them. The first part of the chapter shows how to build a simple proximity detector using only the pieces contained in the kit. More ambitious MINDSTORMS users can build an accurate distance sensor from raw electronic components. I have endeavored to make the instructions for assembly as clear, simple and precise as possible so even those completely unfamiliar with electronics will be able build this powerful sensor. The last part of this chapter shows how to build a classic robot project, the wall follower.

Chapter 10 is the third and final chapter dealing with navigation. This chapter shows how to assemble a compass sensor, which is useful for determining the orientation of the robot using the earths magnetic field. Though more difficult than the proximity sensor, this sensor worked the very first time I plugged the components into the bread board, so most readers shouldn't encounter any problems with this project.

Chapter 11 introduces the topic of communications. The RCX is capable of communicating with other devices that use Infrared signals. This includes the PC, the LEGO Remote Control, and other RCX bricks. The powerful java.io API is available on the leJOS platform, making communications with a PC that much easier. This chapter also shows how to control the RCX brick from a PC across the Internet using a remote program, an embedded applet, or from a plain old web page.

Chapter 12, the final chapter of the book, covers advanced topics. Here you can learn everything you never wanted to know about leJOS. Since memory is always on the mind of an RCX programmer, this chapter describes memory saving strategies that can help you squeeze that last little bit of code on board the RCX. Another interesting aspect of the leJOS JVM is that Java is not the only language that it can execute! The leJOS JVM is also capable of running other languages, such as Forth, NetRexx, and dozens of others. There is also a writeup on how to port leJOS to other processors, something for only the most advanced users.

The appendices will give you some valuable information on leJOS and the RCX. There is a section on ordering sensors, kits, and other parts you may not even have known existed. Ordering electronics parts can be such an artform that an entire Appendix is dedicated to this topic. There is also a section on the burgeoning utilities available for leJOS. Finally, no book on LEGO MINDSTORMS would be complete without a section of web resources.

Companion Web Site

This book has a companion Web site to provide you with updates and other material. It is located at *www.phptr.com/bagnall*.

Acknowledgments

I'd like to express my sincere gratitude to Cay for allowing this book to become part of his Core series of books. I hope the material in this book is up to the high standards set by Core Java and the rest of the series. Thanks also to Greg Doench for coordinating the creation of this snazzy looking book, Eileen Clark for answering all my questions, and MetroVoice for formatting and editing the manuscript. Rendering the instructions for the robots turned out to be more difficult than first anticipated, so special thanks to Harold Cabrera and Jeff Gillespie for persevering through the long and gruelling process.

The electronics projects presented in Chapters 9 and 10 are from two brilliant minds, Philippe "Philo" Hurbain and Claude Baumann. Aside from his other accomplishments, Philo displayed considerable ingenuity to overcome the power limitations of the RCX when designing the proximity sensor interface. Philo definitely has a finely tuned creative spirit. Claude is not only an administrator at a school for young people in Luxembourg, he is also an amateur electronics hobbyist and roboticist. Looking over some of the projects he has organized for these young people makes me wish I attended his school! Thanks to both for helping with the multitude of problems that seemed to crop up for each project. Please feel free to visit their websites, listed in Appendix D, for more examples of their creativity.

Thanks to all those people involved in open source projects. So many excellent software packages would not exist without these people who take time out of their personal lives to create something excellent for the rest of us. Thanks to Jose for spawning leJOS, my favorite open source project bar none. Jose also provided the technical review for this book, and his comments were extremely valuable. Thanks also to Paul Andrews and Jürgen Stuber, who have been leading the leJOS project since Jose "semi-retired" from the scene. Both deserve credit for many large improvements made to leJOS. There are also other open source projects that deserve special mention. LDraw & MLCad are supreme pieces of software for LEGOmaniacs who want to share their models with the rest of the world. The creator of LDraw, James Jessiman, is tragically no longer with us but his program lives on as a tribute to his creativity.

Finally, enormous thanks to LEGO for producing the product that started it all!

—Brian Bagnall

MEET MINDSTORMS

Chapter 1

For the uninitiated, MINDSTORMS might seem like nothing more than a toy, but for inventors, MINDSTORMS plays a more serious role in prototyping. LEGO's Robotics Invention System (RIS) contains all the parts necessary to build and verify the basic design of almost any mechanical invention. This chapter better acquaints you with the major components in the RIS. We look in depth at the RCX computer brick that lies at the center of all MINDSTORMS robots, as well as the official software and electrical parts included. This chapter presents some hands-on projects and experiments to give you firsthand experience of the tools available. Finally, we explore other kits available in the world of MINDSTORMS that can significantly expand your ability to turn your robotic inspirations into reality.

Enter MINDSTORMS

Before LEGO MINDSTORMS it was daunting for a hobbyist to experiment with robotics. Thankfully, LEGO MINDSTORMS has opened up the world of robotics to a larger audience. You can now spend a reasonable amount of money for one of the coolest kits ever devised and within an hour you can be on your way to piecing together your wildest robot creations. It's as if you were given the paints, brushes, and canvas and now you can focus solely on your creative spirit. Before MINDSTORMS, it would have been like collecting minerals and plant dyes, mixing them with oils to create different colors, and mashing up wood into pulp to create paper. MINDSTORMS gives you everything you need to create complex robots *without* the complexity, and with the high degree of quality people have come to expect from LEGO. For people who are yearning to build robots, the kit is revolutionary.

The MINDSTORMS concept was developed by a partnership of the LEGO Group and the Massachusetts Institute of Technology (MIT). The MIT Media Laboratory had been developing a project they called the *Programmable Brick* since about 1987, with heavy sponsorship from the LEGO Group. The main force behind these designs was Fred G. Martin, and between 1987 and 1998 he turned out about four different versions of the Programmable Brick. The final version is a big red brick with four output ports for motors and six input ports for sensors (see Figure 1–1). This version of the Programmable Brick is actually slightly more advanced than the LEGO RCX brick because of the extra ports available, but presumably it drains batteries faster when more devices are hooked up to it.

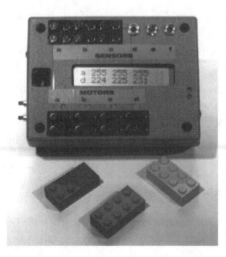

Figure 1–1   The MIT Programmable Brick.

The LEGO Group itself redesigned the RCX brick from the ground up, meaning they used none of the technology developed at MIT, other than basic design philosophy. The result is both sleek and functional. MINDSTORMS was first unveiled commercially in 1998, saving LEGO from a slump in profits. LEGO has stated that 1998 was the first year they did not make a profit since the company was founded in the 1930s. They were able to sell about 80,000 kits for about $200 (U.S.) each in the first three months! The popularity of the kit, especially among technically savvy adults, is at least partially responsible for turning fortunes around at LEGO. At the end of 1998 things were looking much more positive, and 1999 saw the company recover to profitability. With success like that, it is almost guaranteed that MINDSTORMS will continue to evolve for a long time to come.

The Robotics Invention System

MINDSTORMS is actually a family of products from LEGO embracing computer-controlled robotics. At the center of the MINDSTORMS universe is the RIS, a kit that contains more than 700 individual parts. The system allows even nonengineers to piece together a robotic creation using standard LEGO parts such as bricks, pulleys, and gears. In fact, the kit is so easy to use that LEGO suggests it for children ages 12 and up (though the average MINDSTORMS owner is 30). The RIS kit includes motors and sensors, giving LEGO models the ability to move and sense external conditions. Once assembly is complete, even people with limited programming knowledge can sit in front of a desktop computer and program the brains of a LEGO robot. The program is then fed to the robot and it is free to wreak chaos. Like LEGO itself, the concept is simple and brilliant.

LEGO has developed a five-step process they advocate for creating your own robot. This process allows you to focus your attention on each important phase of robot creation. From start to finish, these steps are:

1. **Brainstorm.** Using your imagination, think of the functionality of your robot, and visualize what it will look like.
2. **Build.** Create a chassis for the robot, attach LEGO parts, and connect motors and sensors to the RCX. This is the phase where your design becomes "LEGOized."
3. **Program.** Using your PC, program the logic that will determine the behavior of your robot. This is the step that many people especially savor, because you are infusing your creation with a mind of its own.
4. **Download.** Transfer the program code from your PC to the RCX brick using the infrared transmitter.
5. **Activate.** This is the moment of truth, when you find out if your construction and programming will stand up to the rigors of reality. Usually you will go back to Step 2 or 3 and repeat the process as many times as it takes to perfect your robot.

The RIS kit supplies you with everything you need to accomplish each of these goals. Let's briefly review the major components in the RIS kit and how they can help you achieve your goals. It is a good idea to install the LEGO software if you wish to complete some of the exercises in this chapter, but if you'd rather use a more advanced language right away, feel free to skip the exercises.

Tip:

My only problem with the RIS 1.0 CD software is that it forces you to complete the entire guided tour, step by step, without changing the order of the modules. It does not let you skip any lessons you already know or don't care to tackle. Even worse, you cannot get to the programming environment until you have viewed the entire tutorial, which takes about two hours. You may feel like exploring the programming environment after the first lesson on programming, but the software locks you out. So much for exploration! To get around the lock, hold down the Ctrl key and click the About link. RIS 2.0 owners can easily unlock the software by clicking on the Program button and then placing an X in the window that appears (Figure 1–2).

Figure 1–2   Unlocking the LEGO MINDSTORMS software.

RCX Brick

At the heart of MINDSTORMS is the Robotic Command eXplorer (RCX) brick. This is the brain of the RIS kit, and it gives LEGO robots the ability to be mobile without being tethered to a large PC. The unit itself is only about 6 cm × 10 cm × 4 cm, so it easily fits in the palm of your hand (see Figure 1–3). It is also very light, and weighs about 280 grams with six AA batteries. This lack of mass causes the motors to consume less energy when moving the robot around, giving the batteries a longer life span. I've never felt a particular need to test the limits of RCX durability, but my guess is that it is quite rugged because it uses the same resilient plastic that LEGO uses for its bricks. LEGO is generally known for making high-quality, durable toys. Let's get familiar with the internals of the RCX brick.

Figure 1–3 The RCX brick.

Note:

The RCX 1.0 has an AC adapter port on the back of the brick (see Figure 1–4). This is not used to recharge the batteries; rather, it allows the RCX to be powered from a wall socket using an AC adapter, available separately from LEGO (see Appendix A). This feature is useful for creating stationary robotics that run for a long time, such as a project that monitors lighting and temperature conditions for weeks or more. For this reason the RCX 1.0 has become something of a collectors item, and typically sells for more than the RCX 1.5 or 2.0 on eBay.

Figure 1–4 The AC adapter port.

Central Processing Unit

The RCX brick encloses a Hitachi H8/3292 series microcontroller. The H8 is capable of running at a clock rate of between 10 MHz and 16 MHz, and the RCX uses the highest clock rate of 16 MHz. This is extremely slow compared to modern processors that run at speeds higher than 1,000 MHz, but it's fast enough for most real-world interactions, such as turning motors on and off, reading input from sensors, and computing the next logical move. Real-world events are pathetically slow when compared to computer events, so central processing unit (CPU) speed is generally not much of a factor (with some exceptions). A CPU can switch to a new task in a millionth of a second, whereas a human can't detect differences within a fiftieth of a second.

ROM

The microcontroller chip contains 16 kilobytes (kB) of on-board read-only memory (ROM) and 512 bytes (half a kilobyte) of on-board random access memory (RAM). The ROM contains algorithms for downloading the firmware, displaying data on the liquid crystal display (LCD), and communicating with motors and sensors. This type of hard-wired programming is typically referred to as firmware, but LEGO calls the part of the software that is uploaded to the RCX firmware as well. The ROM also contains some built-in programs that can be used to test the RCX unit (which we demonstrate later in the chapter). The RAM is used for buffering instructions to the CPU.

RAM

The RCX contains 32 kB of external RAM. Two components are stored in the RAM: firmware and user programs. The firmware is essentially an extension of the ROM, except it can be upgraded and replaced to provide different functionality (Chapter 2, "Getting Started with leJOS," describes ways that it can be replaced). The 32 kB of RAM seems relatively small compared to the huge amounts of memory most desktop computers have today, but actually it is ample for most robotics programs. Desktop computers require vast amounts of memory because of the graphics involved in desktop applications, as well as the large documents most applications use. The RCX, on the other hand, displays no real graphics to speak of, so normally it ends up using very little memory. Two anecdotes will help put your mind at ease regarding the seemingly small amount of memory. First, the RCX contains more memory than was used on board the lunar landing module in the moon missions. Second, the Sojourner Mars rover had 160 kB of RAM available to it, but the core program fit into 16 kB of memory. If NASA can achieve something so incredible with this amount of memory, chances are you will also be able to.

Input Ports

The RCX brick contains three input ports that can accept a variety of LEGO sensors such as touch sensors, light sensors, temperature sensors, and rotation sensors. The LEGO group cleverly designed the ports so that a sensor can be connected to the port in any configuration and still work (Figure 1–5). The ports contain tiny LEGO studs that have a metallic connector on about

Figure 1–5   Any sensor configuration works.

half of the circumference. These connectors snap together with the under-side of a LEGO wire to make a connection.

Output Ports

There are also three output ports used to control *actuators* (controllable devices). The ports are primarily used to control motors, but they can control lights, too. People use them to control other actuators such as small LEGO Technic pneumatic valves (see Appendix A) and homemade solenoids. Like the input connectors, an actuator can be connected to an output port in any configuration and still work; however it does affect the direction of the motor. When the wire is at the 6 o'clock or 9 o'clock position and the direction set to forward, the motor will turn clockwise (see Figure 1–6), but when the wire is at the 12 o'clock or 3 o'clock position, the motor will turn counterclockwise. This, of course, also depends on the way the wire is attached to the motor. In this example, the wire is attached going through the groove on the top of the motor. When building a robot, generally you should keep the symmetry of the wire connections consistent to have the wheels rotate in the same direction.

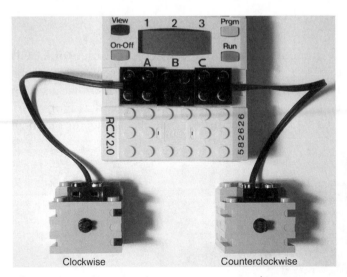

Figure 1–6 Connector orientation vs. motor direction.

Buttons

There are four buttons on the RCX face: On-Off, Run, View and Prgm (see Figure 1–3). These buttons allow limited user interaction with a robot creation, mostly for controlling program execution. The buttons have the following functionality with the standard LEGO firmware:

- **On-Off.** This button allows the power to be turned on or off. Turning the RCX off does not cause on-board programs to be erased.
- **Run.** This button starts running the current program, if one has been uploaded to the RCX.
- **View.** With the standard LEGO firmware, the View button toggles between the current time, the input sensors, and the output ports. Depending on how the sensor is configured, you will see a raw value (0–1023), a percentage (0–100), or a Boolean value (0 or 1).
- **Prgm.** Up to five different programs can be stored by the RCX at one time using the standard LEGO software. The Prgm button is used to select which of the five programs will be executed when Run is pressed.

Infrared Serial Communications Port

The infrared (IR) port is the clear black surface at the top of the RCX brick (see Figure 1–7). The primary purpose of the IR port is to download programs to the RCX brick. The port allows two-way transmission of data, which means the RCX brick can also send data back to the computer. This data can

Figure 1–7 The RCX IR port.

consist of map coordinates, sensor readings, or any other data that the RCX brick recorded. The IR port can also be used to allow two robots to communicate with each other, which can create interesting behavior with groups of robots.

The RCX IR port has two settings: short range and long range. The settings can be configured with the standard LEGO software from a PC. Under short range, the RCX can send a signal that can travel about 96 inches (250 cm). Under long range, the distance is absolutely enormous. I performed several tests with the RCX to see how far it could communicate with the IR port and it was still successful at 25 feet (8 m) when I ran out of room space.

Note:

The RIS 2.0 software allows you to test the range of IR communications in the settings.

Speaker

The speaker is not visible from the outside of the RCX brick. It is located behind the LCD and has a diameter of just 15 mm and a depth of 4 mm. The speaker can produce a variety of simple sounds of variable frequency and duration.

LCD

The LCD can be very useful for testing a program (see Figure 1–8). With the default LEGO firmware it can be used to indicate the internal state of the RCX brick. For example, it can display the values of the input sensors, whether a program is running, or any other numerical output a programmer wishes to send to the display. The RCX has the following segments:

- **Standing Minifig.** This Minifig icon indicates there is a program in memory that is available to be run.

Note:

A Minifig is the name LEGOmaniacs use for the tiny LEGO people available in other LEGO kits.

- **Running Minifig.** This Minifig icon indicates a program is currently running.

- **Caret/Triangle.** This tiny triangle points to the input or output that is currently being monitored. You can cycle the caret to the next input or output by pressing the View button (this applies to the default LEGO firmware only). If a touch sensor is pressed, a small dark triangle appears.

- **Digits.** There are five digits on the display. The standard LEGO firmware uses the rightmost digit to display the program number (1–5) currently ready for execution. The four leftmost digits usually display sensor values.

- **Data Transfer.** This icon shows whether data is being transmitted to the RCX brick. If long-range data transmission is selected for the IR tower, the icon appears larger (see Figure 1–8).

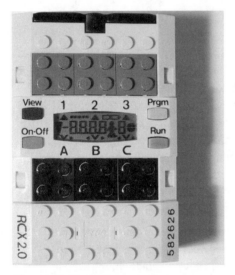

Figure 1-8 LCD segments.

Batteries

The bottom half of the RCX shell can be removed to reveal a compartment for six AA batteries (see Figure 1–9). These batteries take up about half the volume inside the RCX brick. In fact, the 6 cm × 10 cm dimensions of the brick are a direct result of the battery requirements. The batteries also account for about half of the total weight of the RCX.

Figure 1–9   RCX battery compartment.

Tip:

The MINDSTORMS RIS kit does not come with either batteries or a recharging mechanism. This leaves it up to you to decide how you want to supply your RCX with power. The RIS kit needs six AA batteries for the RCX brick and one 9-volt battery for the IR tower (except universal serial bus [USB]). In my case, I purchased an affordable battery recharging station, one rechargeable 9-volt battery, and eight rechargeable AA batteries (they only came in packages of four). The batteries charge in about five hours, and it saves the time and hassle of buying fresh batteries whenever the RCX uses up all the power.

The 9-volt battery is actually a perfect candidate for a (nonrechargeable) lithium-ion battery. The lithium-ion batteries hold a lot more power than regular alkaline batteries, and they do not lose very much charge when unused. In contrast, rechargeable batteries lose their charge while sitting idle. The IR tower only uses up about as much energy as a TV remote control, and as you may have observed, batteries in a TV remote with frequent use can last many years without being changed. One 9-volt lithium-ion battery very well could supply all the power you'll ever need for the life of your IR tower.

IR Tower

MINDSTORMS uses a novel way to send programs from the PC to the RCX brick. Instead of using a direct cable connection, data is transmitted through an IR signal (see Figure 1–10), much like a television remote control. This brilliant design allows for a much faster development cycle because you can simply plunk your robot down in front of the tower to reprogram it, rather than fumbling around with wires and connectors. The IR tower can also be used for exchanging data with the RCX brick while a program is running. The IR tower can even send commands to the RCX brick, allowing the PC to act as a pseudo-remote.

There are two types of IR tower (Figure 1–11): serial port and USB. The RIS 1.0 and 1.5 IR tower connects to the PC through a nine-pin serial port,

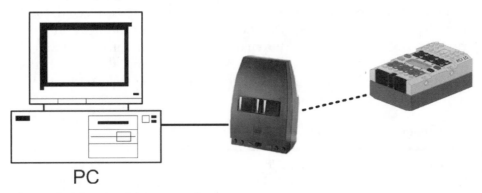

PC

Figure 1-10   PC–RCX data transfer.

Figure 1-11   Serial and USB IR towers.

which is the same type of port used by a serial mouse. Most new computers come equipped with two serial ports, of which at least one should be free. A mouse is also sometimes connected to a serial port, although on newer systems the mouse is more likely to connect to a round PS/2 port. The new RIS 2.0 kit, however, comes with a USB IR tower, which has the advantage of not requiring any batteries.

Note:

The serial IR tower can also connect to a Macintosh using a special cable (see Appendix A).

There is a small switch at the base of the 1.0 and 1.5 IR towers that controls the range of the IR signal. When it is set to short range it is only good for uploading and downloading programs when the RCX brick is situated within about 23 inches (60 cm) of the tower. When long range is selected, the IR tower will send a stronger signal that can be detected by the RCX brick even when it is over 25 feet (800 cm) from the tower. The advantage to setting the switch to short range is that it consumes less power from the 9-volt battery. The new USB tower can be configured in the setting (select LEGO USB Tower from the Windows control panel).

Warning:

When the 9-volt battery in the IR tower becomes weak, programs will start to fail when they are uploaded to the RCX brick. This can sometimes be difficult to identify as the cause of the problem.

Motors

The RIS kit includes two very efficient 9-volt motors (see Figure 1–12), which are the primary drain on battery power from the RCX. The motors are internally geared, meaning they contain an electric motor and some gears that increase the torque to the shaft. This also results in slower shaft rotation. Unfortunately, these motors only have one rate of rotation. It is possible to decrease the power to a motor, but this only makes the output weaker and more likely to stall. The only way to change speed and keep power at 100% is to use additional gears externally to further alter the speed of the shaft. There are also small slots in the side of the motor that allow special 1 × 2 plates to support the motor to a chassis.

Figure 1-12 Technic 9-volt motor.

Sensors

Sensors are able to detect data from the real world and send the data back to the RCX so it can make decisions. Sensors are very important to the robot because they enable it to draw conclusions about the external surroundings and determine what the next move should be. Without sensors a robot would have no link to the external world and would only be able to stumble around blindly. The RIS kit includes two different kinds of sensors: a light sensor and two touch sensors. These are not very refined sensors for navigating, but they are a start.

Light Sensor

The light sensor is primarily for measuring the intensity of light that enters through the tiny lens on the front of the sensor (see Figure 1–13). Dark objects tend to absorb more light, hence they reflect less light back to the light sensor. This means the light sensor can also be used to distinguish dark objects from light. The light sensor also has a small red light-emitting diode (LED) that illuminates the scene in front of the sensor. The light sensor reads values from 0 to 100, with 100 being the brightest.

Typically the light sensor is used to create a robot that will follow a path toward darkness or a bright light. You can even attach a bright light to a moving object (e.g., a pet, another robot) and have your robot track it. The light sensor is also sometimes used to prevent a robot from falling off a table by mounting it in front of the robot pointing directly downward. When the robot gets to the edge of the table, the sensor values generally decrease significantly.

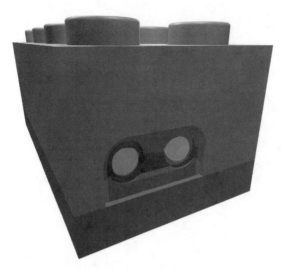

Figure 1-13   Detector lens of the light sensor.

The light sensor is capable of sensing light that is invisible to the human eye, such as the IR light emitted from the RCX brick or IR tower. This feature can be exploited to create a primitive range sensor (see Chapter 9, "Proximity Detection"), but the range values are very inaccurate. Still, it is usually good enough to stop the robot before it crashes into an object.

Hands On:

It's very easy to connect a light sensor and take readings from it.

1.1 Connect the blue light sensor brick to Input 2.

1.2 Turn on the RCX and press the View button until the triangle points at Input 2.

1.3 You will probably see a value between 0 and 1,023. This is called the raw value of a sensor.

1.4 To change the sensor mode to light sensor, select Program 2 and press Run. You can stop the program running at any time, and Input 2 will remain in light sensor mode.

Now you should see a value between 0 and 100. You can walk around your room like Spock with his tricorder, testing various objects for light intensity.

Touch Sensors

The most basic sensor available for MINDSTORMS is the touch sensor. It is typically used in conjunction with a bumper to detect when a robot has come in contact with another object. It can also be used as an extra switch to control a robotic creation or to detect when a moving part such as an arm has moved a specific distance. Touch sensors give a value of either 0 or 1 when in touch sensor mode. The wire brick can be connected to the touch sensor in a variety of ways, but not all will work (see Figure 1–14).

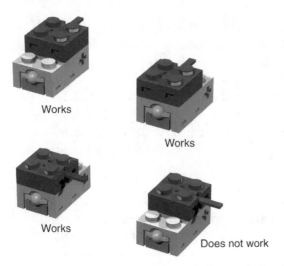

Works

Works

Works

Does not work

Figure 1–14   Wire connections to the touch sensor.

In this exercise we will connect a touch sensor and read the values.

1.1 Connect a short cable to the gray touch sensor.

1.2 Connect the other end of the cable to Input 1.

1.3 Turn on the RCX and press the View button until the caret points at Input 1.

1.4 You will probably see the raw value, something between 0 and 1,023. A raw value of less than 460 is interpreted as 0 (not pressed) and anything greater than 562 is interpreted as 1 (pressed). The Boolean value remains unchanged for any values between 460 and 562.

> **1.5** To change the sensor mode to a touch sensor, select Program 1 and press Run. You can stop the program running at any time, and Input 1 remains in touch sensor mode.
>
> Now you should see a value of 0 when the touch sensor is released and 1 when it is pressed.

LEGO Parts

The RIS kit includes a huge and varied selection of LEGO parts. There has almost never been a time when I wanted to build a component and couldn't find the right parts to make it work. The selection of parts in the kit is near perfect and will probably satisfy most robot projects. This selection is made up of classic LEGO bricks, as well as the more advanced LEGO Technic parts. Technic is a more technical breed of parts than LEGO, including beams, gears, and motors. Let's use these parts to make a very simple robot named Tippy. (This robot is also used in Chapter 2 to test sample code.)

Note:

The RIS 1.0, 1.5, and 2.0 kits contain a different set of parts. Chapter 5, "LEGO 101," explains these parts and the differences between the kits.

Building Tippy

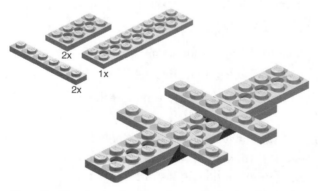

Step 1   The chassis for the robot is made up of five plates.

Step 2 Attach two skid plates to the underside of the chassis. These will skid along the surface, keeping Tippy from tipping over.

Step 3 Add three blocks for the support structure.

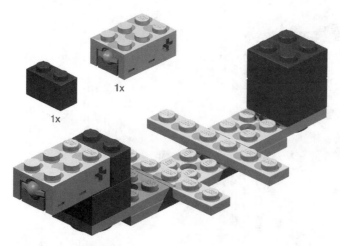

Step 4   Add a touch sensor into the support structure.

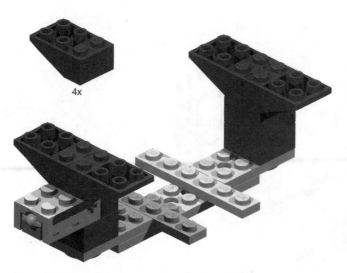

Step 5   Cap off the supports with slope bricks that will support the RCX.

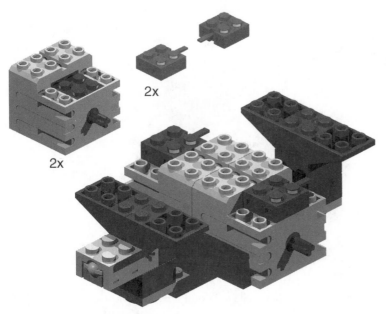

Step 6 Attach two motors to the chassis, then short wires to the tops of the motors. Make sure the motor wires are facing toward the back of the robot.

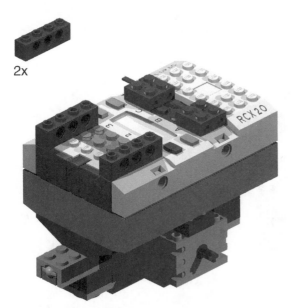

Step 7 Attach the RCX to the top of the slope bricks, then attach the wire bricks from the motor to the output ports. The wire ends should both face to the *right* of the robot when connected. Finally, attach two 1 × 4 beams to the top of the RCX.

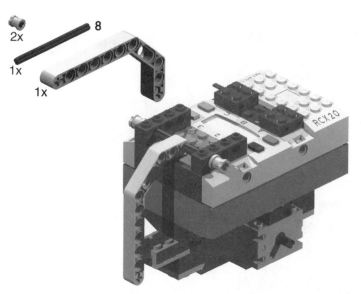

Step 8   The front bumper consists of a yellow lift arm hanging over the front of the robot, like an elephant's trunk.

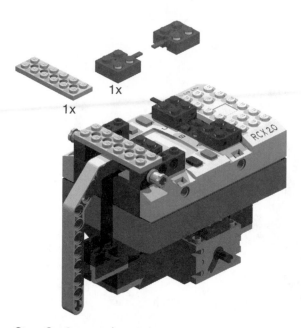

Step 9   Connect the touch sensor to Input 2 using a short wire. The wire should stick out to the left from the touch sensor. Cap the two beams with a plate to add stability and strength to the structure.

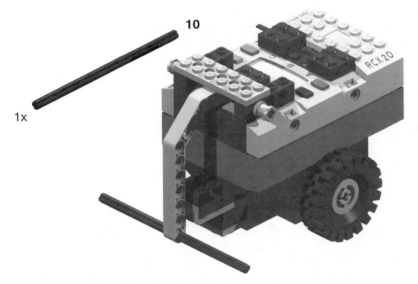

Step 10 Add two large hard-rubber wheels to the motors. Finish off the model by placing a long axle in the lift arm.

Note:

Later in this chapter we will be programming the brains for Tippy.

The RIS CD Software

LEGO calls their latest software the RCX 2.0 Software Development Kit (SDK). There are actually four main parts to the SDK: the tutorial, the integrated development environment (IDE, includes RCX Code), the firmware, and a scripting language they call MindScript. The IDE resides on a desktop computer and allows users to develop and upload code to the RCX brick. The firmware, as previously covered, consists of low-level instructions to control motors and read sensor data, among other things. MindScript (previously called LEGO Script) is a new high-level language that allows the RCX to be programmed without using the graphical IDE for development.

Note:

These are the only official programming tools from LEGO, although their Web site does mention projects that use other programming languages. The LEGO SDK is not used in this book after this chapter. The projects in this book are built around an open source SDK called leJOS, which uses Java for coding.

Note:

The software is currently only available for the Microsoft Windows platform, which doesn't sit very well with the Apple Macintosh user community. RIS 2.0 has the potential to work with Macintosh systems because the USB port for the IR tower can easily connect to both PCs and Macintosh systems, but LEGO has not developed the software yet.

RCX Code

RCX Code is developed using a colorful, graphical style that is very reminiscent of building with LEGO bricks themselves. The programming environment consists of blocks representing one of four categories: commands, sensor watchers, stack controllers, and my (custom) commands. Blocks can be stacked beneath one another to create simple programs. Properties for each block of code can be changed by right-clicking the graphical LEGO block. This brings up a list of changeable settings that varies depending on the type of command.

The purpose of this software is to create a friendly programming environment for children. It is simple to get started with and it's visually colorful. The bricks even make a clicking sound as they lock into place. Kids are likely to feel comfortable with this, and it allows them to begin programming immediately. Best of all, it is very hard to go wrong—in fact, it might be impossible to make a mistake with it. With a more advanced language such as Java, there are many syntax issues that create a steep learning curve for children, and they likely do not have the patience to learn complex Java syntax. Programmers may actually find lower level languages such as Java more intuitive to program with than RCX Code, however. With RCX Code, simple programs are very easy to develop. However, when complex behavior is desired it is sometimes difficult to figure out what steps to take.

RCX Firmware

Most computer hardware contains code that controls lower level functions such as displaying data or accessing the disk drive. This code is usually stored in ROM and exists even before an operating system is installed. The RCX is no different, only it contains code that is responsible for timing events, turning motors on and off, reading data from sensors, activating the speaker, controlling data flow through the IR port, changing programs, and activating the LCD. This code is commonly called firmware, and in the RCX it resides in the ROM. However, firmware also happens to be the name given to the operating system loaded into the RCX RAM. The firmware that is uploaded to the RCX provides routines that can be upgraded. Once firmware is uploaded, it remains in memory until the batteries are removed. If the firmware is removed from memory it must be uploaded again for the RCX brick to accept user programs. The RIS 1.0 firmware only leaves about 6 kB of memory for user programs, which seems quite insignificant, but is in reality adequate for most programs.

The standard LEGO firmware has some major limitations for programmers, however. One of the biggest is the lack of *floating-point numbers*; numbers with decimal places. There is also a limit of 32 variables in a program, and no arrays are allowed. These limitations can be significant, depending on what your goals are for your project.

Mindscript

LEGO has developed a more advanced scripting language for programming the RCX brick. The rationale behind the creation of this language is to provide more advanced LEGO users with an official language to program in. It actually produces the same program data as RCX Code, only it is programmed using a simple text editor. The Mindscript software comes with a simple graphical user interface (GUI) that allows the program to be entered, verified, and uploaded to the RCX (Figure 1–15). This environment will seem a little more familiar to programmers who are used to typing their code as opposed to assembling the objects visually. A typical Mindscript program looks something like this:

```
program Test {
   const max = 50
   output A on 1
   sensor axleRotation on 1
   axleRotation is rotation as angle
   main {
      clear axleRotation
      on A
      while axleRotation < max {
         /* wait for axle to rotate to limit */
      }
      off A
   }
}
```

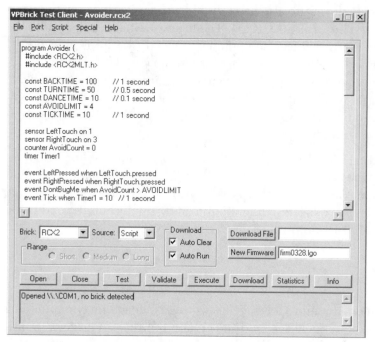

```
VPBrick Test Client - Avoider.rcx2                                    _ □ ×
File   Port   Script   Special   Help

program Avoider {
  #include <RCX2.h>
  #include <RCX2MLT.h>

  const BACKTIME = 100      // 1 second
  const TURNTIME = 50       // 0.5 second
  const DANCETIME = 10      // 0.1 second
  const AVOIDLIMIT = 4
  const TICKTIME = 10       // 1 second

  sensor LeftTouch on 1
  sensor RightTouch on 3
  counter AvoidCount = 0
  timer Timer1

  event LeftPressed when LeftTouch.pressed
  event RightPressed when RightTouch.pressed
  event DontBugMe when AvoidCount > AVOIDLIMIT
  event Tick when Timer1 = 10  // 1 second
```
```
Brick:  RCX2  ▼   Source:  Script  ▼    ┌Download─┐   Download File
                                         ☑ Auto Clear
 ┌Range──────────────────────────┐       ☑ Auto Run    New Firmware  firm0328.lgo
 │  ○ Short  ○ Medium  ○ Long     │

   Open      Close      Test     Validate    Execute   Download   Statistics    Info

 Opened \\.\COM1, no brick detected
```

Figure 1–15 Mindscript IDE.

This code is quite easy to understand, even if you have no familiarity with the Mindscript language. The second line defines a constant called *max* and sets the value to 50. It then defines an output and calls it *A*, and a rotation sensor on Input Port 1 called *axleRotation*. With these variables defined, the code simply turns the motor on, counts 50 rotation counts, and then turns the motor off.

As you can see, this is a little more powerful for writing programs than the visual composition of RCX Code, and more intuitive for seasoned programmers. All code is still limited by the firmware, however, which means there are still limits on the number of variables that can be used, no floating-point numbers, and other limitations. Mindscript might find a niche with some programmers, but I think most would rather use a language they are familiar with rather than learning the quirks of an unfamiliar language.

Note:

There have been three versions of the RIS kit released since 1998: 1.0, 1.5, and 2.0. You can tell which version you have by looking at the box or the edge of your RCX brick. The important thing to remember is that the RCX

internals have not changed in each release. The main differences have come with the RCX software, which has been improved consistently from one release to the next.

For those who desperately want to have the latest version, LEGO supplies an upgrade kit that gives you everything you are missing in the 1.5 or 2.0 version. This includes a new Constructopedia with complete instructions for three robots, new CD software, a user guide, and a large test pad to run your robots on. The main benefit of this kit is that it gives more complete instructions, as well as missing parts.

Programming Tippy

In this section we program Tippy using the standard LEGO software. If you don't wish to install the LEGO software, you can wait until Chapter 2 to program Tippy with Java. Start the LEGO software and enter Program mode, then follow along with Figure 1–16.

1. Click Small Blocks, then on Power. Click an On block onto the main area under the default block (Figure 1–16). Click the small square to the right of the On block to bring up the options. Make sure an X is next to A and C only, then close the Options window.

2. Drag a Set Direction block underneath the On block and click the Options tab. Select A and C only, and make sure forward direction is selected.

3. Click Sensors and drag a Touch Sensor to the middle of the screen. A Wizard will appear. Choose Input 2, and then click Finish.

4. Under the If Click block, drag a Set Direction block, and change the options so the directions for A and C are reverse.

5. Drag a Wait For block, and click the Options tab. Change the delay to 0.5 seconds.

6. Drag a Set Directions block, and change the options so A is reversed and C is forward.

7. Drag another Wait For block, and click the Options tab. Change the delay to 0.5 seconds.

8. Drag a Set Directions block, and change the options so A is once again forward and C is forward.

9. Now save the program by selecting File, Save. Give it the name Tippy. That's it! We can now test the code by clicking Download, then pressing the Run button on the RCX.

Note:

You can view the code you just wrote as Mindscript. Change to the directory you installed the LEGO Software to (e.g. C:\Program Files\Lego Mindstorms). Change to the RIS 2.0\Users directory and look for your user name. In the user directory you will find directory called Vault. Your code appears here with an .lsc extension. Open the code in Notepad to view it.

After assembling and programming Tippy, I think you will agree that building and programming a LEGO MINDSTORMS robot is an amazingly easy process. The robot you just made would probably take months or even years for a single person with no previous electronics or computer engineering experience to build. The learning curve is so steep that most likely all enthusi-

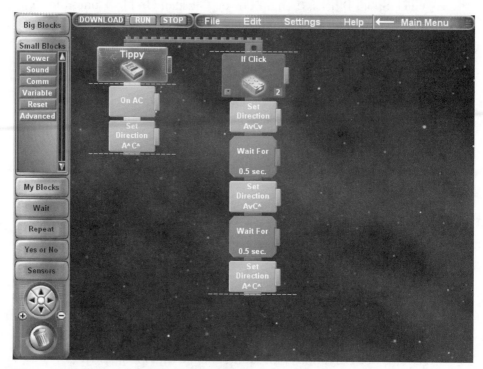

Figure 1-16 Completed LEGO code for Tippy.

asm would be drained within a few short months of starting this project. With MINDSTORMS, you can conceive a new idea in your mind and create a finished robot while your inspiration is still going strong.

The World of **MINDSTORMS**

The availability of parts to expand MINDSTORMS has recently exploded. There are now many commercially available expansion kits and parts that can be purchased to beef up your MINDSTORMS creations. Most are available from LEGO, but some of the more interesting additions can be purchased from third-party companies not directly associated with LEGO. These kits can be a treasure trove of parts, and could be just the thing you need to complete your dream project. Some of these parts can even help you push the envelope with your creations, allowing you to go beyond the toy stage and into research and scientific areas.

Sensors are perhaps the most valuable parts for expanding the functionality of MINDSTORMS. The two touch sensors and the single light sensor included in the RIS are of limited use, and you will soon feel a need for more powerful sensors. By having a larger variety of sensors, you can create robots that react to temperature, humidity, sound, pressure, and other external conditions. These sensors can be difficult to construct for anyone but experts, but thankfully there is a wide variety of commercially available sensors that can plug directly into the RCX brick.

Note:

Some of the products mentioned in this section have been discontinued. If you have problems obtaining them from LEGO or retailers, you might want to try online auction sites, such as eBay.

Note:

See Appendix A for part numbers and ordering instructions.

ROBOLAB™

Pitsco LEGO Dacta is a product line developed by the LEGO Group designed specifically for education. The products are ideal for use in a curriculum setting with an instructor and a group of students. Some project kits are developed specifically for small teams to work on and complete. Within this line of products is ROBOLAB, which uses the RCX.

The main difference between ROBOLAB and the RIS kit (aside from the Constructopedia) is the software. The ROBOLAB software is more advanced than the standard RIS software. It allows programming in a visual environment, but it offers much more programming power. The software can use all kinds of sensors, including the LogIT series of sensors (discussed later). This software can also be used for recording, retrieving, and displaying data recorded by RCX sensors. For example, if you created a small device using the RCX to monitor how often the lights in your bathroom are turned on and off, you could upload the data to the PC using this software and analyze the results. The main kits in this series are discussed in the following sections.

ROBOLAB™ Starter Set

The Starter Set contains enough parts to teach four groups of students: three gear motors, a micromotor, four light bricks, three light sensors, four touch sensors, 14 wires, full-color building instructions, and six sorting trays and element surveys (parts lists). It does not, however, include any RCX bricks or IR towers, so these must be purchased separately.

Team Challenge Set

The Team Challenge Set contains 726 parts, including an RCX, an IR tower, and cables. It also contains step-by-step building instructions for several group challenges such as sumo wrestling or knocking the cans out of a circle. The competitive aspect between groups of students could provide some real motivation for creating functional robotics.

Cities and Transportation Set

This set looks like it has the potential to develop future urban planners and civil engineers. The kit focuses on curricular concepts such as math, science and technology, environmental studies, history, social studies, and geography. There are 389 parts in the kit including a 9-volt motor, two light sensors, two touch sensors, three light elements, four project themes to build on, and a sorting tray.

Amusement Park Set

The Amusement Park Set contains 293 elements including a light sensor, two 9-volt motors, two touch sensors, wires, a sorting tray, and building instructions for five amusement park models.

Web Site:

Also of interest in the ROBOLAB universe is the Invent and Investigate online database. It contains many interesting projects that would appeal to students interested in science. Projects can be accessed from the ROBOLAB software, and new projects can be added to the database. Among the collection is a project to study birds feeding. The RCX is programmed to feed birds as soon as they land on a touch sensor. It also takes pictures and keeps a running log of the time of day the birds were actively feeding, the temperature, and the light conditions. The database can be searched online at www.lego.com/dacta/landl/welcomedatabase.asp.

LogIT Sensors

LogIT sensors are a more advanced breed than the standard LEGO sensors. The ROBOLAB software has been developed to specifically take advantage of these sensors, and other third-party programming environments can also take advantage of them. These sensors are available from a company called DCP Microdevelopments Ltd. There are so many different sensors it almost puts the tricorder from *Star Trek* to shame. Each LogIT sensor plugs into a LogIT-RCX sensor adapter (Figure 1–17), which is available from LEGO Dacta. The

Figure 1–17 LogIT-RCX sensor adapter.

adapter is simply a wire with one end allowing it to connect to an RCX input port, and the other end allowing a LogIT sensor to attach. The sensors themselves are cylindrical and quite small. The LogIT sensors cost a little bit more than regular LEGO sensors, but they provide a greater range of functionality.

ProTemp Sensor

The ProTemp sensor (Figure 1–18) measures temperatures ranging from –30°C to +130°C. The probe does not have to be kept dry, so it is good for measuring liquid or air temperatures. It has an 18-cm stainless steel probe that is used for measuring the temperature. The ProTemp sensor can apparently detect changes in temperature as small as 0.1°C, which allows a user to record very accurate scientific observations.

Figure 1–18   ProTemp sensor.

HumiPro Sensor

The HumiPro sensor (Figure 1–19) measures relative humidity (RH). It can measure the full range from 1% to 100% RH. Large changes in humidity can be detected within 1.5 seconds, and it can measure changes as small as 0.1% RH. It can be used to measure anything from human breath to vehicle exhaust, as long as the temperature remains between –20°C and +80°C.

Figure 1–19   HumiPro sensor.

Sound Level Sensor

A sound level sensor (Figure 1–20) does not record sounds, but rather the sound levels in the decibel (dB) scale. The sensor can measure anything in the range of 50 to 100 dB. A quiet conversation has a noise level of about 50 dB, whereas a loud rock concert is about 100 dB. The dB scale is logarithmic,

Figure 1–20 Sound level sensor.

which means that 100 dB is not double a 50 dB noise. In fact, the sound level doubles every 3 dB to the human ear. This sensor is able to respond to changes in noise level within 0.5 seconds.

pH Amplifier Sensor

The pH Amplifier sensor (Figure 1–21) is able to detect the acidity level in an environment, such as wine, yogurt, or acid rain. It can detect the full range of acidity levels (0–14 pH) with a resolution of up to 0.01 pH.

Figure 1–21 pH Amplifier sensor.

Pressure Sensor

The pressure sensor (Figure 1–22) measures atmospheric pressure in kilo-Pascals (kPa). It can be used to monitor chemical reactions and changes in atmospheric pressure. The sensor does not measure water pressure, however (liquids will damage the sensor). It can measure a range between 0 and 200 kPa.

Figure 1–22 Air pressure sensor.

Movement and Position Sensor

The position sensor (Figure 1–23) measures rotational movement, but it can be used to indirectly detect lateral changes in position. For example, a long

Figure 1–23 Rotational position sensor.

rod could be attached perpendicular to the shaft of the sensor, and then the rod could be attached to an object, such as a plant. As the plant grows, the rod will move upward, causing the sensor shaft to rotate. The sensor can also measure other movements, such as pendulum motion. The sensor can rotate a full 360°, but it can actually only measure 340° (with a 20° "dead" area). Accuracy is ± 2%, which translates to an angle accuracy of ± 7.2°.

Note:

The standard LEGO sensor counts rotations, as opposed to the LogIT sensor, which indicates the absolute position of a point on the shaft (in degrees).

Voltage Sensor

The voltage sensor (Figure 1–24) has two leads a voltage can travel across. It can measure anywhere between –24 and +24 volts (DC). This sensor could be useful for measuring power from solar cells, induced electromagnetic frequency from a coil, or battery charge.

Figure 1–24 Voltage sensor.

Note:

DCP has many other sensors that should be compatible with the RCX. They include a Redox/Ion selective electrode adapter, an accelerometer (measures acceleration), a current probe, a barometric air pressure sensor, a Lux (light intensity) sensor, a radioactivity sensor, a heart pulse monitor, and a designer sensor set for creating your own sensors. These additional sensors do not have ROBOLAB drivers, however, but it is relatively easy to interpret results from raw values.

Web Site:

For more information go to www.dcpmicro.com.

Technic

There are many Technic kits available from LEGO that can be used to enhance your current collection of parts. One of the favorites used in MIND-STORMS projects is pneumatics, which allow powerful lateral movement in robotic creations. Pneumatics are not included in the RIS kit but can be purchased separately from LEGO. A Technic set can really enhance the types of projects you can build and could be a worthwhile investment if you find yourself running out of parts before your robot is finished, or if you need a special-purpose part to perform a specific function.

Note:

If you are interested in pneumatics, everything you've ever wanted to know about LEGO pneumatics can be found at: www.geocities.com/cssoh1/.

Robotics Discovery Set

The Robotics Discovery Set (RDS) is a junior version of the RIS set in every way. At the heart of the RDS is a microcontroller called the Scout (see Figure 1–25), which just as easily could have been called RCX Junior. It is smaller in size than the RCX brick, but contains a larger LCD. The Scout is a little more limited than the RCX because it only has two input and two output ports. Scout contains 32 kB of ROM, and only 1 kB of RAM! Of this 1 kB, only about 400 bytes are available to hold one user program! This might

Figure 1–25   Scout. (Photo courtesy of Zhengrong Zang.)

sound very limiting, but actually the 32-kB ROM contains a library of more than 30 command subroutines, so it could take as little as 1 byte to issue a directive to the Scout microcontroller.

Programs can be developed on the Scout itself, without any external software, using the four buttons and the LCD. Additionally, code can be developed on a PC and uploaded to the Scout using the standard IR tower. The RDS does not include an IR tower or serial cable, however, but these can be purchased separately.

Vision Command

The Vision Command system gives your PC the ability to see. It includes a LEGO Cam, which is really a Logitech QuickCam enclosed in a LEGO shell. The camera is capable of capturing images of 352 × 288 pixels at 30 frames per second and has a small microphone for capturing sound. Keep in mind that the camera itself does not connect to your RCX brick in any way. It connects through a USB port to your computer with a 5-m cord.

The camera has many uses independent of the RCX, such as taking time-lapse films of slow events (plants growing) or making stop-motion animation. It can also be used as an Internet Web cam, just like any normal PC camera. LEGO also provides software with some basic visual algorithms. The software is capable of detecting three types of conditions: motion, brightness, and color. Using the software, you can define different sections in the field of view. Each section can react when a condition occurs within it, triggering an event. For example, you can set the camera up so it is pointing at your wallet.

Then, using the software, you can program it to sound an alarm if anyone moves into the zone around your wallet.

Vision Command also includes software to control the RCX brick. A small program uploaded to the RCX allows the PC to issue commands to the robot. All commands are sent to the RCX through the IR tower, so the RCX must always be facing the tower. This setup is great for controlling stationary RCX robots, but unfortunately it is not very practical to use with mobile robots. A better setup would be to sever the cable completely and send video data using radio frequency (RF). RF has the benefit of traveling all over a room and even into other rooms, so it doesn't matter which way the RCX is facing. I'm a little pessimistic that a low-cost RF transmitter could send video data to the PC rapidly enough, however, which is probably why LEGO decided to go with a cable connection.

RIS Expansion Sets

The classic LEGO business model is founded on selling sets that allow a LEGO user to construct new models. There is a huge range of LEGO bricks, but the bricks are for the most part standard. This makes it necessary for LEGO to sell new sets by including different combinations of the standard parts, along with instructions on how to create new models. Each new set contains more of the same parts, so it's the plans that LEGO is really trying to market.

LEGO first tried the expansion set concept in the MINDSTORMS world with some kits that were released in 1998, around the same time the RIS 1.0 kit was released. These kits feature several projects with a central theme. Each contains some new LEGO parts, but mostly just regular MIND-STORMS parts with different colors. The centerpiece of these kits is a Constructopedia, which is a set of instructions on how to build a variety of robots. The kits also include CD software that cooperates with the original MIND-STORMS software installed on your computer. The software enhances the Constructopedia menu option with hints, tips, and some new multimedia. Let's examine these kits in detail.

RoboSports

This kit provides MINDSTORMS users with the chance to re-create many of the most popular robotics competitions. The kit includes 90 parts, including two balls, two pucks, a large playing-field sheet, and an extra motor. It also contains 12 sports challenges ranging from basketball to soccer. Keep in mind that to stage competitions more than one RCX brick is required.

Extreme Creatures

This kit is supposed to allow you to build creatures that act on instinct. It supplies 140 LEGO parts, but it falls short on supplying useful sensors or actuators. The only additional electronic part included is a light that can illuminate fiber-optic strands. The light can make a robot look more interesting but it adds no practical functionality. If you are a younger LEGO user you may find some novelty in this kit, but more mature LEGO users are advised to steer clear of it.

Exploration Mars

The main goal of this kit is to simulate the tasks of NASA's 1997 unmanned Mars Pathfinder mission. This includes deploying the small rover on the planet (your living room) and taking pictures. Considering the real mission cost tens of millions of dollars and you only have to spend about $260, it's understandable that there are some cutbacks. The software and Constructopedia guide the user through many different mission stages. One of the more interesting aspects is navigation, which introduces the problems encountered in a terrain with many objects like Mars boulders. If you own a LEGO Cam, there is a special project that uses the camera to send pictures back to the PC.

Code Pilot

The Code Pilot (Figure 1–26) uses barcode scanning technology to program a lightweight computer. Programs can be created on a PC, then the barcode printed out to be scanned in by the Code Pilot. This type of toy could be appealing for young children interested in a simple way to program LEGO creations, but it is safe to say the Code Pilot does not approach the power of the RCX.

Figure 1–26   The Code Pilot. (Photo courtesy of Marc Klein.)

Droid Developer Kit

This kit allows children to build some of their favorite robots from the *Star Wars* movies, including everyone's favorite, R2-D2. At the heart of this kit is the Micro-Scout (see Figure 1–27). This device is even smaller than the Scout and is not user programmable. A user can simply select one of seven predefined ROM programs. It contains a built-in motor and a built-in light sensor, but no external devices (motors or sensors) can be attached to it. For RIS users, the Micro-Scout is a step down in complexity and will probably not arouse much interest.

Figure 1–27 The Micro-Scout. (Photo courtesy of Marc Klein.)

It is interesting to note that the Micro-Scout can accept programming instructions from the Scout using the light sensor. It even has its own communications protocol called VLL. Some users on the Web have unlocked the secrets of programming in VLL code, and have devised a way to program the Micro-Scout with up to 15 instructions using a flashlight and barcode transparencies (*www.eaton.dhs.org/lego/*).

Dark Side Developer Kit

This kit allows children to build *Star Wars*-themed droids that walk, such as the four legged AT-AT walker featured in *The Empire Strikes Back*. This kit also uses the Micro-Scout to control the various robots, just like the Droid Developer Kit.

Web Site:

The MINDSTORMS Web site has a very amusing little facsimile of the AT-AT attack from *The Empire Strikes Back*. It features several Dark Side Developer Kit robots attacking little Minifig Rebels who run around in a panic firing laser weapons. For fans of LEGO and *Star Wars*, it is quite a treat, and it's in letter-box format! To access the movie:

1.1 Make sure you have Shockwave installed.

1.2 Go to: *mindstorms.lego.com*

1.3 Click on Products.

1.4 Click on Dark Side Developer Kit.

Enjoy the show!

CyberMaster

CyberMaster is probably the most powerful LEGO computer brick after the RCX (Figure 1–28). The most important feature of the CyberMaster is that it

Figure 1-28 The CyberMaster unit. (Photo courtesy of Jürgen Stuber.)

uses RF instead of IR. This means the PC can communicate with the Cyber-Master even when it is in another room. The CyberMaster communicates at 27 MHz, which is a frequency often used by small remote control toys.

The CyberMaster itself contains two built-in motors (the round protrusions from the side shown in Figure 1–28), one free motor port, and three sensor ports. The kit includes about 900 pieces including one geared motor, three colored touch sensors, an RF tower (Figure 1–29) and a variety of parts. The touch sensors are color-coded because each has a resistor that gives the sensor a unique raw value, so the CyberMaster can tell which color of touch sensor was pressed.

The CyberMaster unfortunately only works with passive sensors, such as touch and temperature sensors. Active sensors that require a power supply, such as the light sensor and rotation sensor, do not work (passive light sensors can be made). Also, the compass and distance sensors in this book are also not compatible, so only simple vehicles with bumpers can be built with the CyberMaster. The ROM firmware of the CyberMaster can't be replaced, so third-party firmware such as leJOS will not work with it.

Figure 1–29 The CyberMaster RF tower. (Photo courtesy of Jürgen Stuber.)

If you haven't heard of the CyberMaster before, you are not alone. It was first released in 1998 around the same time the RIS kit was released, but distribution was limited to Western Europe, New Zealand, and Australia. Most people who own both kits agree the RCX is much more powerful than CyberMaster. Perhaps if active sensors were permitted this would change. Having the unlimited memory, processing power, and network connectivity of the PC would open up LEGO robotics for much more complex artificial intelligence (AI) projects. Direct PC control also gives it the added advantage of not requiring long code downloads. If LEGO ever refines the CyberMaster concept with a new release, the full potential could be realized.

Ultimate Accessory Kit

The Ultimate Accessory Kit (Figure 1–30) contains some popular parts for constructing MINDSTORMS robots. It contains a rotation sensor, another touch sensor, a LEGO Lamp (just a light), a handy remote control, and 45 additional LEGO parts. This is indeed a useful kit and a good value. MIND-STORMS users who are a little more mature and a little more hard-core will appreciate the technology this kit provides, compared to the toy nature of the other expansion kits.

Figure 1–30   The Ultimate Accessory Kit. (Photo courtesy of Marc Klein.)

Ultimate Builders Set

The Ultimate Builders Set (Figure 1–31) is a great expansion set for the RIS. It contains many interesting parts that will allow you to build a physically more interesting robot. There are also instructions for seven impressive robot creations, including a wall climber that uses its two hands to climb up a wire rack, an aerial tram that travels along a string and lowers a winch to pick objects up, a tabletop cleaner that kicks pieces away, a two-dimensional sheet plotter that uses pneumatics to lower a pen, a robot that shoots throwbot discs, and a remote volume control for a stereo.

The kit includes a CD and 316 building elements (many in transparent colors) including pneumatics parts, a 9-volt motor, two white tank tread wheels, clear rectangular frames, a clear worm gear, regular gears, yellow-green bent lift arms, many beams, double-bevel gears, 16-inch-long wire, a large geared turntable with a clear top, some newer Technic flat pieces in the shape of Ds and triangle Ts, many connector pieces, small and large pneumatic pistons, a pneumatic switch, clear tubing, six throwbot discs, and two white axles.

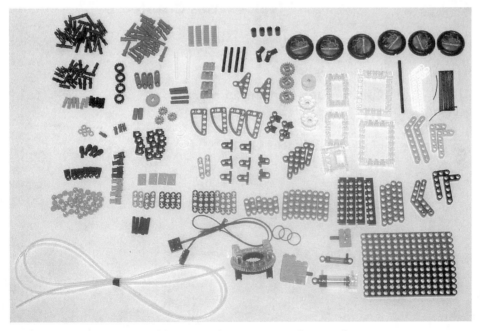

Figure 1–31 Ultimate Builders Set. (Photo courtesy of Marc Klein.)

GETTING
STARTED WITH
leJOS

Topics in this Chapter

- leJOS Overview
- Installing leJOS
- Creating and Running a Program
- Setting Up an IDE
- How leJOS Stacks Up

Chapter 2

The RIS kit is excellent in every respect, but the one thing missing for seasoned programmers is a more mature and well-developed programming language. If you are a Java programmer then you probably already know just how good the Java language is. This chapter introduces what Java programmers have been craving—a Java environment complete with threads, arrays, floating-point numbers, recursion, and total control of the RCX brick, including reprogramming the buttons. This is the second piece of the puzzle that will make your MINDSTORMS robot development truly complete. This chapter also shows how to set up leJOS on your computer, and just as important, how to set up a time saving, frustration saving IDE. At the end of the chapter we review the other third-party RCX programming languages and contrast them with leJOS.

leJOS Overview

leJOS can be compared to the Java 2 SDK that has been released by Sun Microsystems. Both are available for free download on the Internet. Both use compilers that transform your source code into byte-code instructions. (In fact, leJOS uses the Sun Java compiler, *javac*, to produce its byte-code.) Both include a Java Virtual Machine (JVM), which is a small interpreter that reads the byte-code and executes the instructions on the CPU. Both contain an application programming interface (API), which is a set of classes that can be used by programmers to provide advanced functionality. There are also some rather large differences between leJOS and the standard Java 2 SDK. From a product development standpoint, the Java 2 SDK was developed by a huge multibillion dollar company. leJOS was developed by a small handful of pro-grammers over the Internet at no monetary cost. The Java 2 SDK from Sun actually comes in three flavors: Java 2 Standard Edition (J2SE), Java 2 Enter-prise Edition (J2EE) and Java 2 Micro Edition (J2ME). The J2SE and J2EE are both made for powerful computers with megabytes of memory and disk space, whereas J2ME is made for smaller devices, such as pagers, cellular phones, and handheld PCs. J2ME is designed to execute code on platforms with 128 kB to 512 kB of available memory. That's pretty impressive, but leJOS is made to run on a computer (the RCX brick) with only 32 kB of RAM, so leJOS can be thought of as Java micro-micro edition.

Note:

The name leJOS is a play of words on LEGOs, with g replaced by j for Java. The JOS part of leJOS actually stands for Java Operating System, and le means the in several languages, so you can think of the name as meaning "the Java operating system." In Spanish the word leJOS actually means far, and the intention was for leJOS to go very far. (Considering leJOS has been used with an RCX robot that was sent to the International Space Station, it's safe to say this has been fulfilled.) The pronunciation of leJOS is lay-hoss, but English speakers do not pronounce the letter j as an h, so English speakers should pronounce leJOS the way it looks, with the last part sounding like boss.

leJOS Java does pretty much what you would expect it to do on the RCX brick. Like any programming language, it allows you to control the program flow. The leJOS API mirrors the basic functionality of LEGO code, control-ling motors, sensors, and other elements of the RCX brick. leJOS also includes a trimmed-down version of the standard Java API with general classes to help out with programming, such as the vector class. Let's examine the individual parts of leJOS in more detail.

JVM

The JVM is analogous to the standard LEGO firmware; in fact, the JVM *is* the firmware. It is the component that must first be uploaded to the RCX brick to accommodate Java programs. The JVM knows how to interpret byte-code that is uploaded to the RCX and communicate with the onboard firmware (ROM) to make the RCX do what you want it to do. Let's examine the technical specification of the JVM.

Memory

As mentioned before, the RCX has a total of 32 kB of RAM (Figure 2–1). Of that, about 4 kB is off limits because the ROM routines use it. That leaves about 28 kB free to be exploited. leJOS has a footprint of about 16 kB, which means there is a total of 12 kB of free memory for user code. That number is normally more than enough for most robotics programs, unless of course the RCX is heavily collecting and storing data, such as map data.

Floating-Point Numbers

As of this writing, leJOS is currently the only RCX language to allow floating-point numbers (decimal places). This gives leJOS the ability to represent fractional numbers, as well as allowing trigonometric functions such as Tan, Cos, and Sin. Without floating-point numbers it is not very practical to per-

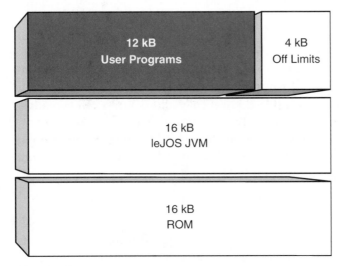

Figure 2–1 The leJOS JVM memory map.

form trigonometric functions, which are vital for navigation. leJOS tries its best to save memory so it does not fully support 64-bit numbers (floating-point or integral numbers).

Warning:

The situation with doubles is a little complicated; they are supported, but not fully. You can do anything with doubles in leJOS, including initializing double variables and performing mathematical operations on them. However, internally they are treated as floats. This means that although it looks like you are using a 64-bit double number, it has the same accuracy as a 32-bit float, so when using very large floating-point numbers, some accuracy may be lost.

Threads

Multithreading allows different parts of a program (threads) to execute at roughly the same time, sharing the CPU. The leJOS thread scheme is very complete, allowing synchronization and interrupting. Because there is a single processor inside the RCX (as opposed to computers containing multiple processors) the threads must take turns using the processor in a preemptive scheme. Threads are normally controlled by a thread *scheduler*, which allows a thread to take control of the processor for a number of instructions. leJOS threads are handled by a very simple scheduler that keeps a list of current threads and simply switches from one thread to the next using a single native C function called switch_thread(). This is all performed automatically by the scheduler. In the latest incarnation of leJOS, each thread is allowed to execute up to 128 instructions before the next thread is given a turn.

In robotics, a thread is usually created to monitor a sensor. Because there are only three sensor inputs, a simple robot project typically has only about three to five threads total, but leJOS theoretically allows up to 255 threads to be created! This is, of course, more than enough threads for most robotics projects, and illustrates the few limitations imposed by leJOS. Keep in mind, however, that every thread you create uses a ton of memory, so it's a good idea to keep them to a minimum in leJOS.

Arrays

Arrays are useful for storing large sequences of related numbers or objects. Arrays are allowed in leJOS, including multidimensional arrays. These are potentially useful for navigation systems that keep track of location using a

two-dimensional grid-based system. With this system, an array could be created to keep track of x and y points of objects it has encountered. Larger
dimensions can also be used, but (without getting into technical detail) not
too many, otherwise the JVM might run out of resources and crash or
become unstable. Programmers rarely use more than two dimensions, however, so this is not a large factor.

Event Model

leJOS is capable of using the Java event model, which includes listeners and
event sources. In the standard leJOS API there are only three objects that use
listeners: Timer (TimerListener), Button (ButtonListener), and Sensor (SensorListener). This model allows for clean, easy-to-understand code when the
RCX needs to wait for an event to occur. In the event model, an object acts as
an event source, such as a sensor (imagine a touch sensor). At the start of the
program execution, one or more objects can register with the sensor to listen
for events. When an event occurs (e.g., the touch sensor being pressed) all listeners are notified of the event and can respond accordingly (Figure 2–2).

Exceptions

Java uses an error-handling scheme to deal with errors (exceptions) when
they occur. The advantage of exception handling is it allows error-checking
code to be separated from the regular program logic. This makes the code
tidy and easy to understand, rather than forming a tangled mess of error-
checking code and logical code. The common term for this is *exception handling*, and it too has been included in leJOS Java.

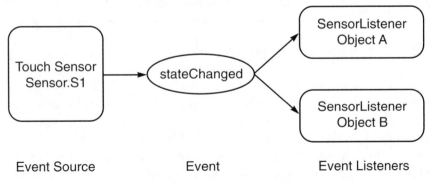

Figure 2–2   Touch sensor event sequence.

The main virtue of exceptions is that they propagate up the call chain, so it is not necessary to write methods with return values that are error codes. For example, exceptions allow you to seamlessly distinguish between a legitimate null return value and a method error. Additionally, Java programs give stack traces instead of crashing the system, which is useful for locating the source of the error. leJOS has its own way of displaying exceptions that is discussed later in the book.

Recursion

Recursion is a programming technique that allows a method to call itself. Java and most other object-oriented languages allow recursion. leJOS is limited in the number of times a block of code can enter itself, however. Currently it can only recurse about 10 levels deep, but if the method is using many local variables, this number will decrease.

Garbage Collection

Object-oriented languages such as Java rely on the creation of new objects to function. When an object is no longer in use by a program it should be removed from memory, a process known as *garbage collection*. Most Java implementations have automatic garbage collection, but leJOS currently does not (although it is being worked on). This is not as big a factor as you might first think. It just requires a programmer to be mindful of reusing objects rather than using the keyword *new* to create new ones. Chapter 12, "Advanced Topics," explores this topic in greater detail.

Note:

Primitive data types such as int and float are not objects, and do not need to be collected when the program is done using a variable.

RCX Platform Extensions

The leJOS API contains the josx.platform.rcx package, which deals specifically with accessing the RCX. The *josx* in the package name stands for Java Operating System eXtension, and these are necessary extensions of the standard Java packages to access and control the RCX brick. Most of the methods in these classes mirror the functionality of the standard LEGO RCX Code. Let's examine the functionality of this package, without going into detail about class and method names in the API (this is covered in Chapter 4, "Learning leJOS").

Output

The three output ports (A, B, and C) can all be controlled under leJOS. Motors can specifically be made to move forward and backward, or a call can be made to reverse the current direction. There are two methods to stop the motors. One stops the motors dead and applies a force to the motor to keep it locked (which uses power). The other method cuts power to the motor but does not lock it, meaning the motor will glide to a stop if it is moving and can be turned freely. The overall power to the motor can also be adjusted, which is demonstrated in a Hands On section later in this chapter.

Input

Reading data from the input ports is slightly more complicated than controlling the output ports. There are two settings that must be specified for each sensor port: *type* and *mode*. The type of sensor that can be connected to the input ports includes the standard LEGO sensors: light, touch, rotation, and temperature sensors. The RCX must be told which type of sensor is connected to a particular input port so the correct algorithm is used to read the data from the sensor. The input ports can also be set to raw type, meaning no algorithm is used to interpret the results and only raw data is collected (between 0 and 1,023).

Mode specifies the type of data collecting the sensor will perform. The temperature sensor, for example, can interpret data in degrees Farenheit or degrees Celsius, so the mode is used to set how the data is interpreted. There are eight modes each input port can use, which are covered in Chapter 4.

RCX Buttons

All buttons except for the On-Off button can be reprogrammed under leJOS. The great part about this is the event model can be used to listen for button presses and react accordingly when one is activated. This makes it easy to separate the user interface portion of your code in an object-oriented style.

System Time

Time is kept on the RCX brick as the number of milliseconds that have elapsed since it was turned on. This can be useful for time-stamping when events have occurred.

Battery Power

leJOS is capable of checking the charge on the batteries. You might think this would give you a percentage of battery power left, but actually it returns a two-digit number representing the voltage of the batteries. For example, it can determine a charge of 7.5 volts, which is common for rechargable batteries, or 9 volts for regular alkaline batteries. If the battery charge starts to fall rapidly, this usually means the RCX is "running on empty."

Note:

The latest beta version of leJOS is now displaying this value as a percentage of battery power left. This may or may not make it into the final release.

Multiple Programs

leJOS allows up to eight programs to be stored on board simultaneously. This is accomplished by uploading more than one class file at a time by specifying a list of class files to be uploaded. Once on board, the program you wish to execute can be selected with the View button.

LCD

leJOS outperforms when it comes to the LCD. Every element on the display can be turned on or off, allowing fine-grained control over the output, and that's not all. leJOS even includes a complete set of arabic letters that can be displayed on screen, much like when students try to spell words on a calculator using just the 10 digits available. Some of these letters are a little wacky, but that's because the RCX LCD only has enough segments to display numbers properly. You will probably find the display is good enough to present debugging information, though.

Web Site:

Tim Rinkens has authored a very cool applet to display leJOS characters to a simulated LCD. Once the applet has completed the introduction, you can start typing characters to see how they will look on the actual RCX. Go to rcxtools.sourceforge.net.

Speaker

leJOS can cause the RCX to play several predefined speaker sounds, including beeps and buzzes. If you want to make your own sounds, leJOS allows complete control over the frequency and duration of a note. Many programmers use this feature to make their robots a little more friendly by belting out short tunes. The sounds can also be used to provide debugging information, which can indicate the point in the program the RCX is executing.

IR Communications

Communications can take place between the RCX brick and the IR tower, between two RCX bricks, or between an RCX brick and the LEGO remote control (see Appendix A). Communication is very simple and consists of sending or receiving byte values (0–255). The communications class can also set the RCX to short range or long range mode, allowing it to stay in touch with the PC even across long distances.

Timers

The RCX has a built-in internal timer to keep track of events. The timer is different from the system time; system time just keeps a running account of the time since the RCX was turned on, but a Timer object will notify all listeners after a certain delay via the event model. The timer can be accessed using the josx.util.Timer class. The number of individual Timer objects that can be created is limited only by the amount of available memory on the RCX.

Java API

The API included in the J2SE is absolutely enormous. It includes packages for programming graphical components, creating applets, JavaBeans development, input/output (I/O), networking, and security (among other packages and classes). For the most part, these classes are not relevant to RCX programming, so it makes no sense to include them in leJOS. Also, the sheer size of some of them makes it impossible for them to run on the RCX in any form. The leJOS Java API can be thought of as a pared-down version of the regular Java API. Where possible, the identical method names and return types have been used by leJOS to keep the environment as consistent as possible with the full-blown Java API. There are currently only three packages in the leJOS Java API that reflect the functionality of the standard Java 2 API. Let's review each of these to get a feel for what they provide.

java.lang

The java.lang package contains classes and interfaces that are fundamental to the Java programming language. Just to give you an idea of how pared down these packages are, the standard java.lang package contains three interfaces, 31 classes, 24 exceptions, and 21 errors. In comparison, leJOS contains one interface, eight classes, eight exceptions, and six errors. We examine these in depth in Chapter 3, "Learning Java in 2.4 Hours!," but for now, let's briefly go over what is included.

- `java.lang.Math`
  The Math class in leJOS is a close approximation of the standard Java Math class. It includes functions for trigonometry, square root, power, random numbers, and others. The standard Java functions often use lookup tables to improve speed, but lookup tables take up a lot of memory, so the leJOS Math class uses raw calculations instead for the most part. This means the functions might not be as fast as regular Java 2 functions (which also run on a faster PC), but for robotics they are still fast enough. None of these functions should take longer than 60 ms to calculate on the RCX.

- `java.lang.String`
  String would probably not be necessary in a pure robotics environment, except for the fact that the RCX has a display screen that can print characters. String can sometimes come in handy if you are outputting text to the LCD. As in regular Java, String objects are immutable, so if you use lots of Strings in your program they can really drain the memory.

- `java.lang.StringBuffer`
  The StringBuffer class does not include as many methods as the standard Java StringBuffer class, but it performs the main function adequately. That function is to allow strings of characters that can be modified dynamically, without creating new String objects. StringBuffer is similar to String, only StringBuffer can be modified using various append methods. If for some reason your program is outputting lots of text and numbers to the LCD screen, it might be a better idea to use StringBuffer.

- `java.lang.System`
  The System class is used for a variety of interactions with the leJOS JVM. It is used to exit a user program, retrieve the

current time, or obtain an instance of Runtime (to calculate free memory).

- `lava.lang.Thread`

  As previously discussed, the Thread class is very full featured and allows complete control over threads.

java.util

The java.util class contains collections (sets of objects) and other miscellaneous utility classes, such as a random number generator. Technically, most of the standard Java 2 utility classes could have been included in the leJOS java.util package (such as java.util.Date), but they would probably find little usage among most RCX programmers. Therefore leJOS just includes some of the more prominent classes and skips those that are unlikely to be useful in a robotics setting. Let's examine the classes it does include:

- `java.util.Bitset`

  The Bitset class is used to represent a series of bits. A Bitset is created with a specific length, then the individual bits can be set to either true or false. Currently Bitset contains the barest elements of the standard Java 2 Bitset class. It doesn't even have a toString() method to display the bit set as a String.

- `java.util.Hashtable`

  A Hashtable allows a collection of objects to be stored and retrieved using a key. The leJOS version of Hashtable is slimmed down, with only two methods to store or retrieve objects. For comparison, the standard Java Hashtable class has 20 methods and four constructors.

- `java.util.Random`

  The Random class is used to produce (pseudo-) random numbers. It is actually easier to generate random numbers using the Math.random() method, which uses an instance of java.util.Random to generate the numbers.

- `java.util.Vector`

  A Vector contains an array of objects that grows dynamically as more objects are added to it. The leJOS Vector class is also extremely pared down compared with the standard Java Vector class.

java.io

The leJOS java.io package is in beta testing as of this writing. It currently contains the Serializable interface, InputStream, OutputStream, DataInputStream, DataOutputStream, and the necessary IOException class. These classes are used by the RCX to transmit data streams through the IR port to another Java enabled RCX brick, or even to a PC through the IR tower. Currently there is no ObjectInputStream or ObjectOutputStream, but the door is open.

Robotics Programming

Because the RCX is most often used for robotics programming, it makes sense to include generic classes and methods to speed up development time and increase program compatibility. These classes were created knowing that robots often have different-sized tires, different turning radii, and sometimes even differences in motor speed. In fact, sometimes robots don't even use wheels to move, but they can still benefit from some of these classes. These types of classes are all stored in the josx.robotics package.

Behavior Control Classes

The most popular cliché in small robotics programming is behavior control programming. This type of programming was pioneered by Rodney Brooks at MIT and has since been refined for use with simple robots. Because it is so pervasive, leJOS has incorporated this with a series of classes and interfaces to make designing the architecture of behavior control programming easier and faster. Chapter 6, "Behavior Control," covers this topic.

Navigation Classes

The navigation package provides classes that speed up development when creating robots that navigate. It provides classes that control movement, so you can easily tell a robot to point in a certain direction, move for a certain distance, or even move to a certain coordinate point. The classes even keep track of the coordinates of the robot relative to its starting point, so it always has some idea where it is. (Chapter 7, "Navigation," and Chapter 8, "Navigation with Rotation Sensors," will cover this topic).

Installing leJOS

Installation for leJOS is relatively simple to accomplish even though the setup is not totally automated. There are a few environment variables that must be set, dependent on the operating system you are using. If you've successfully installed Java on your PC then this should be a breeze because it follows many of the same steps. This section includes instructions for each major operating system, followed by a simple test to make sure everything is working. The following environment variables must be set:

- The PATH to the JDK binary files (javac.exe)

- The PATH to the leJOS binary files (lejosc.exe and lejos.exe)

- A setting called RCXTTY that represents the port to which the IR tower is connected

- The CLASSPATH to your Java classes and packages

Note:

leJOS is fully compatible with the new USB IR tower included in the RIS 2.0 kit.

Windows 98/Windows Me

Warning:

There have been some reports of the IR light staying on when using certain notebook computers running Windows 98. Specifically, the Packard-Bell Easy Note has been cited. Apparently programs will still download properly but the IR light remains on at all times, and the 9-volt battery quickly becomes exhausted. If this is happening to you, the best option might be to unplug the IR cable when you are not uploading RCX Code.

1. If you have not already done so, download and install the Java 2 SDK from the Sun Web site at *java.sun.com.*

Warning:

As of this writing, the JDK 1.4 is not compatible with leJOS. This may change, however, so check the leJOS Readme file to see if this still applies.

2. Add the Java 2 binaries directory to your PATH setting. leJOS relies on the Java binary files to function properly, and they must be accessible from the PATH setting. To do this, edit the Autoexec.bat file and add a line indicating the path to the binaries directory. For example: `path=c:\jdk1.3.1\bin`

3. Download the leJOS Zip file from the leJOS home page at *lejos.sourceforge.net.*

4. There is no installation program for leJOS, so you will have to extract the contents of this file into a permanent directory such as C:\Lejos. For this step, you will need WinZip, which is available at *www.winzip.com.*

5. The leJOS software needs to know which communications port the IR tower is connected to. This is done by adding an environment variable called RCXTTY and specifying the COM port. If the IR tower is connected to Serial Port 2, add the following line to Autoexec.bat: `set RCXTTY = COM2`. The port will likely be COM1 or COM2, but could be as high as COM4.
    If you are using RIS 2.0 with USB, then the setting is as follows: `set RCXTTY = usb`

6. We also add a CLASSPATH variable. First, the leJOS compiler must be told that classes can be found in the current directory (the directory you are compiling from). This is indicated with a single period. The class path is the location of the classes leJOS (and Java) will look to for classes and packages. Again, with the Autoexec.bat file we add the following line: `set classpath=.`

7. You might also want to tell Java the root directory from which all your packages will reside, if you prefer to use the package structure (which is explained more in Chapter 3). Let's assume you are going to give all your projects their own directory, and store those directories in a directory called C:\Java. Then you should add C:\Java to the CLASSPATH: `set classpath=.;c:\Java`

8. You will also probably want to be able to access the leJOS binary files (e.g., the leJOS compiler) from any directory at the command prompt. To do this, we edit the Autoexec.bat file again. Insert a semicolon at the end of the PATH value, then

add the leJOS binary directory: `path=c:\jdk1.3.1\bin ;c:\lejos\bin`

9. Now that everything is set up, reboot the computer to activate the environment variable settings.

That's it! Try the later section called "Testing leJOS" to ensure everything works.

Windows NT/Windows 2000/Windows XP

Warning:

There has been a problem reported with Windows 2000 using certain PC models in which the IR light remains on at all times. When attempting to upload code leJOS.exe will respond with "No response from RCX." This problem is not with leJOS and occurs under the standard LEGO RIS software, too. So far, I have only heard of problems with the Dell Inspiron 5000 under Windows 2000. Some people have even reported that this could damage the IR tower. If you have a Dell Inspiron 5000, your best solution could be to use Windows 98/Me or Windows XP instead.

1. Download and install the Java 2 SDK from the Sun Web site at *java.sun.com*.

2. Add the Java 2 binaries directory to your PATH setting. leJOS relies on the Java binary files to function properly, and they must be accessible from the PATH setting. To do this, open the Control Panel (Start ➤ Settings ➤ Control Panel) and select System. Click the Advanced tab (see Figure 2–3).

3. Click Environment Variables, and you should see the screen shown in Figure 2–4. The top half represents environment variables for the current profile, and the bottom half represents environment variables for the entire system. If you have Power User access or higher you will be able to change the system environment variables; if not you will only be able to change the current profile. Either one will work. Under System Variables, select Path, then click Edit. You should see the window shown in Figure 2–5.

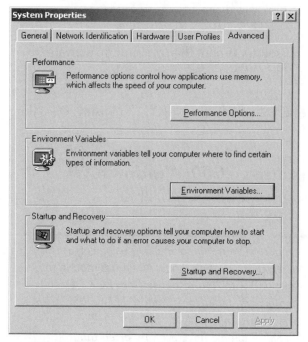

Figure 2–3 Windows 2000 environment variables.

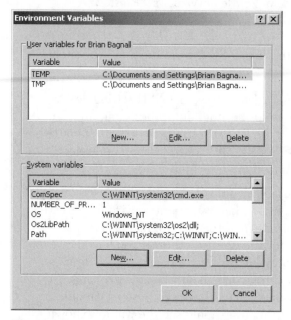

Figure 2–4 Locating the PATH variable.

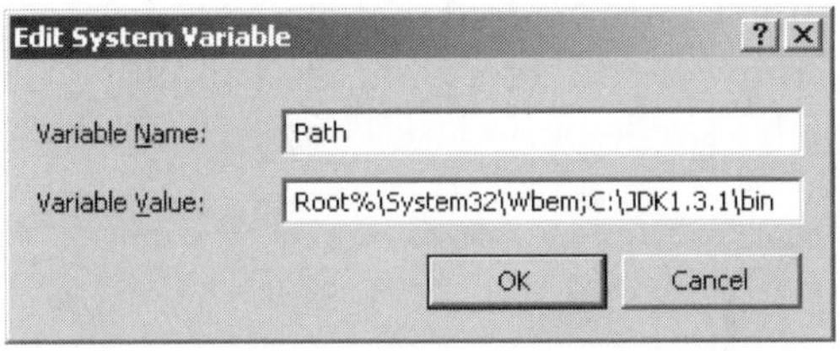

Figure 2-5 Editing the PATH variable.

4. At the end of the variable value, place a semicolon and then the full directory path to the Java 2 binaries directory. For example, if you installed the Java 2 SDK to the C: drive, the path will be something like c:\jdk1.3.1\bin. Click OK on all three windows.

5. Download the leJOS zip file from the leJOS home page at *lejos.sourceforge.net*.

6. There is no installation program for leJOS, so you will have to extract the contents of this file into a permanent directory such as C:\Lejos. For this step, you will need WinZip, which is available at *www.winzip.com*.

7. The leJOS software needs to be able to access the communications port to which the IR tower is connected. This is done by adding an environment variable called RCXTTY and specifying the COM port. Open the environment variables window from Step 2 (Figure 2–6). This time, select New and you should see a window to create a new variable. Fill the first field with RCXTTY and the second field with the COM port that the IR tower is connected to. It will likely be COM1 or COM2, but could be as high as COM4. If you are using RIS 2.0 then the setting should be USB. Click OK.

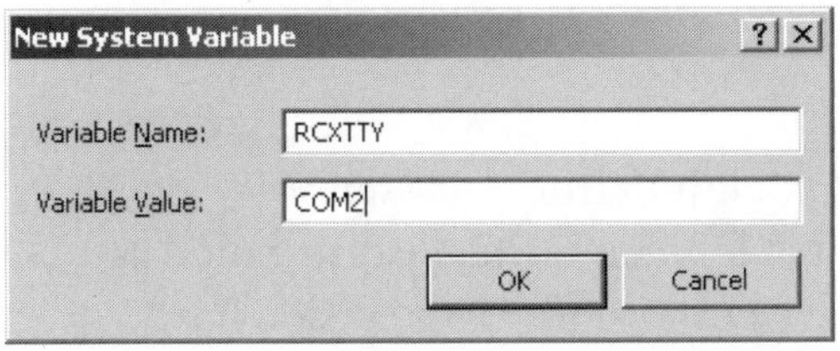

Figure 2-6 Adding the RCXTTY variable.

8. We will also add a CLASSPATH variable. The class path is the location of the classes leJOS (and Java) will look to for classes and packages. Select New again in the environment variables

window. First, the leJOS compiler must be told that classes can be found in the current directory (the directory you are compiling from). This is indicated with a single period (see Figure 2–7).

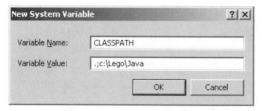

Figure 2–7   Adding the CLASSPATH variable.

9. You might also want to tell Java in which root directory all the packages will reside (which is explained more in Chapter 3). Let's assume you are going to give all your projects their own directory and store those directories within a directory called C:\Lego\Java. Then you would want to add C:\Java to the CLASSPATH (see Figure 2–7). The final value for CLASSPATH would appear as follows: `.;c:\Lego\Java`

10. Once this is done, click OK.

11. You will also probably want to be able to access the leJOS binary files (e.g., the LEGOs compiler) from any directory at the command prompt. To do this, we edit the PATH environment variable again. Insert a semicolon at the end of the PATH value, then add the leJOS binary directory (e.g., C:\Lejos\Bin).

That's it! Now try the later section "Testing leJOS" to ensure everything works.

Linux

1. Download the UNIX version of leJOS from *lejos.sourceforge.net*. The UNIX version of leJOS is normally distributed as a tarball (i.e., a file with a .tar.gz extension). This version has been tested by the developers of leJOS on RedHat Linux, but has also been reported to work on other Linux distributions and Solaris.

2. Unzip and untar the download, for example, by running the following shell commands:

```
cd $HOME/my_download_directory
gunzip lejos_version.tar.gz
cd $HOME
tar xvf $HOME/my_download_directory/
lejos_version.tar
```

A directory named lejos_*version*, containing an uncompiled version of leJOS, should be created after you untar the download.

3. For leJOS to work properly, the bin directory of the JDK should be part of your PATH environment variable. You can check the value of PATH by typing:

```
echo $PATH
```

To add, for example, the directory /usr/java/jdk1.3.1/bin to your PATH, run the following command (assuming bash shell):

```
export PATH=$PATH:/usr/java/jdk1.3.1/bin
```

4. Go to the leJOS installation directory and run:

```
make
```

This step creates tools and scripts necessary to run leJOS. These tools are created under the leJOS *bin* directory, which you may want to add to your PATH environment variable.

5. Set the environment variable RCXTTY to the IR serial port. In a Linux PC the serial port file has the form /dev/ttySn, where n is the port number. This port number is one less than its Windows counterpart. Suppose, for example, that in Windows you would be using COM2 for the IR tower; you would set RCXTTY as follows (assuming bash shell):

```
export RCXTTY=/dev/ttyS1
```

Macintosh OS X

The Macintosh version of leJOS is almost identical to the UNIX version, since OS X uses UNIX at its core. As of this writing it is still in the early stages of testing so please consult the Readme file for installation. See Appendix A for information on obtaining a serial cable (RIS 1.0 and 1.5 only).

Note:

There is no 100% Java version of leJOS yet, (although there has been some talk), but a 100% Java version of TinyVM exists at: ourworld.compuserve.com/homepages/brainstage/mindstorms.htm.

Testing leJOS

Now that leJOS is set up, let's give it a test run. The first thing we should check is the firmware download, which installs the leJOS JVM onto the RCX brick. After that we will see if a sample Java program will compile correctly. Finally, we make sure a program can be uploaded to the RCX brick. For this section we do everything from a command prompt, although later in the chapter you can install an IDE to make things easier.

Uploading the JVM to the RCX

1. Make sure the IR tower is connected to your PC.
2. Place the RCX brick about four to six inches from the IR tower and turn it on.
3. Go to a command prompt.
4. We will first try to upload the firmware in fast mode (which is a lot more enjoyable than slow mode). Type

   ```
   lejosfirmdl -f [enter]
   ```

5. The entire download should take about 50 seconds in fast mode (USB is significantly slower). If the green light appears on the IR tower and it starts downloading, everything is good. If it stops without completing, you might want to try slow mode. Type

   ```
   lejosfirmdl [enter]
   ```

   Slow mode will take about three minutes to download the JVM.
6. When the download finishes you should see a number on the LCD representing the battery charge, and no Minifig (indicating there are no programs on board).

If you have any problems with this section, refer to Table 2–1 for detailed trouble-shooting information.

Table 2-1 Firmware Upload Troubleshooting

Symptom	*Solution*
Message: "Tower not responding"	The cable is not connected properly to either the IR tower or to the serial port at the back of the computer.
	You are using the wrong RCXTTY setting, or this environment variable is not set up properly.
	The IR tower does not contain a battery, or the 9-volt battery is backward.
Message: "'lejosfirmdl' is not recognized as an internal or external command, operable program or batch file"	The leJOS binary directory is missing from the PATH variable. If you installed leJOS on your C drive, the PATH should include C:\Lejos\Bin.
The upload begins but it fails to complete; message: "Transfer data failed"	Most likely the 9-volt battery in the IR tower is getting weak. Try recharging or replacing it.
	The IR tower and/or RCX might be in too much sunlight. Try closing the blinds or moving the setup into a shadier part of the room.

Compiling a Program

1. At the command prompt, change to the leJOS subdirectory Examples\View.
2. We will attempt to compile the file View.java. Type:

```
lejosc View.java [enter]
```

3. The compiler should execute and then bring you back to the command line. When you look in the directory there should now be a file called View.class. If you received an error on this step, consult Table 2–2.

Table 2-2 Troubleshooting Compiling

Symptom	*Solution*
Message: "Unable to execute javac. Return status of exec is -1. Make sure javac is in the PATH, or define JAVAC"	The Java binary files are not set in the PATH environment variable. For example, if the JDK is installed on the C drive, the PATH should include C:\Jdk1.3.1\Bin.
	Java 2 may not be installed on your system. Try downloading and installing it (then add it to the PATH).
Message: "'lejosc' is not recognized as an internal or external command, operable program or batch file" (Windows 2000)	The leJOS binary files are not included in the PATH variable. If you installed leJOS on your C drive, the PATH should include C:\Lejos\Bin.

Uploading a Program to the RCX

1. We will now attempt to upload the View program to the RCX. Make sure the RCX is on and the leJOS JVM has been installed.
2. Place the RCX in front of the IR tower.
3. While in the Examples\View directory type:

```
lejos View [enter]
```

   The light should come on on the IR tower and the program should begin to download to the RCX. You will also see incrementing numbers on the RCX display.
4. Once the download is complete, a Minifig will appear on the RCX display to indicate a program is present and ready to run. If this does not work, refer to Table 2–3.

Table 2-3 Troubleshooting Program Upload

Symptoms	*Solution*
Message: "No response from RCX. Please make sure RCX has leJOS firmware and is in range. The firmware must be in program download mode. Turn RCX off and on if necessary. lejosrun: returned status 1."	Turn on the RCX and make sure it is facing the IR tower. Possibly it is currently running a program, therefore it is not in download mode. To place it in download mode, turn it off then back on.
Program does not finish downloading; message: "Write error: Wrote only -1 of 217 bytes. Probably a resource allocation problem. lejosrun: returned status 1."	The battery in the IR tower is probably very weak. You might even notice the green light on the tower growing dimmer during the download. Recharge or replace the 9-volt battery.
Message: "Fatal: Class View (file View.class) not found in CLASS-PATH: C:\lego\lejos\lib\classes.jar"	The CLASSPATH environment variable must include the current directory, represented by a single period.

Hands On:

The View program you just uploaded is very handy for testing functions of the RCX, such as motors and sensors. In this exercise we use this program to examine the different power settings of the motors.

1.1 Connect a motor to Port A. Preferably, connect a wheel to the motor.

1.2 With the View program uploaded to the RCX, press Run. This starts running the program on the RCX.

1.3 Press View on the RCX until the caret moves to Port A.

1.4 Now press Run to turn the motor on (the rightmost number in the display will change to 1).

1.5 Now increase the power to 7 by repeatedly pressing Prgm. The display will change until you see 7.

1.6 Feel the power of the motor at 7 by lightly grabbing the wheel (but not enough to stop it).

1.7 Now press Prgm again so the power is 0. Lightly grab the wheel to see how easy it is to stop.

1.8 Notice that the wheel turns at about the same rate, even with different power. Power affects the strength of the axle rotation, but not necessarily speed (at least not consistently). As mentioned in Chapter 1, "Meet MINDSTORMS," there is no speed setting available for LEGO motors.

1.9 Now press Prgm until the motor stops. If you try turning the wheel, notice that there is some resistance. (You might need to compare this to a motor that is not in use to detect this.) This resistance shows the difference between the stop() and flt() methods. The stop() method locks the axle in place, which still uses battery power. leJOS also has the option to float the wheels to a stop using flt(), meaning the power is cut off but the wheel may turn freely.

Creating and Running a Program

In Chapter 1 we created a simple robot called Tippy and programmed it using the LEGO software and RCX Code. In this section we write the same program for our robot using leJOS Java. As you might recall, the robot was programmed to move forward until it hit an object, then back up and change direction before moving forward again. In RCX Code this was very easy to program. Let's examine the same routines written in Java:

```
1. import josx.platform.rcx.*;
2. class Tippy {
3.
4.    public static void main(String [] args) {
5.        Motor.A.forward();
6.        Motor.C.forward();
7.        while(true) {
8.            if(Sensor.S2.readBooleanValue() == true)
9.                backUpAndTurn();
10.        }
11.    }
12.
13.    public static void backUpAndTurn() {
```

```
14.      Motor.A.backward();
15.      Motor.C.backward();
16.      try {
17.          Thread.sleep(600);
18.      } catch(InterruptedException e) {}
19.      Motor.A.forward();
20.      try {
21.          Thread.sleep(300);
22.      } catch(InterruptedException e) {}
23.      Motor.C.forward();
24.    }
25. }
```

For those familiar with Java, this program is very easy to understand. Lines 5 and 6 start the robot moving forward. Line 7 begins an endless loop that checks if the sensor has been pressed. If so, the backUpAndTurn() method is called. This causes the motors to reverse for 600 ms, then makes one go forward (with the other still in reverse) for 300 ms. At the end of the method both motors are spinning forward again. The Java code is easy to understand, sometimes more so than the mysteries of LEGO code.

Uploading More Than One Program

The leJOS JVM is capable of storing up to eight distinct programs in memory at the same time. This can be useful if you are demonstrating a variety of programs and don't wish to upload a new program for each one. To try this out we need another program to upload, so we'll use a simple program to move Tippy around in an unpredictable manner:

```
1. import josx.platform.rcx.*;
2. class Tippy2 {
3.    private static final int MAX_DELAY = 1500;
4.    public static void main(String [] args) {
5.        Motor.A.forward();
6.        Motor.C.forward();
7.        while(true) {
8.            move();
9.            spin();
10.       }
11.   }
12.
13.   private static void move() {
14.       // Move forward random distance:
15.       int delay1 = (int)(Math.random() * MAX_DELAY);
16.       try {
17.           Thread.sleep(delay1);
```

```
18.        } catch(InterruptedException e) {}
19.    }
20.
21.    private static void spin() {
22.        // Spin to random direction:
23.        int delay2 = (int)(Math.random() * MAX_DELAY);
24.        Motor.C.reverseDirection();
25.        try {
26.            Thread.sleep(delay2);
27.        } catch(InterruptedException e) {}
28.        Motor.C.reverseDirection();
29.    }
30. }
```

Compile this code and place it in the same directory as Tippy.class. Now type the following:

```
lejos Tippy,Tippy2
```

Both main classes are uploaded to the RCX brick. Once the upload is complete, try pressing the Prgm button. You will notice the program number on the LCD change from 0 to 1. Program 0 is Tippy.class, and program 1 is Tippy2.class. Switch to Program 0 and press Run. When you are done, turn the RCX off and on, then switch to Program 1 and press Run. Pretty easy!

It's worth noting that, to save memory, any classes that are common between the two programs will be shared. In other words, identical classes will not be redundantly uploaded to the RCX. Keep in mind that the number of programs that can be uploaded is also dependent on memory limitations of the RCX brick.

Tip:

It's actually possible to stop a program without turning off the RCX brick. leJOS has a key combination that is very similar to the infamous Ctrl + Alt + Delete (or Ctrl + C) of DOS and older Windows systems. To halt a program, simply hold down the Run button and press the On-Off button. This will stop the program immediately, no matter what it is doing.

Setting Up an IDE

An IDE is a graphical interface that assists with programming and takes away many of the menial tasks of organizing project files and starting the compiler.

A good IDE will make project development faster and eliminate some distractions, such as switching between a text pad and the command line, leaving just you and your code. It's definitely worthwhile to set up a simple IDE, and this section offers some solutions on how to do this.

One of the great features of a good IDE is that it can manage your *workspace*. A workspace can contain many special settings, such as CLASSPATH settings and compiler options. For example, if the computer is shared I could create a workspace for myself and a separate one for my coworker. Also, I could create a workspace for Java 2 programs, and another for leJOS programs. Each of these workspaces can be tailored for the task at hand. A workspace can also manage *projects*, which are simply groupings of all the files belonging to that project. Project management is very useful because it allows you to quickly switch from one project to another easily, rather than having to open and close several scattered files.

There is a range of solutions when it comes to setting up an IDE. Most of these were designed to be used for standard Java development, but they have the option of replacing the compiler (javac.exe) and the JVM (java.exe) with other binary files—in this case, lejosc.exe and lejos.exe. I've picked out the best Windows IDE for leJOS in terms of cost (it's free!) and ease of use.

Note:

leJOS and the JDK must be properly installed and tested to set up an IDE.

JCreator (Windows Platforms)

JCreator is a high-quality Java IDE that consistently receives excellent reviews (Tucows gives it a 5-cow rating). It is a shareware program, which means the maker expects some sort of payment for the latest commercial version. It's obvious that a lot of work and care went into creating this program, and the creator deserves some recognition. There is also the option to download JCreator LE (Light Edition) for free. This version is also quite good but not as well developed as the full-featured JCreator Pro.

JCreator has a very clean, organized interface that pretty much satisfies all the needs of a leJOS programmer. It is very easy to set up, but it makes you extract the setup files first, then run the setup from a temporary directory—one more step than most program setups these days. The interface also allows for easy creation and management of workspaces and projects. Let's go through the steps to acquire and set up this software.

Setup

1. Download JCreator from *www.jcreator.com* (1.9 Mb).
2. Extract the contents into a temporary directory and run the setup.
3. Once JCreator has been installed, open it and we will begin customization for leJOS. Select Configure ➤ Options to open the Options dialog box, then select Tools on the left side of the list (Figure 2–8).

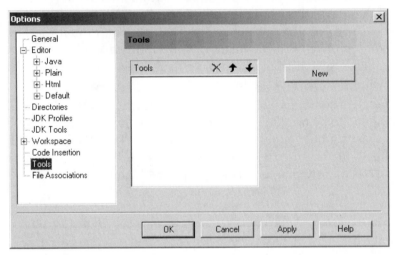

Figure 2–8   Tools setup.

4. Click New, and select Program. A dialog box appears in which you can browse to an executable file. Browse to the `lejos\bin` directory and select `lejosc.exe`, then click Open. You will notice that `lejosc` now appears in the list of tools. Add `lejos.exe` and `lejosfirmdl.exe` in the same manner. You should now have three selections in the Tools window. Click Apply.
5. Now select Tools on the left side, then click the plus sign next to it to expand the list of tools. You should see `lejosc`, `lejos`, and `lejosfirmdl` in the list.
6. Select `lejosc` from the list on the left to bring up a display of options (Figure 2–9). In the arguments field, enter `$[FileName]` (this can also be selected by clicking on the triangle to the right of the field). For initial directory, type `$[FileDir]`. Also, select the Save all documents first and Capture output check boxes. When complete, the form should look like Figure 2–9.

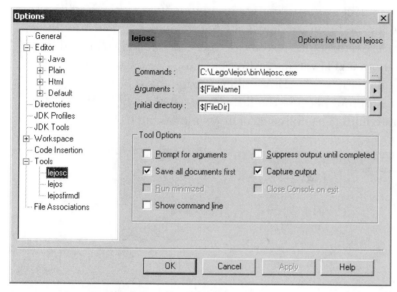

Figure 2-9 Setting up lejosc.exe.

7. Now select `lejos`. In the Arguments field, type `$[CurClass]` and for Initial directory type `$[FileDir]`. Also, select the Capture output check box (Figure 2–10).

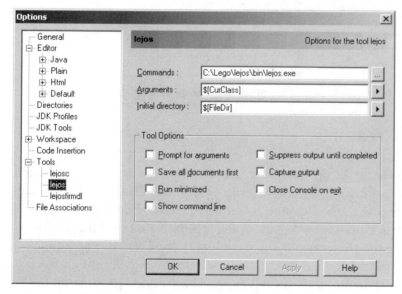

Figure 2-10 Setting up lejos.exe.

8. Finally, select `lejosfirmdl`. For arguments, enter -f to set fast mode for the firmware download. Set the initial directory to the `lejos\bin` directory, just in case this is not already included in the system PATH variable. Also, select the Close Console on exit check box (Figure 2–11). We choose not to have JCreator capture the output because the firmware uploader will print 100 separate lines. The command-line window handles this better.

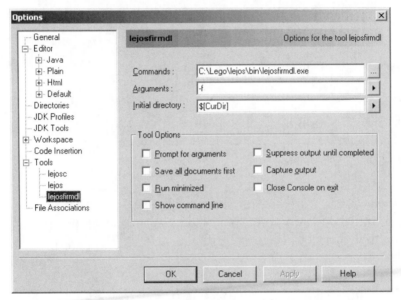

Figure 2-11 Setting up lejosfirmdl.exe.

That's it! You're now ready for some RCX programming.

Using JCreator

Now that you're all set up, using JCreator is simplicity itself. To get started, let's set up a workspace for leJOS projects (you can also set up a separate workspace for Java 2 development if you wish). Select File ➤ New and click the tab labeled Workspaces. We'll use the standard Empty Workspace template, and give the workspace the name leJOS (Figure 2–12). The location in which to save the workspace file can be anywhere—I chose to store the workspace in the root directory for my leJOS projects: C:\Lego\Java. Click OK and the new workspace is created and opened automatically.

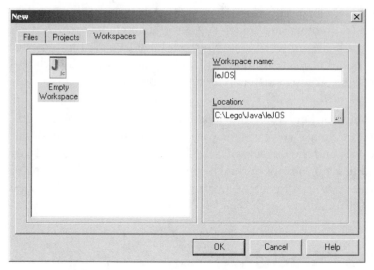

Figure 2-12   Setting up a new workspace.

The next thing to do is add a project to our workspace. Select File ➤ New and click the Projects tab. Select the template icon called Empty Project (see Figure 2–13). For Project Name, type View. You can leave the Location as it is by default, or choose another directory location if you wish. Make sure the Add to current workspace option is selected.

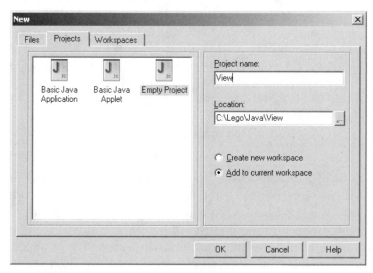

Figure 2-13   Adding an empty project.

To add a file to our project, select Project ➤ Add Files. Browse to the lejos\examples\view directory and select View.java, then click Open. The file now appears beneath the project name (you will have to click the plus sign next to the View name to make it appear). Double-click View.java in the list and the code appears. You can also add a new file by selecting File ➤ New and choosing the "Files" tab.

Let's test compilation and RCX downloading of the View code. On the toolbar, click on the small wrench icon with 1 beside it. The code should compile using leJOS, and the output will say "Process completed." Next, turn on your RCX and place it in front of the IR tower, then click on the wrench 2 icon to upload the code. If all goes well, your RCX brick will have the View program ready for execution.

How leJOS "Stacks Up"

The Internet has spawned one of the most important movements in the field of computing—open source development. In the pre-Internet world, open source projects would have been difficult to create because it would be difficult to recruit enough team members and coordinate programming activities. Now, thousands of die-hard fans of MINDSTORMS can get together online and pool a small amount of their time toward developing awesome programming projects. This process of spontaneous development really shines when it comes to the MINDSTORMS community. There are at least five different programming languages available for the RCX due to open source projects, and all of them are available for free. Each of these projects has also spawned many subprojects, such as GUIs and other tools to help with development (see Appendix C). Let's examine these alternative programming languages for the RCX .

NQC

When it comes to ease of use and installation, it's pretty hard to top Not Quite C (NQC). It even uses the standard LEGO firmware, which has both good and bad points. The good part is that you can store NQC programs as well as RCX Code programs on the same RCX brick. The bad part is there are many limits imposed by the standard LEGO firmware. For instance, there is a limit of 32 variables allowed in a program, there are no floating-point numbers allowed, there are a limited number of tasks (threads) available, there is no access to programming the LCD or the buttons, and it is not object oriented. These shortcomings can seriously limit your programming capabilities. On the upside, most NQC programs download very quickly to the RCX brick, and programs tend not to use as much memory.

pbFORTH

Forth is one of the classic programming languages out there, and many programmers have a fondness for it. The *pb* in pbForth stands for Programmable Brick. This language was one of the first replacement packages available for the RCX. It offers a very basic programming environment using the standard Windows terminal program. It does not come with a firmware uploader program, so it must use the NQC firmware uploader to insinuate itself on the RCX brick. It's more powerful than NQC in many ways; it allows full access to program the LCD and buttons, and there are no variable restrictions (other than memory limits).

There are a few shortcomings to pbForth, however. First, there are no floating-point numbers. Second, most programmers today seem to want to use a more modern programming language. One of the biggest programming innovations to come along is the object-oriented concept. Forth is not an object-oriented language, so Forth programmers are missing out on what makes C++ and Java great languages. There are things to be appreciated about Forth, among them that it is a very simple and elegant language, but there's not a big contingent of people programming their RCX bricks in Forth.

LegOS

LegOS is the most powerful, raw development tool out there for the RCX. It is also the fastest because it actually compiles the code specifically for the Hitachi microcontroller. Other languages for the RCX are interpreted, so they are slightly slower when executing on the RCX brick. The LegOS replacement firmware has a tiny footprint of 8 kB as of version 0.2.4, leaving a (relatively) enormous amount of program space. So far it all sounds good, but LegOS does not have a large following for a number of reasons.

First and foremost is the complexity of everything. It is difficult to set up, especially under Windows. Compiling is such a chore that there are actually a few Web sites where you can send your code and the compiled result is emailed back to you. The API is very empty, offering only the most basic classes and methods. There are no floating-point numbers available (although the author, Marcus Noga, has mentioned he will include this in a future release). So if you are a hard-core C programmer, don't mind working in a difficult programming environment, and don't need floating-point numbers, then LegOS might be for you. Others might want something a little more user friendly.

Visual Basic

It is actually possible to program your RCX brick in Windows with Visual Basic. This is not an open source solution that someone developed, however. This just uses an existing module found in the LEGO MINDSTORMS\System directory called Spirit.ocx. This file allows Visual Basic (or Visual C++ for that matter) to interact with the RCX and send programs to it. You can even use the Visual Basic editors available with many Microsoft products, such as Excel. This solution still uses the standard LEGO firmware, however, so there are the same limitations as standard RCX Code and NQC.

Table 2-4 Comparing RCX Programming Languages

	RCX Code	leJOS	NQC	LegOS	pbForth
Language	Graphical	Java	Not Quite C	C and C++	Forth
Firmware replacement	N/A	Yes	No	Yes	Yes
Floating-point numbers	No	Yes	No	No	No
Programmable display	No	Yes	No	Yes	Yes
Trigonometry and advanced math	No	Yes	No	No	No
Interpreted	Yes	Yes	Yes	No	Yes

Some of these development environments might be preferable to you for a number of reasons. For example, some people might feel more comfortable programming in C because they have been doing it all their lives and see no reason to change. For those people, I would recommend NQC to start with, then if they feel they need more power they could move up to LegOS (and attempt the difficult installation and setup). But when it comes to features, there is nothing that covers everything as fully as leJOS (see Table 2–4). It is a complete object-oriented language with a wide range of primitive types (byte, short, int, char, Boolean, float) and some very useful APIs. leJOS offers the ease of NQC with the power of LegOS, and then some. However, if memory is your biggest concern, and you still want to use Java, then TinyVM might be your best choice.

leJOS vs. TinyVM

TinyVM (Tiny Virtual Machine) is the precursor to leJOS, and can almost be thought of as leJOS micro edition (or Java micro-micro-micro edition). The stated goal of the TinyVM project is not to develop a complete toolbox of features, but rather to keep the memory footprint as small as possible. TinyVM currently has a footprint of just under 10 kB, which leaves a whopping 18 kB of program space.

TinyVM has a relatively complete implementation of the core Java language. For example, it allows threads, recursion, synchronization, arrays, and exceptions. It, of course, allows full access to the RCX brick—it would be pretty useless if it didn't! But it is a little lacking in some areas when compared to leJOS:

- No floating-point numbers
- Limited API
- Math class currently has no fixed-point trigonometric functions
- A smaller following with TinyVM
- No straightforward Windows download

Depending on what you plan on doing, TinyVM could be a better solution for you than leJOS. If you are making very large programs that do not keep track of navigation information, and have no need for floating-point numbers, then TinyVM could be your best choice, but leJOS is definitely a better starting point.

Web site:

TinyVM is located at: tinyvm.sourceforge.net.

LEARN JAVA IN 2.4 HOURS!

Topics in this Chapter

- Java Core Language
- The java.lang Package
- java.util

Chapter 3

This chapter familiarizes you with the Java language, but only as it applies to leJOS. The content of the chapter is written for two kinds of people: those who know Java and those who don't. If you don't know Java, the chapter attempts to familiarize you with the basics of the language. In other words, it will teach you enough Java to be able to program your RCX brick using leJOS. However, what you learn here will also apply to the standard Sun Java language. leJOS *is* Java, in every sense of the word. It just contains a smaller set of API classes, but the core language is identical in syntax to standard Java. After becoming proficient in leJOS you will find it extremely easy to make the jump to programming Java on any computer.

Note:

This chapter should be considered a Java starter kit. There are many good books on the market that teach the Java language in greater depth.

As the title for this chapter indicates, we are attempting the world record for speed-teaching the Java language—and there is some stiff competition. There are books that claim to teach Java in 21 days, and even 24 hours! However, there is a difference between knowing Java and being able to write good code. If this is your first foray into Java, you cannot expect to be able to write good code after just 2.4 hours. In fact, it would be impossible to write good code after 24 hours, or 21 days, or even six months. Good coding comes with experience and gaining new insights into programming, and those things are improved over a lifetime.

For those who already know Java, I suggest skipping over most of the section titled "Java Core Language." This section deals with the absolute basics such as flow control, how to make methods and classes, and all the other topics a seasoned Java programmer is very familiar with. It might be a good idea to pay attention to the Notes and Warnings because they highlight the differences between leJOS and standard Java.

Java Core Language

Every programming language has keywords and symbols used to give it its core functionality. This functionality includes such things as declaring classes, methods, and variables. It also includes manipulating variables, such as adding two variables together. A programming language would be rather boring if it could only run commands one after another. To give a program a branching behavior you need to be able to control program flow—in Java by using if, for, while and do statements. In this section we cover each of these fundamentals and show examples in actual Java code. Before getting into Java it would be a good idea to touch on a fundamental concept to Java: object-oriented programming (OOP).

OOP

OOP is a simple concept to define. To appreciate OOP it should be contrasted with structured programming, which uses one body of code with multiple methods. These types of programs are difficult to manage because methods and global variables are constantly added to the same program. As a program grows larger, it becomes difficult to manage and prone to errors.

OOP has an important difference that leads to powerful implications: Code can be segregated into discrete units. These units, or *objects*, are generally defined by the theme of the code within them. For example, imagine you are trying to program a soccer-playing robot to compete in a tournament. The robot needs to be able to navigate, and also to play soccer. One object could contain functionality centered on the theme of navigation, and another object could contain functionality for playing soccer (Figure 3–1). These units are defined by classes in Java. The Navigation class would contain all the methods to move the robot around the playing field, and the SoccerPlayer class would

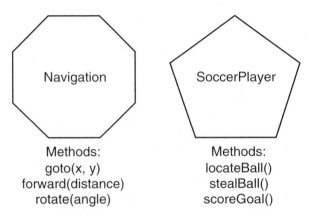

Figure 3-1 Objects in a robotics application.

contain all the methods to make the robot play soccer. Most likely the Soc-cerPlayer class would call methods from the Navigation class to function.

Classes define objects using methods (functionality) and fields (data). Once a class is defined, it can be *instantiated*, which means an object is created that can be manipulated in code. Another powerful feature of OOP is *type extensibility*. This is the ability of classes to inherit data and functionality from other classes. These topics are flushed out further with actual code examples in the following sections.

Source Files

In Chapter 2, "Getting Started with leJOS," you were shown how to set up your development environment and compile some basic code for the RCX. We also had a chance to examine a basic Java class that was a conversion of some RCX Code used in Chapter 1, "Meet MINDSTORMS." We didn't go in depth and explain the code, however, so let's take this opportunity to analyze the contents of a very simple Java source file:

```
import josx.platform.rcx.*;
class Hello {
   public static void main(String [] args) {
      TextLCD.print("HELLO");
      while(true){}
   }
}
```

Try entering this code in a file named Hello.java and compiling it. Once it is compiled, upload it to the RCX and press the Run button to begin execution (refer to Chapter 2 if you are not familiar with how to do this on your system). You should see the word HELLO appear on the LCD. To escape this loop, hold down the Run key and press the On-Off key. The program is not too inspiring, but it is good enough to explain some concepts.

This is about as simple as a leJOS Java source file can get. For now, we'll ignore the import statement in the first line. The second line contains a statement that defines the class name, in this example, Hello. Java is a case-sensitive language, which means it notices if letters are capitalized. To a Java compiler, the name Hello is different from hello. Note the curly brace located after the class declaration and the matching curly brace located at the end of the file. All of the methods and variables contained in the class lie within these two curly braces. In fact, all methods and variables must appear within the curly braces of a class, otherwise it will not compile.

The third line contains a method definition, and as you can see, methods also use curly braces. This method is named main(), and it is the main method that starts the ball rolling. All leJOS programs are started using a main() method. There are also some other keywords in the method definition: public, static, and void. For now, the only thing you should know is that these must be present for the main() method to function properly. There are also some words in the parentheses after the method name, the significance of which is explained later in the chapter.

The statements within the main() method are the heart of the program that provides the functionality of the class. The first line outputs the word HELLO to the LCD, and the next line puts the program in an endless loop. Without this endless loop the program will flash HELLO for a brief millisecond and then go back to the regular battery-power display.

Classes

Classes are the programming structures that define objects in Java, sometimes called *meta-objects*. They are more like templates that are used to create objects, typically by using the new keyword. One class can make a multitude of objects, much like a rubber stamp can create copies of the same design. For example, String is a class contained in the java.lang package. To create several String objects, we can use the following code:

```
String s1 = new String("String A");
String s2 = new String("String B");
String s3 = new String("String C");
```

Once an instance of an object is created, it is possible to call methods on that object or access variables. The following line of code uses the toCharArray() method to retrieve a character array of the String object just created:

```
char [] name = s1.toCharArray();
```

This is the essence of OOP. Objects contain all the data and methods they require in one place. This makes the code easier to understand, especially when compared to structured "spaghetti code," in which methods and data are all thrown together.

Until now we have only seen some very basic class definitions, but classes can also be modified by a number of keywords. For example, the following class contains a declaration using several keywords:

```
public abstract class Hermes extends Navigator
implements SensorListener {}
```

Let's examine each of the keywords available to class definitions.

Class Access

Classes can be either public or default (nothing). A public class is visible to all other classes, meaning another class can interact with the class, doing such things as creating an instance of the class and accessing its methods. Default (sometimes referred to as package access) classes are only visible to other classes within the same package.

Extending Classes

One of the most useful concepts of OOP is that a class can extend another class. Imagine that you program a class that controls a robot arm to move up and down. You decide to call this class Arm. Let's examine a very simplified version of what this class might look like:

```
import josx.platform.rcx.*;
class Arm {
    public void armUp() {
        Motor.B.forward();
    }
    public void armDown() {
        Motor.B.backward();
    }
}
```

Now imagine you create an enhanced robot arm that still moves up and down, but it also has a claw attached to it that opens and closes. It would be

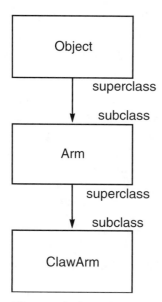

Figure 3–2 Superclass and subclass.

preferable to be able to reuse the code in the Arm class instead of starting from scratch. It also seems a little cumbersome to copy and paste the old Arm code. Java provides an elegant solution of being able to *extend* the Arm class to inherit all the functionality of Arm, as well as being able to add new methods and data to handle the claw. In our example we call this new class ClawArm. ClawArm extends Arm, so Arm is the superclass and ClawArm is the subclass (Figure 3–2). All classes in Java extend the Object class by default, as you can see in Figure 3–2. If you follow the hierarchy of any Java class, the class at the top is always Object.

When a subclass extends another class, it inherits all of the functionality of the superclass. In Java code, the syntax for extending another class is as follows:

```java
import josx.platform.rcx.*;
class ClawArm extends Arm {
    public void openClaw() {
        Motor.C.forward();
    }

    public void closeClaw() {
        Motor.C.backward();
    }
}
```

The extends keyword is used here to indicate the superclass. Now anyone using the ClawArm object will be able to call the two methods of Arm, as well as the methods introduced in ClawArm:

```
ClawArm myRobot = new ClawArm();
myRobot.armDown();
myRobot.openClaw();
```

Abstract Classes

An abstract class is a class that (possibly) contains some functional methods, but also declares method names with no functional code. In a way, an abstract class is like a half-finished class: Some methods are already provided, but others are just defined and must be filled in later. Because an abstract class is not complete, it cannot be instantiated. Let's examine an abstract class to see what they are about. We'll use the Arm class again:

```
import josx.platform.rcx.*;
abstract class Arm {
   public abstract void spinArm();
   public void armUp() {
      Motor.B.forward();
   }
   public void armDown() {
      Motor.B.backward();
   }
}
```

Note in the second line that the Arm class is now declared as Abstract. It contains the same two functional armUp() and armDown() methods as before, but it also defined a third method called spinArm(). Notice this method has semicolons at the end of the definition, but no curly braces. If we try to instantiate this class in code, the leJOS compiler responds with "Arm is abstract; cannot be instantiated." The purpose of an abstract class is that it is a higher level superclass that will be used by other subclasses. The subclasses all share the same code, making it more efficient and logical to program. In this case, Arm is the general class and the subclasses are more specific types of Arm (Figure 3–3).

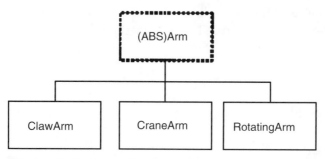

Figure 3–3   Hierarchy of Arm classes.

Final Classes

As we saw before, a class can be extended; all classes, that is, except for final classes. Any class that is declared final may not be extended. Let's examine the ClawArm class again, only this time we make it final:

```
final class ClawArm extends Arm {
   public void openClaw() {
      Motor.C.forward();
   }

   public void closeClaw() {
      Motor.C.backward();
   }
}
```

The ClawArm class can still be used, only now if we attempt to extend this class we will receive the compiler error "Cannot inherit from final ClawArm." Final classes are used for two reasons:

- To enforce an API when you do not want a class extended
- To make the code run slightly faster

In Java, the Math class is declared final for the purpose of making it run faster. Programs often use many math functions, so there can be a significant time savings by making it final. However, it is probably of no use to make a class such as ClawArm final because the motor movements are extremely slow anyway, and the code in the class is simple.

Objects

Objects form the basis of OOP. An object is an instance of a class that contains variables and methods. Put another way, objects contain the data and functionality of a class. A class is not a full-fledged object, but a programmer can use a class to create an object by using the *new* keyword to call a constructor on the class. The new object can also be assigned to a variable if the object needs to be referenced in later lines of code. The following lines of code show an object being initialized, and another assigning an object to a reference variable:

```
new ControlGUI(); // initialized but not assigned
String name = new String("Maximillion"); // initialized
and assigned to 'name'
```

All Java classes are extended from the class Object. This class contains methods common to all Java objects, such as toString() and equals(). The toString() method provides a string representation of an object, and the equals() method compares two reference variables to see if they refer to the same object.

Note:

In leJOS the toString() method is rarely implemented in classes because robotics programming does not use strings as much as desktop PC programming, so it would be a waste of memory. The main reason these methods are defined is to satisfy the Java compilers.

In Java, objects can be accessed by *reference*. This means it is possible for two or more variables to refer to the same object, as the following pseudo-code demonstrates:

```
MyObject a = new MyObject();
MyObject b = a;
MyObject c = b;
```

As you can see, all three reference variables (a, b, and c) are now referring to the same object. Imagine a method is called using Variable b, such as:

```
b.setValue(25);
```

This means the value will be changed for the object that a and c refer to as well, because they all refer to the same object. Now if you call getValue() on a, it will retrieve a value of 25:

```
int x = a.getValue(); // x = 25
```

It gets even more confusing. All arguments are passed to methods by value, including references. This is a notoriously confusing but important issue. When an argument passes a reference by value, both the callee and the caller have a handle on the same object instance, which is a good thing. Examine the following snippet of code:

```
MyObject c = new MyObject();
myMethod(c);
```

The method call myMethod(c) can't possibly modify the value of the c variable. This is why we say even reference arguments are passed by value. Let's look inside the method to see an example of a reference being changed:

```
public void myMethod(MyObject my) {
    my = new MyObject();
}
```

The second line of the method assigns the variable to a new object. Does this mean c now refers to a new object as well, outside the method? No. It can interact with the object referenced by c, including modifying the contents of the object, but it cannot reassign c to another object.

Interfaces

Java does not allow a class to extend more than one class, which can be somewhat limiting for a programmer. Normally, with object-oriented design, it is a good idea for a class to be responsible for only one type of behavior. If you try to make a single class perform all kinds of tasks, it usually makes things unnecessarily complex. However, sometimes it is necessary to make a class with multiple behaviors. In these cases, interfaces are the solution. An interface can define methods and variables, but the methods do not contain any functional code. Because there is no functional code, an interface may not be instantiated (similar to an abstract class). The following is an example of an interface:

```
interface Steerable {

    public void turnLeft();

    public void turnRight();

    public void driveForward();

    public void applyBrakes();

}
```

As you can see, there is no functional code here, only method definitions. So how does this help you as a programmer? Imagine a class that contains a method to steer any type of steerable robot around a track. We'll call this class RaceCar. Pretend the RaceCar class has a method that steers a car around the track by using the steering and driving methods contained by Steerable objects. We'll say the method definition looks like this:

```
public void drive(Steerable carSteering)
```

By having your robot code implement Steerable, it can be used by the Race-Car class. It can also extend another class if need be (but this is not necessary). In the following example, we also have the class extend the Thread class:

```
import josx.platform.rcx.*;
class MyCar extends Thread implements Steerable {
    public void turnLeft() {
        Motor.B.backward();
        pause(200);
        Motor.B.stop();
    }

    public void turnRight() {
        Motor.B.forward();
        pause(200);
        Motor.B.stop();
    }

    public void driveForward() {
        Motor.A.forward();
        Motor.C.forward();
    }

    public void applyBrakes() {
        Motor.A.stop();
        Motor.C.stop();
    }

    public void run() {
        // Sensor watching code here
    }

    private void pause(int mSeconds) {
        try{
            Thread.sleep(mSeconds);
        }catch(InterruptedException e){}
    }
}
```

As you can see, there are now complete method definitions for turnLeft(), turnRight(), driveForward() and applyBrakes(). Now the RaceCar class will

be able to use the MyCar class and guide it around the track using a few lines
of code to get things going:

```
MyCar speedy = new MyCar();
RaceCar.drive(speedy);
```

RaceCar now has an instance of MyCar, which I called speedy. RaceCar
knows it has a Steerable, so it can now call the proper methods to drive the
car around the track.

Import and Package Statements

You may have noticed the following statement at the top of the MyCar class:

```
import josx.platform.rcx.*;
```

This is an import statement, and it is responsible for allowing the MyCar
class access to all classes contained in the josx.platform.rcx package. Keep in
mind this statement does not cause all these classes to upload to the JVM.
Only the classes used in your code will end up taking any extra memory. In
Chapter 2 we discussed some of the packages in the leJOS API, such as
java.lang and java.util. These packages contain an assortment of classes that
perform functions, according to the theme of the package. The main theme
of josx.platform.rcx is that all the classes in that package give you access to
the RCX platform, such as Motor and Sensor. These classes cannot be
accessed by your code until the import statement is used, however. The
advantage of the package system is that other classes can be hidden as well as
sorted, but called out of hiding only when you need to use them. You can also
import just a single class from a package. For example, if we only want to use
the Motor class, we can use the following syntax:

```
import josx.platform.rcx.Motor;
```

Conversely, we could also access a class in a package without using an
import statement by drilling down to it. The following line could be used to
call a method directly from Motor:

```
josx.platform.rcx.Motor.B.forward();
```

Note:

*The java.lang package is always imported automatically by Java because
the classes used in this package are central to the use of the Java language.
It contains such important classes as Thread, System, String, and Math,
which are frequently used. The josx.platform.rcx package is also extremely*

important, and all leJOS programs must import it to interact with the RCX, but leJOS does not import it automatically because leJOS can also be used on other non-RCX platforms.

So how can you make your own packages? First, you must create a directory structure that matches the package name. This directory structure must start at a CLASSPATH directory. For example, let's say you want to make a package called robot.flying. If you have included C:\Java in your CLASS-PATH, it would be logical to make the following directory:

```
C:\Java\robot\flying
```

Now let's say you are making a class called AirShip and you want it to appear in the package robot.flying. First, include the package declaration at the top of your source file:

```
package robot.flying;
import josx.platform.rcx.*;
class AirShip {
    /// Rest of code...
}
```

The package statement must appear before any other code, otherwise the compiler produces an error. Also, once this class is created, to import it, the class file must appear in the directory C:\Java\robot\flying. Normally I just store the source code file in the same directory as the package classes so that when it compiles it automatically dumps it here, but you could move the class file here on your own.

Note:

The main purpose of packages is to organize code. On large projects with hundreds of classes, this can be very important. When creating leJOS programs there are usually very few classes because you are only working with 32 kB. Usually there are fewer than five user-defined classes for any given project. For this reason it might not be useful to create your own packages.

Methods

A method gives a class its functionality. All methods must be contained within a class, and there is no such thing as a global method in Java. Methods have two important defining characteristics—return types and arguments. Let's examine a typical Java method definition:

```
public int readDistance() {
    return Sensor.S2.readValue();
}
```

The first line of this method declares a return type of the primitive int, so by definition the code within the curly braces must return an integer value. If a method declares it will return a value but the code does not return anything, the compiler produces an error. Methods can just as easily return objects, too. As you can see, the parentheses are empty and contain no arguments. Let's examine a method that does use arguments:

```
public void setMotors(Motor left, Motor right) {
    leftDrive = left;
    rightDrive = right;
}
```

This method has no return type, as indicated by using the keyword void. This method uses two arguments, left and right, which can be objects (in this case, two Motor objects) or primitives.

Note:

Recursion is allowed in leJOS. This is an advanced programming technique of having a method call itself (often several hundred times) before a criteria is satisfied and the methods all return. Recursion is very memory-intensive however, and is not recommended in RCX robotics.

Constructor Methods

A constructor method is a special method used to initialize an object when it is created. The code within a constructor can contain absolutely anything the programmer wants, but generally it is limited to setting variables and preparing the object to work when a programmer starts calling methods. The following class shows a properly defined constructor method:

```
1. class Kangabot {
2.     int jumpCentimeters;
3.     public Kangabot(int jumpDistance) {
4.         jumpCentimeters = jumpDistance;
5.     }
6.
7.     public static void main(String [] args) {
```

```
8.       Kangabot roo = new Kangabot(5);
9.   }
10. }
```

The constructor method starts at Line 3. As you can see, it has the same name as the class name, and it has no return type (not even void). In this case the constructor is simply used to initialize a programmer-defined variable jumpCentimeters. All objects use a constructor method, but if you don't specifically create one, the object will have a default no-arguments constructor implicitly defined by Java.

Note:

When you call the constructor method from another body of code, that body of code will stop its execution until the constructor returns. This means that if your constructor starts running methods that never end, your program will effectively freeze. This is a classic error that new programmers often make.

Static Methods

A static method is a method that can be called without creating an instance of a class. To contrast static methods with member methods, let's examine the following code:

```
MyRobot merl = new MyRobot();
merl.attack();
```

This code demonstrates how a method is normally called from an object. With static methods, however, there is no need to create an instance first. If we changed the attack() method just shown to a static method, we could call it straight from the class as follows:

```
MyRobot.attack();
```

There are many Java classes that contain exclusively static methods, such as the java.lang.Math class. Because no data needs to be kept in an object for Math methods to work, there is no reason to go to the trouble of creating an instance of Math. So methods are called directly from the class instead, as follows:

```
int result = Math.sin(0.5);
```

It is easy to write a static method, but there are a few rules that must be obeyed for it to work properly:

- A static method may not directly call an instance (nonstatic) method.
- A static method may not directly use an instance (nonstatic) variable.

Let's examine a static method that will not compile for a variety of reasons:

```
class StaticTest {
    public final int MAXIMUM = 1000;

    public double getRandomUnder100() {
        return Math.random() * 100;
    }

    public static void main() {
        double r = getRandomUnder100();
        r = r + MAXIMUM;
    }
}
```

In this case the static method we are using is the main() method, although it just as easily could be another method such as public static void doCalc()—it all works the same. Notice that the static main() method tries to call the nonstatic getRandomUnder100() method. This violates the first rule and produces a compiler error. The next line in the main() method tries to use the nonstatic variable MAXIMUM, but once again this variable is nonstatic so we violate the second rule.

There are a few ways to fix these problems. The first is to make the getRandomUnder100() method and the MAXIMUM variable static, as follows:

```
class StaticTest {

    public static final int MAXIMUM = 1000;

    public static double getRandomUnder100() {
        return Math.random() * 100;
    }

    public static void main() {
        double r = getRandomUnder100();
        r = r + MAXIMUM;
    }
}
```

This seems like an easy fix, but it often starts the class down the long road of making every single method and variable static, which is not a very good object-oriented solution because this would prohibit you from making more StaticTest instances. The other solution is to create an instance of the class first, then use that instance to access methods and variables:

```java
class NotStaticTest {

    public int count;

    public double getRandomUnder100() {
        return Math.random() * 100;
    }

    public static void main() {
        NotStaticTest test = new NotStaticTest();
        double r = test.getRandomUnder100();
        r = r + test.count;
    }
}
```

As you can see, the main() method creates an instance of NotStaticTest called *test*, then proceeds to access the nonstatic methods and variables using this instance. This is not always the best solution, but in most cases it's a good starting point.

The main() Method

As we saw before, the main() method starts the ball rolling. This method is called by the JVM itself to initiate program execution. For a main() method to work properly it needs a very specific definition, otherwise it will not work. The following is an example of a legal main() method definition:

```java
public static void main(String [] args) {}
```

Let's analyze why each of these keywords is used. First, the method is public so the method is visible outside of the package. Technically, the JVM is not in this package so the method must be public for the JVM to see it. The method is static because there is no instance of the class created yet to call an instance method, so only static methods can be called by the JVM to start things off. It is void because the JVM is not interested in any returned variables from the main() method. Once all programmer threads (called *nondaemon threads*) are done executing, the JVM terminates. The args variable represents an array of Strings. In Java, these arguments are given at the command line and passed to the main() method by the JVM.

Note:

Currently there is no way to pass arguments to a leJOS main() method.

Overloading Methods

It's possible to create two methods with the same name, as long as the argument types are unique for each method. These sets of arguments are called a *signature*. For example, a method using (int, int) has a different signature from one using (int, String). When more than one method exists with the same name it is called an *overloaded method*. This can be very useful to a programmer when it is necessary to create a variant of a method to perform the same functionality as the original, yet uses a different set of parameters to perform the function. Let's examine a possible example of some robot code that uses overloading:

```
1.  import josx.robotics.Navigator;
2.  import josx.platform.rcx.*;
3.
4.  class Wendelbot {
5.     String [] lookupTable = {"Kitchen", "Dining room",
           "Bedroom1"};
6.     int [] lookupX = {200, 560, 900};
7.     int [] lookupY = {10, 60, 1200};
8.     Navigator nav;
9.
10.    public Wendelbot() {
11.       nav = new Navigator(Motor.A, Motor.C, 2.5, 2.5);
12.    }
13.
14.    public void goToLocation(int x, int y) {
15.       nav.gotoPoint(x, y);
16.    }
17.
18.    public void goToLocation(String location) {
19.       int x=0;
20.       int y=0;
21.
22.       boolean match = false;
23.       for(int i=0;i<lookupTable.length;++i) {
24.          if(lookupTable[i].equals(location)) {
25.             x = lookupX[i];
26.             y = lookupY[i];
27.          }
28.       }
29.       goToLocation(x, y);
30.    }
```

```
31.
32.    public static void main(String [] args) {
33.        Wendelbot wb = new Wendelbot();
34.        wb.goToLocation("Kitchen");
35.        wb.goToLocation(0, 0);
36.    }
37. }
```

This class allows the robot to travel to a location using the goToLocation() method, but there are two of them to choose from. The method at Line 14 accepts two coordinate values to determine its goal, whereas the second method at Line 18 accepts a String argument that allows it to travel to a pre-defined location. As you can see, the goToLocation(String) method uses a lookup table to determine which coordinates to travel to, then it ends up calling the goToLocation(int, int) method to actually travel to those coordinates.

Note:

The return type of a method does not affect overloading. This means creating two methods with the same name and arguments but different return types is illegal, as the interpreter will not be able to discern which method call is intended.

It's also possible to overload constructor methods, just like normal methods. When overloading constructors, it is sometimes beneficial to call another constructor as well. This is achieved using the *this* keyword:

```
class GoalKeeper {

    Color myTeamColor;

    public GoalKeeper(Color teamColor) {
        this();
        myTeamColor = teamColor;
    }

    public GoalKeeper() {
        // More initialization code here
    }
}
```

As you can see, the GoalKeeper(Color teamColor) constructor method calls the other constructor in Line 6 by using this(). Java has a rule that when a constructor calls another constructor, the line must appear at the very top of the constructor code. If we try to exchange Lines 6 and 7, the compiler produces an error.

Overriding Methods

As we learned previously, when one class extends another class, the subclass inherits all the methods from the superclass. However, sometimes it is beneficial to change one of the existing superclass methods to provide the subclass with altered or enhanced functionality. For example, imagine you create a robotic arm with LEGO MINDSTORMS (Figure 3–4a). You also need to program a class to control that arm, so you program various methods to control the two-jointed arm. Imagine the simplified API for the arm looks like this:

```
class RoboArm {

    public void goToPoint(int x, int y, int z) {
        // Code to move hand to 3-dimensional coordinate
    }

    // More methods...
}
```

Assume your code is able to move the hand to any coordinate in three-dimensional space. Now pretend you add an extra joint on the robot arm around the wrist area (Figure 3–4b). This means you need to alter the program code to accommodate the physical change. A good object-oriented way to do this would be to extend the RoboArm class and then replace the goToPoint() method with new code. Replacing an existing method defined in a superclass is called *overriding* a method. There's not much to it, as the following example demonstrates:

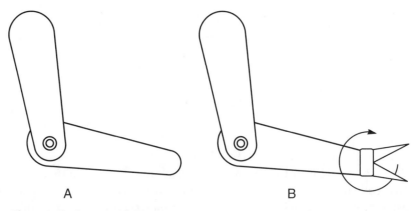

A   B

Figure 3–4   Simplified robot arms.

```
class SuperArm extends RoboArm {
   public void goToPoint(int x, int y, int z) {
      // New code to move 3-jointed arm in 3-dimensional
space
      }
   }
}
```

In Java it is also possible to provide new constructor methods for an extended class, but the superclass constructor is always called in one form or another. If the superclass has a default no-arguments constructor, Java will automatically call that constructor. However, if the superclass has a constructor that requires arguments, then it is up to the subclass constructor to implicitly call that constructor. This can be done using the keyword *super*. Let's take a look at a new definition of RoboArm and the subclass SuperArm:

```
1.  import josx.platform.rcx.*;
2.  class RoboArm {
3.     Motor shoulderJoint;
4.     Motor elbowJoint;
5.
6.     public RoboArm(Motor shoulder, Motor elbow) {
7.        shoulderJoint = shoulder;
8.        elbowJoint = elbow;
9.     }
10. }
11.
12. class SuperArm extends RoboArm {
13.
14.    Motor wristJoint;
15.
16.    public SuperArm(Motor shoulder, Motor elbow, Motor
          wrist) {
17.       super(shoulder, elbow);
18.       wristJoint = wrist;
19.    }
20. }
```

In this example the SuperArm class requires a constructor using an additional Motor. To initialize the superclass, it calls the superclass constructor using the keyword *super* in Line 17. This call allows the SuperClass code to become initialized, then allows the subclass to initialize its own variables (in this case, wristJoint).

Warning:

The rule that a constructor can't call another constructor anywhere except for the first line also applies to super(). What if you want to call super() and this() in the same constructor? You can't. To accomplish this, generally you would call another overloaded constructor using this(), and the overloaded constructor would call super(), as follows:

```
class SuperArm extends RoboArm {
    public SuperArm() {
        this(Motor.A, Motor.B);
    }

    public SuperArm(Motor shoulder, Motor elbow) {
        super(shoulder, elbow);
    }
}
```

Fields and Variables

A variable is simply a symbol composed of characters (e.g., myCount) assigned to a data structure in programming. There are two varieties of variables in Java: primitives and object references. Both of these types have their own characteristics and in some cases must be handled differently.

In OOP terminology, a *field* is a type of data (object or primitive) belonging to an object. When talking about fields, we say these compose the *attributes* of an object. The set of fields (including fields contained in the superclass) is referred to as the state of an object. They are really properties that define the state of an object at a specific point in time. There are two varieties of fields: static fields and (nonstatic) fields. Static fields (also referred to as *class fields*) can be thought of as existing in the class object, or meta-object. Nonstatic fields (instance variables) are fields that can only be accessed from an instance of a class—an object. Then we have local variables and arguments, which are not classified as fields. These live only for the duration of a method call and belong exclusively to the current thread of execution.

Primitive Data Types

leJOS allows code to declare all eight primitive types (although only six are fully implemented—see note later). There are four integral numbers, two floating-point numbers, a character type, and a Boolean type. Table 3–1 shows these types and their sizes. As of this writing, mathematical operations are not allowed with longs, however. To do anything with long values, they must be cast to ints. The long type is used so methods like currentTimeMillis() and Thread.sleep() have the same signature as their Java counterparts. Full support for longs is being worked on as of this writing and may be implemented in the next release, provided memory is not overtaxed.

Table 3-1 Java Primitives

Keyword	Minimum	Maximum	Default	Bits
byte	-2^8	$2^8 - 1$	0	8
short	-2^{16}	$2^{16} - 1$	0	16
int	-2^{32}	$2^{32} - 1$	0	32
long	-2^{32}	$2^{32} - 1$	0	64
float	Varies	Varies	0.0	32
double	Varies	Varies	0.0	64
boolean	None	None	False	2
char	'\U00000'	'\U65535'	'\U00000'	16

Note:

leJOS gives the illusion of allowing all eight Java primitives, but in fact it only fully supports six. The 64-bit numbers long and double are actually not completely supported, although you can still declare variables as long and double. For example, even though your code may look like it created a double value, the underlying primitive is a float. Likewise, any long literals are truncated to int.

In some languages, such as Visual Basic, it is possible to declare a variable without specifying the type of the variable. Java, on the other hand, is a *strongly typed* language, which means all variables must be declared as belonging to a specific data type. The following class shows each of the primitive variables declared and initialized with a value:

```
class Primitives {

    byte b = 127;
    short s = 32767;
```

```
        int i = 2147483647;
        long l = 2147483647;

        float f = 100.123f;
        double d = 100.123;

        char c = 'M';

        boolean boo = true;
    }
```

All of these variables are declared at the class level. Note in the eighth line it is necessary to place an *f* after the literal number. This is because literals are treated as double values by default, and it is illegal to assign a double value to a float variable.

Variables do not need to be initialized in the same line as they are declared, however. The following code shows a variable declared at class level and initialized with a value in the constructor. It also contains a variable declared at method level:

```
1. class DumpTruck {
2.     float radius; // instance variable
3.
4.     public DumpTruck() {
5.         int mult = 56; // local variable
6.         radius = 100.123f * mult;
7.
      }
8. }
```

This example shows the variable *radius* declared at class level and the integer *mult* declared at the local (method) level. There is a distinction to be made between local and class-level variables. All class-level variables are initialized with a default value, but if a local variable is to be used, it must be implicitly initialized with a value somewhere in the code. For example, the following code does not compile due to the seventh line:

```
1. class DumpTruck {
2.
3.     float radius; // Initialized with default value of zero
4.
5.     public DumpTruck() {
6.         int mult; // Not initialized
7.         float result = radius * mult; // Error due to mult
      }
8. }
```

Note:

Primitives are passed into methods (as arguments) by value. *When a variable is passed in this manner it is just like a copy of the variable was passed into the method. Therefore, if the value is changed within the method, it is not reflected outside the scope of the method:*

```java
import josx.platform.rcx.*;

class ByValue {
    public static void main(String [] args) {
        float height = 72f;
        float metricHeight = getCentimeters(height);
        LCD.showNumber((int)height);
    }

    public static float getCentimeters(float inches) {
        inches = inches * 2.6f;
        return inches;
    }
}
```

This code passes the value of variable height to the method getCentimeters. Inside the method, the value of the variable is multiplied by 2.6, but this does not mean the actual variable height is also multiplied. Because a copy of the variable is passed to the method, height is not affected.

Sometimes it is necessary to convert from one type of primitive to another. This can be done by *casting*, as in when a ceramics artist casts plaster into a shape by using a mold. In Java, casting can convert a smaller primitive to a larger number type, or conversely, a larger value to a smaller primitive type. Let's examine how both of these look in code:

```java
short x = 500;
int y = x; // implicit cast
int a = 500;
short b = (short)a; // explicit cast
```

Notice that to convert a short number to an int requires no special syntax. Why? Because a smaller 16-bit primitive (short) will always fit within a larger 32-bit primitive (int). If you have a 16-gallon jug and a 32-gallon jug, the contents of the 16-gallon jug will always fit in the 32-gallon jug no matter how full the 16-gallon jug is. However, in the third and fourth lines, to convert the int to a short it must be explicitly stated that the conversion is occurring. If the larger primitive type contains a number larger than the smaller primitive can store there could be problems. If the number is too large to store in the smaller primitive, the number will be truncated.

It is also possible to cast floating-point numbers into integrals and vice versa. When converting a float to an int, the decimal places are chopped off out of necessity. The following code demonstrates this:

```
float a = 555.555f;
int b = (int)a; // explicit cast - decimal places lost
int x = 25;
float y = x; // implicit cast
```

Warning:

One of the most common programmer errors with leJOS is trying to use a double value where a float is required. This produces a compilation error if attempted. Examine the getCentimeters() method again:

```
import josx.platform.rcx.*;

class ByValue {
    public static void main(String [] args) {
        float metricHeight = getCentimeters(5.7);
    }

    public static float getCentimeters(float inches) {
        inches = inches * 2.6f;
        return inches;
    }
}
```

The code might look fine as it is, but actually it will produce an error. Floating-point literal numbers, such as 5.7 in the fifth line, are double by default. So 5.7 is assigned a type double, but the method requires a float number. To indicate 5.7 is a float, place an f after the number:

```
        float metricHeight = getCentimeters(5.7f);
```

Arrays

An array is a collection of objects or primitives that can be accessed using an index number. An array is an object in every sense of the word. It contains all the methods of the Object class such as equals() and toString(), and it has a variable called length that indicates how many elements it contains. The only difference is that it is initialized in a different manner from a regular object or primitive as the following two examples demonstrate:

```
int [] x = new int[20];
boolean [] boo = {true, false, false, false, true, false};
```

Note:

The equals() and toString() methods don't work in arrays as you would probably expect them to. The toString() method doesn't produce usable results because Strings are not used much in leJOS and they waste memory. The equals() flaw occurs in standard Java, too, and is well known.

If you pass an array into a method as an argument and change one of the variables in the array, this is also reflected outside of the method. So, like any object, an array is accessed by reference.

Naming Rules

As a programmer, it is up to you to give your classes, methods, and variables a unique name. There are several rules about naming these elements in code:

- The name must *begin* with a letter (uppercase or lowercase), an underscore (_), or a dollar sign ($).

Warning:

The $ sign is not recommended because the compiler generates special methods and inner classes with names containing $. This ends up wasting more memory than using a standard character.

- The name may only contain numbers, or the characters just mentioned.
- The name may not be a keyword (e.g., *true, false,* or *null*). Table 3–2 shows a complete list of keywords.

Table 3-2 Java Keywords

abstract	default	if	private	this
boolean	do	implements	protected	throw
break	double	import	public	throws
byte	else	instanceof	return	transient

Table 3-2 Java Keywords (continued)				
case	extends	int	short	try
catch	final	interface	static	void
char	finally	long	strictfp	volatile
class	float	native	super	while
const	for	new	switch	
continue	goto	package	synchronized	

Operators

Operators lie at the very core of programming because they perform the actual calculations, which is what a computer is designed to do. Operators essentially perform low-level math calculations involving bits.

Mathematical Operators

The basic mathematical operators usually function the same across all programming languages, so most people are quite familiar with them. They are as follows:

- addition (+)
- subtraction (-)
- multiplication (*)
- division (/)
- remainder (modulo division; %)

The most unfamiliar operation here for most new programmers is the modulo division operator. It produces the remainder of integral number division; that is, the amount that was not able to divide evenly into a number and was thus left over. Modulo can be used for both integer numbers and floating-point numbers. Examine the following code:

```
class MathTest {
    public static void main(String [] args) {
        int result1 = 15 % 2; // yields 1
        float result2 = 15 % 2.3f; // yields 1.2
    }
}
```

Tip:

If you have a hard time remembering whether to use the backslash (\) or the forward slash (/) for division, remember that the division symbol tilts in the same direction as the % symbol on the keyboard.

Note:

There is no power operator in Java, such as the calculation 3^9. To perform a power calculation you must use the Math.pow() method, as follows:

```
Math.pow(3, 9)
```

Increment and Decrement Operators

Individual variables can be incremented and decremented by a value of one without using the equal assignment operator. This is done as follows:

```
x++ // postfix increment
++x // prefix increment
x-- // postfix decrement
--x // prefix decrement
```

The postfix operator works differently from the prefix operator. This is best explained through an example. First, let's examine how the prefix operator works:

```
int x = 8;
int y = ++x
```

The prefix operator is quite predictable. Looking at the preceding code, what does y equal after this line executes? The answer is 9, and of course x also is equal to 9 when this completes. Now let's look at the postfix operator:

```
int x = 8;
int y = x++;
```

Now what does y equal after this code executes? The answer is 8, because the value of x is used to assign a value to y; then the increment occurs. As before, x will equal 9 after this code has executed.

Comparison Operators

Comparison operators are used to compare two variables. All comparison operators return a Boolean value to indicate if the comparison is true or not.

Comparison operators are most often used in looping constructs, such as if–then and while (described later). The following comparison operators are used in Java:

```
==        // equals
>=        // greater than or equal to
<=        // less than or equal to
>         // greater than
<         // less than
!=        // not equal
```

Comparisons can be made as follows:

```
boolean a = 25 > 24; // true
boolean b = 25 == 24; // false
```

Boolean Operators

Some operators are specifically for numbers (greater than, less than), some are for Boolean comparisons only (&& and ||), and some can be used for both numbers and Boolean (!= and ==). The following can be used with Boolean operands:

```
&&        AND
||        OR
^         Exclusive OR (XOR)
!=        Not equal
==        Equal
```

Let's examine these in some code:

```
boolean a = (25>24)||(12==13); // true
boolean b = (25>24)&&(12==13); // false
boolean c = a == b; // false
boolean d = a != b; // true
boolean e = a ^ b; // true
boolean f = a ^ d; // false
```

Most people are familiar with AND, OR, Not Equal, and Equal. Exclusive OR (XOR) is different from OR, however. Let's first contrast this with OR. OR is true if one or the other, or both operands are true. XOR is only true if one or the other are true. If both are true, then XOR produces false.

Program Flow Control

A program that executed statements one after another in the same order each time it was run would be a rather boring and predictable program. It is the branching quality of a program that gives it power and flexibility. This quality is known as program *flow control*.

If Statements

If statements are very easy to use and very powerful. A typical if statement examines a Boolean value and executes a block of code if the Boolean value is true. The following is a typical example of an if statement in leJOS code:

```
if(x == 10) {
    Sound.beep();
}
```

Notice there is no then keyword used. All conditional code must appear in the curly braces. Alternatively, if there is only one statement to execute, the braces are not required:

```
if(x == 10)
    Sound.beep();
```

You can also use an else statement to execute a block of code should the Boolean value equal false:

```
if(x==10) {
    x = 0;
    Sound.beep();
} else {
    Sound.buzz();
}
```

Any code can be placed within the conditional code, including other if statements. This type of code construct is called a nested if statement:

```
if(x==10) {
    if(y == 5)
        Sound.beep();
}
```

Note:

Switch statements are currently not supported by leJOS, but these can easily be replaced by if–else statements. For example:

```
if (c == 'a') {
    ...
} else if (c == 'b') {
    ...
} else if (c == 'c') {
```

```
    ...
} else {
    // default behavior
}
```

For Loops

Conditional loops are used to repeat a code block a number of times until a condition is met. One of the most popular loop constructs is the for loop. This loop repeats a block of code a predetermined number of times until a condition is satisfied. A for loop consists of three main parts:

- Counter initialization
- Boolean condition
- Counter increment

These parts are stated in the following order:

```
for(counter initialization; boolean condition; counter
increment)
```

A statement such as for(A;B;C) roughly translates into the following:

```
A;
while (B) {
    ...
    C;
}
```

Let's examine a for loop in some actual code:

```
import josx.platform.rcx.*;
class SoundLoop {

    public static void main(String [] args) {
        for(int freq=500;freq<1000;freq += 50) {
            Sound.playTone(freq, 30);
        }
        try{
            Button.RUN.waitForPressAndRelease();
        } catch(InterruptedException e) {}
    }
}
```

The preceding example declares and initializes a variable called `freq`, checks if the variable satisfies the condition, executes the block of code, then increments the freq integer by 50 and rechecks the condition until it evaluates to false.

Note:

If the Boolean condition is empty, it's assumed to be always true, so it will repeat in an endless loop, as the following code demonstrates:

```
for(;;) {}
```

While and Do-While Loops

While loops are actually very similar to for loops, but they are not constructed specifically for incrementing a variable a set number of times. The while loop evaluates one Boolean value, as follows:

```
while(boolean condition)
```

The following code uses a while loop to keep a robot moving forward until it gets to a dark area:

```
1.  import josx.platform.rcx.*;
2.
3.  class CockroachBot implements SensorConstants{
4.
5.     public CockroachBot() {
6.         Sensor.S2.setTypeAndMode(SENSOR_TYPE_LIGHT,
             SENSOR_MODE_PCT);
7.         Sensor.S2.activate();
8.     }
9.
10.    public static void main(String [] args) {
11.        CockroachBot bot = new CockroachBot();
12.        Motor.A.forward();
13.        Motor.C.forward();
14.        while(bot.isBright()) {
15.            // Keep moving forward
16.        }
17.        Motor.A.stop();
18.        Motor.C.stop();
19.    }
20.
21.    public boolean isBright() {
22.        return (Sensor.S2.readValue() > 55);
23.    }
24. }
```

It is also possible to make the while loop execute the block of code at least once, then evaluate the condition. This is done using the *do* keyword, as follows:

```
do {
    // code body
} while(boolean condition)
```

Exception Handling

Exception handling is one of the features of Java that makes it so popular with programmers. With exception handling, the error-checking part of your code can be segregated from the rest of your functional code. This makes code neater and easier to understand. Java accomplishes this by enclosing method calls that may throw exceptions within a try–catch block. The following pseudo-code shows how this works:

```
try {
    // method that may throw exception
}
catch(Exception Type) {
    // code to deal with exception
}
```

The try block is where a method prone to throwing an exception must be called. The catch block is where the error is dealt with. There is a third, optional part of this, a finally block. The finally block is executed once either the try or catch block has finished executing:

```
try {
    // method that may throw exception
}
catch(Exception Type) {
    // code to deal with exception
}
finally{ // Optional
    // code that is always executed no matter what
}
```

For the most part, using leJOS the only time you'll really deal with exceptions is when using the Thread.sleep() method, as follows:

```
try {
    Thread.sleep(100);
} catch(InterruptedException e) {
    interrupted = true;
}
```

Reading Exceptions

In regular Java, when an exception is thrown and it isn't caught, the JVM can display its trace on the console. This allows a programmer to visibly identify what has occurred internally to the program. In leJOS this is not so easy because the LCD only has space for five numbers, so it must do something special to signal the exception to you. When an uncaught exception is thrown, you will see two numbers displayed on the LCD screen. For example:

```
0052^3
```

How is this deciphered? The first number represents the method the exception occurred in and the second number represents the exception class that was thrown. We need some sort of listing of method numbers (signatures) and class IDs to understand the exception. This can be generated with lejos.exe using the verbose option:

```
lejos -verbose myTest
```

This causes the lejos.exe program to output all the classes and signatures to the screen, as follows:

```
Class 0: java/lang/Object
Class 1: java/lang/Thread
Class 2: java/lang/String
Class 3: java/lang/Runtime
Class 4: java/lang/Throwable
Class 5: java/lang/Error
Class 6: java/lang/OutOfMemoryError
Class 7: java/lang/NoSuchMethodError
Class 8: java/lang/StackOverflowError
Class 9: java/lang/NullPointerException
Class 10: java/lang/ClassCastException
Class 11: java/lang/ArithmeticException
Class 12: java/lang/ArrayIndexOutOfBoundsException
Class 13: java/lang/IllegalArgumentException
Class 14: java/lang/InterruptedException
Class 15: java/lang/IllegalStateException
Class 16: java/lang/IllegalMonitorStateException
Class 17: java/lang/ThreadDeath
Class 18: josx/util/Test
Class 19: MyTest
Class 20: java/lang/System
Class 21: java/lang/RuntimeException
Class 22: java/lang/Exception
Signature 0: main([Ljava/lang/String;)V
```

```
Signature 1:  run()V
Signature 2:  <init>()V
Signature 3:  <clinit>()V
Signature 4:  notify()V
Signature 5:  notifyAll()V
Signature 6:  wait()V
Signature 7:  wait(J)V
Signature 8:  getDataAddress(Ljava/lang/Object;)I
Signature 9:  start()V
Signature 10: yield()V
Signature 11: sleep(J)V
Signature 12: currentThread()Ljava/lang/Thread;
Signature 13: getPriority()I
Signature 14: setPriority(I)V
Signature 15: interrupt()V
Signature 16: interrupted()Z
Signature 17: isInterrupted()Z
Signature 18: setDaemon(Z)V
Signature 19: isDaemon()Z
Signature 20: join()V
Signature 21: join(J)V
Signature 22: currentTimeMillis()J
Signature 23: exit(I)V
Signature 24: freeMemory()J
Signature 25: totalMemory()J
Signature 26: getRuntime()Ljava/lang/Runtime;
Signature 27: getMessage()Ljava/lang/String;
Signature 28: callRom(S)V
Signature 29: callRom(SS)V
Signature 30: callRom(SSS)V
Signature 31: callRom(SSSS)V
Signature 32: callRom(SSSSS)V
Signature 33: readMemoryByte(I)B
Signature 34: writeMemoryByte(IB)V
Signature 35: setMemoryBit(III)V
Signature 36: resetSerial()V
Signature 37: readSensorValue(II)I
Signature 38: setPoller()V
Signature 39: setThrottle(I)V
Signature 40: setSensorValue(III)V
Signature 41: assert(Ljava/lang/String;Z)V
Signature 42: assertEQ(Ljava/lang/String;II)V
Signature 43: equals(Ljava/lang/Object;)Z
Signature 44: hashCode()I
Signature 45: toString()Ljava/lang/String;
Signature 46: getClass()Ljava/lang/Class;
```

```
Signature 47: isAlive()Z
Signature 48: <init>(Ljava/lang/String;)V
Signature 49: <init>([CII)V
Signature 50: toCharArray()[C
Signature 51: valueOf(Ljava/lang/Object;)Ljava/lang/
              String;
Signature 52: getCentimeters(I)F
Signature 53: arraycopy([CI[CII)V
```

We can tell right away that Signature 52 is where the error occurred, which is the getCentimeters() method. But what kind of exception was it? Recall in our hypothetical example the LCD said it was 3. This number is actually the class id mod 10, so the number 3 only narrows down the list of possible exceptions. In other words the exception could be class 3 or 13 (Runtime or IllegalArgumentException). It's basically up to you to decide which exception it was, but this is usually pretty easy to determine just by looking at the code in the method that is responsible. In this example, because Runtime is not an exception, clearly we're dealing with IllegalArgumentException.

The java.lang Package

The previous sections dealt with Java language fundamentals. Now we can have a look at the actual Java API included in leJOS. The first package we examine is the java.lang package. As you saw in Chapter 2, the java.lang package contains classes that are fundamental to the Java programming language. As such, all classes in java.lang are imported automatically into all Java code, so there is no need to specifically import this package. Let's examine the classes in this package.

Math

The Math class is the place to go when you need complex mathematical functions. Some of these functions can be very useful in robotics where it is necessary to keep track of distances, angles, and coordinates. The leJOS Math class contains every method in the standard Java 2 Math class except methods with dubious worth, such as IEEEremainder() and rint().

Note:

All methods in the leJOS Math class use double values, but internally they are converted to float numbers to perform the math.

Tip:

The Math class contains many methods, all of which are imported if your class uses the Math class. If the RCX is constantly running out of memory, you can save memory by chopping out some of these methods from the source code and recompiling. Refer to Chapter 12, "Advanced Topics," for details on how to accomplish this.

`java.Lang.Math`

* `public static final double E`

  The double value that is closer than any other to e, the base of the natural logarithms.

* `public static final double PI`

  The double value that is closer than any other to π, the ratio of the circumference of a circle to its diameter.

* `public static double sin(double a)`

  Returns the trigonometric sine of an angle.

  Parameters: a   Angle value in radians.

Note:

All of the trigonometric functions return values in radians, as does the standard Java 2 package. This means instead of getting a value of 180°, the value will equal pi, or about 3.1416 (360° equals 2 pi in radians). If you prefer working in degrees you can use the Math.toDegrees() method for quick conversions.

* `public static double cos(double a)`

  Returns the trigonometric cosine of an angle.

  Parameters: a   Angle value in radians.

* `public static double tan(double a)`

  Returns the trigonometric tangent of an angle.

  Parameters: a   Angle value in radians.

* `public static double asin(double a)`

  Returns the arc sine of an angle, in the range of –pi/2 to pi/2.

  Parameters: a   Angle value in radians.

- `public static double acos(double a)`
  Returns the arc cosine of an angle, in the range of 0.0 through pi.

  Parameters: a   Angle value in radians.

- `public static double atan(double a)`
  Returns the arc tangent of an angle, in the range of –pi/2 to pi/2.

  Parameters: a   Angle value in radians.

- `public static double toRadians(double angdeg)`
  Converts an angle measured in degrees to the equivalent angle measured in radians.

  Parameters: angdeg   Angle value in degrees.

- `public static double toDegrees(double angrad)`
  Converts an angle measured in radians to the equivalent angle measured in degrees.

  Parameters: angrad   Angle value in radians.

- `public static double exp(double a)`
  Returns the exponential number *e* (i.e., 2.718...) raised to the power of a double value.

  Parameters: a   Double value.

- `public static double log(double a)`
  Returns the natural logarithm (base *e*) of a double value.

  Parameters: a   Double value.

- `public static double sqrt(double a)`
  Returns the correctly rounded positive square root of a double value.

  Parameters: a   Positive double value.

- `public static double ceil(double a)`
  Returns the smallest (closest to negative infinity) double value that is not less than the argument and is equal to a mathematical integer.

  Parameters: a   Double value.

- `public static double floor(double a)`
  Returns the largest (closest to positive infinity) double value that is not greater than the argument and is equal to a mathematical integer.

  Parameters: a   Double value.

- ```
  public static double atan2(double a, double b)
  ```
  The regular atan() method accepts a value calculated by using y/x. The problem is, if either x or y is negative, the result of the fraction will also be negative but will not give a clue about which quadrant the angle is in. The atan2() method converts rectangular coordinates x, y (b, a) to polar (r, theta). This method computes the phase theta by computing an arc tangent of a/b in the range of –pi to pi.

  Parameters: a   The y value in a coordinate system.

  b   The x value in a coordinate system.

- ```
  public static double pow(double a, double b)
  ```
  Returns the value of the first argument raised to the power of the second argument.

  Parameters: a   The base number.

  b   The power to raise the base number to.

- ```
  public static int round(float a)
  public static long round(double a)
  ```
  Returns the closest int to the argument. The result is rounded to an integer by adding 1/2, taking the floor of the result, and casting the result to type int. In other words, the result is equal to the value of this expression:

  ```
  (int)Math.floor(a + 0.5f)
  ```

  Parameters: a   Value to round.

- ```
  public static double random()
  ```
  Returns a double value with a positive sign, greater than or equal to 0.0 and less than 1.0. Returned values are chosen pseudo-randomly with (approximately) uniform distribution from that range. When this method is called, it uses a static instance of a pseudo-random-number generator, exactly as if by the expression:

  ```
  new java.util.Random();
  ```

  This method is properly synchronized to allow correct use by more than one thread.

  Parameters: a   Double value.

- ```
  public static int abs(int a)
  public static double abs(double a)
  ```
  Returns the absolute value of an int value. If the argument is not nega-
  ```

tive, the argument is returned. If the argument is negative, the negation of the argument is returned. Note that if the argument is equal to the value of Integer.MIN_VALUE, the most negative representable int value, the result is that same value, which is negative.

Parameters: a   An int or double value.

- ```
  public static int max(int a, int b)
  public static double max(double a, double b)
  ```
  Returns the greater of two int values; that is, the result is the argument closer to the value of Integer.MAX_VALUE. If the arguments have the same value, the result is that same value.

  Parameters: a   First number.

                     b   Second number.

- ```
  public static int min(int a, int b)
  public static double min(double a, double b)
  ```
  Returns the smaller of two float values; that is, the result is the value closer to negative infinity. If the arguments have the same value, the result is that same value. If either value is NaN, then the result is NaN. The floating-point comparison operators consider negative zero to be strictly smaller than positive zero. If one argument is positive zero and the other is negative zero, the result is negative zero.

  Parameters: a   First number.

                     b   Second number.

Object

In Java, all objects are subclasses of the Object class, even if the code does not declare that the class extends Object. If you follow the hierarchy of any class all the way to the top you will find the Object class. There are eight methods in the Object class, of which six have any importance to a casual programmer: toString() and equals() do not

java.lang.Object

- ```
  public boolean equals(Object aObject)
  ```
  The equals method compares two reference variables and tests if they refer to the same object. To compare two objects, call the method from one of them and use the other object as an argument:
  ```

```
boolean match = firstObject.equals(secondObject);
```

Parameters: `aObject`   Object to compare with.

- `public String toString()`

Normally this method returns a string representation of an object, but in leJOS it just returns an empty string, unless you override this method yourself. Once again, strings are not very important in robotics so this would only waste memory if it was implemented.

- `public final void wait(long timeout)`

Parameters: `timeout`   Maximum time in milliseconds to wait. Zero means forever.

Waits until notified. The block of code must be synchronized on this object, otherwise an IllegalMonitorStateException will be thrown. The wait can terminate if one of the following occurs:

- notify() or notifyAll() is called.
- The calling thread is interrupted.
- The timeout expires.

- `public final void wait()`

This is the same as calling wait(0).

- `public void notify()`

Wakes up one thread blocked on a wait(). The block of code must be synchronized on this object, otherwise an IllegalMonitorStateException will be thrown. If multiple threads are waiting, higher priority threads will be woken in preference; otherwise the thread that gets woken is essentially random.

- `public final void notifyAll()`

Wakes up all threads blocked on a wait(). The block of code must be synchronized on this object, otherwise an IllegalMonitorStateException will be thrown.

Runtime

The Runtime class is one of the newer additions to leJOS and it's a lifesaver. The only reason for the existence of Runtime is to check on memory in the RCX. The following two methods show how this works:

```
public static void showFreeMemory() {
    Runtime rt = Runtime.getRuntime();
    int free = (int)rt.freeMemory();
    LCD.showNumber(free);
}

public static void showTotalMemory() {
    Runtime rt = Runtime.getRuntime();
    int total = (int)rt.totalMemory();
    LCD.showNumber(total);
}
```

java.lang.Runtime

- `public static Runtime getRuntime()`

  This method returns an instance of Runtime because the freeMemory() and totalMemory() methods are not static.

- `public long freeMemory()`

  This method returns the amount of free memory in the heap. The heap is the amount of memory the user program has access to (this is explained further in Chapter 12).

- `public long totalMemory()`

  This method returns the total memory of the heap.

String

The String class simply contains an array of char primitives and methods to access those characters. String is given special status in Java in that it is not necessary to use the new keyword to create a String object (although the option to use it is open):

```
String island = "Tahiti";
```

It is also possible to create a string by joining two other strings together as follows:

```
String island = "Pit" + "cairn";
```

java.lang.String

- `public char[] toCharArray()`

  Returns an array of characters representing the string.

- `public String toString()`

  Returns itself.

- `public static String valueOf(Object aObj)`

  Returns the string representation of the Object argument.

  Parameters: aObj   Object to obtain string representation from.

StringBuffer

In Java, a String object is immutable, meaning characters in the string cannot be added or removed once the string is initialized. To create a new set of characters a new String object must be created, which uses memory. The StringBuffer, on the other hand, can be modified after creation, so it is more flexible and has the potential to save memory. Most of the methods in the leJOS StringBuffer class have to do with appending characters to a character array.

java.lang.StringBuffer

- ```
  StringBuffer append(boolean aBoolean)
  StringBuffer append(char aChar)
  StringBuffer append(int aInt)
  StringBuffer append(long aLong)
  StringBuffer append(float aFloat)
  StringBuffer append(double aDouble)
  StringBuffer append(String aString)
  StringBuffer append(Object aObject)
  ```

  Used to append a data type to the StringBuffer. If an object is used, the string representation of the object is used by calling toString().

  Parameters: a   Data to append to the String.

- `public char [] toCharArray()`

  Returns an array of characters representing the StringBuffer.

System

The System class allows a programmer to interact with the operating system and retrieve information from it. In leJOS the only thing that can be retrieved is the system time:

java.lang.System

- `public static long currentTimeMillis()`

  Returns the number of milliseconds since the RCX was turned on.
  ```

Threads

Threads allow a program to execute several pieces of code simultaneously. They are very useful for robotics programming because each thread can be used to control a separate behavior. For example, you can use one thread per sensor that needs to be monitored. A single thread could be used to monitor the light in a room, and another could monitor a touch sensor. You can also use threads to control different parts of your robot. For example, I could create one thread to control a gun turret or robot arm, and another thread to control wheel movement. Threads are very easy to create in Java; you simply extend the abstract Thread class and place the main code for your thread in the run() method. To demonstrate this, let's make a program that does two tasks at once—counting to 1,000 and playing random music:

```java
import josx.platform.rcx.*;

class BadMusic extends Thread {

    public static void main(String [] args) {
        new BadMusic().start();
        new Counting().start();
    }

    public void run() {
        while(true) {
            int freq = (int)(Math.random() * 1000);
            int delay = (int)(Math.random() * 40) + 10;
            Sound.playTone(freq, delay);
        }
    }
}

class Counting extends Thread {
    public void run() {
        for(int i=0;i<1000;++i) {
            LCD.showNumber(i);
            LCD.refresh();
            try{Thread.sleep(1000);
            } catch(Exception e) {}

        }
    }
}
```

This example will play random, disjointed, Shatneresque "music" and is sure to be a favorite for many years to come. As you can see in this code, the program has two threads: BadMusic and Counting. BadMusic plays a random note for a random duration, one after another, in a never-ending loop. The Counting class counts from 0 to 1,000, pausing for a second after each number. Both of these methods are started in the main() method. Keep in mind that the main() method is its own thread, often called the *primordial thread*, so when you create a thread it runs concurrently with the main() code. Even though the main() method ends, the program does not terminate because the other two threads are still alive.

In Java it's possible to interrupt a thread that is either waiting or sleeping by calling the interrupt() method on the thread. An object can go into wait mode by calling Object.wait() within its own code, and it can subsequently be woken up if another method calls Object.notify() or Object.notifyAll(). The interrupt() method will also cause wait() to return.

If you create a central thread coordinating the others it would be a good idea to run it at MAX_PRIORITY by using the setPriority() method. The main thread can then call yield() often to allow other threads to take a turn executing.

Tip:

Threads use a surprisingly large amount of memory, so go easy on them and try to keep the number below eight.

Note:

There is no Runnable interface in leJOS as there is in standard Java. This means all threads must extend the abstract Thread class and override the run() method.

java.lang.Thread

- `public static Thread currentThread()`

  Returns an instance of the current thread, which will, of course, be the thread the line of code is running in.

- `public int getPriority()`

  Returns the priority of a Thread object.

- `public void interrupt()`

  Sets the interrupt flag on a thread.

- `public static boolean interrupted()`

  Checks whether the current thread has been interrupted.

- `public boolean isAlive()`

  Tests if this thread is alive.

- `public boolean isDaemon()`

  Checks whether this thread is a daemon thread (i.e., not a user-created thread).

- `public boolean isInterrupted()`

  Checks whether this thread has been interrupted.

- `public abstract void run()`

  This method should be implemented with the main code for the thread.

- `public void setDaemon(boolean on)`

  Marks this thread as either a daemon thread or a user thread.

- `public void setPriority(int priority)`

  Sets the priority of the thread. Use the Thread constants to set the priority.

- `public static void sleep(long milliseconds)`

  Causes the thread to pause for a specific time.

- `public void start()`

  Begins the thread execution. (Remember not to call run() to start the method!)

- `public static void yield()`

  Causes the current thread to give way for another thread.

Throwable

The Throwable class is merely the superclass for all Error and Exception classes. It contains one method called getMessage() that displays an error message.

Note:

java.lang.Class and java.lang.Clonable are not at all functional in leJOS. They are present merely because compilers require them to function properly.

java.util

The java.util package contains four classes to aid with programming in general. Three of the classes are used to store data types in collections, and one is a random number generator. All of these classes have standard Java counterparts, but the leJOS classes have had all but the most important methods stripped away to save memory.

BitSet

The BitSet object is used to represent a series of bits. The number of bits is specified in the constructor, and each bit is represented by a Boolean value.

java.util.BitSet

- `void clear(int n)`

  Clear the bit (set it to false) at the nth position.

- `boolean get(int n)`

  Get the Boolean value of the bit at the nth position.

- `void set(int n)`

  Set the bit at the nth position to true.

Hashtable

The Hashtable class is used to store objects (not primitives) in a collection. These objects are not sorted, but they can be stored and retrieved according to a key. Keys are specified by using another object, which is normally an Integer object, or a String. As you might imagine, a Hashtable object can use up a lot of memory, because every object is stored using another object for the key.

java.util.Hashtable

- `Object get(Object aKey)`

  Retrieve the object from the collection with the key aKey. If no object exists with that key, the method returns null.

- `void put(Object aKey, Object aValue)`

  Store an object in the collection using a key.

Random

The Random class is a random number generator. This class is used by the Math.random() method to generate a random floating-point number between 0 and 1. The class is instantiated by giving it a seed number from which to start generating random numbers (normally the RCX clock counter is used for this).

java.util.Random

- `Random(long seed)`

  Creates a single instance of Random by seeding it with a long number (which is actually an int with leJOS).

- `int nextInt()`

  Used to retrieve a random integer number.

Vector

The Vector class is one of the most popular collection types used in programming. It stores a collection of Objects, sorted according to the order in which they are added. Objects can be retrieved using an index number. The API for Vector has been hugely expanded in the latest release of leJOS and includes almost every method of the actual J2SE Vector class.

java.util.Vector

- `void addElement(Object aObj)`

  Adds an Object to the Vector.

- `int capacity()`

  Returns the current capacity of this Vector.

- `void clear()`

  Removes all of the elements from this Vector. The Vector is empty after this call returns (unless it throws an exception).

- `Object elementAt(int aIndex)`

  Retrieves an element, specified by the index number. The index number is determined by the order in which objects are added to the Vector.

- `void ensureCapacity(int minCapacity)`

  Increases the capacity of this Vector, if necessary, to ensure that it can hold at least the number of components specified by the minimum capacity argument.

  If the current capacity of this Vector is less than minCapacity, then its capacity is increased by replacing its internal data array, kept in the field elementData, with a larger one. The size of the new data array will be the old size plus capacityIncrement, unless the value of capacityIncrement is less than or equal to zero, in which case the new capacity will be twice the old capacity. If this new size is still smaller than minCapacity, then the new capacity will be minCapacity.

- `boolean equals(Object aObj)`

  Compares the specified Object with this Vector for equality. Returns true if and only if the specified Object is also a Vector, both Vectors have the same size, and all corresponding pairs of elements in the two lists are equal. Two elements e1 and e2 are equal if the following expression is true:

  ```
  e1==null ? e2==null : e1.equals(e2).
  ```

  In other words, two Vectors are defined to be equal if they contain the same elements in the same order.

- `int indexOf(Object aObj)`

  Searches for the first occurrence of the given argument, testing for equality using the equals method.

- `int indexOf(Object aObj, int aIndex)`

  Searches for the first occurrence of the given argument, beginning the search at index, and testing for equality using the equals method.

- `void insertElementAt(Object aObj, int aIndex)`

  Inserts the specified object as a component in this Vector at the specified index. Each component in this Vector with an index greater than or equal to the specified index is shifted upward to have an index one greater than the value it had previously.

  The index must be a value greater than or equal to zero and less than or equal to the current size of the Vector. (If the index is equal to the current size of the Vector, the new element is appended to the Vector.)

  This method is identical in functionality to the add(Object, int) method (which is part of the List interface). Note that the add() method reverses the order of the parameters to more closely match array usage.

- `boolean isEmpty()`

  Tests whether this Vector has no components.

- `void removeAllElements()`

  Removes all components from this Vector and sets its size to zero.

  This method is identical in functionality to the clear method (which is part of the List interface).

- `boolean removeElement(Object aObj)`

  Removes the first (lowest indexed) occurrence of the argument from this Vector. If the object is found in this Vector, each component in the Vector with an index greater than or equal to the object's index is shifted downward to have an index one smaller than the value it had previously.

- `void removeElementAt(int aIndex)`

  Deletes the component at the specified index. Each component in this Vector with an index greater than or equal to the specified index is shifted downward to have an index one smaller than the value it had previously. The size of this Vector is decreased by 1.

  The index must be a value greater than or equal to 0 and less than the current size of the Vector.

  This method is identical in functionality to the remove method (which is part of the List interface). Note that the remove method returns the old value that was stored at the specified position.

- `void setElementAt(Object aObj, int aIndex)`

  Sets the component at the specified index of this Vector to be the specified object. The previous component at that position is discarded.

  The index must be a value greater than or equal to zero and less than the current size of the Vector.

  This method is identical in functionality to the set method (which is part of the List interface). Note that the set method reverses the order of the parameters to more closely match array usage. Note also that the set method returns the old value that was stored at the specified position.

- `void setSize(int aSize)`

  Defines the initial size of the Vector. As the Vector grows, the size is increased automatically.

- `int size()`

  Returns the number of objects stored in the Vector.

- `Object[] toArray()`

  Returns an array containing all of the elements in this Vector in the correct order.

- `void trimToSize()`

  Trims the capacity of this Vector to be the Vector's current size. If the capacity of this Vector is larger than its current size, then the capacity is changed to equal the size by replacing its internal data array, kept in the field elementData, with a smaller one. An application can use this operation to minimize the storage of a Vector.

THE LEJOS API

Chapter 4

The brief introduction to Java in the previous chapter was presented for one reason—so you can use Java to interact with the leJOS API. Specifically, the information presented in the last chapter allows you to use the classes in the josx.platform.rcx package, including the Motor and Sensor classes. This section lays the groundwork on how to use the leJOS API, but for reference purposes you should probably get used to referring to the actual leJOS API Javadocs (Figure 4–1) which can be downloaded along with leJOS. These documents will be your best friend when it comes to checking out the classes and methods available to you for robotics programming.

For those familiar with regular Java programming and objects, be warned there are some differences when coding for a real-world object such as a motor. All the motors and sensors are similar to global variables, because all objects have access to the exact same resource. This goes against the wisdom of OOP—keeping objects modular. There is nothing you can do to prevent another object from accessing the Motor, but there are ways to avoid conflicts by using the Behavior classes (which we explore in Chapter 6, "Behavior Control"). For now, let's get started with the basics of robotics programming with leJOS.

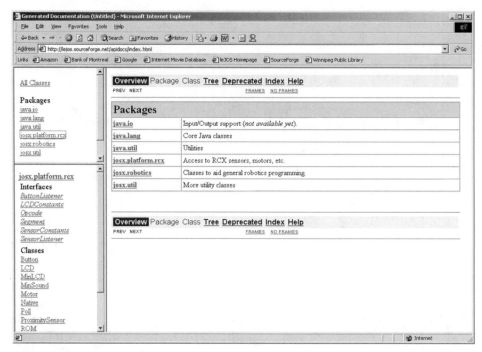

Figure 4–1   The leJOS Java docs.

Web Link:

It's handy to keep a link to the online Java docs on your desktop so that when you need to quickly reference them, they are just a click away. The docs can be found at lejos.sourceforge.net/apidocs/index.html. You can also download them separately from the leJOS Web site.

Warning:

Changes to open source projects such as leJOS usually come fast and furious. If you are using the latest version of leJOS, keep an eye out for changes to the API.

josx.platform.rcx

The josx.platform.rcx package is where all the action happens on the leJOS platform, namely motor movement and sensor reading. For this reason, 100% of your RCX programs will import this package, or at least some of the classes from this package. Without it, any program you run on the RCX has no visible or audible way of showing you it is running. You will find that most methods in this package are static. There is a subtle and interesting reason why: The objects on the RCX are finite. There are physically only three input ports, three output ports, one speaker, one LCD, one IR port, and four buttons. Contrast this with regular desktop PC programming, where there are usually an unlimited number of *virtual* objects that can be created. If a game needs one more enemy soldier, it simply creates a new instance of an enemy soldier object. Not so in leJOS! You can't create another instance of a Run button because physically there is only one Run button. It can only be accessed from a singleton, or by using static methods. For this reason, none of the classes in the josx.platform.rcx package have a visible constructor available. Let's take a look at these classes.

Button

The Button class only allows access to three of the four buttons, with the On-Off button unavailable for programmer control. There are four fields that can be used to obtain a reference to a button: BUTTONS, PRGM, RUN, and VIEW. The variable BUTTONS is an array containing all three Button objects. A typical method call for a Button looks like this:

```
// Stops code until Run pressed
try{
   Button.RUN.waitForPressAndRelease();
} catch(InterruptedException e) {}
```

Notice the try–catch block in case the program needs to interrupt the thread waiting for the button to be pressed. This can be interrupted by calling the member method interrupt() on the thread object this code belongs to (see "Threads" section in Chapter 3). There are no constructors for Button but you can easily obtain a reference variable to a Button object as follows:

```
Button runButton = Button.RUN;
```

One of the great things about Java technology is the use of event listeners. We briefly touched on this concept in Chapter 2, "Getting Started with

leJOS," and now we examine how this is actually done in code. Java can initiate an action, or several actions, that are dependent on an event occurring
(e.g., an event when a user presses a button). There can be more than one listener waiting for an event to happen, and when the event occurs, all the
classes that are listening are notified, and can thus execute the appropriate
code. The following example shows how an event listener is created:

```
import josx.platform.rcx.*;
class PlaySound implements ButtonListener {
    public void buttonPressed(Button b) {
        Sound.beepSequence();
    }

    public void buttonReleased(Button b) {} // Do nothing
}
```

This class implements the ButtonListener interface, which contains two
method definitions: buttonPressed() and buttonReleased(). All interface
methods must be defined in the class implementing the interface. When the
button that is registered with this listener is pressed, the RCX plays a cascad-
ing series of beeps. Now let's examine a class that registers this listener:

```
1. import josx.platform.rcx.*;
2. class ButtonTest {
3.     public static void main(String [] args) {
4.         Button.RUN.addButtonListener(new PlaySound());
5.         while(true){} // Never ending loop
6.     }
7. }
```

As you can see in the fourth line, the RUN button has an instance of the
PlaySound button listener registered with it (more than one button listener
can also be registered if desired). The next line puts our main() method into a
never-ending loop, but it could just as easily have continued our program. We
could also have opted to do this all in one class by having ButtonTest implement the ButtonListener interface, then add an instance of itself to the RUN
button. It's quite easy to use the event listeners and this is often the most efficient way to check for events such as button presses, because a listener will
rarely miss an event from an event generator such as a button.

josx.platform.rcx.Button

- `public void addButtonListener(ButtonListener aListener)`
  Adds a listener of button events.

- `public boolean isPressed()`
  Checks to determine if the button is currently pressed.

- `public static int readButtons()`
Low-level method that reads the status of buttons.

- `void waitForPressAndRelease()`
Stops program execution at this line until the button is pressed and released. This can be interrupted using the interrupt() method on the thread this method is executing.

LCD

The LCD class can be used to display numbers (not letters) and other elements on the RCX display. Every element of the LCD is completely under your control in leJOS, which allows a lot of flexibility. You can use the display to present messages from your robot, or you can even use it for debugging purposes. The following methods are available for controlling the LCD:

`josx.platform.rcx.LCD`

- `static void clear()`
Clears the display.

- `static void clearSegment(int aCode)`
Clears an LCD segment.

  | *Parameters:* | `aCode` | Integer constant representing the segment to clear (see Segment interface). |

- `static void refresh()`
Refreshes LCD.

- `static void setNumber(int aCode, int aValue, int aPoint)`
Sets a number to be displayed on the LCD. aPoint refers to the position in which to display a decimal point (0x3002 to 0x3005).

Parameters:	`aCode`	Allow signed numbers = 0x3001 Use program (fifth) digit = 0x3017 Only allow unsigned = 0x301f
	`aValue`	Number to display. Normally only the first four digits will be displayed.
	`aPoint`	The position in which to place the decimal point. Must be a hexadecimal value between 0x3002 (rightmost decimal) and 0x3005 (leftmost decimal).

- `static void setSegment(int aCode)`

  Sets an LCD segment.

  Parameters: `aCode`   The segment to activate, indicated by an int constant (found in the Segment interface).

- `static void showNumber(int aValue)`

  Shows an unsigned number on the LCD. Keep in mind it uses only the first four digits to the left of the Minifig to display a number. The fifth number is used by showProgramNumber() (see next).

  Parameters: `aValue`   Value to display. If the number is greater than 9999, the display shows 9999.

- `static void showProgramNumber(int aValue)`

  Shows a digit in the Program section of the LCD.

  Parameters: `aValue`   Value to display. Only the first digit is used.

To control the individual segments, such as the walking Minifig, it is necessary to supply the setSegment() method with a numerical constant. These constants can be found in the josx.platform.rcx.Segment interface. The following code demonstrates how the Segment interface constants are typically used:

```
1.  import josx.platform.rcx.*;
2.  class LightUpLCD implements Segment{
3.      public static void main(String [] args) {
4.          LCD.setSegment(ALL);
5.          LCD.refresh(); // Very important!
6.          try{
7.              Button.RUN.waitForPressAndRelease();
8.          } catch(InterruptedException e) {}
9.      }
10. }
```

Although the fourth line could have lit up individual segments such as WALKING and BATTERY, it chooses Segment.ALL, which lights everything up (for a complete list of segments, see the leJOS API docs).

Warning:

The LCD remains unchanged until the LCD.refresh() method is called.

MinLCD

The MinLCD class is a pared-down version of the LCD class with only two methods: setNumber() and refresh(). Both of these methods are identical to their counterparts in the LCD class. This is a good memory-saving alternative if you just want to display numbers and are not interested in the other segments.

Motor

The Motor class is used to control a DC current to the output ports on the RCX. Most of the following methods are tailored toward controlling motors, but they can be used to control almost any actuator, such as a light bulb.

`josx.platform.rcx.Motor`

- `void backward()`
  Causes motor to rotate backward.

- `void flt()`
  Causes motor to float to a stop.

- `void forward()`
  Causes motor to rotate forward.

- `char getID()`
  Get the ID of the motor. One of "A," "B," "C."

- `int getPower()`
  Returns the current motor power setting.

- `boolean isBackward()`
  Returns true if the motor is rotating backward.

- `boolean isFloating()`
  Indicates if the motor is in float mode.

- `boolean isForward()`
  Returns true if the motor is rotating forward.

- `boolean isMoving()`
  Indicates if the motor is presently moving.

- `boolean isStopped()`
  Returns true if the motor is stopped.

- `void reverseDirection()`
  Reverses direction of the motor.

- void setPower(int aPower)

  Sets motor power to a value between 0 and 7, with 7 being the highest power level.

  Parameters: aPower   Power level, between 0 and 7.

- void stop()

  Causes motor to stop pretty much instantaneously, and continues to apply force to keep the wheel from spinning. This is good if you stop your RCX on an incline or keep an arm locked.

There is nothing very complicated about controlling the motors, as we've already seen in several examples from previous chapters. Keep in mind that Motor objects exist as static variables, so a typical line of code to call a method from Motor is as follows:

```
Motor.A.forward();
```

ROM

The ROM class provides access to some ROM routines embedded in the microprocessor that fall into a miscellaneous category. If you wanted to program your robot to come home when the batteries got low, the getBatteryPower() method could be useful to you. There are two methods in the ROM class.

josx.platform.rcx.ROM

- static int getBatteryPower()

  Indicates the raw battery power. This does not produce the same number displayed by leJOS in the LCD by default, which is voltage in volts (V). To get the value in volts, multiply by 10 and divide by 355. To convert this number to millivolts, multiply by 43,988 then divide by 1,560. These are the "official" mathematical algorithms used by leJOS and LEGO code.

- void resetMinuteTimer()

  Resets two-byte timer in the RCX.

Sensor

The Sensor class has one of the more complex APIs in the josx.platform.rcx package. The complexity arises from the number of different types of sensors and modes of data that each one can read. For example, there are five different sensor types known to leJOS (touch, light, rotation, temperature, and raw). There are also different modes for some types of sensor, such as Fahrenheit or Celsius temperature readings. Let's examine the Sensor methods.

josx.platform.rcx.Sensor

- void activate()

  Some sensors, such as the light sensor, require electricity to function. By switching into active mode, the input port acts like an output port too, providing power to sensors that need it. It does this by providing power for 3 ms, then switching over and reading data for 0.1 ms. The electronics in the light sensor smooth out the pulses to provide a steady stream of power, so no flicker is noticed in the LED of the light sensor.

- void addSensorListener(SensorListener aListener)

  Much like the button listener, sensors can also have sensor listeners. The listener is notified anytime the sensor data reading changes from the last reading. This is sometimes more practical for touch sensors than sensors that read continuously changing data, such as rotation sensors. It is still practical for light and temperature sensors in some situations when these conditions are relatively constant.

  Parameters: aListener   The SensorListener to register with the sensor.

- void passivate()

  Turns off the supply of power to the output port (the opposite of activate). This is useful for writing drivers for passive sensors, such as the touch sensor.

- boolean readBooleanValue()

  Reads the Boolean value of the sensor (true or false).

- int readRawValue()

  Reads the raw value of the sensor (from 0–1,023).

- static int readSensorValue(int aSensorId, int aRequestType)

  Low-level API for reading sensor values.

  Parameters: aSensorId   The ID of the sensor to read (0–2).

  aRequest-   The type of data to retrieve.
  Type   0 = raw value, 1 = canonical value, 2 = Boolean value

- int readValue()

  Reads the canonical value of the sensor, which is the filtered data value from the sensor. This value depends on what the sensor type and mode have been set to. For example, for the thermometer sensor if you choose Celsius as the sensor mode, you will receive data in degrees Celsius.

- `void setPreviousValue(int aValue)`

Resets the canonical sensor value of a sensor. This can be useful for resetting the count of a rotation sensor.

Parameters: `aValue`   The canonical value to reset the sensor to.

- `void setTypeAndMode(int aType, int aMode)`

Sets the sensor's type and mode. The type is either light, rotation, touch, temperature, or raw sensor.

Parameters: `aType`   The sensor type, an integer found in the SensorConstants interface.

`aMode`   The mode for the sensor, also found in the SensorConstants interface.

The mode can be one of eight data types (see Table 4–1). These constants can be found in the SensorConstants interface.

Table 4-1 Sensor Modes

Mode	*Function*
Angle	Counts the rotations made.
Boolean	Touch sensor released or pressed (0 or 1).
Degrees Celsius	Temperature using metric system.
Degrees Farenheit	Temperature using imperial system.
Edge counter	Counts number of times state on touch sensor changes from on-off or off-on.
Percent	Generally used as a light scale of brightness (0–100).
Pulse counter	Counts number of complete clicks of touch sensor.
Raw	Raw reading from 0 to 1,023

Let's examine a typical program that counts the number of times the touch sensor has been pressed. For this example we take advantage of the edge counter mode:

```
1. import josx.platform.rcx.*;
2. class EdgeCounter implements SensorConstants, SensorLis-
   tener {
3.    public static void main(String [] args) {
4.        Sensor.S1.setTypeAndMode(SENSOR_TYPE_TOUCH,
              SENSOR_MODE_EDGE);
5.        Sensor.S1.addSensorListener (new EdgeCounter());
6.        try{
7.            Button.RUN.waitForPressAndRelease();
8.        } catch(InterruptedException e) {}
9.    }
10.       public void stateChanged (Sensor src, int oldValue,
              int newValue) {
11.        // Will be called whenever sensor value changes
12.        LCD.showNumber (newValue);
13.        LCD.refresh();
14.    }
15. }
```

This program counts the number of times an edge is encountered. An edge is when the data goes from one range to another abruptly (Figure 4–2). Every time you press the touch sensor down, a steep edge is created and the counter adds one. When it is released, the sensor creates another steep edge and it adds another to the counter.

Note:

If this program is restarted (by pressing the Run and On-Off buttons) or the RCX is turned off and back on, the edge counter still retains the values where it left off. This is one of the properties of Sensors. In order to reset the value, use SetPreviousValue(0).

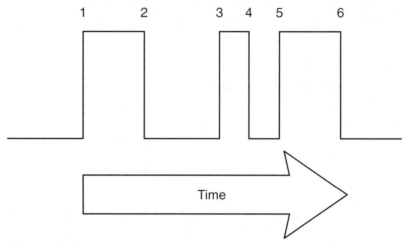

Figure 4-2   Edges from a touch sensor.

Serial

The Serial class is used for IR communications from the IR serial port *on the RCX*. This includes sending data to other RCX bricks or to a PC. The only data type that the Serial class may send is byte, so larger primitive types such as float and int cannot be sent using this class.

Note:

leJOS currently has a beta version of a higher level communications API in the josx.platform.rcx.comm package.

`josx.platform.rcx.Serial`

- `static boolean isPacketAvailable()`
  Checks to see if a packet is available.

- `static int readPacket(byte[] aBuffer)`
  Reads a packet received by the RCX, if one is available.

- `static void resetSerial()`
  Resets serial communications.

- `static void sendPacket(byte[] aBuffer, int aOffset, int aLen)`
  Sends a packet to the IR tower or another RCX.

- `static void setDataBuffer(byte[] aData)`
  Sets the buffer that will be used to save data transferred with opcode 0x45.

- `static void setRangeLong()`

  Sets long-range transmission (over 5 m).

- `static void setRangeShort()`

  Sets short range transmission (about 60 cm).

Note:

Chapter 11, "RCX Communications," will explain communications more thoroughly.

Sound

The Sound class is capable of producing many simple, predefined sounds, and it can also generate custom sounds (and even tunes). Let's examine the static methods of the Sound API.

`josx.platform.rcx.Sound`

- `static void beep()`

  Beeps once.

- `static void beepSequence()`

  Produces a sequence of downward tones.

- `static void buzz()`

  Produces a low buzz, which is almost inaudible.

- `static void playTone(int aFrequency, int aDuration)`

  Plays a tone, given its frequency and duration. Frequency is measured in hertz (Hz). The duration is in hundredths of a second (centiseconds), not milliseconds like the rest of the API. The aDuration argument is accepted as an integer but it actually gets truncated at 256, so a single tone will only last for a maximum of 2.56 seconds.

  Parameters: aFrequency   The frequency, in hertz.

                   aDuration   The duration, in centiseconds.

- `static void systemSound(boolean aQueued, int aCode)`

  Play a system sound.

  Parameters: aQueued   Indicates whether or not the ROM should queue the request and play the sound in the background.

aCode   The code number for the sound (see
               Table 4–2).

There are six predefined system sounds, as shown in Table 4–2).

Table 4-2 leJOS System Sounds

aCode	Resulting Sound
0	Short beep
1	Double beep
2	Descending arpeggio
3	Ascending arpeggio
4	Long, low beep
5	Quick ascending arpeggio

- `static void twoBeeps()`

  Beeps twice.

The speaker on the RCX is actually capable of producing a wide range of frequencies. The following code outputs a series of frequencies starting with 1 Hz and ending with 32,000 Hz. The upper limits are only audible by dogs, and the lower sounds don't become audible until about 31 Hz:

```
import josx.platform.rcx.*;
class ToneDeaf {
   public static void main(String [] args) {
      for(int i=1;i<=32000;i=i*2){
         Sound.playTone(i, 30);
         LCD.showNumber(i);
         LCD.refresh();
         try{Thread.sleep(500);
         } catch(Exception e) {}
      }
   }
}
```

MinSound

The MinSound class is a smaller, memory-saving alternative to the Sound class. It contains one deprecated method, playTone(). This method is identical to the method in the Sound class. *Deprecated* means the method (in this case, the whole class) may be removed in future releases of the language and should not be relied on.

TextLCD

One of the coolest aspects of leJOS that is not duplicated in regular RCX Code is the ability to display text to the LCD. This feature is not entirely useful and not entirely economical, yet somehow it seems very impressive. It demonstrates the ability of custom languages such as leJOS to push the RCX brick beyond its original abilities. All 26 letters of the alphabet are represented in one form or another using the seven segments of an LCD digit display. Seven segments is not nearly enough detail to accurately depict all 26 letters, so the leJOS developers had to be very creative to represent many of the letters, which require a stretch of the imagination to identify in some cases.

`josx.platform.rcx.TextLCD`

* `static void print(char[] text)`

  Prints up to the first five characters of a char array to the LCD.

* `static void print(String str)`

  Prints a string on the LCD.

* `static void printChar(char the_char, int pos)`

  Prints a character to a given position (0–4).

The josx.util Package

The Timer class is the one lonely, but useful, class in the josx.util package. However, it will soon be joined by classes for object recycling.

Timer

The Timer class is a great class if you want your robot to repeat an action in increments of time. For example, you could use this class to make your robot stop every 10 seconds and point back at the IR tower to see if there are messages. Those familiar with the javax.swing.Timer class will have no problem using this class, because it attempts to mirror it. The Timer class works in conjunction with the TimerListener interface, which will be notified repeatedly after a specified delay until the timer is stopped. A Timer is a virtual object, so it has a constructor. Let's examine the methods used to create a Timer object with a specific delay and a listener.

josx.util.Timer

- `Timer(int theDelay, TimerListener el)`

  Creates an instance of Timer and defines the time delay and listener.

- `public int getDelay()`

  Accesses how many milliseconds between timedOut() messages.

- `void setDelay(int newDelay)`

  Changes the delay between timedOut messages.

- `void start()`

  Starts the timer, telling it to send timeOut() methods to the TimerListener.

- `void stop()`

  Stops the timer.

josx.util.TimerListener

- `void timedOut()`

  Called every time the Timer fires.

josx.robotics

In robotics there are some ideas that, out of necessity, are used over and over again. The josx.robotics package attempts to group these robotics clichés together so programmers don't constantly have to reinvent the wheel every time they sit down to write code for a new robot. The josx.robotics package contains classes and interfaces for two types of frequent robotics code: navigation and behavior programming. Because of the complex nature of using some of these classes, they are dealt with in separate chapters. Chapter 6 deals with behavior control, and Chapter 7, "Navigation," and Chapter 8, "Navigation with Rotation Sensor," deal with navigation.

java.io and josx.platform.rcx.comm

Communications between the RCX and other IR devices (e.g., another RCX brick or the IR tower) expand the potential of robotics enormously. leJOS uses two packages to deal with communications: java.io, which includes some of the standard Java I/O classes, and josx.platform.rcx.comm. This topic is discussed completely in Chapter 11, "RCX Communications."

LEGO 101

Topics in this Chapter

- RIS Parts Library
- Common LEGO Structures
- Building Philosophy 101

Chapter 5

The RIS kit contains both standard LEGO parts and more advanced LEGO Technic parts. LEGO is a simplified engineering system and, like any engineering system, there are rules, shortcuts, tips, and well-known design patterns. Every part in the LEGO kit was designed with specific uses in mind. To learn these you could play around for hours trying different combinations, or you can read this chapter, which is a sort of LEGO 101 course. This chapter is intended to take away some of the pain of learning how Technic parts fit together, and to help new LEGOmaniacs create their own designs. More experienced LEGOmaniacs might find this chapter helpful as a parts reference for the RIS kit, as every part is explained. Those who are just mad about programming robots but don't really care about constructing may opt to skip this chapter completely. If you are in this category you will probably just want to choose a good wheeled robot from this book and use it as the basis for your projects.

For this chapter, you might find it useful to have the box of LEGO parts next to you as you read. This will allow you to test the structures for yourself. As the Chinese proverb states, "Tell me and I will forget, show me and I may remember, involve me and I understand." Nothing drills home an idea more than actually doing it. This is also the part of the book where you will actually feel what *LEGO-finger* is all about: a non-life-threatening redness around the tips of the fingers as described by Douglas Coupland (*Microserfs*, HarperCollins, 1995).

RIS Parts Library

LEGO does not include very much documentation with their kits. This is not an oversight on the part of the LEGO Corporation; their philosophy is to learn by experimentation. Most of their kits are designed with younger people in mind, so documentation is not the best answer for people with short attention spans. They also don't provide names for their parts in the documentation, so it is sometimes difficult to communicate the name of a part. The following sections attach names to all the parts in the RIS kit and describe how the parts work and interact with each other. You can usually tell how important a LEGO part is by the quantity included in the RIS kit. For example, one of the tiniest parts is the Technic Bush, but the LEGO kit includes 40 of them! This is a good indication you will be using (or losing) a lot of these pieces when creating robots.

Note:

The names for the parts are taken from the official LDraw library.
www.ldraw.org.

Bricks

The most basic unit of LEGO is the LEGO brick. All bricks (and plates) are measured by the number of studs on the top of the brick. The smallest brick in the RIS kit is 2×1 in size, and the largest is 2×8 (RIS 1.0 only). There are two kinds of bricks: standard LEGO bricks, and Technic bricks with holes in them that allow axles, pins, and pegs to be inserted. These type of bricks are sometimes called *beams*. Beams are always one stud in width, so beams can be identified solely by their length. The smallest beam is 2 units long, and the longest is 16 units long. Beams also have studs that are cylindrical in shape, like a stud with a hole in the center. This gives beams a slightly snugger fit when coupled with another brick. Let's examine the various species of brick available to us.

Tip:

The overall structure of your creation can be made stronger by overlapping the contacts of LEGO bricks where possible, much like a brick layer does when creating a wall.

Classic LEGO Bricks

Surprisingly, the classic rectangular bricks (Figure 5–1) are not used very frequently in MINDSTORMS designs. The most frequent use of the standard brick is as filler to build up height in a model.

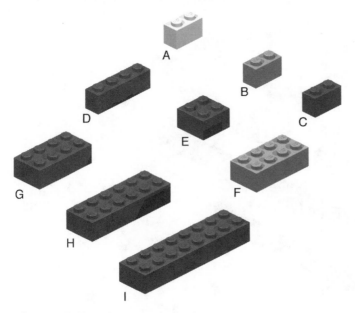

Figure 5–1   Classic LEGO bricks.
A, B, and C: 1 × 2 brick (4 yellow; 4 green, RIS 1.0 only; 20 black)
D: 1 × 4 brick (6 black, RIS 1.0 only)
E: 2 × 2 brick (20 black)
F and G: 2 × 4 brick (1 green, RIS 1.0 only; 25 black, 1.0; 5 black, 1.5 & 2.0)
H: 2 × 6 brick (6 black, RIS 1.0 only)
I: 2 × 8 brick (8 black, RIS 1.0 only)

Note:

The information in parentheses gives the quantity of parts included in the RIS kit, followed by the color of the part.

Technic Beams

Beams are most often used for making a chassis for the robot (see Figure 5–2). All beams have an even number of studs, with one less beam hole than there are studs, so a beam with six studs will only have five holes. The holes in the beams are most often used to support gears, axles, and pulley systems.

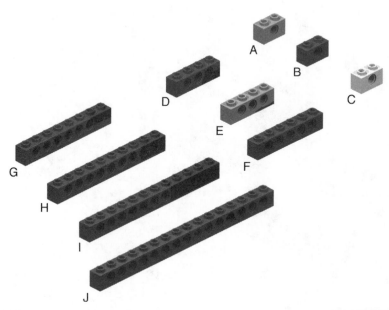

Figure 5–2   Beams.
A, B, and C: 2-unit beam (4 yellow; 8 green, RIS 1.0 only; 12 black)
D and E: 4-unit beam (2 green, 10 black)
F: 6-unit beam (8 black)
G: 8-unit beam (8 black)
H: 10-unit beam (8 black)
I: 12-unit beam (6 black)
J: 16-unit beam (6 black)

Specialized Bricks

The RIS kit contains a variety of bricks for special purposes (Figure 5–3). These bricks are often infrequently used (except the brick with the axle hole), or used as decoration only.

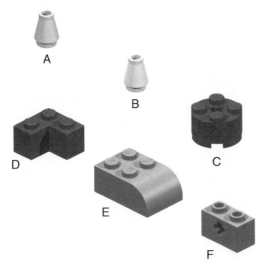

Figure 5–3 Specialized bricks.
A and B: 1 × 1 cone (2 yellow, 2 white)
C: 2 × 2 round brick (8 black)
D: 2 × 2 corner brick (4 black, RIS 1.0 only)
E: 2 × 3 brick with curved top (4 green, RIS 1.0 only)
F: 1 × 2 brick with axle hole (8 green)

The cone bricks are primarily decorative. They are capable of gripping on to a single LEGO brick stud, or held in place between four LEGO brick studs. The interior of the cone has an X shape that allows it to be attached to the end of an axle.

Despite being round, round bricks connect to square bricks with no problems. The round bricks are often used as supporting legs for stationary robots. They can also be used to smoothly contact a touch sensor.

The 2 × 2 corner brick is a special-purpose brick for creating strong corners. The corner plate is actually more useful than the corner brick for creating rectangular frames using beams, which is why the corner brick was discontinued in the RIS 1.5 and 2.0 kits.

The curved brick has only four studs on top, but the footprint is 2 × 3. This is one of the few pieces with an odd-number unit length. This brick can sometimes be useful when a moving part such as an arm must smoothly contact a touch sensor.

The brick with axle hole is very useful when a part needs to be locked to an axle (e.g., the rear wheel of the robot in Chapter 9, "Proximity Detection"), causing the structure to rotate when the axle rotates. It is also useful for locking an axle in place, making it stationary. The axle is gripped quite tightly by this part, preventing it from sliding back and forth.

Slope Bricks

The slope bricks (Figure 5–4) are measured by the angle of the slope, as well as the footprint they create. These bricks are often used aesthetically to remove sharp corners from your robot. They can also be used for making feet on a robot.

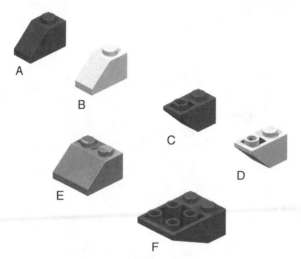

Figure 5–4   Slope bricks
A and B: 45-degree 2 × 1 slope brick (4 yellow, 12 black)
C and D: 45-degree 2 × 1 inverted slope brick (4 yellow, 4 black)
E: 45-degree 2 × 2 slope brick (3 green, RIS 1.0 only)
F: 33-degree 3 × 2 inverted slope brick (4 black)

Plates Overview

A plate is like a flattened brick. A plate is exactly three times thinner than a brick, so stacking three plates produces the same height as a brick (Figure 5–5). The RIS kit contains classic LEGO plates (Figure 5–6) as well as Technic plates with holes along the top. There are also many specialty plates that perform unique functions, which are described later.

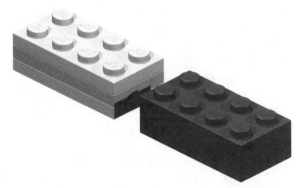

Figure 5-5   Three plates are the same height as a single brick.

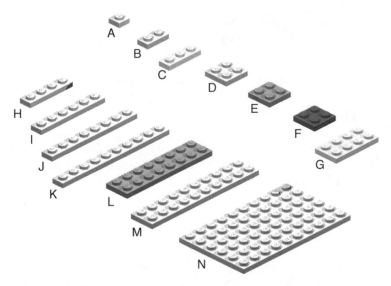

Figure 5-6   Classic LEGO plates.
A: 1 × 1 plate (8 gray)
B: 1 × 2 plate (20 gray)
C: 1 × 3 plate (2 yellow)
D, E and F: 2 × 2 plate (2 green, 4 blue, 8 gray)
G: 2 × 4 plate (6 yellow)
H: 1 × 4 plate (10 gray)
I: 1 × 6 plate (10 gray)
J: 1 × 8 plate (8 gray)
K: 1 × 10 plate (6 gray)
L: 2 × 8 plate (4 green)
M: 2 × 10 plate (6 gray)
N: 6 × 10 plate (1 gray)

Rectangular Plates

The classic rectangular plates (Figure 5–6) are most often used to fortify other bricks. For example, if you place two bricks on a structure, the bricks will fall off when sufficient stress is placed on them. By sandwiching the bricks between pairs of plates with the plate covering the seam of the bricks (Figure 5–7) the bricks become much more difficult to separate.

Figure 5–7   Using plates to strengthen connections between beams.

Technic Plates

The Technic plates (Figure 5–8) contain holes that run vertically through the plate. These holes can be used for inserting axles, straws, or even pins and pegs. Most often the holes are used when an axle needs to run vertically, such as with a *castor* wheel.

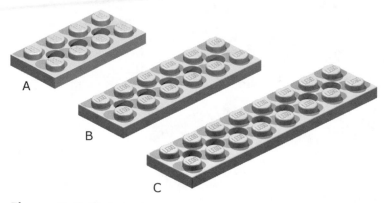

Figure 5–8   Technic plates.
A: 2 × 4 plate (4 gray)
B: 2 × 6 plate (4 gray)
C: 2 × 8 plate (8 gray)

Specialty Plates

The RIS kit comes with an assortment of plates in odd shapes to suit a special purpose (see Figure 5–9).

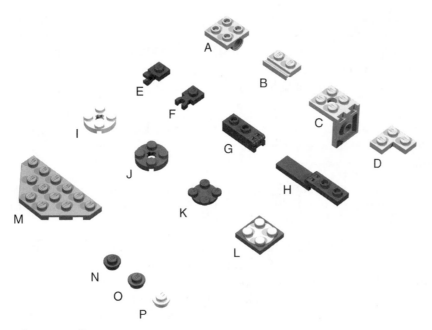

Figure 5–9 Specialty plates.
A: 2 × 2 plate with holes (2 gray, RIS 1.0; 4 gray, RIS 1.5 and 2.0)
B: 1 × 2 plate with door rail (8 gray)
C: 2 × 2–2 × 2 bracket (2 gray)
D: 2 × 2 corner plate (8 gray, 1.5 and 2.0 only)
E and F: 1 × 1 plate with clip (2 black horizontal, 2 black vertical)
G and H: hinge assemblage (2 black plates and 2 black tiles)
I and J: 2 × 2 round plates (2 blue, 2 white)
K: 2 × 2 skid plate (2 black)
L: 2 × 2 turntable plate (2 blue-gray)
M: 3 × 6 plate without corners (2 green)
N, O, and P: 1 × 1 round plates (2 white, 2 blue, 2 black)

The holes that run along the underside of the 2 × 2 plate with holes allow an axle to rotate under the plate. This creates a hinge that allows a brick to attach directly to the length of an axle. This can be useful for creating teeter-totter structures. The holes also will accept a pin, which allows axle pins and wheels to attach to the plate.

The 1 × 2 plate with door rail was originally part of the LEGO train set and was intended to be used to create a rail for sliding doors on box cars. In the RIS kit this part is used to hold down the motor securely. When a motor turns it often creates a lot of torque that can pry it out of its position. These pieces can be inserted into the slots on the side of the motor to pin it down.

The 2 × 2 bracket plate has another 2 × 2 plate that hangs perpendicular to it. This is useful when you need to change the direction of construction 90°. The most frequent use of this brick in MINDSTORMS is to point the light sensor downward, toward the ground (e.g., when using the sensor for line following). The plate contains a hole in the center, so it can also be used to support an axle.

The corner plate is the counterpart to the corner brick. The corner plate is useful for sandwiching together beams to make a rectangular frame (Figure 5–10).

The 1 × 1 plates with clips are similar to the Minifig hands. In the RIS kit they are primarily used for attaching wing decorations or thin straws to LEGO structures.

The hinge assemblage is created by joining two parts: the 1 × 2 hinge plate with three fingers and the 1 × 2 hinge tile with two fingers. This assemblage is useful for mounting the light sensor because it allows you to adjust the angle of elevation of the sensor points. The hinge can be assembled in two ways (see G and H in Figure 5–9) depending on what it is being used for.

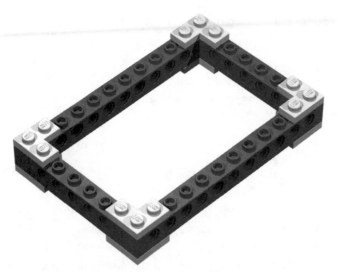

Figure 5–10   Creating a rectangular frame.

The 2 × 2 round plates can be useful when used with the 2 × 2 round bricks to build up the height of the brick. They also have axle holes (in the shape of an X) so they can lock onto an axle.

When placed on the underside of a robot, the skid plate provides a relatively frictionless contact with the ground. Robots with only two wheels can use this piece as a third (or third and fourth) balance point. RCX robots are generally light enough for this piece to slide without slowing the robot down.

The turntable plate spins in place, allowing for rotation along the vertical axis without the use of an axle. Any piece that is clamped to the top of this plate will rotate (e.g., the 2 × 2 round brick); however, the rotation cannot take large stresses because it is not strongly locked in place.

The 3 × 6 plate without corners has two corners removed, making the plate ideal for creating a robot with an angled front and back. Aesthetically it's a good piece for removing some of the boxiness of a model.

The 1 × 4 round plates are purely decorative. LEGO often uses them for eyes by sticking them in the center of the 2 × 2 round plate. The 1 × 1 plate is capable of gripping on to a single LEGO brick stud, or can be held in place between four LEGO brick studs.

Pins

Technic pins (Figure 5–11) come in two varieties: pins that are used for rotation and pins that are used to lock beams together. The rotating pins are always gray in color, and they fit loosely within the beam hole, allowing free rotation. The black pins, on the other hand, have small elevated surfaces that cause friction on the pin so it does not rotate. This allows black pins to "weld" beams together for an extremely strong connection.

Tip:

Pins can also be used to secure rubber bands.

The axle pin can be your best friend when working with complicated gear systems. It plugs right into a beam, allowing you to attach a gear or thin wheel. Gears attached in this manner are referred to as *idler gears* because they pass the force on to the next gear, rather than transmitting the force to an axle (Figure 5–12).

Tip:

Axle pins are sometimes difficult to remove from wheels and gears because they are tiny and hard to grip between fingers. You will probably have better luck pushing them out from the other side using another axle.

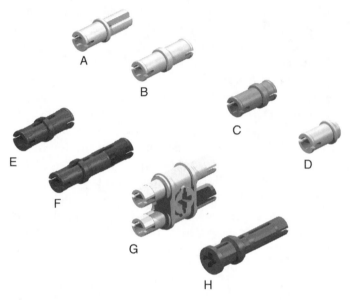

Figure 5-11   Technic pins.
A: axle pin (16 gray)
B: pin (24 gray)
C: 3/4 pin (16 dark gray)
D: 1/2 pin (8 gray)
E: friction pin (24 black)
F: long friction pin (8 black)
G: double pin (2 yellow, 1.5 and 2.0 only)
H. long pin with stop bush (4 blue, 1.5 and 2.0 only)

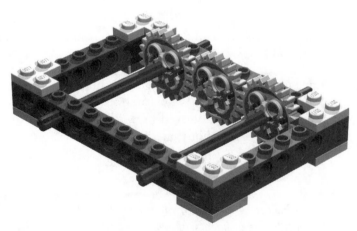

Figure 5-12   An idler gear between two drive gears.

The full-sized gray pins are useful for many functions. Because they rotate freely, pins can be used to create a hinge joint between two beams (see Figure 5–13 for an interesting demonstration). They can also just as easily be used between a beam and a lift arm to give the lift arm mobility. The rotating pin can also be used in the holes of gears. This can create an off-center rotation, or even just provide a small handle to use to turn the gear. Various LEGO pieces such as angle connectors and the 2×2 bracket have holes that allow the gray pin to lock in and rotate freely.

Figure 5–13   An extending arm using pins.

The 3/4 pin rotates freely, just like the other gray pins. This pin is useful for attaching a variety of thin gray lift arms to beams (Figure 5–14a) or the holes of the thin wedge belt pulley wheel (Figure 5–14b). The most popular use of the 3/4 pin is to lock the RCX brick to the chassis of the robot (Figure 5–14c).

Note:

The 3/4 pin looks like it would snap into the hole of a Technic plate, but it is not quite long enough.

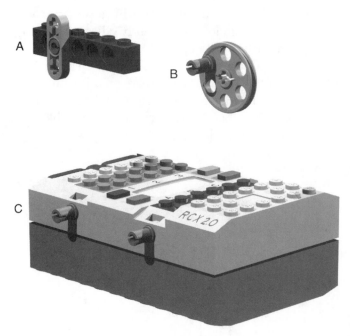

Figure 5–14   Using the 3/4 pin.

The 1/2 pin has one full-sized connector to fit into a beam and another half that is actually a stud. By placing several 1/2 pins into the side of a beam, you can build the LEGO perpendicular to the main robot (Figure 5–15a). It is also possible to insert 1/2 pins into gears to create a surface that other LEGO parts can attach to, such as a sensor (Figure 5–15b).

The black friction pin is one of the most frequently used pieces in the RIS kit. It is primarily used to connect two beams together, or to attach lift arms to beams. It can also be connected to a beam with one end sticking out to restrict movement of a hinged LEGO part.

Tip:

If you run out of black friction pins you can use the gray pins instead, although they create a looser connection.

The long black friction pin is useful for connecting three beams together to create a stronger connection between beams. This will stop the rattling sound from occurring in your chassis. You might consider using these where possible, just so you don't run out of regular-sized friction pins.

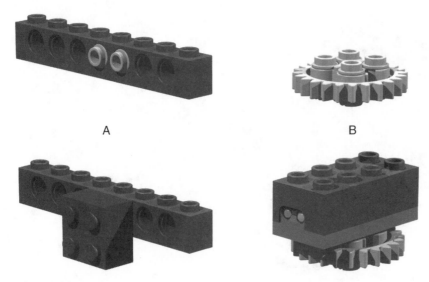

Figure 5-15   Using 1/2 pins to attach LEGO bricks.

The yellow double pin is actually three units long. The main use of the double pin is to join the clear blue connector block (see "Axle Accessories" section) together with another connector brick, or with a beam. It can also be useful for locking together two beams, leaving a gap in between for gears. The double pin also has an X along the side in which an axle can be locked in place.

The blue long pin with stop bush is a friction pin, so it does not rotate freely. At the end of the pin is a bush that accepts an axle or axle pin. This is a specialty part, useful in situations when you are using the same axis to connect beams and attach an axle pin.

Tires, Wheel Hubs, and Treads

The RIS kit contains an excellent assortment of wheels. When choosing the type of wheel for your robot, there are essentially two factors to consider: floor surface and clearance needed. The type of wheel you choose should vary according to the terrain your robot will be driving in. For hardwood or linoleum floors, it is a good idea to use a hard wheel because they lose less energy than softer tires. It is the most efficient tire for a hard surface and will not drain your batteries as quickly as a softer tire. On rougher terrain with small bumps and rocks, a softer tire works better because it absorbs the shock of driving over small bumps. Then there is the ultimate in conquering rough terrain—the tank tread. We discuss each of these types of locomotion separately.

Figure 5-16 Tires, wheel hubs, and treads.
A: tank tread (4 sprocket wheels, 2 treads)
B: wedge belt wheel (4 pulley wheels, 2 rubber tires)
C: 30.4 × 14 mm wheel (2 white)
D, F, and G: solid wheel hubs (10 yellow, RIS 1.0; 6 yellow, RIS 1.5 and 2.0)
D: large solid tire (2 black rubber)
E: 49.6 × 28 mm wheel (2 white)
F: small solid tire (2 black rubber)
G: medium solid tire (4 black rubber)
H: 81.6 × 15 mm motorcycle wheel (4 white)

The tank tread is a good mode of locomotion for very rough terrain. The advantage of a tank tread is that it covers a larger area than a wheel. A wheel occasionally will come off the ground and spin in place, but with a tread there will always be some surface area on the ground to keep forcing your robot forward. Keep in mind that, unlike a full-sized tank, a LEGO tank uses a tiny motor, so it will not be able to push itself over all obstacles unless you use gears to decrease the speed of rotation. Also, the tread itself can usually only manage to climb small bumps, so something as large as a standard LEGO brick could halt the tank. Most tank treads use two sprocket wheels, but if you have another kit (e.g., Ultimate Builder's Set) containing more sprocket wheels, you can make a triangular tread configuration (Figure 5–17) that will allow it to climb over larger obstacles.

The wedge belt wheel is also a pulley wheel. It has a small, solid rubber tire. The advantage of this tire is that it is extremely thin, so if you are lacking space on your robot this might fit better than some of the other tires in the kit.

Figure 5–17 Three-sprocket tank tread.

All tires with white hubs have an air cavity, making them springy and shock absorbent. These 30.4 × 14 mm wheels are excellent for rough terrain.

Wheels with yellow hubs have solid rubber, so they absorb bumps to a lesser degree than balloon tires, which makes them less efficient on bumpy terrain. They are efficient on hard, flat floors however. All the yellow hubs are the same size, so it is the tire itself that determines the circumference.

Note:

There are two fewer tires than hubs in the RIS 1.0 kit, so you will have two extra hubs. Conversely, the RIS 1.5 and 2.0 kits contain two fewer hubs than tires, so two tires will be without hubs.

Axles

Axles are just the right size to turn freely in the standard-sized holes of various LEGO bricks. Looking along the length of the axle reveals an X shape. This shape allows wheels and gears to lock onto the axle, at the same time allowing them to rotate freely in holes. Axle length is measured in studs (Figure 5–18), just like regular LEGO bricks. All axles in the RIS kit (see Figure 5–19) are of even length, except for the 3-unit axle. The 3-unit axle is handy to connect two wheels on either side of a single beam, or conversely a single wheel sandwiched between two beams. Axles are also sometimes used as robot legs.

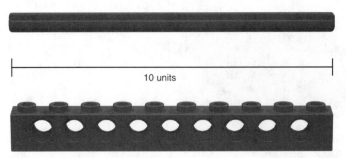

Figure 5-18   Length of axles is also measured in studs.

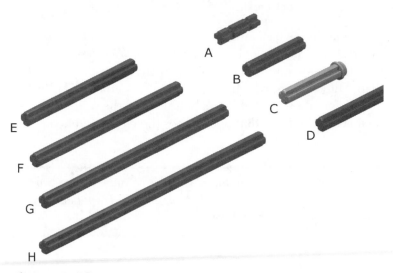

Figure 5-19   Axles.
A: 2-unit notched axle (8 black)
B: 3-unit axle (3 black)
C: 3-unit axle with stud (2 dark gray)
D: 4-unit axle (2 black)
E: 6-unit axle (6 black)
F: 8-unit axle (6 black)
G: 10-unit axle (4 black)
H: 12-unit axle (2 black)

The 2-unit axle is notched, allowing certain parts such as gears to snap into place.

The 3-unit axle with stud is a special axle with a stud on the end. This allows the axle to be placed through a beam hole without the need for a securing bush (Figure 5–20a). Another beam can also lie flush against the stud on the end of the axle (Figure 5–20b).

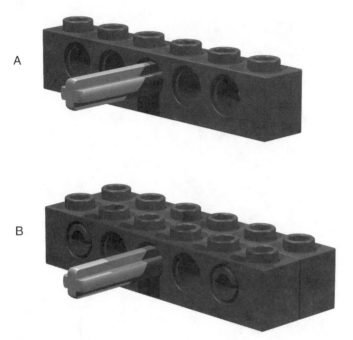

Figure 5–20 The 3-unit axle with stud.

Axle Accessories

All the parts listed as axle accessories (see Figure 5–21) join with an axle in one way or another. The majority of the axle accessories are concerned with making a connection between two axles in a variety of different configurations.

The 180-degree angle connector contains two cross-axle connectors at each end. In between the axle connectors there is a round axle hole at a perpendicular angle to the other holes. This piece can also be used as an axle extender, connecting two axles into one longer axle.

The T-angle connector contains a round hole and a cross-axle connector. When axles are inserted in the connector, it makes a T shape.

It actually takes two crankshaft parts and three axles to make a complete crankshaft (Figure 5–22a). This creates a bend in the axle that, when rotated, creates a reciprocal motion. Another axle can be attached to the middle with an axle connector to translate the reciprocal motion to lateral movement (Figure 5–22b), much like a piston.

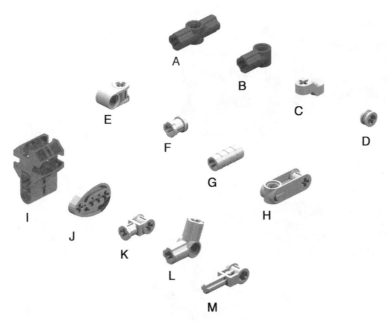

Figure 5–21   Axle accessories.
A: 180-degree angle connector (2 blue, RIS 1.5 and 2.0)
B: T-angle connector (4 blue)
C: engine crankshaft center (2 gray)
D: smooth Technic half bush (16 gray, RIS 1.0; 18 gray, RIS 1.5 and 2.0)
E: perpendicular axle joiner (2 gray)
F: Technic bush (40 gray)
G: axle joiner (2 gray; 4 gray, RIS 1.5 and 2.0)
H: long perpendicular axle joiner (2 gray, RIS 1.0)
I: connector block (4 transparent blue, RIS 1.5 and 2.0)
J: cam (2 gray)
K: connector with axle hole (2 gray)
L: 120-degree angle connector (4 gray)
M: pole reverser handle (2 gray)

The smooth Technic half bush performs the same function as the regular Technic bush, except it is thinner. Despite its small size, the half bush actually grips onto the axle stronger than the regular bush. The half bush also doubles as a small pulley wheel.

The perpendicular axle joiner has one round hole and one cross-axle hole. When axles are inserted, the configuration makes a cross shape.

A bush is used to lock parts onto an axle to keep them from slipping off, or to keep an axle in place without slipping out of the beam holes. The Technic bush also has one side that fits in between four LEGO brick studs vertically, locking it in place (Figure 5–23).

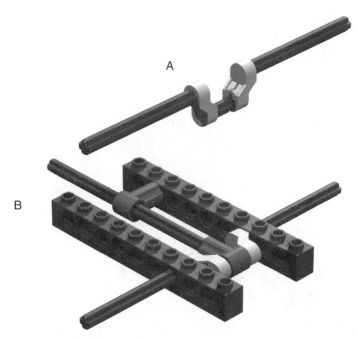

Figure 5-22 Engine crankshaft.

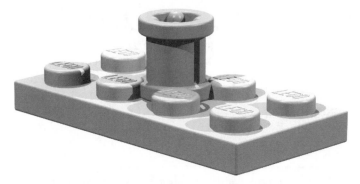

Figure 5-23 Locking a Technic bush to a plate.

The axle joiner creates a sturdy connection between two axles, allowing very long axles to be created. This includes extending the axle on the motor shaft, which is one of its most frequent uses.

The long perpendicular axle joiner provides identical functionality to the regular-sized perpendicular axle joiner, except the spacing between the axles is about double.

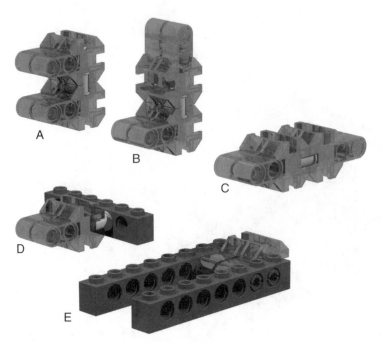

Figure 5-24   Using the yellow double pin to attach a connector block.

The connector block is useful for connecting assemblages such as bumpers and castor wheels to a robot. The yellow double pin is tailor made to be used in the holes of the connector block. They can be used to clamp connectors to one another in a variety of configurations (Figure 5–24a, b, c). The yellow double pin can also join a connector block to a beam (Figure 5–24d). There are also two axle holes on one arm of the connector block that allow beams and lift arms to attach using either axles or pins (Figure 5–24e).

Note:

When using the double pin with the connector block, make sure to push the double pin in all the way until you hear a snap. It takes more force than most LEGO parts, but the connection is likewise much stronger.

In a combustion engine, cams are attached to an axle to drive the axle as the pistons move up and down. Conversely, in LEGO the cam is used to change a circular motion into a *reciprocal* motion (back and forth movement). In most robots in which I've seen the cam used it was to raise or lower a LEGO part, frequently an arm or beam. The smooth egg shape of the cam allows it to slide easily along the underside of a hinged beam as it applies force to it.

The connector with an axle hole is similar to the blue angle connector, except both holes in the connector are cross-axle connectors, so the axle may not rotate. This accessory locks two axles into a T configuration.

The 120-degree angle connector contains two cross-axle connectors at each end and forms a 120-degree angle. In between the axle connectors is a round axle hole at a perpendicular angle to the other holes. When connected, this accessory forms a wide V.

The pole reverser handle contains an axle on the bottom of the T and a cross-axle connector hole perpendicular to the axle. It is very similar to the connector with an axle hole, except the pole reverser handle can fit into an axle hole itself.

Gears

Gears can seem complicated, probably because they evoke images of complex industrial machinery, but LEGO makes gear systems incredibly easy to work with. The gears in LEGO are sized according to the number of teeth. The RIS kit contains gears with as few as 8 teeth and as many as 40 teeth. Gears are excellent for keeping moving parts synchronized. Gear teeth never slip when the gears are aligned properly, so they are excellent when timing is important, such as for walking robots. To contrast this, pulley systems slip frequently. In walking robots, synchronization would soon be lost with pulleys and the robot would squirm hopelessly.

When two gears are interlocked, rotation applied to one gear causes the other gear to rotate as well. This can be useful in transferring motion from one axle to another. If both gears have the same number of teeth, then one full rotation of one gear causes the same rotation in the other gear (Figure 5–25a). If one gear has twice as many teeth as the other gear, however, then the gear with half as many teeth will rotate its axle twice for every rotation the larger gear makes. For example, if one gear has 24 teeth and the other gear has only 8 teeth, then the small gear will rotate three times for every rotation the larger gear makes (Figure 5–25b). If the gear with 8 teeth is attached to the motor axle and the gear with 24 teeth is attached to a wheel axle, then the wheel will turn three times slower than the motor output, but it will also generate three times as much torque. *Torque* is a word used for rotational force. This produces a trade-off of speed for increased torque, called *gear reduction*.

Gear reduction always uses pairs of interlocking gears. When more than a single pair of gears is used, it is called *gear ganging*. In each pair, one of the gears shares the same axle as one of the gears in the next pair, thus overlap-

1:1

3:1

Figure 5–25   Gear ratios.

Figure 5–26   A gear train with 125:1 reduction.

ping each other (Figure 5–26). These gears form a gear train, which can produce impressive gear reductions and a lot of torque. The gear train in Figure
5–26 produces a gear reduction ration of 125:1, meaning one rotation from
the final axle is caused by turning the pulley wheel 125 times.

Figure 5–27 Idler gears make no difference in gear ratio.

A gear can be placed between a pair of axles using an axle pin. This third gear does not drive an axle, so it is known as an *idler gear*. Idler gears can be used to reverse the rotation of a point in a gear train. Keep in mind that it doesn't matter what the size of an idler gear is; the number of teeth on an idler gear has no bearing on the final output. For example, if a pair of gears is separated by an idler with 40 teeth (Figure 5–27a), and another pair of gears is separated by a gear with 8 teeth (Figure 5–27b), which end gear will rotate faster? They both rotate at the same speed. The first and third gear turn at the same rate, no matter what size the idler gear is.

Standard Gears

The standard LEGO gears (Figure 5–28) lock onto axles, much like wheels. The larger gears (24 teeth and 40 teeth) contain holes in them that allow pins to be inserted. As previously shown, a 24-tooth gear with four 1/2 pins was used to attach a sensor (Figure 5–15). The smaller 16-tooth gear has holes, but they are too small for a pin to fit in. Gear spacing is determined by the spacing of the holes in the beams. Only the 8-, 24-, and 40-tooth gears will mesh together properly when placed horizontally along the same beam (Figure 5–29a). The 16-tooth gears can only be used with each other on a beam,

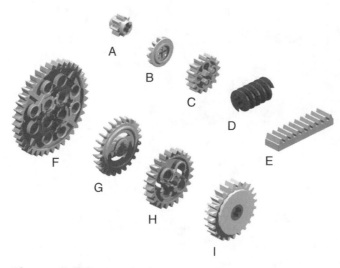

Figure 5-28 Standard gears.
A: 8-tooth gear (6 gray)
B: 12-tooth bevel gear (8 gray)
C: 16-tooth gear (4 gray)
D: worm screw (4 black)
E: gear rack (4 gray)
F: 40-tooth gear (4 gray)
G: 24-tooth crown gear (4 gray)
H: 24-tooth gear (4 gray)
I: 24-tooth clutch gear (1 white, RIS 1.5 and 2.0 only)

Figure 5-29 Only 8-, 24-, and 40-tooth gears interact along a plane.

and are incompatible with all other RIS gears (Figure 5–29b) because the teeth fail to connect. The only way 16-tooth gears can interact with the others is if they meet at an angle to one another on different beams.

Bevel gears provide about the same function as the crown gear; they change the axis of rotation by 90 degrees. The main difference is that bevel gears can only be used with each other, so the gear ratio is always 1:1. Also, bevel gears are quite compact so they can be useful in small places (e.g., inside the differential, as discussed later).

The 16-tooth gear is also used inside the tread sprocket (tank tread wheel) to lock the sprocket to the axle.

The worm screw fits over an axle and meshes with standard LEGO gears (see Figure 5–30). A single rotation of the worm screw causes the gear to rotate by only one tooth, so you can get incredible gear reduction in a limited space. The 40-tooth gear and the worm screw provide a 40:1 gear reduction in a relatively compact space. There is a unique property of the worm screw that can be used to the advantage of robot builders: The axle of the worm screw can drive the gear axle, but the gear cannot drive the worm screw. If you attempt to turn the gear it will lock. This property can be applied in situations in which an arm must lift an object and lock in place when the motor stops. Worm screws can also be added to the same axle to make a longer worm screw, but this should not be necessary in most cases because a single worm screw can adequately accommodate even the largest gear (40 teeth).

The gear rack has gear teeth, just like a round gear, only they are laid flat on a 1 × 4 LEGO plate. In construction, typically a round gear is meshed with the gear rack, and when the gear turns it causes lateral movement. Gear

Figure 5–30   A worm screw meshing with a 24-tooth gear.

racks can be joined together into longer gear racks for longer ranges of movement. The gear rack has a variety of uses, especially in creating scanner and plotter devices. It can also be used to raise or lower assemblages.

The largest gear available in the RIS kit, the 40-tooth gear can be meshed with the 8-tooth gear to provide a 5:1 gear reduction ratio.

The 24-tooth crown gear contains teeth that stick up perpendicular to the gear face. This allows the crown gear to interlock with any standard gear at a perpendicular angle (Figure 5–31), which changes the axis of rotation by 90 degrees.

Tip:

The 24-tooth crown gear is just as good as a 24-tooth standard gear on a flat plane, so if you run out of regular 24-tooth gears you can substitute the crown gear.

The clutch gear is extremely useful for robotics when there is a danger of damaging the LEGO model due to force exerted by gears. This gear is often called a *slip gear* for a reason. There is a clutch inside that keeps the axle from slipping until a certain force is reached. Once too much force is exerted on the gear the axle will begin to slip, dissipating the force harmlessly. On the side of the gear it says 2.5–5.0 Ncm, which stands for newton centimeters. In other words, a force of between 2.5 and 5.0 Newtons applied over a distance of 1 cm

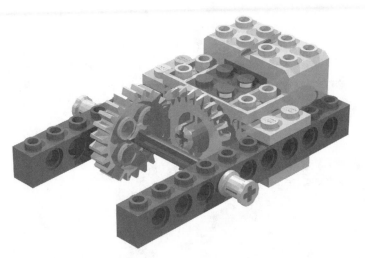

Figure 5–31   Using a crown gear to change the axis of rotation.

will cause the gear to slip. Not many people have a clear grasp of what a Newton is, however, so it is best to just try it out in an assemblage to see how it works. Imagine a robot hand that closes to grip something. If you use a clutch gear in the drive train, once the hand is closed the gear will slip, stopping the hand from destroying itself and the motor from stalling.

Differential Shell (1 dark gray)

The differential (Figure 5–32) is a complex mechanism that is actually not very difficult to understand. Let's first examine the theory of a differential. A differential has essentially one axle that is split in the middle, so one half of the axle can move independently of the other half. The unbreakable rule of the differential, firmly grounded in physics, is that the sum of the speeds of the two axles will always average the speed of the differential shell. If one axle is rotating at one revolution per second, and the other axle is stationary, the differential shell will rotate at half a rotation per second. If one axle is rotating clockwise at one rotation per second, and the other axle is rotating counterclockwise at one rotation per second, the differential shell will not rotate at all (the counterrotations cancel each other out). Looking at the actual LEGO differential, notice the shell has gear teeth. This is what gives the differential real power. There are essentially three ways to drive or receive torque from the differential: the left axle, the right axle, and one of the differential gears. By applying force to any two areas we can derive an output from the third area.

The LEGO differential has two gears built into the shell: a 24-tooth gear and a 16-tooth gear. Only one of the two gears on the shell is typically used, depending on what type of gears are in place. The mechanism is not complete until you add two axles (to create a split axle) and three bevel gears (Figure 5–32). Try assembling this and then we can try some quick experiments. First, turn both axles in the same direction. The result probably seems obvious, but now try to apply force to the differential shell. Notice that the shell resists any attempt to slow it down. Now try turning one axle and holding the other stationary. The shell now rotates at half the speed of the rotating axle, even when you try to slow it down. For a final observation, try turning one axle clockwise and the other axle counterclockwise. The differential shell will now remain fixed. This is all very interesting, but what good is this for robotics? As we discussed in Chapter 1, "Meet MINDSTORMS," the RCX is limited to three output motors. It is possible to use the differential to control two separate axles with only one motor, which can often overcome the limitation of only having two motors (see the section "Single Motor Navigation" near the end of this chapter).

Figure 5–32   The differential.

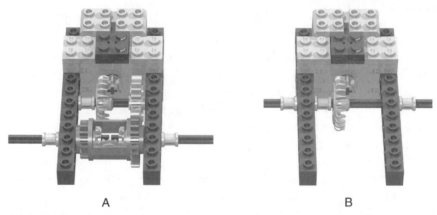

A   B

Figure 5–33   The differential really makes a difference.

The most popular use of the differential is in automobiles. A single axle shared between two wheels can cause problems. When a car is making a turn the outer wheel will travel farther than the inner wheel. The two wheels will skid and bump as the car makes the turn, causing rubber to wear from the tires and preventing a very sharp turn. By using a differential, the outer wheel is allowed to turn faster than the inner wheel. Philo, the robot in Chapter 9, uses a differential drive to allow very sharp turns using analog steering. A reduced model of the differential drive used by Philo is shown in Figure 5–33a. If you want to see the power of the differential, try removing the differential from Philo (Figure 5–33b) and running it on a hard surface. Without it, the robot bounces and shimmies as the forces come into conflict.

Pulleys

Pulleys (see Figure 5–34) and gears share a similar purpose: to transmit force to axles. There are a few notable differences, however. Pulleys are connected by stretchy pulley belts, so the spacing of the pulley wheels is not as rigid as with gears. Also, a pulley setup can transmit a force over a larger distance in a

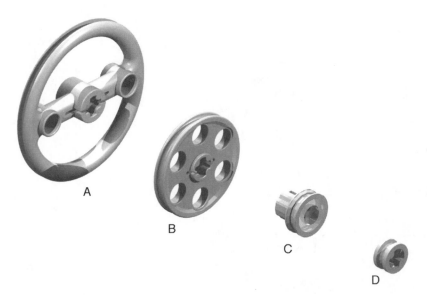

Figure 5–34 Pulleys.
A: large pulley (2 gray)
B: wedge belt wheel (4 gray)
C: micromotor pulley (4 gray, RIS 1.0; 2 gray, RIS 1.5 and 2.0)
D: smooth half bush/small pulley (16 gray)

thinner space. The main downfall of pulleys is that their belts slip minutely, so they are not good at keeping moving parts synchronized. Also, the pulley drive belt is not as capable of transmitting torque, so when the force gets very large the pulley belt tends to slip. This often means that when creating a gear train, only the connection from the motor to the first axle can be a pulley system. Pulleys can still perform basic gear reduction, however. Instead of counting gear teeth to formulate the gear reduction, measure the circumference of each pulley to determine the pulley reduction. Fortunately, each pulley has an equivalent gear size (except for the micromotor pulley). For example, the large pulley is the same size as the 40-tooth gear. Thus you can calculate gear reduction ratios in the same manner as calculating gears, with the number of teeth (see Figure 5–35).

The large pulley is the equivalent of the 40-tooth gear. It contains one spoke with an axle connector and two holes. This piece is often used for the steering wheel on LEGO kits. If you ever make a gear train and need a handle to act as a crankshaft, you can add a pin in one of the holes for a small handle.

The wedge belt wheel is thinner than the large pulley wheel and is equivalent to a 24-tooth gear. It also doubles as a wheel (see "Tires, Wheel Hubs, and Treads").

Figure 5–35   Pulley sizes and equivalent gears.

The micromotor pulley is about equivalent to a 12-tooth gear. If you look closely at the center of the wheel you will notice a rubberized end. This is used to clip on to a micromotor shaft (see Appendix A). The shaft on the micromotor is the size and shape of a single stud, so this pulley will also attach snugly to the stud on a brick. There is also a regular cross-axle hole, so an axle will fit through the center as well.

The small pulley is equivalent to an 8-tooth gear. It is so small that, unless the belt is sufficiently tight, it will often slip without turning the pulley wheel. This piece also doubles as an axle bush (as discussed earlier).

Pulley Drive Belts

Drive belts are used to connect pairs of pulley wheels. Ideally the pulley belt should be just tight enough to turn the pulley. If it is too tight, the rubber band is apt to break. If it is too loose, there will not be enough frictional force to turn the pulley wheel. Take some care when choosing the size of pulley belt. Alternately, the rubber bands can be used to allow limited movement of a part. Usually the rubber band is attached to a pin connected to a beam or lift arm in this case. The RIS kits include a small rubber band (1 white), small pulley belts (2 black), medium rubber bands (2 blue), and large rubber bands (3 yellow).

Lift Arms

Lift arms (Figure 5–36) are special beams with no studs on top and rounded ends. The smaller, gray lift arms are half the thickness of the larger black and yellow lift arms, so the dark gray 3/4 pin is used with them rather than the full-sized gray pin. Typically these pieces are attached to an axle and used to generate lifting movements. Another popular use of the lift arms is as front bumpers for roving robots.

The black 1 × 7 lift arm contains seven holes and no axle connectors, making it ideal for acting as a hinge for beams.

The 1 × 5 lift arm has five holes and no axle connectors, similar to the 7-unit lift arm.

The 1 × 4 lift arm has two axle connectors and two beam holes. One of the axle connectors is surrounded by a cylinder, which gives it the thickness of a regular beam and adds support to the axle.

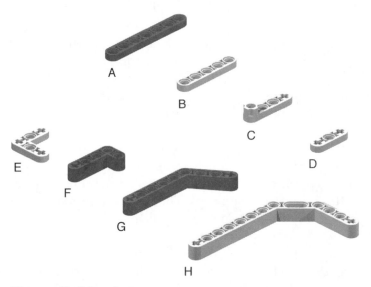

Figure 5–36 Lift arms.
A: 1 × 7 lift arm (4 black, 1.5 and 2.0 only)
B: 1 × 5 lift arm (2 gray, RIS 1.0; 4 gray, RIS 1.5 and 2.0)
C: 1 × 4 lift arm (2 gray)
D: 1 × 3 lift arm (2 gray, RIS 1.0; 4 gray, RIS 1.5 and 2.0)
E: 3 × 3 L-shape lift arm (4 gray, 1.5 and 2.0 only)
F: 2 × 4 L-shape lift arm (2 black, 1.5 and 2.0 only)
G: 1 × 9 bent lift arm (2 black, RIS 1.0; 4 gray, RIS 1.5 and 2.0)
H: 1 × 11.5 double bent lift arm (4 yellow)

The 1 × 3 lift arm has two axle connectors and one central hole. Because of this symmetry, this piece is ideal for acting as a rotor (e.g., a helicopter blade).

The 3 × 3 L-shape lift arm is thin like the previous ones with a 90-degree bend.

The 2 × 4 L-shape lift arm is thicker than the previous arms and bent closer to one end at a 90-degree angle.

The black 1 × 9 bent lift arm is bent after the third unit and contains an axle connector on both ends of the arm. The bend is slightly more than 45 degrees, so in certain situations it is not compatible with the 11.5-unit lift arm.

Each bend in the yellow 11.5-unit double bent lift arm is 45 degrees. There are eight holes in the entire arm, as well as an axle connector at each end of the arm. There is also a slot, as opposed to a hole, in the middle segment of the arm. This allows a pin to snap in place and slide laterally along the arm. The 1 × 9 and 1 × 11.5 lift arms are often used for legs, arms, and bumpers on MINDSTORMS robots.

Other Parts

The ribbed straws (Figure 5–37) are mostly for decoration. They can be attached to LEGO blocks by inserting a pin in one end, then attaching the other end of the pin to any round LEGO hole. I have also seen them joined together using pins to make a large circle. The circle is then attached to the robot so that when the circle contacted an obstacle it depressed a touch sensor, creating a 360-degree bumper.

The thin straws are good for creating antennae on robots. You can even make them functional by attaching a touch sensor, so when the antenna bumps an object the touch sensor is depressed. Thin straws can be attached to LEGO objects by the 1 × 1 plates with clips. They can be inserted into the small cylinder studs on Technic bricks, into 1 × 1 cone bricks, or into a Technic bush, which can then be attached to the top of a brick.

The fiber optic passes light from one end of the tube to the other. The advantage of this is light can be bent, allowing you to direct the course of the light through your LEGO structure. For example, you could attach the light sensor facing forward, and use the fiber optic to redirect light from behind the robot into the light sensor. This would allow the robot to monitor light signals from the front and back at the same time. There is quite a lot of degradation of the light signal, however, which is why the tube is not very long. Light intensity is usually about one quarter of the original source. Typically the tube is attached to LEGO structures by inserting 1/2 pins into the holes of Technic beams, then inserting the tube into the 1/2 pins.

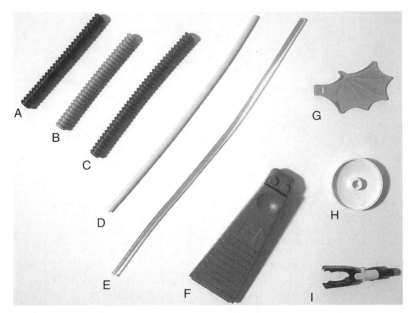

Figure 5–37 Other parts.
A, B, and C: ribbed straws (4 black, 7 cm; 4 topaz, 7 cm; 4 purple, 9.5 cm)
D: thin straws (2 yellow)
E: fiber optic (1 clear, RIS 2.0)
F: brick separator (1 dark gray)
G: dragon wings (2 clear orange)
H: satellite dish (2 white)
I: claws (2 black and yellow)

As promised, I will now reveal the use of the mystery part. This is the least LEGO-looking part in the whole kit and it is, in fact, not a part. It is actually an incredibly helpful tool known as a brick separator. It can be used to pry apart even the smallest plates from bricks, saving your fingers and fingernails, as well as preventing you from leaving teeth marks in your LEGO parts. To separate a plate, just attach the top or bottom of the tool to the edge of the plate (Figure 5–38), then pry off the plate, similar to using a bottle opener. If you have two plates stuck to each other, it is difficult to grasp a plate with enough force from your fingers. In these situations it's helpful to first attach the plates to some larger bricks, then use the brick separator to pry the plates off.

Many LEGO users like to attach the dragon wings as a final flourish, much like painting the flames on a hot-rod.

The satellite dish can give your robot that high-tech look, as though it's communicating with planet Earth. The concave side contains an axle cross connector, so if your robot uses axle legs it is possible to use these for feet.

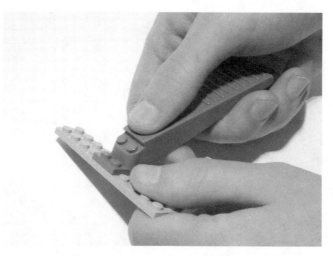

Figure 5–38   Using the brick separator to pry plates apart.

Each claw is assembled from four different parts. The claw is strong enough to hold onto most small round objects in the RIS toolkit, such as pins and bushings.

Tip:

In the interest of getting organized, it is a good idea to buy a large plastic sorting box or toolbox in which to store your LEGO parts. Having the parts pre-sorted, especially the smaller ones, can really help speed assembly.

Common LEGO Structures

There are some structures used over and over by LEGO builders. Being familiar with these can help you in your own designs, and possibly allow you to push well-known designs even further. Even wildly unconventional robots, such as a robot that navigates through a maze of PVC pipes, uses many of these same structures in their designs. There are several discreet units that go into a robot design: chassis, bumpers, drive system, and occasionally caster wheels. The LEGO Constructopedia does an excellent job of describing several of these units. For example, the bumpers described are quite well designed. The following sections attempt to go over topics left out by the Constructopedia.

Chassis

When you start building a MINDSTORMS robot, the first priority is usually building a platform or, for a mobile robot, a chassis. The chassis is what holds the wheels, gears, and RCX brick together, as well as supporting other structures. The type of chassis you build depends on the function of your robot. If it will be gaining high speeds, rolling over bumps, or encountering rough movement, then the chassis needs to be both durable and stable.

An excellent chassis can be created by four long beams and some plates for structural support (Figure 5–39). This type of chassis allows axles and pins to be inserted through any beam holes, and there is plenty of room for creating gear trains. If you use 16-unit beams then it is the perfect length to attach the RCX to the front and two drive motors at the rear (Figure 5–40). The drive motors are precisely 4 × 4 units, so they fit back to back on the 4 × 8 unit plates. 3/4 pins are used in the holes on the side of the RCX to clamp the RCX unit to the chassis, ensuring that the RCX will not come loose or rattle.

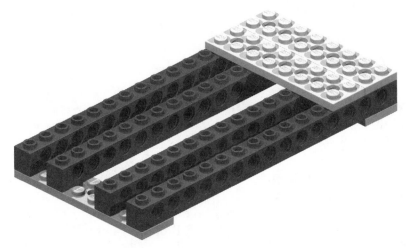

Figure 5–39   A chassis with beams and plates.

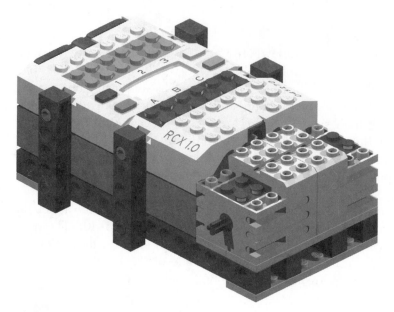

Figure 5–40   The RCX and motors attached to the chassis.

Caster Wheels

A caster wheel is a small, swiveled wheel. These types of wheels are common on shopping carts, chairs, and tables because you can push the object in any direction and the caster wheel will self-adjust accordingly. One of the most common forms of steering with a MINDSTORMS robot is differential steering. A robot can turn one wheel forward and one in reverse, turning the robot within its own footprint. These types of steering systems generally use a caster wheel to keep the robot balanced. The caster wheel in Figure 5–41 is a good design because the wheel is centered, so the robot will not drift to one side. The robot in Chapter 8, "Navigation with Rotation Sensors," uses this caster wheel.

Note:

It is very important to attach the caster wheel firmly to the chassis of the robot. The caster wheel is repeatedly subject to forces that are liable to rip the plate away from the chassis. To reinforce it properly, it is usually necessary to overlap other plates onto the caster wheel plates, or at the very least make sure there are at least four studs holding each plate to the chassis.

Figure 5–41 A properly balanced caster wheel.

Ratchets

A ratchet is a simple but useful device for allowing rotation of a gear in one direction but not the other. A ratchet mechanism can be devised with LEGO using a gear and a small beam with a hinge pin (Figure 5–42). The beam will slide off the gear when it turns in one direction, but if the gear attempts to turn in the other direction the beam prevents movement. Adding an elastic over the hinged beam will allow the ratchet to work no matter what the orientation, even upside down.

Figure 5–42 A simple ratchet.

Single Motor Navigation

The following structure is probably one of the most complicated you are likely to encounter in LEGO. It uses the differential and a ratchet to achieve steering using only a single motor (Figure 5–43). When the motor rotates forward, both wheels also rotate forward. When the motor goes backward, only one of the wheels will rotate backward. This causes differential turning, allowing the robot to alternately rotate and drive forward.

Note:

Wheels must be placed on the axles.

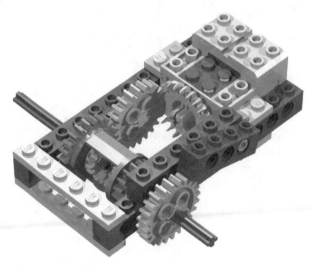

Figure 5–43   Steering and driving with only one motor.

Walking Mechanism

By using several parts (the angle connector, an axle, a connector with axle hole, and a gear) a rudimentary walking leg can be constructed (Figure 5–44). This construction is similar to a train piston, but the tip of the axle (leg) will produce an elliptical motion, perfect for a walking gait.

Figure 5–44 A simple walking mechanism.

Building Philosophy 101

Before starting this section, let's review the rules that must be adhered to when building LEGO creations:

-
-
-

As you can see, there are no rules! LEGO is a supposed to be a creative activity where you can let your imagination rule. If you want to build a tree out of LEGOs that grows and sprouts branches, build a tree. If you want to build a scary creature that frightens people, do it. New ideas are not discovered by people who follow the rules. The best way to invent with LEGO is to just sit down and play.

Don't buy into the rule that all LEGO creations must use 100% LEGO parts. Many LEGOmaniacs insist on this, as if using non-LEGO parts in a creation is a sin. This is an artificial constraint, so why impose it on your creations? LEGO is incredible, but it just can't create every type of material a robot may need. How are you going to make a floating blimp robot if you can't use helium and a light mylar envelope? Don't limit your inventions by limiting the parts to LEGO only.

There are actually a few guidelines that LEGOmaniacs like to follow when building robotic creations. These guidelines are sometimes used to evaluate how well a robot is designed and can help to raise the bar on the quality of your robot:

- **Strength.** Without the RCX or sensors attached, try dropping your robot from a height of about six inches onto a carpeted surface. If pieces fall off, things could be stronger.
- **Stability.** The robot should not be prone to tipping over.
- **Easy access to batteries.** Some robot designers like easy access to the RCX batteries without removing a lot of parts.
- **IR port free.** To upload programs to the robot, the IR port should be free from obstructions.
- **Using the minimum number of pieces.** One of the unwritten design goals of any engineered object is to use the minimum number of parts possible. A design that achieves this is more efficient than one containing superfluous pieces. When you can no longer remove any pieces, consider your robot finished.

The important thing when designing with LEGO is to relax and be creative. You can tell when you have really entered the zone when you experience *LEGO time*, a compressed form of time. This phenomena is similar to when objects travel near the speed of light or near a large gravitational mass. LEGO time is capable of turning several hours into mere minutes. It's a unique experience!

BEHAVIOR CONTROL

Chapter 6

Over the years programmers have noticed a pattern of program architectures that seem to evolve over and over again. The reason an idea is used repeatedly is because it is the best solution for a particular problem. These ideas have come to be known as *programming patterns*, a collection of commonly repeated program structures. The patterns are object-oriented models that describe the main objects and the relationships between the objects. Programming robots is much different from programming an application for a user, so the robotics field has also developed its own set of patterns. One of the most popular for small, limited memory, "insect"-level programming is known as *behavior control*.

Behavior Control Theory

Behavior control was first defined by Rodney Brooks at the MIT Artificial Intelligence Laboratory. The strategy of behavior control is in contrast to most AI programming styles before it, which tend to rely on large data models of the world, and can also be slow to react to changes in the environment. Brooks took his strategy from the insect world. He noticed that insects are able to perform in the real world with excellent success, despite having very little in the way of brains. If we were to compare an insect to a computer, we would conclude that the insect possessed only a small amount of working memory. After all, it has been shown that insects do not remember things from the past, and cannot be trained in Pavlovian style. Insects thus rely on a strategy of many simple behaviors that, when alternated with one another, build into complex behavior that can react quickly to changes. These strategies are effectively "hard-wired" into the insect and are not learned in the way mammals learn their behavior. Brooks adapted this strategy, observing it in nature and then transforming it into the world of computers. It was originally developed under the name *subsumption architecture*, but it has since been renamed to the much more recognizable *behavior control*.

There are essentially two discrete structures that build a behavior: sensors (inputs) and actuators (outputs). This is true of any organism, not just robots. For example, imagine a mosquito sitting on a wall. At all times it is monitoring its current situation through a variety of sensors. If certain sensors are stimulated, a trigger occurs that causes the mosquito to react in some fashion. It might be only one sensor that triggers a reaction, but more likely it will take input from a few sensors for the mosquito to determine that something is happening and it should react. If the wind blows and a few bristles on the legs of the mosquito are stimulated, it would not be logical to take off and flee. For the survival of the mosquito it is important that the reaction to a trigger is appropriate to the situation that caused the sensors to be stimulated. These pairs of conditions and actions are called *behaviors* (Figure 6–1).

Behavior actions can be very simple, such as moving forward, or they can be complex, such as mapping the data in a room. A behavior is just a program the robot (or organism) follows for a period of time. You can think of the behavior control concept as changing modes. When you are writing an e-mail to someone, you are in letter-writing mode, but then when your stomach starts to grumble you go to the kitchen and switch to eating mode. Letter-writing mode requires a different set of instructions than eating mode. By building up several simple behaviors you can theoretically achieve a complex logical model.

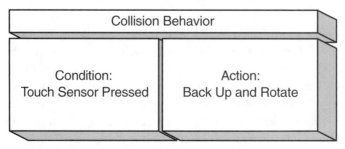

Figure 6–1 Diagram for a collision behavior.

Sensors are not just restricted to determining when to switch from one mode to another. In fact, they can be used within the action portion of the code as well. If the behavior is to map the boundaries of a room, then it will have to use sensors to determine if there is a wall next to it. This sensor can also be used by other behaviors, both for the controlling the action and determining the conditions. Sensors can also be shared for determining conditions. For example, a firefighting robot could share a single temperature sensor to control more than one reaction. The robot could actively move toward areas with greater heat to help it locate the fire. If it moves forward in a direction and the temperature sensor indicates it is warmer, then it tries another step in that direction. If it gets cooler, then it tries another direction. But assuming there is actually a fire, there will come a time when the temperature gets so hot that our robot would melt if it kept homing in. To counter this, we could use the same sensor with a higher level behavior to back off if the temperature got close to the melting point of plastic (Table 6–1).

Table 6-1 Fire-Fighting Behavior Control

Behavior	Condition	Action	Priority
Seek heat	Temperature hotter in another area	Move toward heat	Low
Extinguish flames	Ultraviolet light sensor detects flame	Spray CO_2	Medium
Avoid flames	Temperature > 160°	Move away from heat	Highest

A behavior takes over when a condition becomes true, and it does not have to depend on an external sensor for a behavior to kick in. For example, the robot could monitor an internal condition such as time. When 2 minutes have elapsed, a higher level behavior could become active. In a way, the timer is a time sensor. Other factors can also be monitored, such as counting the number of bricks the robot has picked up. Once a robot has collected 10 bricks, a higher level behavior of seeking home and dumping the bricks could become active. Any condition, internal or external to the robot, can activate a behavior.

This doesn't have to be for practical behaviors only. I have seen robots that switch from one emotional mode to another. For example, there is an R2-D2 type of robot that switches from happy mode to bored mode, or sad mode. The bored mode kicks in if the robot has been wandering around for a while without encountering anything. Each of these emotional states is dependent on what the robot senses of its surroundings, which is really not that different from complex organisms such as humans.

There will be times when more than one behavior will seek to be activated. For the robot to determine which mode to break into, the different behaviors need to have priorities. For example, an animal has several basic goals, such as eating, mating, defending itself, exploring, and protecting its young. Some of these behaviors are more important than others, but all are necessary for the overall survival of the species. One of the most important behaviors is eating, because starvation prevents an organism from completing any of the other important goals. We would thus say eating is a high-level priority for an animal. However, if another ferocious animal is attacking it then it should not continue eating. Defending itself (attack mode/retreat mode) would be the highest level behavior for this animal. Likewise a robot is no good if it runs out of battery power, so it could have explore as a lower level behavior, and when the battery level gets too low it could seek the battery recharging station. It is important that the code interrupts the current action if a higher level action needs to take over. When this happens, we say that the lower level behavior has been *suppressed*. Rodney Brooks came up with a standard diagram for representing these sorts of hierarchies of behaviors (Figure 6–2). A typical diagram for this shows the behavior and the order of priorities. When a behavior suppresses other behaviors it is indicated with an S. The rule for behavior control is that all lower level behaviors are suppressed when a higher level behavior takes over. This means only one behavior can be running at any given time. At first this might seem like it limits a

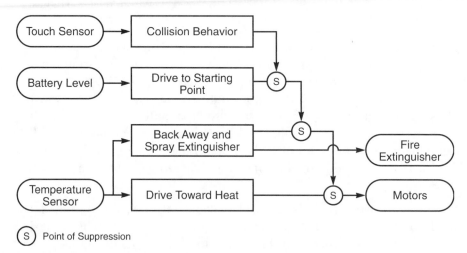

Figure 6–2   Hierarchy of behavior.

robot, but organisms really only do one thing at a time. If you want to perform more than one behavior at a time, then a single behavior must include more than one function within it.

Programming Behavior with leJOS

Most people, when they start programming their robot, will think of the program flow as a series of if–thens, which is reminiscent of structured programming (Figure 6–3). This type of programming is very easy to get started in and hardly requires any thought about design beforehand. A programmer can just sit at the computer and start typing. The problem is that the code can end up as spaghetti code, all tangled up and difficult to expand. The behavior control model, in contrast, requires a little more planning before coding begins, but the payoff is that each behavior is nicely encapsulated within an easy-to-understand structure. This will theoretically make your code easier to understand for other programmers familiar with the behavior control model. More important, it becomes very easy to add or remove specific behaviors from the overall structure without negative repercussions for the rest of the code. Let's examine how to do this in leJOS.

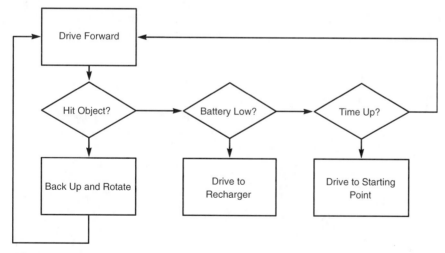

Figure 6–3 Structured programming visualized.

The Behavior API

The Behavior API is very simple, and is composed of only one interface and one class. The Behavior interface is used to define behaviors. It is very general, so it works quite well because the individual implementations of a behavior vary widely. Once all the behaviors are defined, they are given to an arbitrator to regulate which behaviors should be activated. All classes and interfaces for behavior control are located in the josx.robotics package. The API for the Behavior interface is as follows:

`josx.robotics.Behavior`

- `boolean takeControl()`

  Returns a Boolean value to indicate whether this behavior should become active. For example, if a touch sensor indicates the robot has bumped into an object, this method should return true.

- `void action()`

  The code in this method initiates an action when the behavior becomes active. For example, if takeControl() detects the robot has collided with an object, the action() code could make the robot back up and turn away from the object.

- `void suppress()`

  The code in the suppress() method should immediately terminate the code running in the action() method. The suppress() method can also be used to update any data before this behavior completes.

As you can see, the three methods in the Behavior interface are quite simple. If a robot has three discrete behaviors, then the programmer will need to create three classes, with each class implementing the Behavior interface. Once these classes are complete, the code should hand the Behavior objects off to the arbitrator to deal with:

`josx.robotics.Arbitrator`

- `public Arbitrator(Behavior [] behaviors)`

  Creates an Arbitrator object that regulates when each of the behaviors will become active. The higher the index array number for a behavior, the higher the priority level.

  Parameters: `behaviors`   An array of Behaviors.

- `public void start()`

  Starts the arbitration system.

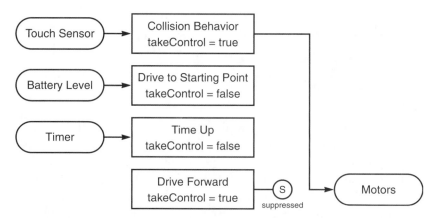

Figure 6–4 Higher level behaviors suppress lower level behaviors.

The Arbitrator class is even easier to understand than Behavior. When an Arbitrator object is instantiated, it is given an array of Behavior objects. Once it has these, the start() method is called and it begins arbitrating, or deciding which behaviors should become active. The Arbitrator object calls the take-Control() method on each Behavior object, starting with the object with the highest index number in the array. It works its way through each of the Behavior objects until it encounters a behavior that wants to take control. When it encounters one, it executes the action() method of that behavior once. If two behaviors both want to take control, then only the higher level behavior is allowed (Figure 6–4).

Now that we are familiar with the Behavior API under leJOS, let's look at a simple example using three behaviors. For this example, we program some behavior for Tippy (see Chapter 1, "Meet MINDSTORMS"), a simple robot with differential steering. This robot will drive forward as its primary low-level behavior. When it hits an object, a high-priority behavior will become active to back the robot up and turn it 90 degrees. We will also insert a third behavior into the program after the first two have been completed. Let's start with the first behavior.

As we saw in the Behavior interface, we must implement the methods action(), suppress(), and takeControl(). The behavior for driving forward takes place in the action() method. It simply needs to make Motors A and C rotate forward:

```
public void action() {
   Motor.A.forward();
   Motor.C.forward();
}
```

That was easy enough! Now the suppress() method will need to stop this action when it is called, as follows:

```
public void suppress() {
    Motor.A.stop();
    Motor.C.stop();
}
```

So far, so good. Now we need to implement a method to tell Arbitrator when this behavior should become active. As we outlined earlier, this robot will always drive forward, unless something else suppresses it, so this behavior should always want to take control (it's a bit of a control freak). The take-Control() method should return true, no matter what is happening. This may seem counterintuitive, but rest assured that higher level behaviors will be able to cut in on this behavior when the need arises. The method appears as follows:

```
public boolean takeControl() {
    return true;
}
```

That's all it takes to define our first behavior to drive the robot forward. The complete code listing for this class is as follows:

```
import josx.robotics.*;
import josx.platform.rcx.*;

public class DriveForward implements Behavior {

    public boolean takeControl() {
        return true;
    }

    public void suppress() {
        Motor.A.stop();
        Motor.C.stop();
    }

    public void action() {
        Motor.A.forward();
        Motor.C.forward();
    }
}
```

The second behavior is a little more complicated than the first, but similar. The main action of this behavior is to reverse and turn when the robot strikes an object. In this example, we would like the behavior to take control only when the touch sensor strikes an object, so the takeControl() method is defined as follows:

```
public boolean takeControl() {
    return Sensor.S2.readBooleanValue();
}
```

For the action, we want the robot to back up and rotate when it strikes an object, so we define the action() method as follows:

```
public void action() {
    // Back up:
    Motor.A.backward();
    Motor.C.backward();
    try{Thread.sleep(1000);}catch(Exception e) {}
    // Rotate by causing one wheel to stop:
    Motor.A.stop();
    try{Thread.sleep(300);}catch(Exception e) {}
    Motor.C.stop();
}
```

Defining the suppress() method for this behavior is quite easy in this example. The action() method is the sort of method that runs very quickly (1.3 seconds) and is usually a high priority. We can either stop it dead by stopping motor movement, or we could wait for it to complete the backing up maneuver. To keep things simple, let's just stop the motors from rotating:

```
public void suppress() {
    Motor.A.stop();
    Motor.C.stop();
}
```

The complete listing for this behavior is as follows:

```
1. import josx.robotics.*;
2. import josx.platform.rcx.*;
3.
4. public class HitWall implements Behavior {
5.     public boolean takeControl() {
6.         return Sensor.S2.readBooleanValue();
7.     }
8.
9.     public void suppress() {
10.        Motor.A.stop();
11.        Motor.C.stop();
12.    }
13.
14.    public void action() {
```

```
15.        // Back up:
16.        Motor.A.backward();
17.        Motor.C.backward();
18.        try{Thread.sleep(1000);}catch(Exception e) {}
19.        // Rotate by causing only one wheel to stop:
20.        Motor.A.stop();
21.        try{Thread.sleep(300);}catch(Exception e) {}
22.        Motor.C.stop();
23.    }
24. }
```

We now have our two behaviors defined, and it's time to make a class with a main() method to get things started. All we need to do is create an array of our Behavior objects, and instantiate and start the Arbitrator as shown in the following code listing:

```
import josx.robotics.*;

public class BumperCar {
    public static void main(String [] args) {
        Behavior b1 = new DriveForward();
        Behavior b2 = new HitWall();
        Behavior [] bArray = {b1, b2};
        Arbitrator arby = new Arbitrator(bArray);
        arby.start();
    }
}
```

This code is fairly easy to understand. The first two lines in the main() method create instances of our behaviors. The third line places them into an array, with the lowest priority behavior taking the lowest array index. The fourth line creates the Arbitrator, and the fifth line starts the arbitration process. When this program is started, the robot will scurry forward until it bangs into an object, then it will retreat, rotate, and continue with its forward movement until the power is shut off.

This seems like a lot of extra work for two simple behaviors, but now let's see how easy it is to insert a third behavior without altering any code in the other classes. This is the part that makes behavior control systems very appealing for robotics programming. Our third behavior could be just about anything. We'll have this new behavior monitor the battery level and play a tune when it dips below a certain level. Examine the completed Behavior:

```
1. import josx.robotics.*;
2. import josx.platform.rcx.*;
3.
4. public class BatteryLow implements Behavior {
```

```
5.    private float LOW_LEVEL;
6.    private static final short [] note = {
         2349,115,  0,5,  1760,165,  0,35,  1760,28,  0,13,  1976,23,
         0,18,  1760,18,  0,23,  1568,15,  0,25,  1480,103,  0,18,
         1175,180,  0,20,  1760,18,  0,23,  1976,20,  0,20,  1760,15,
         0,25,  1568,15,  0,25,  2217,98,  0,23,  1760,88,  0,33,  1760,
         75,  0,5,  1760,20,  0,20,  1760,20,  0,20,  1976,18,  0,23,
         1760,18,  0,23,  2217,225,  0,15,  2217,218};
7.    public BatteryLow(float volts) {
8.        LOW_LEVEL = volts;
9.    }
10.
11.   public boolean takeControl() {
12.       float voltLevel = (ROM.getBatteryPower() * 10 / 355);
13.       int displayNum = (int)(voltLevel * 100);
14.       LCD.setNumber(0x301f, displayNum, 0x3004);
15.       LCD.refresh();
16.
17.       return voltLevel < LOW_LEVEL;
18.   }
19.
20.   public void suppress() {
21.       // Nothing to suppress
22.   }
23.
24.   public void action() {
25.       play();
26.       try{Thread.sleep(3000);}catch(Exception e) {}
27.       System.exit(0);
28.   }
29.
30.   public static void play() {
31.       for(int i=0;i<note.length; i+=2) {
32.           final short w = note[i+1];
33.           Sound.playTone(note[i], w);
34.           try {
35.               Thread.sleep(w*10);
36.           } catch (InterruptedException e) {}
37.       }
38.   }
39. }
```

The complete tune is stored in the note array at Line 6 and the method to play the notes is at Line 30. This behavior will take control only if the current battery level is less than the voltage specified in the constructor. The take-Control() method looks a little inflated, and that's because it also displays the battery charge to the LCD. The action() and suppress() methods are comparatively easy. Action makes a bunch of noise, then exits the program as soon as it is called. Because this behavior stops the program, there is no need to create a suppress() method.

To insert this behavior into our scheme is a trivial task. We simply alter the code of our main class as follows:

```java
import josx.robotics.*;

public class BumperCar {
    public static void main(String [] args) {
        Behavior b1 = new DriveForward();
        Behavior b2 = new BatteryLow(6.5f);
        Behavior b3 = new HitWall();
        Behavior [] bArray = {b1, b2, b3};
        Arbitrator arby = new Arbitrator(bArray);
        arby.start();
    }
}
```

Note:

The voltage level of the RCX at rest is different from the voltage when in action. The voltage level at rest might be 7.8 V, but when motors are activated they naturally cause a drop in the voltage reading. Make sure the voltage threshold used in the BatteryLow constructor is low enough.

This beautifully demonstrates the real benefit of behavior control coding. Inserting a new behavior, no matter what the rest of the code looks like, is simple. The reason for this is grounded in object-oriented design; each behavior is a self-contained, independent object.

Tip:

When creating a behavior control system, it is best to program each behavior one at a time and test them individually. If you code all the behaviors and then upload them all at once to the RCX brick, there is a good chance a bug will exist somewhere in the behaviors, making it difficult to locate. Programming and testing them one at a time makes it easier to identify where the problem was introduced.

Behavior coding is predominantly used for *autonomous robots*, robots that work independently, of their own free will. A robot arm controlled by a human would likely not use behavior programming, although it would be possible. For example, a robot arm with four joystick movements could have a behavior for each direction of movement. As you may recall, however, behaviors are ordered with the highest order taking precedence over lower order behaviors. Who is to say that pushing left on the joystick would take precedence over pushing up? In other words, behavior control in anything other than autonomous robots is largely overkill.

Advanced Behavior Coding

It would be nice if all behaviors were as simple as the preceding examples, but in more complex coding there are some unexpected results that can sometimes be introduced. Threads, for example, can sometimes be difficult to halt from the suppress() method, which can lead to two different threads fighting over the same resources—often the same motor! Another problem that can potentially occur in multithreaded programs is that events go undetected, such as touch sensor hits. These are a few of the pitfalls we examine in the following sections. Let's start by looking at what is generally the least complicated of the three behavior methods to implement: the takeControl() method.

Note:

The behavior control API used by leJOS is a modified version of the model proposed by Rodney Brooks. His model is all done at the lowest level possible, the motors. This prevents higher level classes from being used in behaviors. For example, the Navigator class accesses the motors of the RCX directly, so with the original behavior control model Navigator could not be used. Also, if both motors are moving forward and a higher level behavior takes command, it is not clear if all lower level motor movements should be stopped. What if the higher level behavior uses only one of the motors? Should the other keep moving forward? Will this lead to odd behavior? These are the problems the leJOS Behavior Control API tries to address.

Coding Foolproof takeControl() Methods

It is very important for takeControl() methods to be responsive in behavior control systems. When a bumper collides with an object, the robot must stop or reverse direction immediately; otherwise it will continue to move forward into the object. Sometimes when an event occurs, such as a touch sensor press, the program misses the event because the RCX is executing another thread. By the time it gets to the takeControl() method, the sensor has been released and the program misses its opportunity to activate the proper behavior action. In this section we learn how to make foolproof takeControl() methods.

In the earlier example using Tippy, we used single indicators of whether or not to take control. For example, it took one reading from the Sensor class to check if the touch sensor was hit. The takeControl() method can also make a decision to take control based on a number of different values. It could initiate an action if it is facing east, the light reading is greater than 60, and the temperature is less than 20°:

```
public boolean takeControl() {
    boolean pass = false;
    if(direction == EAST)
        if(Sensor.S1.readValue() > 60)
            if(Sensor.S2.readValue() < 20)
                pass = true;
    return pass;
}
```

Likewise, a different behavior could just as easily check on the same data, only react differently based on different values. For example, another behavior could initiate a different action if the robot is facing west, the light reading is less than 60, and temperature is greater than 20°. Therefore, a robot can initiate an unlimited number of responses with only a few sensors at its disposal. This leads us to another salient point about implementing the takeControl() method.

With the arbitrator cycling through all the takeControl() methods, there could be a significant delay in checking a condition, such as whether a touch sensor has been pressed. It's a feature of the imperfect world we live in that, when the robot strikes an object, the touch sensor may not remain depressed for long. It sometimes bounces off the object into a position where the bumper is no longer pressing on the touch sensor. You may have noticed in the example we used for Tippy that it relies on checking touch very often. What if the touch sensor is momentarily activated, but the arbitrator misses this fact? The solution is to use a SensorListener, and have it set a flag to indicate the event has occurred. Let's take the HitWall behavior from the preceding Tippy example and modify it so it uses a SensorListener:

```
1. import josx.robotics.*;
2. import josx.platform.rcx.*;
3.
```

```
4. public class HitWall implements Behavior, SensorListener {
5.     boolean hasCollided;
6.
7.     // Constructor:
8.     public HitWall() {
9.         hasCollided = false;
10.         Sensor.S2.addSensorListener(this);
11.     }
12.
13.     public void stateChanged(Sensor bumper, int oldValue,
            int newValue) {
14.         if(bumper.readBooleanValue() == true)
15.             hasCollided = true;
16.     }
17.
18.     public boolean takeControl() {
19.         if(hasCollided) {
20.             hasCollided = false; // reset value
21.             return true;
22.         } else
23.             return false;
24.     }
25.
26.     public void suppress() {
27.         Motor.A.stop();
28.         Motor.C.stop();
29.     }
30.
31.     public void action() {
32.         // Back up:
33.         Motor.A.backward();
34.         Motor.C.backward();
35.         try{Thread.sleep(1000);}catch(Exception e) {}
36.         // Rotate by causing only one wheel to stop:
37.         Motor.A.stop();
38.         try{Thread.sleep(300);}catch(Exception e) {}
39.         Motor.C.stop();
40.     }
41. }
```

This code implements a SensorListener, and hence implements the state-Changed() method. It is important to add the SensorListener to Sensor.S2, as shown in Line 10. Notice the stateChanged() method does not simply return the value of the bumper Sensor; rather, if the Sensor value is true then it changes the hasCollided variable to true. If, on the next pass, the Sensor value is false then hasCollided will remain true until takeControl() has seen the hasCollided value. Once takeControl() sees there has been a collision, then hasCollided is reset back to false (Line 20). With this new code, it should be almost impossible for the robot to miss collisions with the bumper!

Coding Solid action() and suppress() Methods

To code functional action() and suppress() pairs, it is necessary to understand how arbitration works. Arbitrator cycles through each of its behaviors, checking the takeControl() method to see if the action() for a behavior should be executed. It starts with the highest priority method and goes down to the lowest priority behavior. As soon as it comes across a behavior that wants to take control, it executes suppress() for the previous behavior (assuming it is not a higher level thread), then runs the action() method for the current behavior. As soon as the action() method returns, it then starts looping again, checking each behavior. If takeControl() from the previous behavior continues to say true, it does *not* run action() again. This is important; a single behavior cannot be executed twice in a row. If it could, it would constantly be suppressing itself. If arbitrator moves on to another behavior, when that behavior completes then it calls action on the lower level behavior again.

Tip:

If you would like to remove any mystery about what goes on in the Arbitrator class, take a look at the source code. It is located in leJOS/ classes/josx/robotics/Arbitrator.java. The code is not very complicated and may prove enlightening.

To program individual behaviors, it is important to understand the fundamental differences between types of behaviors. Behavior actions come in two basic varieties:

1. Discrete actions that finish quickly (e.g., back up and turn)
2. Actions that start running and keep going for an indefinite period until they are suppressed (e.g., driving forward, following a wall)

Discrete actions execute once and return from the action() method call only when it has completed its behavior. These types of behaviors generally do not need any code in the suppress() method because once the action is done there is nothing to suppress. The second type of action sometimes runs in a separate thread, although not always. For example, the Motor.A.forward() method call acts like a thread because the motor keeps turning after the method returns. In actuality, this is not a thread; the RCX just turns on an internal switch to activate the motor. An example of a true thread would be complex behavior, such as wall following. The action() method could start a thread to begin following a wall until the suppress() method is called. Be careful of never-ending loops! If one were to occur within the action() method, the program would become stuck.

So why use the Behavior API? The best reason is because in programming we strive to create the simplest, most powerful solution possible, even if it takes slightly more time. The importance of reusable, maintainable code has been demonstrated repeatedly in the workplace, especially on projects involving more than one person. If you leave your code and come back to it several months later, the things that looked so obvious suddenly don't anymore. With behavior control, you can add and remove behaviors without even looking at the rest of the code, even if there are 10 or more behaviors in the program.

Another big advantage of behavior control is code reusability. Reusability in OOP was talked about for a long time, but it didn't seem to really take hold until well into the '90s. There is the potential in robotics for code reusability, but in my opinion several factors need to be addressed before it can become a reality. The primary obstacle is differences in robot hardware. True, LEGO uses standard parts, but everyone build their robots differently. Something as simple as the orientation of a wire can cause the motor to spin in the wrong direction. This sort of difference can be addressed in the constructor, but sometimes there are so many factors it becomes confusing. Also, there are different families of robots, such as traveling robots and stationary arms, so a body of code might only be useful to a certain family of robot. Until a standard grouping of robots is agreed on, reusable code may not be achievable. If these obstacles can be overcome, the advantages of being able to use complex, prefabricated AI classes with robots is obvious.

Web site:

The Rossum Project is an open source movement with the goal of creating a library of code for robots. More information is available at: rossum.sourceforge.net.

Although this is the end of the chapter, it is not the end of the topic of behavior control. The next few chapters use behavior control in the code used for navigation, so there will be many more examples to observe.

NAVIGATION

Chapter 7

One of the most exciting, baffling challenges in robotics is navigation, which is important to mobile robots for obvious reasons. Without it, a robot will only be capable of wandering around aimlessly. Before we get into the finer points of navigation it is useful to define what we mean when talking about Navigation. In previous chapters we experimented with a small bumper-car robot that could move around a room with a moderate degree of success. It drove forward, and if it encountered an object it would back up and head off in another direction. Is this navigation? By strict definition, navigation is the science of directing the course of a vehicle. With robot navigation, a robot should be able to go from one point to another and have the ability to return to the original point. Furthermore, it should be able to find another position relative to the original position. This requires keeping track of where the robot is in one form or another, so a simple bumper-car robot would not be considered a navigator. With our task defined, let's get on with discovering navigational methods. This chapter, as well as Chapter 8, "Navigation with Rotation Sensors," and Chapter 10, "Navigation with a Compass Sensor," all give progressively more competent methods of RCX navigation, but each successive chapter requires additional components and a higher level of sophistication. In this chapter, the only thing you need is the basic RIS kit.

Understanding the Problem of Navigation

Why is navigation so difficult to program into robots? It seems like it should be easy to program accurate navigation; after all, navigation is extremely easy for humans. As an experiment, try navigating around your living room. As you do this, pay attention to the strategies that allow you to accurately move from one location to another. Try walking to one corner, then follow the wall to the other corner, then walk toward an object such as a television. These steps are easy for you because you are packed with sensors. Your sensors give you, among other things, a visual picture of where you are in relation to objects, and your sense of touch informs you when you brush against another object. You also have tons of memory (AI pioneer Alan Turing estimated a human has 10,000 million bits of memory, or 1.25 GB), so you can store (amazingly inaccurate) maps of your surrounding area; in fact most people have an adequate internal map of the city they live in. However, navigation within a small, visible space does not rely on any of this map data. The visual picture you see of your living room overrules any map representation you may have previously stored. To walk toward the television you don't simply point toward it, estimate how many steps you will take, then close your eyes and start walking. Instead, as you move toward it you are constantly self-correcting your direction, much like a missile homes in on a target. Now let's examine how this compares to the RCX.

We'll try to imagine your living room from the perspective of a robot. Our robot Tippy, from previous chapters, is equipped with a single touch sensor that is either on or off. It also has two motors it can control, and an internal timer that functions like a stopwatch. To put yourself in the robot's shoes, imagine climbing into a yellow box about one cubic meter in size. When the box is closed everything about the outside world becomes unknown. The box is equipped with a small control panel that contains a three-way switch (forward, stop, reverse) for the left wheel, another three-way switch for the right wheel, a stopwatch, and a light bulb (Figure 7–1). The light bulb will go on only when the bumper hits an object. We will also add the presence of a benevolent giant who exists outside the box. He may, according to his whim, give you small pieces of information that can help you in your task. Furthermore, we must introduce some pseudo-physics into this scenario. If the box scrapes by an object you will not hear it. If you back into an object, you will not be jostled or feel your momentum change. If you run over some objects on the floor, you will not feel a bump. If a wheel becomes stuck in

Figure 7-1 Life inside the box. (Artwork courtesy of Wil Glass.)

midair, rotating freely, you will be unaware of this. This is exactly how Tippy experiences the world, and it is a very dark place.

Now let's see how well we can navigate within this scenario. Imagine you have a piece of paper and a pencil inside this box. The first thing you can do is mark an X representing your starting point. The strategy we employ is to measure the forward and backward movement using a stopwatch. We aren't really sure how fast the robot moves, but we do know that moving forward for four seconds is twice as far as moving for two seconds. Units are not really important to us because we have no idea of the scale of the outside world. One second could represent a centimeter, a meter, or 20 inches. To us it is irrelevant, so all measurements will be measured in seconds. Now it's time to boldly go forth, so we start the watch and switch both motors to forward. It's a little scary, knowing that at any moment the box could go plunging down a flight of stairs. After a time the touch sensor light goes on, so we halt the stopwatch and record the time. In this case, we have moved forward for four seconds, so we draw a line—say four inches long—due east from the X. This is our new position. We can also indicate on our piece of paper that an object was struck at that point by placing O_1 next to the point. Now, because we are trying to emulate Tippy's world, our only recourse is to back up and turn in a new direction. Backing up is no problem—we just back up an arbitrary amount of, say, one second. To rotate we drive one motor forward and one in reverse, but we need to know how many degrees we have rotated. To calculate this, we need to know how long it takes to complete one full rotation. In our case, the giant has given us a piece of paper that tells us it takes four seconds to rotate 360 degrees. Thus, we decide to rotate to the right 90 degrees, or one second. Now we can carry on our way, navigating around the room and keeping track of when we bump into objects. After a while, we might even be able to make inferences about the room, such as where doorways and walls exist. At any time we can attempt to head back to our starting point, or to one of the other points within the area, using the coordinates we have written on the paper.

So, as you can see, we can perform some rudimentary exploration with little external information. The main source of external data is the light bulb—one bit—which is either on or off, but much can be inferred from changes in this state. This doesn't guarantee we are in fact where we believe we are, though. For all we know, the giant, in one of his more puckish moods, could be holding the box off the ground and pressing the touch sensor at random intervals (Figure 7–2). Barring any anomalies such as this, we should have a pretty good

Figure 7–2   External conditions can affect accuracy. (Artwork courtesy of Wil Glass.)

idea of our location at any given time. We could even go so far as to navigate to a specific section of the house. For this to succeed we have to ensure the starting point and orientation are always the same. The external giant could even hand a piece of paper through a slot that tells us the coordinates of the kitchen, bathroom, bedroom, and living room. By receiving some external data, it is possible for Tippy to get from one known location to another.

To really understand what the RCX robot sees, I heartily recommend navigating around your own living room. By involving yourself in what the robot experiences you can really start to understand how limited its perceptions of the world are. To do this you need to shut off as many senses as possible by turning off sources of sound such as a TV, a radio, an air conditioner, or a ticking clock. Better yet, use ear-plugs. You may want to blindfold yourself so you aren't subconsciously navigating by the brightness of a local light source. Please take extreme care if you decide to perform this experiment. I don't want to be responsible for intrepid roboticists falling down flights of stairs while blindfolded!

Navigation Theory

The method just described is called *dead reckoning* (sometimes called *orienteering*), a method of navigation used by all animals, older sailing vessels, geologists, forest rangers, and hikers. The only pieces of information needed for dead reckoning are direction and distance. Direction is usually obtained using a magnetic compass and distance (odometry) can be found in a number of ways, such as keeping count of paces and knowing the distance of each pace. A geologist entering a thick forest essentially has no visual references to follow because the trees block off almost everything on the horizon. Essentially it is the same situation as navigating an ocean, with few landmarks to help identify position. A geologist typically wants to find an outcrop of rock in the forest, usually identified by an aerial map of the location. Because trees themselves are not landmarks, the geologist must plot the distance as a straight line from the starting point (usually a road) to the destination (the outcrop). Once the path is plotted, the geologist takes a direction measurement directly toward the goal and starts pacing off the distance. The method is as good as the person pacing off the distances and scoping the direction, but generally it only brings the geologist to within 100 feet of the target—not very accurate!

There are some advantages and disadvantages to using this type of navigation for a robot. The advantages for a robot are obvious: A robot's ability to pace distances is vastly more accurate than that of a human, at least on a smooth floor. With wheels and accurate timers, a robot (like any machine) will outperform a human. It is still estimating by timing and, although it is better than a human, this can lead to low accuracy. The accuracy of calculating and storing coordinate points is also better than that of humans, although a pad of paper often helps humans with better memory recall. There is a downside to robots, however: Most robots are unable to self-correct their course by analyzing the situation. They also have no ability to visually recognize a target or landmark. Finally, the RIS kit does not contain a compass to help with navigation (see Chapter 10). These shortcomings are addressed here through firsthand demonstrations.

Trigonometry

The goal with navigation is to accurately know the current location, and the easiest way to represent this is with a coordinate system. For our navigation purposes we will employ simple x, y coordinates to indicate a position in a two-dimensional space. Let's examine how these coordinates can be calculated. A *rectangular coordinate system* consists of an x and y axis. Both of these axes start at zero and include positive and negative numbers. The x and y axis divide the system into four quadrants (Figure 7–3). Any point in a two-dimensional area can be plotted in this space using x and y.

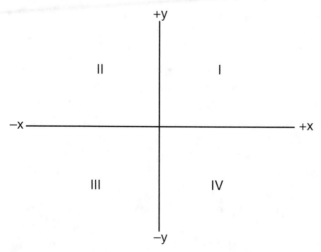

Figure 7–3   A rectangular coordinate system.

The angle can be measured in two ways. The first, most common form is degrees. A complete rotation is 360 degrees. Engineers, scientists, and mathematicians prefer using radians because the units are not arbitrarily arrived at. A complete rotation in radians is given the value 2π or about 6.28 radians. You can use whichever system you are more comfortable with, and there are methods in the Math class for conversion between the two (see the leJOS API docs). In the coordinate system, zero degrees (or zero radians) always runs along the x axis, and positive rotation occurs counterclockwise (Figure 7–4). Thus, when the robot is pointing up along the y axis, it is at 90 degrees.

Trigonometry is simply a branch of mathematics dealing with the relationships of the sides of triangles with angles. For our navigational purposes we use only the very simplest form of trigonometry: right angle trigonometry. Every time a robot moves a distance, the x and y coordinates also change. For example, if the robot rotates 60 degrees to the left and travels 20 cm, as it is moving both the x and y values will increase (Figure 7–5). As you can see, this movement creates a triangle with a right angle. In trigonometry, when there is a right-angled triangle with all angles known, and the length of one side is known, it is possible to calculate the lengths of all sides.

The side of the triangle opposite the right angle is called the *hypotenuse*, the side opposite the angle in the calculation is the *opposite*, and the remaining side is the *adjacent* (Figure 7–6). As stated before, our robot will always keep track of the angle, and it will pace off the distance traveled (the hypotenuse). To calculate the new location we will need to calculate x (the adjacent) and y (the opposite).

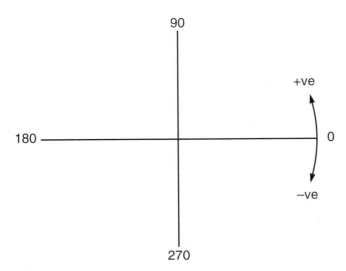

Figure 7–4 Rotation.

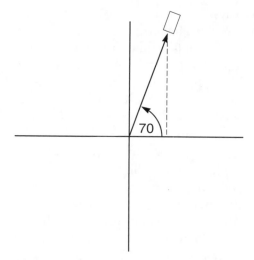

Figure 7–5   Right angle trigonometry.

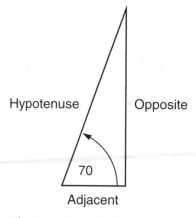

Figure 7–6   The three sides of a right-angle triangle.

In high school math you probably learned tangent, cosine, and sine (tan, cos, and sin). These functions are used to solve for the lengths of sides on a triangle. Many people use the mnemonic SOH, CAH, TOA to remember the following equations:

$$\sin(\text{angle}) = \text{opposite/hypotenuse}$$
$$\cos(\text{angle}) = \text{adjacent/hypotenuse}$$
$$\tan(\text{angle}) = \text{opposite/adjacent}$$

We only need to know the opposite and adjacent, so only the first two equations are useful to us. Let's replace the technical terms with variables and rearrange the equations to make things simpler. The distance traveled by the robot, the hypotenuse, will be replaced by distance:

$$x = \cos(\text{angle}) \times \text{distance}$$
$$y = \sin(\text{angle}) \times \text{distance}$$

We can now use these equations to figure out the x and y coordinates after a robot has moved a distance across the floor. Let's imagine the robot has started at 0,0 and rotates positive 70 degrees (counterclockwise), then moves 25 cm (Figure 7–5). In order to find new coordinates simply plug our values into the preceding equations to get:

$$x = \cos(70) \times 25$$
$$y = \sin(70) \times 25$$

If you are using a calculator, make sure it is in degrees (DEG mode) and not radians (RAD mode). The resulting x and y coordinates are 8.55 and 23.49.

In Java code, it is very easy to figure out how these will look. Just use the calculus methods from the Math class, as follows:

```
double x = Math.cos(Math.toRadians(70)) * 25;
double y = Math.sin(Math.toRadians(70)) * 25;
```

Note:

All methods in the java.lang.Math class use radians for angles. There are two methods available to convert back and forth between degrees to radians: Math.toRadians() and Math.toDegrees().

Using the Navigator API

The leJOS Navigator API provides a convenient set of methods to control a robot. There are methods for moving to any location and controlling the direction of movement. A Navigator object automatically keeps track of the current angle and x, y coordinates after every movement. The great part about this class is that it can be used by any robot with differential steering, regardless of the construction of the robot. Differential steering has one requirement: The robot must be able to turn within its own footprint; that is, it must be able to change direction without changing its *x* and *y* coordinates. The robot can have wheels with a diameter of 8 cm or 3 cm, or no wheels at all (treads, legs), or it can be fast or slow—it doesn't matter! These sorts of physical parameters are addressed by the constructor of the Navigator class. Once these parameters are set, the Navigator class works the same for all differential robots. Let's examine the actual interface:

`josx.robotics.Navigator`

- `public void forward()`

  Moves the RCX robot forward until stop() is called.

- `public void backward()`

  Moves the RCX robot backward until stop() is called.

- `public void travel(int distance)`

  Moves the RCX robot a specific distance. A positive value moves it forward and a negative value moves it backward. The method returns when movement is done.

  Parameters: `distance`   The distance to travel, in inches or centimeters.

- `public void stop()`

  Halts the RCX robot and calculates new *x*, *y* coordinates.

- `public void rotate(float angle)`

  Rotates the RCX robot a specific number of degrees, in a positive or negative direction (+ or −). The angle can be any positive or negative integer. For example, rotate(720) will cause two complete rotations counterclockwise. This method returns only once the rotation is complete.

  Parameters: `angle`   The angle to rotate in degrees. A positive value is counterclockwise and a negative value is clockwise.

- `public void gotoAngle(float angle)`

  Rotates the RCX robot to point in a specific direction. It will take the shortest path necessary to rotate to the desired angle. The method returns once rotation is complete.

  Parameters: `angle`   The angle to rotate to, in degrees.

- `public void gotoPoint(float x, float y)`

  Moves to any point on the coordinate system. The method rotates the

RCX robot toward the target point and travels the required distance. The stop() method can be called at any time to stop movement and recalculate the x, y coordinates.

Parameters: x   The target x coordinate.

                y   The target y coordinate.

- `public float getX()`

  Returns the current x coordinate of the robot. If the robot is moving it calculates the present coordinate and returns the value.

- `public float getY()`

  Returns the current y coordinate of the robot. If the robot is moving it calculates the present coordinate and returns the value.

- `public float getAngle()`

  Returns the current angle the robot is facing. If the robot is rotating it does not calculate the present angle, so make sure the robot is stopped when calling this method.

The Navigator interface is used for two classes in the josx.robotics package: TimingNavigator and RotationNavigator. For this chapter we use TimingNavigator exclusively because it is the easiest to use and requires no additional LEGO parts. TimingNavigator relies on keeping track of coordinates by measuring movement in terms of the number of seconds it has traveled or rotated. Robots have different wheel radii, different gearing, different motor strengths, and different axle lengths, so the timing constants for a particular robot will differ. To accommodate this, the TimingNavigator class requires the time it takes for the robot to move any given distance and the time it takes to rotate any given angle. Both of these numbers could be given in the form of speeds, but to make things easier the constructor just asks for the time it takes to travel 100 units (inches or centimeters, whatever you prefer to use), and the time it takes to complete one full rotation. The constructor also requires two Motor objects, one for the left wheel and one for the right. This is to let it know which output ports are being used to drive the movement. The constructor is as follows:

`josx.robotics.TimingNavigator`

- `public TimingNavigator(Motor right, Motor left, float time-OneMeter, float timeRotate)`

  Allocates a Navigator object and initializes it with the left and right wheels. The x and y values will each equal zero on initialization, and the starting angle is 0 degrees.

Parameters:	right	The motor used to drive the right wheel (e.g., Motor.C).
	left	The motor used to drive the left wheel (e.g., Motor.A).
	time-OneMeter	The number of seconds it takes the robot to drive 100 units.
	timeRotate	The number of seconds it takes the robot to rotate 360 degrees.

- `public void setMomentumDelay(short delay)`

Sets a variable that adds extra time (in milliseconds) to each rotation. This gives the robot more time to overcome momentum when starting a rotation. Proper use of this variable increases accuracy dramatically.

Creating a Navigator Robot

Let's build a robot so we can try out some simple navigation. Tippy seems like it could be good for navigation, because it rotates within its own footprint, but in fact Tippy is too fast! Fast robots like Tippy are actually not good for timing navigation because the wheels skid when starting and stopping. Also, it takes Tippy a few milliseconds to build up enough force to start moving, which can throw off our timing measurements. What we need is a robot that doesn't skid and starts moving immediately when it is instructed to move. Slow rotation is vital, so for this chapter we will build a robot that uses tank treads to achieve differential steering.

Building the Trilobot

This section shows you how to build a robot using tank treads. The robot moves relatively slowly, and makes slow turns, making it ideal for use with the TimingNavigator class. The robot is named Trilobot because it resembles an extinct animal known as a trilobite (Figure 7–7). Both trilobot and trilobite have wraparound antennae, they are low to the ground, they have a hard outer shell, and both have arthropod-level intelligence.

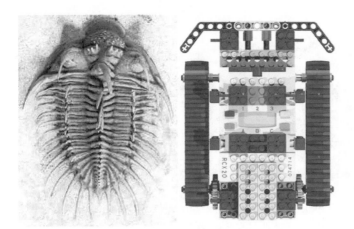

Figure 7–7 Trilobite vs. Trilobot.

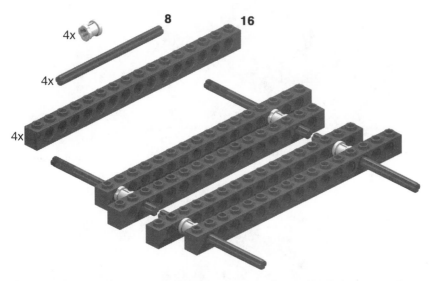

Step 1 Join two 16-unit beams together with two 8-unit axles, spacing them with a bush. Repeat the same for the other side.

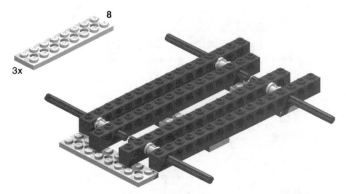

Step 2   Clamp three 2 × 8 plates to the underside of the chassis, joining the two halves together. The front plate should hang over the edge by one unit.

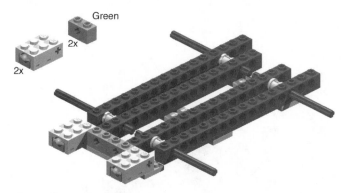

Step 3   Attach two touch sensors and two 1 × 2 beams with axle connectors to the front plate.

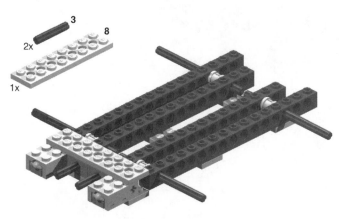

Step 4   Clamp a 2 × 8 plate over the assemblage. Insert two 3-unit axles into the green axle connectors.

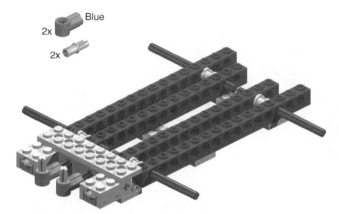

Step 5   Attach two axle connectors to the front of the robot and insert two axle pins into the top. These will be used to support the front bumper.

Step 6   Attach two black lift arms to the axle pins. At this point they should swing freely.

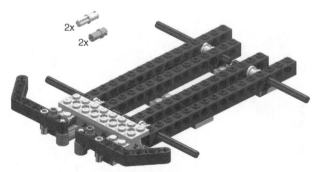

Step 7   Attach two dark gray 3/4 pins in the hole closest to the axle pins. These will be used to secure a bar to keep the bumpers from moving forward too much. Next, insert two axle pins to the underside of the bumper.

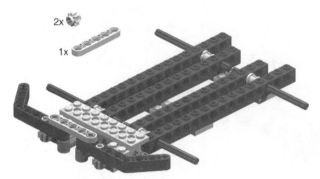

Step 8   Attach two 8-unit gears to the axle pins on the underside of the bumper. Clip on the 5-unit lift arm, which will act as a restraining bar for the bumper. This will allow the bumpers some movement back and forth without swinging all the way out.

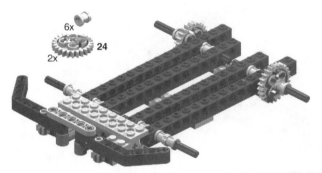

Step 9   Attach two bushes to each of the two front axles. On the rear axles, attach a 24-tooth gear and a bush.

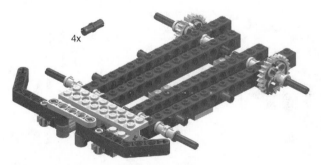

Step 10   Attach four friction pins to the outer beams. These will be used to secure the RCX brick to the chassis.

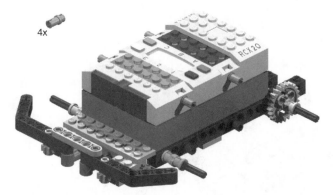

Step 11   Clamp the RCX brick to the top of the chassis. Make sure it fits snugly to the top of the beams. Insert four 3/4 pins into the holes of the RCX brick.

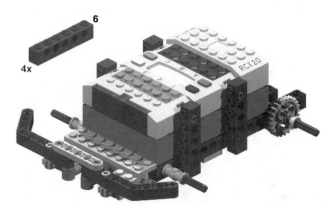

Step 12   Attach four securing beams to the sides of the robot to lock the RCX down.

Step 13   Place a rubber tread over two sprocket wheels and insert the wheels onto a pair of axles. Repeat for the other side.

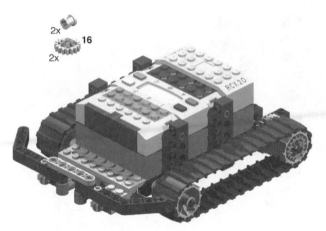

Step 14   Secure the front sprocket wheels with Technic bushes. The rear sprocket wheels should be secured with 16-tooth gears, which will cause the wheel to turn with the motorized axle.

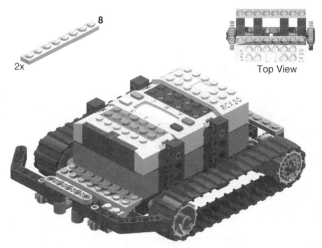

Step 15 Attach two 1 × 8 plates to the rear of the chassis. This prepares a surface to clamp down two motors, as the bottom of the motor is not flat.

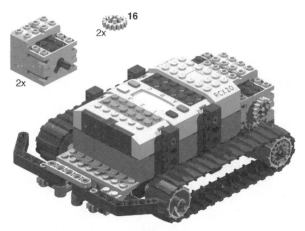

Step 16 Attach a 16-tooth gear to each motor, then attach them to the rear of the chassis, back to back.

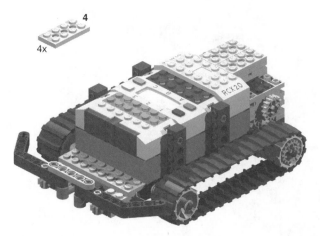

Step 17 Attach two 2 × 4 plates across the gap between the two motors (difficult to see in this picture). On top of these plates, attach two more 2 × 4 plates perpendicular to the first pair. This provides added strength to the unit.

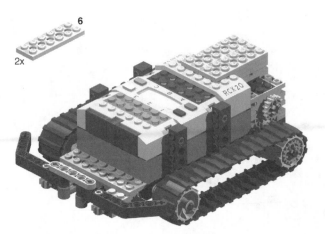

Step 18 Attach two 2 × 6 plates to the top of the robot. This secures the motors in place when force is applied to the gears.

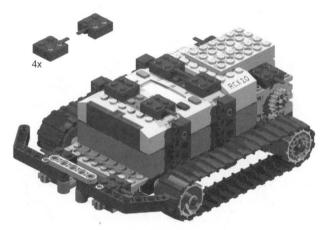

Step 19   Attach two short wire bricks to the front sensors, keeping the wires to the outer sides of the robot. Attach two more short wire bricks to the rear motors, with the wires facing outward. When you attach the wires to Ports A and C, make sure the wires face inward.

Programming Trilobot

Now that we have the Trilobot built, it is time to give it some intelligent navigation abilities. TimingNavigator requires us to figure out how long it takes to travel one meter, and how long it takes to rotate 360 degrees. The first part is easy; all we need to do is make a simple program to get it moving forward and then time it:

```
import josx.platform.rcx.*;
class TravelTest {
   public static void main(String [] args) {
      Motor.A.setPower(7); // Change to equalize motors
      Motor.C.setPower(7); // Change to equalize motors
      Motor.A.forward();
      Motor.C.forward();
   }
}
```

This code has two lines for setting the power to each motor. Generally the motors do not produce the same torque, which can cause your robot to veer off in one direction. When I first tested Trilobot, it veered off significantly to the left, indicating that Motor C is turning faster than Motor A. By playing around with the aPower argument in the setPower() method, I came up with the following revised code:

```
import josx.platform.rcx.*;
class TravelTest {
    public static void main(String [] args) {
        Motor.A.setPower(7);
        Motor.C.setPower(4); // Decreases power
        Motor.A.forward();
        Motor.C.forward();
    }
}
```

It is very important to balance the two motors! If they are not balanced the robot will be thrown off course. Now we need to create a small track for Tri-lobot by measuring out a meter (100 cm) on the floor. If you want, you can measure out 100 inches if you are more comfortable using the imperial system of measurement, but just make sure you consistently use inches with all measurements. If you use inches in the constructor, the TimingNavigator class will use inches for the x and y coordinates.

For better accuracy, instead of measuring 100 units, you can measure out 400 units, and then divide the final result by four to get the average. Keep in mind the surface the robot travels on affects speed. My test on a carpet produced different times than when it was done on a hard surface. The total four meter trip took 21.9 seconds on carpet, so we will use the value of 5.475 seconds per meter. Next, we need to measure the time it takes to rotate 360 degrees. For this, I'm going to make it rotate four times and average them out. The code is the same as the previous example, only one of the motors will move backward:

```
import josx.platform.rcx.*;
class RotateTest {
    public static void main(String [] args) {
        Motor.A.setPower(7);
        Motor.C.setPower(4); // Decreases power
        Motor.A.forward();
        Motor.C.backward();
    }
}
```

Four complete rotations took 16.0 seconds, so one rotation is about 4.0 seconds. I also tried rotating counterclockwise to see if it produced a different result, but it was quite similar at 16.27 seconds for four rotations, or 4.0675 seconds per rotation. I'll use a final average of 4.03 seconds. Now that we have our two required values we can create a TimingNavigator object and try some simple functions.

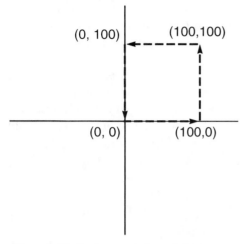

Figure 7–8   Test path for Trilobot.

Our first test will make Trilobot spin 360 degrees (so we can see how accurate we were with the calibrations), then trace out the shape of a square. The path will look similar to Figure 7–8. To trace the square, we will make it go to the following coordinates: (100,0) (100,100) (0,100) (0,0):

```
1. import josx.platform.rcx.*;
2. import josx.robotics.*;
3.
4. class Trilobot {
5.
6.     public static void main(String [] args) {
7.         Motor.A.setPower(7);
8.         Motor.C.setPower(5);
9.
10.        TimingNavigator n = new TimingNavigator(Motor.C,
                Motor.A, 5.475f, 4.03f);
11.        n.rotate(360);
12.        n.gotoPoint(100,0);
13.        n.gotoPoint(100,100);
14.        n.gotoPoint(0,100);
15.        n.gotoPoint(0,0);
16.    }
17. }
```

Warning:

The third and fourth parameters in this constructor will likely be different for you than the values here (5.475 and 4.03). These values are dependent

on the motor strengths and battery charge of your robot. If your robot uses lithium batteries the wheels will probably turn faster, so the parameters in the constructor will likely be smaller than for a robot that uses rechargeable batteries.

In this code we have retained the method calls to setPower() to equalize the motors. If all goes well the robot should complete a full square and then stop. If you notice that Trilobot rotates more than 360 degrees, you might want to consider lowering the rotate argument in the TimingNavigator constructor; likewise, if it doesn't rotate enough it should be increased. Once this is straightened out as close as possible (it will never be perfect) we can move on to some more serious programming using behavior control.

In this example, and the rest of the book, we use behavior control as the architecture for robotics programming. Behavior programming gets a little more challenging with high-level classes such as Navigator, but not much more. Trilobot will have four behaviors it will use to navigate. The lowest level behavior will randomly go from one point to another within a square 150×150 cm (Figure 7–9). At any time while the robot is moving to a point, if one of the bumpers hits an object it reacts, based on the bumper. If the left bumper detects an object, the robot backs up 20 cm and makes a buzz. If the right bumper detects an object, the robot backs up 20 cm and makes a beep. After more than 30 seconds elapse, the robot makes a sound then returns to the point of origin, stops, and pauses for five seconds before continuing. Each one of these reactions will be in a separate Behavior object (Table 7–1), and each behavior will share the same Navigator object for its own purposes

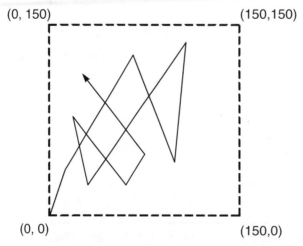

Figure 7–9   Trilobot confines itself to a square.

to keep track of coordinates. In this example it will be interesting to place a reference object, such as a dime, at the point of origin to see how close it comes after 30 seconds.

Table 7-1 Behavior Descriptions for Trilobot		
Condition	*Action*	*Suppress*
Always	Move to random points within a square region	Stop traveling and update coordinates
Left bumper collision	Make noise and back up 20 cm	Stop moving backward
Right bumper collision	Make noise and back up 20 cm	Stop moving backward
30 seconds	Seek point of origin	Stop moving to origin

Let's begin with the lowest level behavior first. We use the TimingNavigator class to control all operations in all classes. The method gotoPoint() will serve our purpose of moving about randomly within a square 1.5 m × 1.5 m, as follows:

```
1. import josx.robotics.*;
2. public class Move implements Behavior {
3.     private boolean active; // Indicates behavior is active
4.     private Navigator nav;
5.
6.     public Move(Navigator nav) {
7.         this.nav = nav;
8.         active = false;
9.     }
10.
11.     public boolean takeControl() {
12.         return true;
13.     }
14.
15.     public void suppress() {
16.         active = false;
17.         nav.stop();
18.     }
19.
20.     public void action() {
21.         active = true;
22.         while(active) {
23.             float x = (int)(Math.random() * 150);
```

```
24.            float y = (int)(Math.random() * 150);
25.            nav.gotoPoint(x, y);
26.        }
27.    }
28. }
```

Notice this class uses an instance of TimingNavigator in the constructor. This object will be shared by many behaviors. The main action for the Move behavior takes place starting at Line 20. The while loop will repeat until active is false, which will occur as soon as suppress() is called. The suppress() method also stops the robot by calling Navigator.stop(), and the Navigator object automatically updates the internal positional coordinates when this occurs. Now let's create some classes to handle collisions with other objects.

The Trilobot robot has two separate touch sensors, one for the left bumper and one for the right bumper. The code actually reacts the same for the left and right bumpers, so only one bumper is necessary for this program, but I included a split bumper so that Trilobot could be reprogrammed with more interesting behavior based on the side the collision occurred on. For the purposes of this program, we want Trilobot to stop and back up when a collision occurs. The suppress() code will stop Trilobot backing up, and the takeControl() method will only take control when the bumper hits an object. We use a SensorListener, as described in the previous chapter, so collisions are never missed. The left bumper behavior is as follows:

```
1. import josx.robotics.*;
2. import josx.platform.rcx.*;
3.
4. public class LeftBump implements Behavior, SensorListener {
5.     private Navigator nav;
6.     private boolean hasCollided;
7.
8.     public LeftBump(Navigator nav) {
9.         this.nav = nav;
10.        hasCollided = false;
11.        Sensor.S1.addSensorListener(this);
12.    }
13.
14.    public boolean takeControl() {
15.        if(hasCollided) {
16.            hasCollided = false; // reset value
17.            return true;
18.        } else
19.            return false;
20.    }
21.
```

```
22.     public void suppress() {
23.         nav.stop();
24.     }
25.
26.     public void stateChanged(Sensor bumper, int oldValue,
            int newValue) {
27.         if(bumper.readBooleanValue() == true)
28.             hasCollided = true;
29.     }
30.
31.     public void action() {
32.         // Back up:
33.         Sound.buzz();
34.         nav.travel(-20);
35.     }
36. }
```

This code is quite straightforward. When the touch sensor is hit, Line 28 changes the hasCollided value to true. Then, when takeControl() is called the method returns true. Line 16 resets the hasCollided flag. Likewise, the right bumper behavior is almost identical:

```
1. import josx.robotics.*;
2. import josx.platform.rcx.*;
3.
4. public class RightBump implements Behavior, SensorListener {
5.     private Navigator nav;
6.     private boolean hasCollided;
7.
8.     public RightBump(Navigator nav) {
9.         this.nav = nav;
10.        hasCollided = false;
11.        Sensor.S3.addSensorListener(this);
12.    }
13.
14.    public boolean takeControl() {
15.        if(hasCollided) {
16.            hasCollided = false; // reset value
17.            return true;
18.        } else
19.            return false;
20.    }
21.
22.    public void suppress() {
23.        nav.stop();
24.    }
```

```
25.
26.     public void stateChanged(Sensor bumper, int oldValue,
           int newValue) {
27.         if(bumper.readBooleanValue() == true)
28.             hasCollided = true;
29.     }
30.
31.     public void action() {
32.         // Back up:
33.         Sound.beep();
34.         nav.travel(-20);
35.     }
36. }
```

Our fourth behavior is the most complex of all. It requires the robot to go back to the point of origin when 30 seconds have elapsed. To do this, we will use the josx.util.Timer class and the josx.util.TimerListener interface. Timer-Listener will be notified by the timer every 30 seconds via the timedOut() method. We'll make our behavior implement TimerListener, and the timed-Out() method will simply change a Boolean value to indicate the time is up, as follows:

```
1.     public void timedOut() {
2.         timeUp = true;
3.     }
```

The takeControl() method will then return true only if the time is up:

```
1.     public boolean takeControl() {
2.         return timeUp;
3.     }
```

The action() method is very easy to implement. It simply calls the method gotoPoint(0,0) to make Trilobot return to the point of origin. The completed module for this behavior is as follows:

```
1. import josx.robotics.*;
2. import josx.platform.rcx.*;
3. import josx.util.*;
4.
5. public class GoHome implements TimerListener, Behavior {
6.
7.     Navigator nav;
8.     boolean timeUp;
9.
10.    public GoHome(Navigator nav) {
11.        this.nav = nav;
12.        timeUp = false;
```

```
13.        Timer t = new Timer(30000, this);
14.        t.start();
15.    }
16.
17.    public void timedOut() {
18.        timeUp = true;
19.    }
20.
21.    public boolean takeControl() {
22.        return timeUp;
23.    }
24.
25.    public void suppress() {
26.        nav.stop();
27.    }
28.
29.    public void action() {
30.        Sound.beepSequence();
31.        nav.gotoPoint(0,0);
32.        Sound.twoBeeps();
33.        try {Thread.sleep(5000);}catch(InterruptedException
               e) {}
34.        Sound.beep();
35.        timeUp = false; // reset time up
36.    }
37. }
```

As you can see, the methods are all very simple and straightforward. Now we merely need to create a main class to start the process:

```
1. import josx.platform.rcx.*;
2. import josx.robotics.*;
3.
4. class TrilobotMain {
5.    public static void main(String [] args) {
6.        Motor.A.setPower(7);
7.        Motor.C.setPower(5);
8.        TimingNavigator nav = new TimingNavigator(Motor.C,
               Motor.A, 5.475f, 4.03f);
9.
10.        Behavior b1 = new Move(nav);
11.        Behavior b2 = new LeftBump(nav);
12.        Behavior b3 = new RightBump(nav);
13.        Behavior b4 = new GoHome(nav);
14.
15.        Behavior [] bArray = {b1, b2, b3, b4};
```

```
16.        Arbitrator arby = new Arbitrator(bArray);
17.        arby.start();
18.    }
19. }
```

Warning:

Lines 6, 7, and 8 should be tailored to your specific robot. These variables are dependent on relative motor strengths, battery level, and other factors.

That's it! Notice all four Behavior objects share the same Navigator object (nav). Little by little we have built up many simple steps to create some relatively complex behavior. Upload the code to Trilobot and see how well it performs. Hopefully, after 30 seconds, Trilobot will come close to the point of origin. Now let's examine the accuracy of the results we can achieve with TimingNavigator.

TimingNavigator Accuracy

The results from testing the preceding code vary greatly. After 30 seconds Trilobot is supposed to return to the point of origin, but in reality it only comes close. I performed a test by dropping a coin on the ground at the point of origin after letting the robot go. Sometimes it came back to within 50 cm, but other times it was off by as much as 90 cm! This sort of discrepancy seems hard to account for, but after performing a few experiments the reason for the inaccuracy is clear. Examine Figure 7–10. This is a small course I set up for Trilobot on carpet by placing a coin at each point. There are five individual vectors to this course, each labeled in Figure 7–10 by a number. The code to make Trilobot follow this course is as follows:

```
1. import josx.platform.rcx.*;
2. import josx.robotics.*;
3.
4. class TrilobotMain {
5.
6.     public static void main(String [] args) {
7.         Motor.A.setPower(7);
8.         Motor.C.setPower(5);
9.
10.        TimingNavigator nav = new TimingNavigator(Motor.C,
               Motor.A, 5.475f, 4.03f);
11.
```

```
12.        nav.gotoPoint(75,75);
13.        nav.gotoPoint(0,150);
14.        nav.gotoPoint(75, 150);
15.        nav.gotoPoint(75,0);
16.        nav.gotoPoint(0,0);
17.    }
18. }
```

This looks like a relatively simple series of movements, but as you can see from Figure 7–11 Trilobot didn't handle it very well. When Trilobot executed the initial 45-degree rotation it didn't quite rotate enough—probably closer to 40 degrees than 45. Not too bad so far. Next comes Vector 2. It executes the 90-degree turn, but once again it underrotated, causing it to wander off drastically to the right. By the time it stops at what it thinks is 0, 150 the orientation of the robot is off by about 15 degrees and the x coordinate is off by about 40 cm. This vector seems to be the worst one of all five. If Vector 2 ended up at 0,150 as it was supposed to, the overall path would be much more accurate. Vectors 3, 4, and 5 are not bad, but their small errors also cause a cumulative effect on the positional estimate. The final position was off by about 15 cm from the point of origin—not bad, considering. Accuracy was probably regained because the errors in the lefthand turns were made up by countererrors in the righthand turns. So what caused all these errors?

Errors fall into two camps by definition. *Systematic errors* are introduced in the design of the robot and the methodology. This includes errors due to inaccuracies in parameters used in the program and errors caused by the

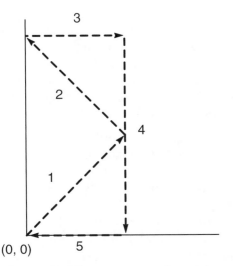

Figure 7–10   A test course for Trilobot.

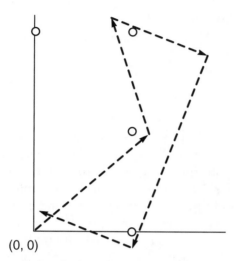

(0, 0)

Figure 7–11   Trilobot's interpretation of the course.

design of the robot itself. *Nonsystematic errors* are errors that are introduced because of the real world. Errors in this camp include uneven floors, wheel slippage, and cats walking in front of the robot. Let's try to identify the errors that hamper the accuracy of TimingNavigator.

Systematic Errors

The most obvious systematic error introduced into TimingNavigator is the accuracy of the travel and rotate times used in the constructor. Because the whole premise of navigation using timing relies on these, inaccuracies will cumulatively throw off the positioning. For example, the angle parameter requires the time it takes to rotate 360 degrees. If the actual rotation time is 4.2875 seconds and you give a value of 4.4425 seconds it will cause a rotation of 360 degrees to be about 12 degrees off. This disparity will add up quickly after the robot has been traveling for a time.

The biggest problem with accuracy, as we observed, was underrotation. Each time the robot attempted to rotate a discreet angle, it would consistently fall short. How can we explain this, especially after being so careful when timing a complete 360 degree rotation? For an answer we need to look to Newton's first law of motion: objects at rest tend to stay at rest. It takes a certain amount of time and force to overcome the momentum of the stationary robot. So when we tell the robot to rotate right 90 degrees it takes a small amount of time to get moving, in Trilobots case about 0.06 seconds. Because of this factor, larger angles of rotation, such as a 180 degree turn, are likely to be more accurate than smaller rotations, such as a 5-degree turn. This accounts for the observed angle being smaller than the projected angle. As with all systematic errors, it should be possible to correct this through code. Timing by hand with a stopwatch is so inaccurate it is best to start with an estimate for the delay, then refine it with a few trials. Adding the following line of code at line 11 will accomplish this:

```
nav.setMomentumDelay(60);
```

The momentum variable (which had been set to 0) will now cause the robot to delay an extra 0.06 seconds for each rotation, giving it enough time to overcome momentum. To refine this, have the robot rotate 90 degrees and stop, then note how accurate it seems. If it rotates too much, decrease this value and if it underrotates, increase the value. Now when the test course is run, accuracy should be improved.

Warning:

If you use the setMomentumDelay() method, the time variable in the Timing Navigator constructor should measure only one full rotation. Do not try to average four rotations otherwise the delay caused by momentum will be divided.

One of the biggest problems with achieving accurate parameters is that the battery slowly loses power, and thus the output speed of the motors changes. I've noticed several times that when the RCX is turned on it may have a charge of 7.6 V, and then by the time the program ends the battery power is at 7.3 V. Then, after shutting down for a few minutes, I turn it on and the voltage once again reads 7.6 V. This change really throws rotations off. The worst part is once you think you have the TimingNavigator parameters honed and the motors balanced, the battery charge lessens and the settings are no longer valid. One way to negate this effect is to use freshly charged batteries.

Nonsystematic Errors

Differences in motor speed between the A motor and the B motor also affect accuracy greatly. One of the noticeable problems encountered in the course just presented is the inability of the robot to drive straight. Just when I thought I had the motors balanced it would start drifting to the right. Then, later in the same run, it would mysteriously straighten up for some stretches! This effect can be attributed to frictional differences in the structure of the robot.

A comparatively minor source of errors likely results from the surface the robot is on. Carpet and rough surfaces are likely to introduce more errors than a smooth floor such as hardwood.

Contact with external objects also introduces error into the positional esti- mate. When the bumper hits an object it has the potential to turn the robot slightly out of alignment. This can be minimized by slowing down the robot, or by detecting objects before the robot strikes them using a proximity detec- tor (see Chapter 9, "Proximity Detection").

Summary

As you can see, systematic errors and nonsystematic errors both conspire to degrade accuracy. The main problem seems to be the inaccuracies in turning. If Trilobot was able to execute an accurate turn, the overall navigation would be improved drastically. Also, one wheel turning faster than the other causes the robot to move in an arc rather than a straight line. The root cause of this seems to be uneven motor speed. Even small mechanical differences in the friction caused by an axle can contribute to this problem. The next chapter introduces methods to cope with most of these problems, increasing the accuracy of movement greatly. But it comes with a price—the cost of two rotation sensors!

NAVIGATION WITH ROTATION SENSORS

Topics in this Chapter

- Understanding Rotation Sensors
- Using the RotationNavigator Class
- Creating a Navigator Robot
- RotationNavigator Accuracy

Chapter 8

I n the previous chapter we built a robot that performed some very basic navigation using dead reckoning. Distances and angles were measured using timing because the RIS kit does not contain any sensors for measuring distances. This chapter introduces a sensor available from LEGO that counts the number of times an axle has rotated, which can dramatically improve the accuracy of robot navigation. In the previous analysis of navigation using timing, we encountered errors building up due to the robot wandering to one side or the other as it traveled. Using two rotation sensors we will be able to ensure the robot travels in a relatively straight path, as well as improve the turning accuracy.

Understanding Rotation Sensors

The rotation sensor looks similar to the light sensor in that it is blue and has its own wire connector (as opposed to the touch sensor, which does not). The light sensor is exactly one brick and one plate in height, but the rotation sensor is a full two bricks in height (Figure 8–1). The rotation sensor is an active sensor, meaning it must be supplied with an electric current, much like the light sensor. The rotation sensor has an axle hole that allows an axle to be loosely inserted. There is also a groove along the back of the sensor so the

Figure 8-1   The rotation sensor (center).

wire can be tucked away, allowing the back of the rotation sensor to lie flush with another brick. LEGO designed the position of the axle hole to align properly with other axle holes in beams and other LEGO parts.

The rotation sensor is used for counting rotations of an axle. For every 22.5 degrees rotated the sensor will add one to a cumulative rotation count (Figure 8–2). This means a full 360-degree rotation will add 16 to the total count. The counter range is between –32,768 and 32,767, so anything surpassing these numbers will cause the counter to roll over. Turning the axle in one direction causes the rotation count to increment and the other direction causes it to decrement. Starting with a count of 0, if we rotated an axle 360 degrees clockwise, then 360 degrees counterclockwise, the rotation sensor value will equal 0. This should be contrasted with the LogIT angle sensor (Chapter 1, "Meet MIND-STORMS"), which simply gives a value indicating the current angle of an arm on the sensor. The rotation sensor can also be used to give a very accurate reading of the angle of an arm by using gear reduction, as we shall see later in this section.

Note:

The orientation of the wire connection to the input port on the RCX has no effect on the values produced by the rotation sensor.

When addressing accuracy there are two separate factors to examine: angle accuracy and speed. As already discussed, the sensor measures each rotation in increments of 16 (22.5 degrees per increment), so at any time the rotation count is accurate ±22.5 degrees. There is also the speed factor. The rotation sensor itself does not have memory to count rotations, so the RCX must continually monitor it and keep a running total. If the axle spins too quickly for the RCX to keep up with, it will lose track of the count, and inaccuracies will result. As of this writing leJOS can accurately count intervals at a rate of 9,600 per minute, which is equal to 600 rotations per minute (RPM) or 10 complete rotations per

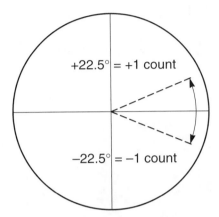

Figure 8-2   Rotation increments are 22.5 degrees.

second. To put this in perspective, an ungeared LEGO motor spins at about 350 RPM, so it should be well within the limits for most robotics applications. Problems can occur with gear reduction, however (as discussed later). If we use gear reduction so the rotation sensor axle spins three times for every single turn of the drive axle, then the rotation axle will spin at 1,050 RPM, which is too fast for leJOS to keep up with. There are ways to address this problem, however. Let's examine some common ways of using the rotation sensor.

Trailer Odometer

The simplest way to measure distances with one rotation sensor is to construct a trailer containing the rotation sensor (Figure 8–3). The trailer attaches to the back of the robot so that it swings freely up and down, allowing it to conform to the terrain without interfering with the existing drive wheels.

Figure 8-3   A trailer to measure distance.

Handheld Odometer

For testing purposes, let's build a simple digital measuring stick. A wheel will measure distances and display the distance on the LCD.

Step 1   Insert a 6-unit axle into a large motorcycle wheel, leaving about 1.5 units sticking out the other side. Secure the wheel using two half bushes.

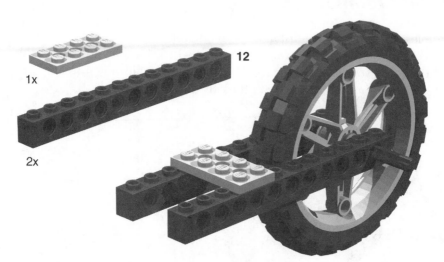

Step 2   Attach the wheel to two 12-unit beams. Lock the beams together using a single 2 × 4 plate.

1x

1x

1x

Step 3   Slide the remainder of the axle into a rotation sensor. Clip the sensor to the beam arm using a 2 × 4 plate and a 1 × 4 plate.

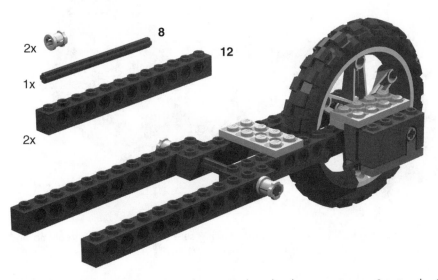

2x

8

1x

12

2x

Step 4   Attach two more 12-unit beams to the other beams using an 8-unit axle. Secure the axle to the beams using two Technic bushes.

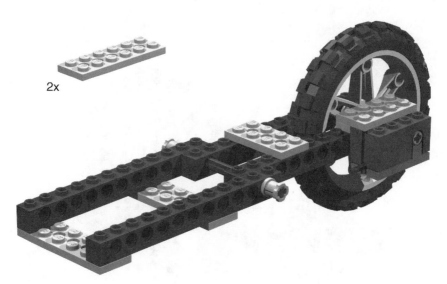

Step 5   Clamp two 2 × 6 plates to the underside of the second set of arms. The entire arm unit should swing freely, allowing the measuring wheel to conform to the terrain.

Step 6   Attach the RCX brick to the arms, making sure the wheel swings freely up and down. Connect the rotation sensor to RCX input Port 2.

We want our odometer to measure out distances in meters, so it is necessary to determine how many centimeters each of the 16 intervals equals. To do this, we need to know the circumference of the wheel. In this case, LEGO has included the diameter on the side of the tire—81.6 mm, or 8.16 cm. From this we can conclude the circumference is 25.64 cm (8.16π). This means each 1/16th of a rotation measures 1.6025 cm. With this known, the actual code for the odometer is easy to write:

```
1.  import josx.platform.rcx.*;
2.  class MeasuringStick implements ButtonListener, SensorCon-
        stants {
3.      /**
4.       * The circumference of the motorcycle wheel (8.16 * pi).
5.       */
6.      private final float WHEEL_CIRC = 8.16 * Math.PI;
7.      private final float CMS_PER_INTERVAL = WHEEL_CIRC / 16;
8.
9.      public MeasuringStick() {
10.         Sensor.S2.setTypeAndMode(SENSOR_TYPE_ROT,
                SENSOR_MODE_ANGLE);
11.         Sensor.S2.setPreviousValue(0);
12.         Sensor.S2.activate();
13.
14.         Button.PRGM.addButtonListener(this);
15.     }
16.
17.     public static void main(String [] args) {
18.         new MeasuringStick().measure();
19.     }
20.
21.     public void measure() {
22.         while(true) {
23.             int count = Sensor.S2.readValue();
24.             int centimeters = (int)(count * CMS_PER_INTERVAL);
25.             LCD.setNumber(0x3001, centimeters, 0x3004);
26.             LCD.refresh();
27.         }
28.     }
29.     public void buttonPressed(Button b) {
30.         Sensor.S2.setPreviousValue(0);
31.         Sound.beepSequence();
32.     }
33.
34.     public void buttonReleased(Button b) {}
35. }
```

When using a rotation sensor, it is important to initialize it properly. The code in the constructor (Lines 10–12) performs this by setting the type to rotation and mode to angle. It is also important to call the activate() method, otherwise the sensor will be unpowered. The code also includes a button listener for the Prgm button. When this is pressed the counter will reset to zero, as shown in Line 30. To assess the accuracy of the measuring stick device I measured out one meter on a hard surface using a meter stick and then compared the measurement with our homemade odometer. The results indicate the LEGO odometer is actually remarkably accurate!

On-Axle Odometers

The most straightforward method of measuring distance is placing the rotation sensor directly on the wheel axle (Figure 8–4). This gives a 1:1 ratio between wheel rotation and sensor rotation. For robots using differential drive steering (i.e., most robots) rotation sensors can be placed on each axle to measure the distance traveled by each wheel, resulting in greater accuracy.

Figure 8–4   A rotation sensor placed directly on an axle.

Off-Axle Odometers

It is also possible to indirectly measure the rotation of an axle by using gears to translate movement (Figure 8–5). Sometimes it is necessary to use this kind of setup where there is not enough room to place the rotation sensor directly on the main axle, but it can also be used with different gear ratios to achieve greater accuracy. Placing a smaller gear on the rotation sensor axle causes it to turn more times than the wheel axle, which results in finer readings.

Figure 8-5   A rotation sensor placed beside the main axle.

Angle Measurement

The rotation sensor can also be used to measure an angle directly, much like the LogIT position and movement sensor. A long arm is connected to the main axle, resulting in a pendulum motion. Using trigonometry (see Chapter 7, "Navigation," for overview), it is possible to determine linear movement from angular rotation (Figure 8–6). This can be useful for performing a number of experiments, including monitoring the growth of plants.

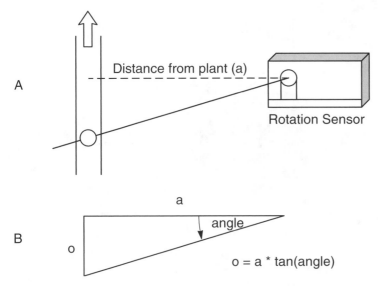

Figure 8-6   Using trigonometry to calculate height from angle.

Say, for example, you have planted a sunflower seed and a small sprout has developed. You would like to record growth periods of the sunflower seedling. By hooking up an angle sensor to the plant it would be possible to record this growth (Figure 8–6a). With the RCX brick you could record growth rates and correlate them with light intensity using the light sensor. This would indicate the period of day the sunflower grows the most, and the effect of light intensity. In this theoretical experiment the reading of the angle and the light intensity could be taken every half-hour and stored to an array for later analysis.

The LogIT sensor is made specifically to output an angle, but with some LEGO parts and some simple code we can build a poor man's angle sensor.

Note:

It has been reported that the rotation sensor has problems counting at extremely low speeds. More information as a fix can be found at www.philohome.com/sensors/legorot.html.

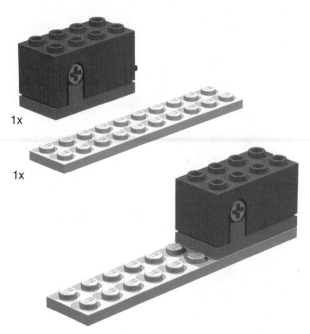

1x

1x

Step 1   Attach a rotation sensor to a 2 × 10 plate.

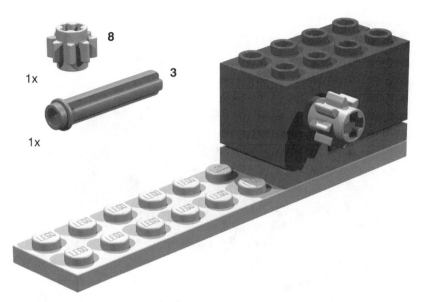

Step 2   Insert a 3-unit axle with stud end into the rotation sensor and secure it with an 8-tooth gear.

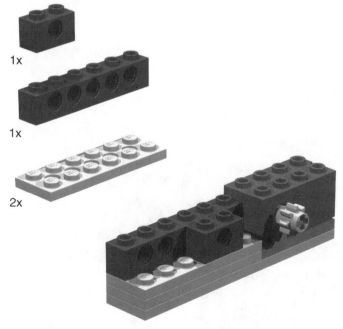

Step 3   Build up the surface of the base plate with two 2 × 6 plates. On top of this place the gear train support: a 1 × 6 brick and a 1 × 2 brick.

Step 4   Insert a 3-unit axle with stud end into a beam hole and secure it with a 24-tooth gear.

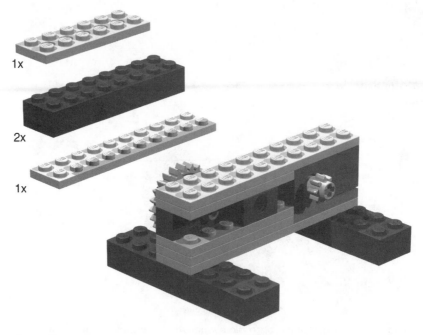

Step 5   Secure the gear train with a 2 × 6 plate and a 2 × 10 plate.

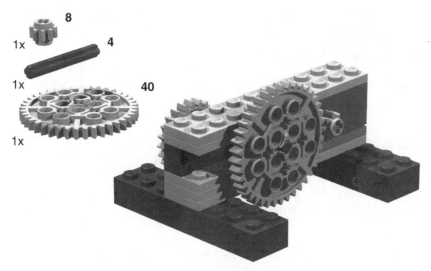

Step 6   Insert a 4-unit axle into the fourth hole from the front (right next to the 24-tooth gear). Attach an 8-tooth gear to the axle (not shown) so it interlocks with the 24-tooth gear. Cap the other side with a 40-tooth gear so it interlocks with the other 8-tooth gear.

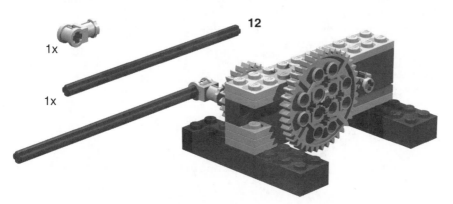

Step 7   Attach a Technic connector with axle hole to the 24-tooth gear axle. Insert either a 12-unit axle or even better, the long yellow straw (not pictured).

The gears in this plan cause more resistance, especially from the 40-tooth gear, but the arm provides sufficient leverage to turn the sensor axle. The 8-tooth to 40-tooth gears provide a 5:1 reduction and the 8-tooth to 24-tooth gear gives a 3:1 reduction, for an overall reduction of 15:1. This means for every complete rotation of the straw the rotation sensor axle rotates 15 times. Because the rotation sensor measures in increments of 16, each rotation of the straw produces 240 increments on the rotation sensor! Therefore each increment is equal to 360 degrees divided by 240, or 1.5 degrees per increment. The code for the sensor is almost identical to the previous code:

```
1.  import josx.platform.rcx.*;
2.
3.  class AngleMeasure implements ButtonListener, SensorCon-
        stants {
4.
5.      /**
6.       * The number of teeth for each gear.
7.       */
8.      private final int SMALL_GEAR = 8;
9.      private final int MEDIUM_GEAR = 24;
10.     private final int LARGE_GEAR = 40;
11.
12.     /**
13.      * The calculation of the intervals for each rotation.
14.      */
15.     private final float REDUC1 = (LARGE_GEAR/SMALL_GEAR);
16.     private final float REDUC2 = (MEDIUM_GEAR/SMALL_GEAR);
17.     private final int INTERVALS = 16;
18.     private final float TOTAL_INTERVALS = REDUC1 * REDUC2 *
            INTERVALS;
19.     private final float DEGREES_PER_INTERVAL = 360 /
            TOTAL_INTERVALS;
20.
21.     public AngleMeasure() {
22.         Sensor.S2.setTypeAndMode(SENSOR_TYPE_ROT,
                SENSOR_MODE_ANGLE);
23.         Sensor.S2.setPreviousValue(0);
24.         Sensor.S2.activate();
25.
26.         Button.PRGM.addButtonListener(this);
27.     }
28.
29.     public static void main(String [] args) {
30.         new AngleMeasure().measure();
31.     }
32.
33.     public void measure() {
34.         while(true) {
35.             int count = Sensor.S2.readValue();
36.             int angle = (int)(count * DEGREES_PER_INTERVAL);
37.             LCD.setNumber(0x3001, angle, 0x3002);
38.             LCD.refresh();
39.         }
```

```
40.      }
41.
42.      public void buttonPressed(Button b) {
43.          Sensor.S2.setPreviousValue(0);
44.          Sound.beepSequence();
45.      }
46.
47.      public void buttonReleased(Button b) {}
48. }
```

This code contains all the calculations, with constants, so that any changes to the LEGO model will be easy to change in code. Each gear has a constant describing the number of gear teeth, making the gear ratio easy to calculate (Lines 15–19). The current accuracy is ±1.5 degrees, or ±0.4 %. This compares favorably with the LogIT sensor, which has an accuracy of ±2%. The main difference is there is much less resistance with the LogIT sensor. I assume a plant would be able to generate enough torque to move the straw arm, but the LogIT sensor has almost no torque, making it interfere less with the subject of the experiment. To reduce torque (at the expense of accuracy) it is possible to replace the 40-tooth gear with a 24-tooth gear. This also requires changing Line 15 by replacing the LARGE_GEAR constant with MEDIUM_GEAR.

Tip:

There are only three input ports on the RCX, which limits the number of sensors that can be attached to the RCX brick, so it is sometimes necessary to use "hacks" to achieve the desired results. One such programming hack is to use rotation sensors for collision detection. When the robot collides with an object the wheels should slow down or stop. When monitoring the wheel axles, any slowdown in rotation can be interpreted as a collision.

Using the RotationNavigator Class

The RotationNavigator class contains all the methods of the Navigator interface, so using it is similar to the TimingNavigator discussed in Chapter 7. Using two rotation sensors, one for each wheel, the RotationNavigator can judge distances much more accurately than with timing. It still has problems judging distances on different surfaces, however, because a bumpy surface

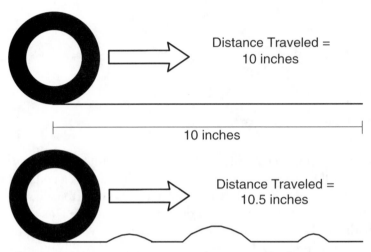

Figure 8-7   Wheels travel farther over bumpy surfaces.

actually causes a robot to travel longer distances than a smooth surface (Figure 8–7). As we will see shortly, this can be evened out by testing the robot on the surface, such as carpet, and refining the parameters in the constructor. Rotation counts are accurate, but with only 16 increments per rotation the sensor is not fine grained enough on its own to provide accuracy to ±1 degree. It is possible to use gears to increase the rotations of the sensor to provide greater accuracy, but the RCX can't quite keep up with the counting speed at the level required for ±1 degree. Even with this limitation, it is still more accurate than TimingNavigator. Another benefit of using rotation sensors in navigation is the ability to keep the robot on a straight path. This was one of the biggest weaknesses of TimingNavigator. With RotationNavigator, even on something as rough as carpet the robot stays arrow straight!

The RotationNavigator assumes a few things about your robot. First, it assumes that when a motor rotates forward the wheel will also carry the robot forward. If you find your robot moves backward when it should be going forward, the best solution is usually to just reverse the connectors to the output ports by 180 degrees for both motors. The second assumption it makes is that when the wheels move forward the rotation sensors will record positive increments. This is not as easy to fix because changing the wire configuration has no effect. If this is a problem, the best way to fix it is to either reverse the direction of the rotation sensor in the robot chassis or add an extra idler gear between the drive axle and the rotation sensor. This effectively reverses the rotation to the sensor axis without altering the rotation count. Let's examine RotationNavigator in more detail.

`josx.robotics.RotationNavigator`

- `public RotationNavigator((float wheelDiameter, float drive-Length, float ratio, Motor leftMotor, Motor rightMotor, Sensor leftRot, Sensor rightRot)`

  Allocates a RotationNavigator object and initializes it with the proper motors and sensors.

Parameters:	`wheel-Diameter`	The diameter of the drive wheels, in centimeters.
	`drive-Length`	The distance from the center of the left tire to the center of the right tire, in centimeters.
	`ratio`	The ratio of sensor rotations to wheel rotations. e.g. 3:1 = 3
	`leftMotor`	The motor used to drive the left wheel.
	`rightMo-tor`	The motor used to drive the right wheel
	`leftRot`	Sensor used to read rotations from the left wheel.
	`rightRot`	Sensor used to read rotations from the right wheel.

- `public RotationNavigator(float wheelDiameter, float drive-Length, float ratio)`

  This constructor is the same as the previous one, except it assumes the following about the robot: the left motor is Motor.A, the right motor is Motor.C, the left rotation sensor is Sensor.S1, and the right rotation sensor is Sensor.S3.

There are essentially three parameters the RotationSensor class needs to calculate movement for a robot:

- Tire diameter
- Drive length
- Ratio of sensor gear to drive wheel gear

Tire diameter is the measurement of the diameter of the wheel, out to the furthest extent of the rubber tire. Once RotationSensor has this information it simply multiplies diameter by Math.PI to get the circumference of the wheel. With this it knows that for every single rotation of the wheel the robot will travel the circumference in distance. The tire diameter is easy enough to acquire, because LEGO prints the diameter right on the side of the balloon tires. Even the tank tread acts like a wheel. By measuring the diameter from top to bottom of the tread around the wheel sprocket you can get a fairly accurate parameter. The other wheels in the RIS kit can be measured with a ruler, or you can use the measurements I obtained in Table 8–1.

Table 8-1 Wheel Diameters

Small yellow	2.4 cm
Medium yellow	3.0 cm
Large yellow	4.3 cm
Small white	3.04 cm
Medium white	4.96 cm
Large white	8.16 cm
Gray pulley wheel	3.0 cm
Tank tread	2.8 cm

The drive length is essentially the entire length of the split axle (Figure 8–8) from wheel to wheel. There should be a theoretical point where the wheel contacts the ground, but some LEGO tires are quite wide, which causes some discrepancy between theory and reality. It can be somewhat difficult to determine if this measurement should be from the inside of the tires or the outside. Theoretically, if each wheel had virtually no width, it would be easy to measure where the tire contacted the ground, but in the real world we should probably measure from dead center of the left wheel to dead center of the right wheel. The "center" of the tire actually depends on the surface the robot is moving on. If the robot is traversing carpet then the drive length should be slightly wider, whereas on a hard floor the drive length should be measured slightly closer to the inner edge of the tire. We'll examine the differences that surfaces make when we build a robot later in this chapter.

The gear ratio is relatively easy to come up with. All you need to determine is the number of times the rotation sensor axle will rotate for every full rotation the wheel makes. For example, if the sensor axle rotates three times for every time the wheel rotates (Figure 8–5) then this ratio is 3:1, or simply 3. Conversely, if the drive wheel rotates three times for every rotation of the

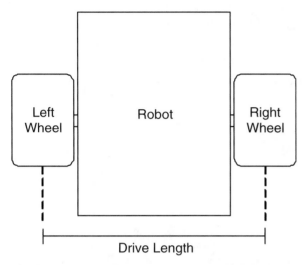

Figure 8-8 The drive length is measured from wheel to wheel.

sensor axle, then the ratio is 1:3 or 0.333. The latter is an unlikely scenario, however, because usually you want to increase the number of rotations of the sensor axle to improve accuracy. If the rotation sensor is directly on the axle (Figure 8–4) or uses the same-sized gear as the drive axle, then the ratio is 1:1, or simply 1. Now that we know how RotationNavigator works, let's build a robot so we can test it.

Creating a Navigator Robot

Building Instructions

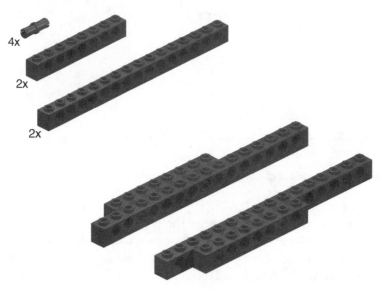

Step 1   Attach an 8-unit beam to a 16-unit beam. Mirror this for the other side.

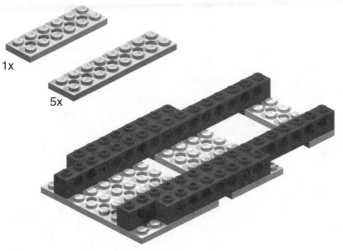

Step 2   Attach five 2 × 8 plates and one 2 × 6 plate, as shown.

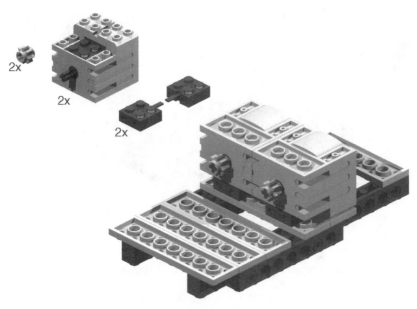

Step 3   Attach two RCX wires to the motor with the wire ends sticking out the back. Turn the chassis over and attach the motors to the chassis. Add two 8-tooth gears to the motor shafts.

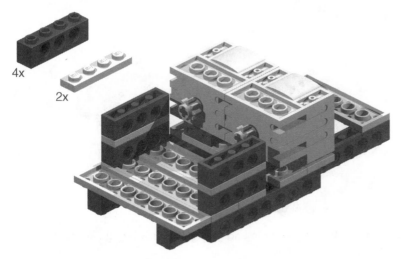

Step 4   Build a support structure for the gear train.

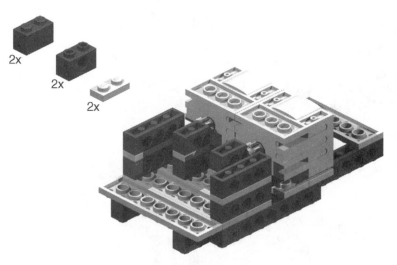

Step 5   Build smaller gear supports close to the center, as shown.

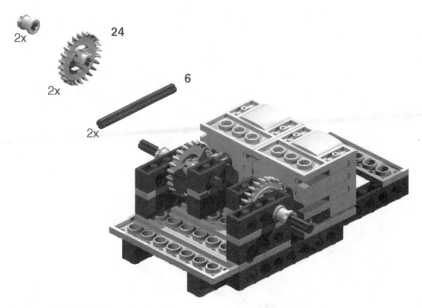

Step 6   Slide the axle into the gear train and through the crown gear. Repeat for other side and cap both with Technic bushes.

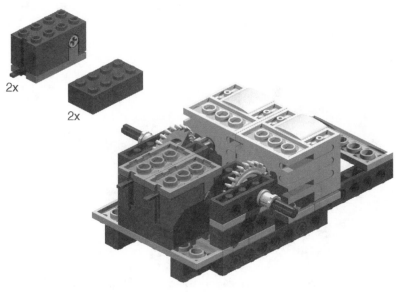

Step 7 Attach two 2 × 4 bricks to the chassis and attach both rotation sensors.

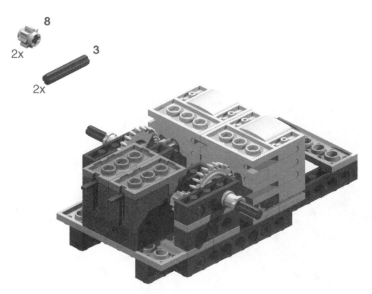

Step 8 Slide the axle into the gear train beams, through the 8-tooth gear, and into the rotation sensor. Repeat for the other side.

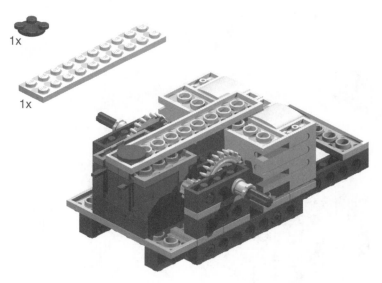

Step 9   Secure the motors to the rotation sensors using a 2 × 10 plate. This gives the structure more strength. Attach a skid plate to the end of the long plate.

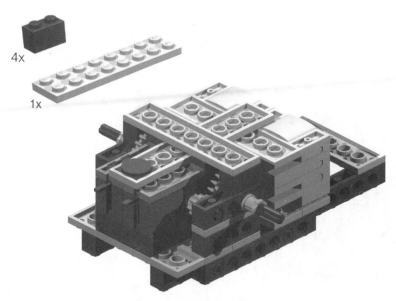

Step 10   Add four 2 × 1 bricks all in a line on top of the gear train beams. Cap it off with a 2 × 8 plate for additional strength.

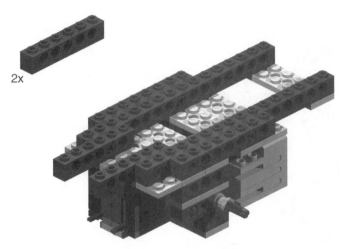

2x

Step 11 Attach two 6-unit beams to the front of the chassis to hold the bumper in place.

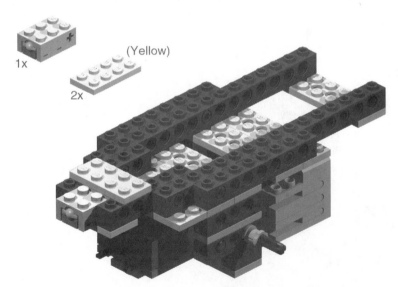

1x

(Yellow)

2x

Step 12 Sandwich a touch sensor between two 2 × 4 plates, as shown.

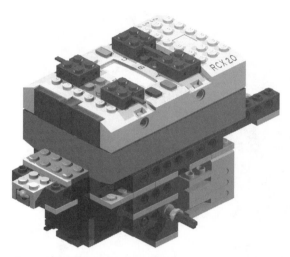

Step 13   Secure the RCX brick to the top of the chassis, making sure it is pressed firmly in place. Attach the wires from the motors to Ports A and C, threading them through the space between the beams on the rear of the robot. Make sure the wires face inward, otherwise the robot will travel backward. Attach the rotation sensors to Input Ports 1 and 3.

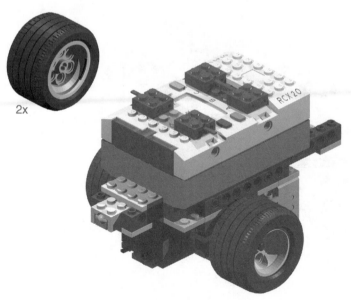

Step 14   Attach two wheels to the side axles.

Step 15 Attach an RCX wire from the touch sensor to Input 2. The wire should face forward on both connections.

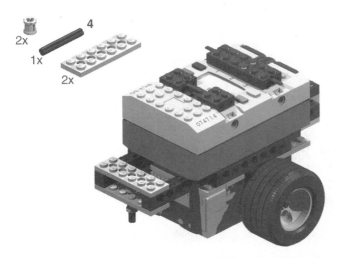

Step 16 Connect two 2 × 6 plates to the rear of the robot. Insert a 4-unit axle into the hole, through a Technic bush (making sure the rounded part of the bush faces down) and secure the bottom with another Technic bush.

Note:

RIS 1.0 owners will need to use a 6-unit axle for this step because there are only two 4-unit axles in the kit.

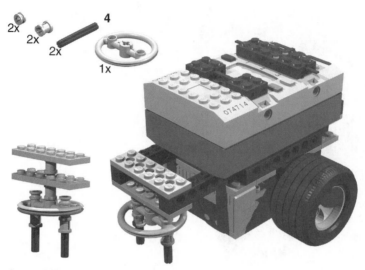

Step 17   Add the large pulley wheel to the axle. Insert two 4-unit axles into the holes and secure each with a Technic bush on the bottom and a half bush on top.

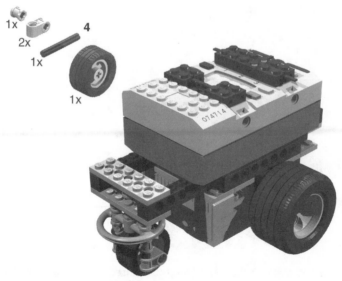

Step 18   Slide the wheel onto a 4-unit axle and add a single Technic bush on the axle to even out the symmetry of the wheel. Secure the wheel axle to the two support axles.

Note:

RIS 1.0 owners will need to use a 6-unit axle for this step because there are only two 4-unit axles in the kit.

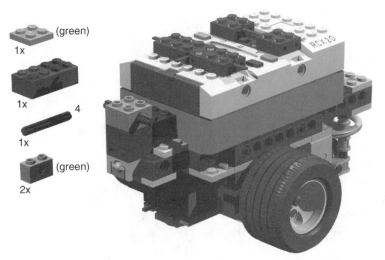

Step 19 Attach a 2 × 2 plate to the yellow 2 × 4 plate. Place a 2 × 4 brick on top of this, as shown. Attach two 1 × 2 green axle bricks on top and slide a 4-unit axle through the axle holes.

Note:

RIS 1.0 owners will need to use a 6-unit axle for this step because there are only two 4-unit axles in the kit.

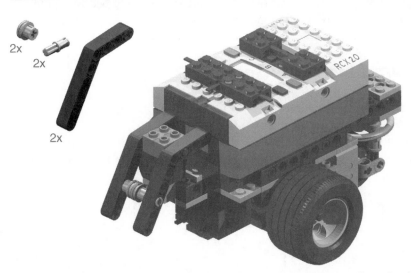

Step 20 Slide two lift arms onto the bumper axle. Attach two pulley wheels to the arm using axle pins. The pulleys should make contact with the touch sensor when the arms are in the downward position.

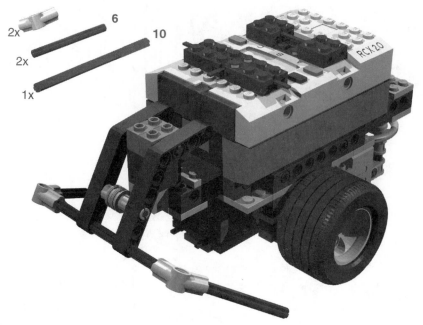

Step 21   Using axles, attach the bumper as shown.

Note:

RIS 1.0 owners will need to use two 8-unit axles for this step because there are no more 6-unit axles left in the kit.

Programming Tippy Senior

We'll try a few pieces of code to test out navigation with our new robot, Tippy Senior. First, let's implement the same code we used in the last chapter. You might think it would take a lot of tiny changes to make this happen, but actually it is very simple and only involves changing a few lines in the main code. Recall the main class for Trilobot from Chapter 7:

```
1. import josx.platform.rcx.*;
2. import josx.robotics.*;
3.
4. class TrilobotMain {
5.    public static void main(String [] args) {
6.       Motor.A.setPower(7);
7.       Motor.C.setPower(5);
```

```
8.      TimingNavigator nav = new TimingNavigator(Motor.C,
            Motor.A, 5.475f, 4.03f);
9.
10.     Behavior b1 = new Move(nav);
11.     Behavior b2 = new LeftBump(nav);
12.     Behavior b3 = new RightBump(nav);
13.     Behavior b4 = new GoHome(nav);
14.
15.     Behavior [] bArray = {b1, b2, b3, b4};
16.     Arbitrator arby = new Arbitrator(bArray);
17.     arby.start();
18.   }
19. }
```

Converting this code for use with RotationNavigator is very simple. There is now no need to try to balance the motors (Lines 5 and 6) because the rotation sensors will ensure that the robot drives in a straight path. The constructor for RotationNavigator is different from TimingNavigator, so Line 8 must change, but other than that the rest of the code can remain intact! The new code is as follows:

```
1. import josx.platform.rcx.*;
2. import josx.robotics.*;
3. class TippySr {
4.    public static void main(String [] args) {
5.        // float driveLength = 8.45f; // linoleum/hard wood
6.        float driveLength = 10.17f; // carpet
7.
8.        RotationNavigator nav = new RotationNavigator(4.96f,
            driveLength, 3);
9.
10.       Behavior b1 = new Move(nav);
11.       Behavior b2 = new LeftBump(nav);
12.       Behavior b3 = new RightBump(nav);
13.       Behavior b4 = new GoHome(nav);
14.       Behavior [] bArray = {b1, b2, b3, b4};
15.       Arbitrator arby = new Arbitrator(bArray);
16.       arby.start();
17.   }
18. }
```

Note:

The drive length is the most important variable for accuracy. To hone this variable, try using rotate(720) to make the robot rotate twice. Place a coin at the front of the robot to mark the direction the robot is facing. If the

robot rotates less than it is supposed to, increase the driveLength variable slightly. If it rotates more than expected, decrease the value slightly. To achieve the best accuracy, it is necessary to hone this number to two decimal places.

The reason this works so well is because the four behavior classes Move, LeftBump, RightBump, and GoHome all use a Navigator object in their constructors. RotationNavigator and TimingNavigator both implement Navigator, therefore they can be interchanged freely because they contain the same set of methods. The three behavior classes don't even need to be recompiled to accommodate this. When you run this code, Tippy Senior should behave as Trilobot did, only it should be a little more accurate. Now for something a little more interesting.

Let's attempt to make Tippy Senior navigate a small race course in your house, much like a ship in a sailing regatta navigates buoys. To set up the course you will need: half a dozen small coins, a notepad, a pen, and a ruler. The coins will act as buoys for the robot to turn on. By placing these on your floor you will be able to tell how accurately the robot is making its turns. We need to tell Tippy Senior when to make its turns, so after you lay down a coin, measure out the distance and write down the distance and angle for the next turn. If you stick to 90-degree turns it will make things a lot easier, and I would recommend using the corner of a book to make sure you keep the turns at precisely 90 degrees. You can also use a coordinate system instead of direct measurements. I decided to create my race course from a chair in the living room to a light stand in the bedroom (Figure 8–9). My list of measurements is as follows:

1. Forward 70 cm

2. Right 90 degrees

3. Forward 160 cm

4. Right 60 degrees

5. Forward 100 cm

6. Right 30 degrees

7. Forward 330 cm

8. Left 90 degrees

9. Forward 150 cm

10. Stop

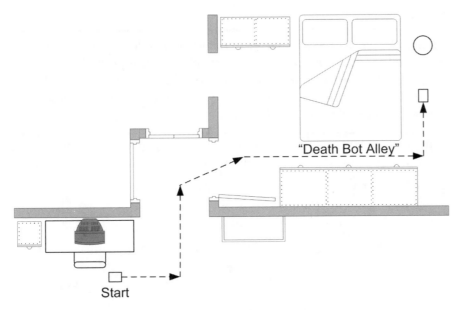

Figure 8-9 The test course for Tippy Senior.

Now all we need to do is convert these measurements into code. The best way to organize our measurements would probably be in an array. Each forward movement is always followed by an angle, so we will use an array to store movements and angles. The code for this is easy to write:

```
1. import josx.platform.rcx.*;
2. import josx.robotics.*;
3. class Regatta {
4.     static final int [] distance = {70, 160, 100, 330, 150};
5.     static final int [] angle = {0, 90, -60, -30, 90};
6.
7.     //static final float driveLength = 8.45f; // linoleum/
           hard wood
8.     static final float driveLength = 10.2f; // carpet
9.
10.    public static void main(String [] args) {
11.        RotationNavigator nav = new RotationNavigator(4.96f,
               driveLength, 3);
12.        for(int i=0;i<distance.length;++i) {
13.            nav.rotate(angle[i]);
14.            nav.travel(distance[i]);
15.        }
16.    }
17. }
```

Note:

These code samples must be altered to run within your home. The course designated by Lines 4 and 5 should be customized to your particular floor plan. Also, if the floor is carpeted you can leave Lines 7 and 8 alone, but if you are using a hardwood or linoleum surface, remove the // symbols next to Line 7 and add them next to Line 8.

As an alternate strategy, the robot can navigate using a coordinate system. The following code uses an array for the *x* and *y* coordinates, as follows:

```
1. import josx.platform.rcx.*;
2. import josx.robotics.*;
3. class Regatta2 {
4.     static final int [] x = {70, 70, 157, 487, 487};
5.     static final int [] y = {0, 160, 210, 210, 360};
6.
7.     //static final float driveLength = 8.45f; // linoleum/
           hard wood
8.     static final float driveLength = 10.2f; // carpet
9.
10.     public static void main(String [] args) {
11.         RotationNavigator nav = new RotationNavigator(4.96f,
               driveLength, 3);
12.         for(int i=0;i<x.length;++i) {
13.             nav.gotoPoint(x[i], y[i]);
14.         }
15.     }
16. }
```

So how did Tippy Senior handle this course? Well, you'll have to read the next section on accuracy to find out, but I'll give you a hint: The narrow area between the bed and dresser is called Death Bot Alley for a reason.

RotationNavigator Accuracy

For the most part, Tippy Senior had a good run through the course (Figure 8–10). The robot didn't stop directly over any coins, but it more or less kept to the proper path. Going into the bedroom it came alarmingly close to the left edge of the door frame, then straightened and looked like it had a good chance of making it through Death Bot Alley, but the weight of the dresser seemed to have curved the carpet, sucking Tippy Senior toward it. On only

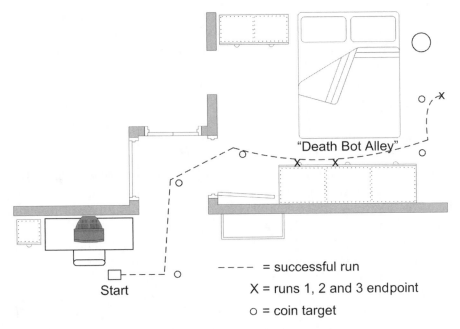

"Death Bot Alley"

---- = successful run

X = runs 1, 2 and 3 endpoint

o = coin target

Start

Figure 8-10   The journeys of Tippy Senior.

one in three runs did it actually make it through this section properly. The robot's final position is actually quite close to the target—within 10 cm. Rotation sensors are indeed a good improvement over timing, but they are not perfect. Let's examine the systematic and nonsystematic errors that caused Tippy Senior to deviate from the proper course.

Systematic Errors

In the last chapter there were many errors that were eradicated here by using rotation sensors. The relative strengths of the two motors does not matter anymore because rotations are now being counted. The robot no longer pulls to one side or another (noticeably) as it moves, unless the terrain is curved (as the carpet is around the dresser and walls). Also, if the batteries are getting weak and start slowing things down, distances are no longer affected. Now the robot can move at any speed and the only thing that matters is counting wheel rotations.

There are some systematic errors that are within our control. The first is when we measure the course, lay out our coins, and write down the appropriate coordinates. The measurement of distances is likely to be quite accurate, but any angles you make are apt to be off unless you use a compass. Overall, however, your course is not likely to be more than a few centimeters off from beginning to end. An important but relatively simple systematic error is the direction the robot is initially facing when the program is started. If the robot is slightly to the left or right on the x axis when it begins, it can translate to a very large error, especially when traveling long distances.

The accuracy of distances is also a concern. There is no doubt the rotation sensor accurately keeps track of axle rotations, but how accurate is it when the resolution is only 16 increments for every rotation of the axle? This is largely dependent on the internal gearing of Tippy Senior, which has a 3:1 gear ratio between rotation sensor and wheel axle. For every rotation of the wheel, the sensor axle turns three times, or 48 times for a complete rotation of the wheel. Because the resolution of the rotation sensor is one increment, we can't be sure if the axle has rotated closer to 48 or 49 times. In other words, it might have rotated 48.001 times or 48.999 times. Therefore, the accuracy is within 1/48 of a rotation or ±2.08% for each complete wheel rotation. In our example, the wheel has a circumference of 15.58 cm (at 48 increments per rotation), so for each line of movement it makes it has an accuracy of ±0.32 cm (3.2 mm). If Tippy Senior moves two wheel rotations, or 31.16 cm, the accuracy is also ±3.2 mm. In other words, whether Tippy Senior moves 5 m, or 5 cm, the accuracy of that line of movement will be ±3.2 mm, theoretically at least.

Now what about the more important question of rotation accuracy? As we just calculated, after each movement Tippy Senior has an accuracy of ±3.2 mm. We also determined the drive length (diameter from wheel to wheel) is about 9.7 cm. For Tippy Senior to turn in a complete circle each wheel must travel 9.7 times pi, or 30.47 cm. This means to rotate 360 degrees is the equivalent of 94 increments of a rotation sensor. Because it is always ±1 increment, the complete rotation can be off as much as 1/94th of 360, or 3.83 degrees. Thus, every rotation made, whether it is 90 degrees or 9 degrees, will be off as much as 3.83 degrees. That's not too bad, really, but the accuracy of Tippy Senior will not last for very long if it moves for long periods of time.

Nonsystematic Errors

The nonsystematic errors that plagued Trilobot in the previous chapter are back. Any curvature in the floor, such as the unevenness in the rug near the dresser, is apt to cause Tippy Senior to deviate from a straight path. Minute wheel slippage is also likely occurring, but the slow speed of Tippy Senior should obviate this effect. The biggest problem is that the current angle of movement is easy to throw off, especially after much movement. Any interaction with objects causes the angle to be thrown off. Whether Tippy Senior is colliding with large objects or running over small objects, they all serve to diminish accuracy, causing the internal angle to differ from the actual angle of movement. In every sense of the word, when Tippy Senior hits an object it becomes disoriented. In the next chapter we will create a sensor that can detect objects before a collision, which will go a long way toward solving some of these nonsystematic errors.

PROXIMITY DETECTION

Topics in this Chapter

Chapter 9

Lego includes only one type of sensor for detecting objects in the path of a robot—the touch sensor. This poses some problems with navigation. As we learned in previous chapters, when a robot collides with an object it tends to get jostled and loses its assumed orientation (like a person who has been struck, it becomes disoriented). It's just not very elegant for a robot to navigate around by crashing into objects. A better solution would be for a robot to detect an object in its path before a collision. LEGO does not provide a standard part for detecting objects in this manner but we can create a makeshift proximity detector using existing RIS parts. This proximity detector is a little limited, so the last half of the chapter demonstrates how to build a more accurate distance sensor using raw electronic components.

Creating a Simple Proximity Sensor

The MINDSTORMS light sensor is capable of detecting more than just visible light; it can also detect light on the IR portion of the light spectrum. This includes light generated by the RCX IR port. To the light sensor, the light emitted from the IR port (when set to long range) probably looks like a flashlight going on and off very quickly. Using this fact, we can make the IR port light pulse. If it reflects off an object in front of it, this can be picked up by the light sensor. When the light sensor detects a strong change in light it interprets this as an object in its path.

The Serial class is used to send numerical messages through the IR port. Sending a single number causes the IR port to flash for a brief period of time. This has been recorded with IR-sensitive video cameras and it has been found that the light stays on for about one to two frames of video. At 25 frames per second, this means the light remains on for about 1/25th of a second, or 40 ms. We want to pulse the light, however. Our strategy is to take a reading without the IR port on, then turn on the "IR flashlight" and take another reading. Any large changes will indicate there is something in front of the robot reflecting light back to the light sensor. If there are no objects in front of the robot the light should dissipate into the distance and not be reflected back very strongly. The trick is to look for a large change in the light reflected back. Building this sensor requires four simple LEGO parts (Figure 9–1).

Now that we have a mechanism to work with, let's try some test code to see how this strategy works. The Sensor class has a method for sending a packet of byte values. In our case, we just want to send one byte, and we'll pick the largest byte we can for Java (127, because bytes are signed). As we theorized, the IR pulse will last for about 40 ms so we have a small window to take a reading. It's possible the IR pulse doesn't become active immediately, however, so we include a small 5-ms delay after calling this method in the hopes

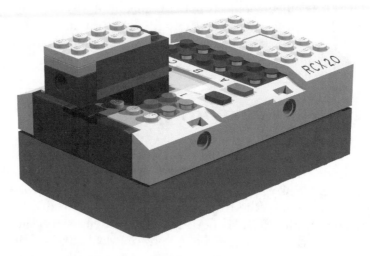

Figure 9–1   A simple proximity sensor.

that the RCX will take a reading while the IR light is on. Let's review the code to do this:

```
1.  import josx.platform.rcx.*;
2.  class IRTest extends Thread implements SensorConstants {
3.      private final byte [] packet = {127};
4.
5.      public IRTest() {
6.          Sensor.S2.setTypeAndMode(SENSOR_TYPE_LIGHT,
                  SENSOR_MODE_RAW);
7.          Sensor.S2.activate();
8.          Serial.setRangeLong();
9.          this.start();
10.     }
11.
12.     public void run() {
13.         int oldValue;
14.         int newValue;
15.         while(true) {
16.             oldValue = Sensor.S2.readValue();
17.             Serial.sendPacket(packet, 0, 1);
18.             try{Thread.sleep(5);}catch(Exception e){}
19.             newValue = Sensor.S2.readValue();
20.             int diff = Math.abs(oldValue - newValue);
21.             if(diff > 80) {
22.                 Sound.playTone(diff, 20);
23.                 LCD.showNumber(diff);
24.             }
25.             try{Thread.sleep(160);}catch(Exception e){}
26.         }
27.     }
28.
29.     public static void main(String [] args) {
30.         new IRTest();
31.     }
32. }
```

This code is run as a never-ending loop in a separate thread. Line 6 initializes the sensor as a light sensor that will read raw values. Line 8 is crucial to the operation of our proximity sensor because it sets the serial port to long-range mode. In the default short-range mode the IR port sends a very weak signal that does not cause a large enough change for the light sensor to detect. Remember in previous chapters that long range was able to send an IR signal right across a room to the IR port, whereas short range could only transmit about 250 cm. Once the light sensor has been activated, the thread is started. Line 16 takes a quick reading of the current lighting conditions (oldValue), then Line 17 sends a byte to the serial port. After a small 5-ms delay, Line 19 takes another reading (newValue). The difference between oldValue and newValue is determined, and if it is larger than 80, the LCD notes it.

Line 22 produces an aural clue as to the distance, much like a submarine receiving a ping. A strong change in light value will cause a high pitch frequency, but if the object is barely registering, the ping will be deeper. This device is a little like a digital white stick that could be used by the blind. (If you decide to try navigating around your house while blindfolded, please stay away from stairs or other dangerous areas.)

With the program running, try walking around your house and holding the RCX in front of objects. The first thing you will notice is that when the RCX is farther from an object it produces less frequent pings. Move closer and the RCX produces almost five pings per second, as would be expected. This variable frequency of pings is something we have to contend with when programming robots to use this sensor. The second noticeable effect is that a consistent difference is not produced by the detector. When I place the RCX brick in front of a wood door, the values range anywhere from 83 to 157, even with it sitting in the same spot. There seems to be some consistency to these numbers, but there is a random element as well. Number grouping is occurring, in which common numbers keep reappearing. For example, on a given surface the numbers may change between 80, 100, and 120. This might be caused by the IR port altering the frequency of the IR wave, causing changes in light intensity. Obviously we cannot use these numbers individually as an indication of distance, but we might be able to average them out or use peak numbers to estimate distance from an object.

The surface of the object in front of the RCX brick also affects the reading because light intensity is completely dependent on an object's ability to reflect IR light. As you have probably observed, when shining a flashlight around a room, white or light-colored objects reflect much better than black or dark-colored objects. The surface texture also affects the amount of light reflected back to the light sensor. Table 9–1 shows the peak values of various surfaces measured from different distances. As you can see, light-colored, solid, hard, smooth surfaces tend to give stronger readings than dark, soft, rough surfaces.

The size of object in front of the proximity detector also matters. A small object such as a 2×4 LEGO brick just doesn't have very much surface area to reflect light back, so it produces a very small signature when it is far from the light sensor. Figure 9–2 shows a setup of various LEGO targets used to test

Table 9-1 Peak Values from Various Surfaces

	40 cm	30 cm	20 cm	10 cm	5 cm
Stained wood	82	95	120	195	223
White wallboard	82	100	152	200	227
Black wood	None	85	93	170	190
Blue leather	None	None	88	128	151
Off-white refrigerator	None	81	110	185	190
Mirror	93	135	168	245	264
Glass window	None	90	121	170	212

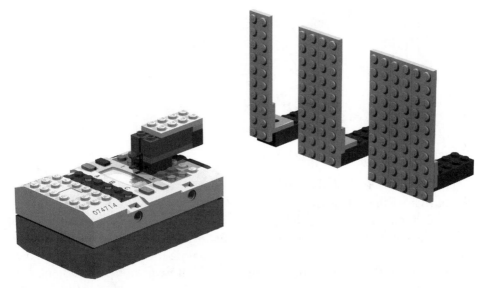

Figure 9–2   Reflection is affected by the size of targets.

light reflectance. As expected, larger targets produce a stronger signal than smaller ones (Table 9–2). The height of the target from the ground also matters. A target of one to two LEGO units in height will not register a ping at any distance, but three LEGO units will register pings.

Table 9-2 Size of Object vs. Reflection Strength

LEGO Wall	40 cm	30 cm	20 cm	10 cm	5 cm
2 × 10	None	None	102	182	220
4 × 10	None	82	116	207	241
6 × 10	None	83	133	182	207

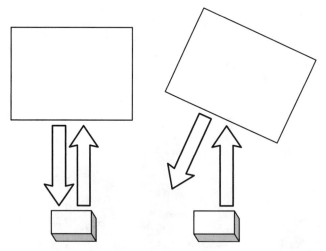

Figure 9–3   IR light is easily deflected.

The field of view of the proximity sensor is actually quite limited. Any object that was not directly in front of the sensor was not detected. At a distance of 20 cm, if a 2 × 10 gray plate was moved 1 to 2 cm to the left or right, it became undetectable. This occurs even when removing the blinder we placed over the light sensor. It's interesting to note the angle the plates faced was crucial to getting a good reading. If the plate was not perpendicular to the direction the sensor was facing it did not register a signal, probably due to most of the IR light being deflected away (Figure 9–3).

Programming the Sensor

Now that we have a better understanding of the capabilities of the proximity sensor we can put it into action. To make it truly useful, we will create a class in true object-oriented fashion that is easy to incorporate into source code.

The most useful design pattern we can use in Java is a listener, which will be notified every time the proximity detector detects an object. The first step to creating this design is to create a ProximityListener interface. This class is quite simple, and resembles the SensorListener interface in many ways:

```
public interface ProximityListener {
    /**
     * Called when the proximity sensor detects an object
     * @param ping The strength of the detected signal.
     */
    public void objectDetected(int ping);
}
```

The interface uses only two functional lines of code. The objectDetected() method is called every time the sensor thinks it has spotted an object. This method contains a ping variable to indicate the strength of the reflected light from the object.

Now that we have a listener defined, we need to create a ProximityDetector class that will actually be able to detect objects and notify all registered ProximityListeners. As with any listener architecture, it is necessary to have a method to add listeners. This method simply adds the listener to an array of ProximityListener objects. We also need a method to notify the listeners when an object is detected. This method is located at Line 43 in the following code, which is the full code for the proximity detector:

```
1.  import josx.platform.rcx.*;
2.  import java.util.*;
3.
4.  public class ProximityDetector extends Thread implements
        SensorConstants{
5.
6.      private final byte [] packet = {127};
7.
8.      private Sensor lightSensor;
9.      private Vector proximityListeners;
10.
11.     public ProximityDetector(Sensor lightPort) {
12.         proximityListeners = new Vector(2,2);
13.
14.         lightSensor = lightPort;
15.         lightSensor.setTypeAndMode(SENSOR_TYPE_LIGHT,
                SENSOR_MODE_RAW);
16.         lightSensor.activate();
17.
18.         Serial.setRangeLong();
19.
```

```
20.        this.start();
21.    }
22.
23.    public void run() {
24.        int oldValue;
25.        int newValue;
26.        while(true) {
27.            oldValue = Sensor.S2.readValue();
28.            Serial.sendPacket(packet, 0, 1);
29.            try{Thread.sleep(5);}catch(Exception e){}
30.            newValue = Sensor.S2.readValue();
31.            int diff = Math.abs(oldValue - newValue);
32.            if(diff > 80) {
33.                notifyListeners(diff);
34.            }
35.            try{Thread.sleep(160);}catch(Exception e){}
36.        }
37.    }
38.
39.    public void addProximityListener(ProximityListener lis-
               tener) {
40.        proximityListeners.addElement(listener);
41.    }
42.
43.    private void notifyListeners(int ping) {
44.        for(int i=0;i<proximityListeners.size();++i) {
45.            ProximityListener prox = (ProximityListener)prox-
                   imityListeners.elementAt(i);
46.            prox.objectDetected(ping);
47.        }
48.    }
49. }
```

As you can see, the code for the run() method of the thread is lifted almost exactly from our previous test class. The only difference is Line 33, which notifies the listeners using the notifyListeners() method if it detects a strong enough signal. Now that we have a useful listener-notifier architecture in place, let's make a simple class to control a robot:

```
1. import josx.platform.rcx.*;
2.
3. class ProximityTest implements ProximityListener {
4.
5.    public ProximityTest() {
6.        Motor.A.forward();
7.        Motor.C.forward();
```

```
8.      }
9.
10.     public static void main(String [] args) {
11.         ProximityDetector pd = new ProximityDetector(Sen-
                sor.S2);
12.         pd.addProximityListener(new ProximityTest());
13.         try {Button.RUN.waitForPressAndRelease();
14.         }catch(Exception e){}
15.     }
16.
17.     public synchronized void objectDetected(int ping) {
18.         Motor.A.backward();
19.         Motor.C.backward();
20.         try{Thread.sleep(500);}catch(Exception e){}
21.         Motor.A.forward();
22.         try{Thread.sleep(700);}catch(Exception e){}
23.         Motor.C.forward();
24.     }
25. }
```

This code is a simple bumper car routine. The robot drives forward until it encounters an object, then it reverses and turns to face a new direction. I used the Trilobot robot found in Chapter 7, "Navigation," but it will work with any robot using differential steering. Overall the robot seems to work quite well, as long as it comes up to well-distinguished objects. Smaller objects are a problem for the robot, however, so it would be a good idea to use a backup bumper system just in case.

Reliability

The detector just described is somewhat of a hack, derived from basic LEGO parts that weren't really made for detecting the proximity of another object. Most times it detects objects quite well, but once in a while it does not, and ends up getting stuck. It does fantastic when approaching white objects, such as a wall or door. The detector seems to have the most trouble with approaching black objects at an angle. If it is driving straight toward a black object with a flat surface it has no problem detecting it, but it appears blind to anything off center. This is because we programmed the detector to look for a large change in signal—greater than 80 raw units. Sometimes a black object just doesn't reflect that much. We could, of course, lower this threshold to about 50, but then it starts detecting objects from too far a distance, which hinders movement and progress. It's a bit of a balancing act. Problems with reliability can be overcome by creating a range sensor that does not rely on signal strength, which we examine in the next section.

Note:

This design works much better with an IR filter placed on the light sensor. For details, see www.philohome.com/sensors/ir_sensitivity.htm.

Creating a Distance Sensor

In this section we are going to build and program a custom sensor to accurately measure the distance to an object. Compared to the previous projects in this book, it is not going to be easy. The end result, however, is well worth it. Unlike the proximity sensor we made in the last section, this sensor does not depend on the strength of the returned signal to estimate distances (this is explained later). The sensor can be attached anywhere on your robot relative to the RCX, and it can point in any direction. This sensor is also small enough that it can be attached to a motor and made to rotate, much like radar. In fact by rotating, theoretically it could traverse a room by methodically moving in rows (like mowing the lawn) and mapping objects in your home. With our previous sensor, rotation was not possible. Finally, the range sensor does not tie up the IR serial port, so the serial port will be free at all times for communications. These advantages make it a great addition to your arsenal of robotic sensors.

Note:

If you would rather not build this sensor from scratch you can buy it online already assembled. The source is not a large company, however (one person), so availability is in no way guaranteed. See Appendix B for ordering information.

The Sharp GP2D12 Sensor

Sharp produces a popular series of range sensors. Most sensors, such as the one described earlier in this chapter, rely on the strength of a signal (or sometimes timing a sonar signal) to determine the distance to an object. The problem with this is that the strength of the signal is dependent on the color and

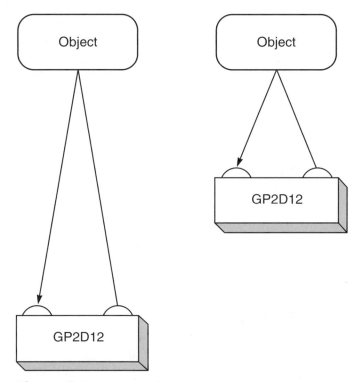

Figure 9–4 Emitter and receiver.

other surface characteristics of an object. The Sharp GP2D series of sensors use a technique in which light is emitted from one part of the sensor, bounces off an object, and then returns to the receiver of the sensor. The emitter, reflected object, and receiver form a triangle (Figure 9–4). The angle at which the light is received is used to determine the distance, so the strength of the signal is largely irrelevant.

The GP2D series sensors actually emit a beam of light straight ahead (Figure 9–5). When the beam strikes an object it is scattered in all directions (unless the object is a perfect mirror). Some of this light reaches the receiver lens, and the beam gets concentrated to a point. This point of light strikes the *position-sensitive detector* (PSD) inside the sensor. The output voltage of the sensor varies depending on where the light beam hits the PSD. The GP2D12 sensor can only measure between 10 cm and 80 cm. If the object is too far away, the signal will either be too weak to be measured, or the PSD will not be able to discriminate differences in the angle accurately enough. If the object is too close the lens cannot focus the beam on the PSD (in other words, the light beam overshoots the PSD). For this reason you should

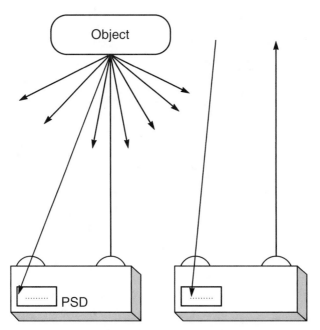

Figure 9–5   Light from the sensor is scattered.

mount the sensor about 10 cm from the front of the robot so it can detect objects right up to the bumper.

There are four sensors in the GP2D series family of sensors: GP2D02, GP2D05, GP2D12, and GP2D15. These sensors superficially look similar, but there are some key differences. The GP2D0x sensors (GP2D02 and GP2D05) are digital sensors, and they communicate using strange signal patterns. The signal pattern to communicate is somewhat difficult to use, and the sensor ports for the RCX are made for analog signals (voltage changes), so digital signals are not the best way to go. The GP2Dx5 sensors (GP2D05 and GP2D15) are just proximity sensors. They do not tell anything about the distance to an object; rather, they indicate if an object is within the range of the sensor (either true or false). The GP2Dx2 sensors on the other hand (GP2D02 and GP2D12) give a signal that indicates the distance to an object, within 10 cm to 80 cm. Given this information it seems obvious the best sensor for our purpose is the GP2D12 because it's easiest to interface with the RCX and it gives an accurate distance measurement.

Note:

For GP2D12 ordering information, see Appendix B.

A Primer in Electronics

Electronics can seem a little scary at first. There are thousands of components available, each capable of performing some mysterious little function. There are schematic diagrams containing symbols that must be understood to assemble a circuit. The components are so tiny they are often difficult to handle, and the print on them is difficult to read. There are theories of electricity including current flow, resistance, power, and quiescent current. There is another whole language to learn including volts, amps, ohms, and farads. Once a circuit is assembled, if something is not working then a novice is probably going to have a difficult (if not impossible) time trying to figure out what is wrong. But take heart, because the aim of this section is not to teach you everything about electronics, but rather to teach just enough to get the interface circuit assembled.

Note:

For anyone interested in learning electronics from square one, I recommend a book available from Radio Shack, Getting Started in Electronics, *by Forrest M. Mimms, III. It starts with the basics of electricity and covers everything from semiconductors to schematic diagrams.*

Keep in mind an understanding of electronics is not at all necessary to assemble the circuits in this book. All you need to do is to connect a handful of small parts, plug the circuit into the RCX, and—probably to your own amazement—the circuit will work. It is very difficult to damage the RCX by connecting your own circuit because the RCX has built in protections. All power comes from the RCX batteries, so there is probably not going to be enough current capable of damaging anything. The hardest part of completing a project like this is obtaining the correct parts! Once you have the parts, attaching them is actually relatively straightforward. It is often difficult to find parts for small robotics projects because the components used are low voltage and low current, meaning they run from batteries. Most electronic component stores, however, stock parts made to run from high-voltage, high-current applications, such as VCRs and televisions, which use household electricity. If you encounter problems trying to locate the parts locally, your best bet might be to order online.

Electronic Components

There are a few things you should know about parts and parts distributors before you go hunting. First, most semiconductors have a part number, such as LM78L05 or LM324. These are industry-standard parts and are manufactured by a variety of companies (e.g., Phillips, Fairchild). The manufacturer should not be important when ordering the parts. Another factor to consider is differences in regional availability. Europeans are often supplied by different manufacturers than in North America. Some parts, mainly from the rangefinder circuit in this chapter, are difficult to obtain in North America, so a list of alternative parts is listed in case you have difficulty obtaining the primary part. For example, the BC558B transistor is a European part, but it can be substituted with an NTE17 or NTE234 transistor, which are more common in North America.

Parts distributors can vary in the variety of stock they carry. Radio Shack can be a good place to obtain tools and very basic components, but many of the newer stores seem to be emphasizing consumer electronics and not dealing in electronics components. Even when ordering parts from the Radio Shack catalog, the selection of components is very slim (see Appendix B for an excellent list of parts distributors). In general, parts distributors can also vary in their friendliness to the hobbyist—most do not want to be bothered by questions about your circuit, so be ready to order your parts and nothing more. There are also shipping fees if you are ordering. For this reason it is a good idea to order all of the parts together, both for this chapter and Chapter 10, "Navigation with a Compass Sensor" (if you plan on building the compass sensor). Some mail-order companies also require a minimum order (e.g. $50 U.S.). This is another reason to place one large order rather than several small orders. There can also be a minimum order quantity required for individual components. When I was purchasing my resistors I had to buy 100 of each type of resistor, but thankfully 100 resistors only cost a few dollars. It is also a good idea to order duplicates of each part, just in case something breaks during assembly. Costs are very low for most components, so order about double what you really need. The costs for the main sensors, on the other hand, are much higher. The compass sensor in Chapter 10 costs about $35 U.S. per unit, though the Sharp range sensor in this chapter is a little cheaper, at about $12 U.S. per unit.

Tools

As the saying goes, a carpenter is only as good as his tools, and the same applies to electronics. Most of these tools are relatively cheap, however, and several can be found around the house already, so it shouldn't be difficult to obtain them.

The breadboard is a device used for prototyping a circuit (Figure 9–6). This device is a must when assembling a circuit for the first time. If you like, once the circuit is working you can keep using the breadboard, or you might want to move to a more permanent fixture (which is explained later). The breadboard allows standard electronics components to be inserted or removed in a matter of seconds. The board itself contains hundreds of tiny holes that accept the thin wire *leads* (pronounced leeds) of components. Underneath the surface there are continuous electrical paths. Rows of holes are separated from each other. Also, the middle of the board breaks the circuit, so holes on the top half of the row are not connected to the holes on the bottom half. There are also rows running lengthwise that are used for the positive and negative current of the circuit. Figure 9–7 shows what the circuit looks like underneath the surface of the board.

A soldering iron is necessary if you want to make your circuit permanent, but you do not need it for the prototyping stage. Soldering irons can be purchased for under $10 U.S. from Radio Shack, and the kit also includes electrical solder and some other soldering tools. You will also want a wet sponge for

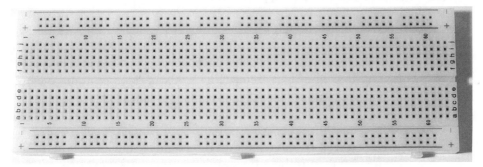

Figure 9–6   An experimenter's breadboard.

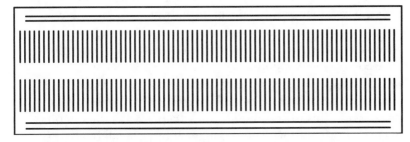

Figure 9–7   Row and column circuits.

cleaning off the solder when working, and a piece of sandpaper for sanding off carbon deposits from the solder bit (do this only when it is cool, however).

A pair of needle-nose pliers can come in handy for manipulating the small components. The pliers can be used to bend the leads on electrical components and they can also come in handy for breadboard work. When assembling the circuit I sometimes find it difficult to fit my fingers into spaces between components, but with pliers it's easy to push them into the breadboard. Most needle-nose pliers also include a blade at the hinge joint that is useful for cutting wires and component leads.

A small knife will also be useful for this project. You will use it to slice through the webbing of the electrical brick wire to separate the left wire from the right wire, as this wire does not just pull apart like some wires do. The knife is also used to score the punchboard to separate it into pieces (later on in the permanent assembly). An inexpensive disposable utility knife will suffice.

A small wire stripper is also handy, but it will only be used once in this project for stripping the wires on the electrical brick wire. You could get away with slicing the plastic around the wire with a blade, but the wire stripping tool will make it easier.

A Crash Course in Schematics

This section reviews just enough about schematics to make sense of the circuits used in this book. Take a look ahead in this chapter to Figure 9–13, which shows the interface circuit for the distance sensor. There are about 10 unique symbols to describe this circuit (Figure 9–8). Let's examine each of these symbols and find out how each component is related to the symbol.

- *Resistor.* A resistor has two leads, neither of which is positive or negative, so it can be connected to the circuit in any direction. Resistance is measured in ohms, so if you see 330K next to a symbol it means the resistance of the component is 330,000 ohms. The actual resistor has colored bands around it that indicate the resistance, but you won't really need to know how to read these because the resistors come in labeled bags. If you do mix up a resistor, there are internet sites that describe how to read the colors (see Appendix D).
- *Diode.* A diode permits electricity to flow one way but not the other. Diodes are polarized, meaning there is a positive end and a negative end. This means diodes must be placed in the circuit in the correct orientation. The diode itself has a small band painted closer to one end (Figure 9–9). If you look closely at the

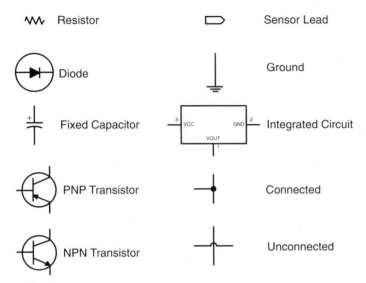

Figure 9-8 Schematic symbols.

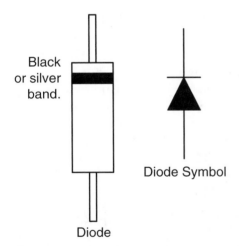

Figure 9-9 Diodes have a band indicating current flow.

diode symbol in Figure 9–8 you can see it has a triangle with a line. This line corresponds to the band painted on the diode, so if the line is to the right of the triangle then the band should also be to the right in the circuit.

- *Capacitor.* Capacitors are like rechargeable batteries—they store a charge and can release it when the current drops. Ceramic capacitors are not polarized so it doesn't matter in

A   B

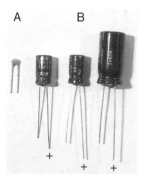

Figure 9–10 Nonpolarized (A) and polarized (B) capacitors.

which direction it is connected in the circuit (Figure 9–10a). The symbol for a capacitor sometimes has a + sign, indicating which lead is positive. Electrolytic capacitors (the type that is cylindrical in shape) are polarized, so there are positive and negative terminals. The positive lead is always longer than the negative lead (Figure 9–10b).

- *Transistor.* A transistor has three leads: base, emitter, and collector. These three leads are normally labeled B, E, and C, respectively, on schematics. It's not necessary to know anything about transistors for assembling the circuit, but if you are curious, read on. A transistor is like an electronic on–off switch; it can stop or start current flow depending on whether a current is flowing through the emitter to the base. If some current is flowing, it will also allow higher current to flow through the emitter to the collector (Figure 9–11). As you can see in this figure, when the current is flowing through E–B, the current is also allowed to flow through E–C. When no current is flowing through E–B it is stopped at E–C. There are two kinds of transistors we will be using for this project—PNP and NPN.

- *Sensor lead.* This symbol represents either the positive or negative wire coming from the RCX. In our project we will be cutting one of the long wires in half to obtain this part.

- *Ground.* In Figure 9–13 you will notice the ground symbol in many places on the schematic. The ground symbol means the wire should connect to the negative terminal of the power source. On a breadboard this is the row that runs along the top or bottom, marked negative. As you can see in the schematic, the negative sensor lead goes straight to ground.

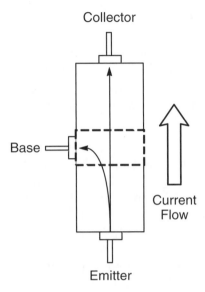

Collector

Base

Current
Flow

Emitter

Figure 9-11 An NPN transistor current flow.

- *Integrated circuit.* Integrated circuits (ICs) are just small circuits contained within one component. There are many possible functions of ICs. For example, in this project the GP2D12 is classified as an IC, but normally ICs are small circuits encased in ceramic package cases. Figure 9–12 shows an LM324 IC, which is used in the compass circuit in Chapter 10. ICs can be enclosed in a variety of cases, including cases that resemble transistors.

Figure 9-12 An integrated circuit.

- *Connected wires.* A dot represents a junction between two or more wires where the wires should be connected.
- *Unconnected wires.* The unconnected symbol shows the wire curving over the adjacent wire if they are not meant to be connected.

Building the Distance Sensor

This circuit is fairly simple to build and should not pose too much of a problem for a beginner. As long as you have ordered all the correct parts, the chance of the circuit working is good. We'll be building what is known as an *interface*, which is a circuit used to feed the proper amount of electricity to the sensor and obtain readings from the sensor.

There is a special challenge with using the GP2D12 sensor with the RCX brick, however. The GP2D12 sensor uses 35 mA (milliamps) of current, but the RCX only produces about 14 mA! Current can't just be created out of thin air, so a special design had to be made to provide the correct supply. The solution is to store energy in a capacitor (which is like a battery) for a fraction of a second, then release the combined energy at once to the GP2D12 sensor. We can use code to make the RCX charge the capacitor, then switch to reading the sensor. The code is designed to charge the capacitor for 250 ms, then take 50 ms to read the sensor value. Normally the GP2D12 sensor can take a reading every 50 ms, but because of the charge phase, our circuit will take 300 ms. This is much better than having to use additional batteries to

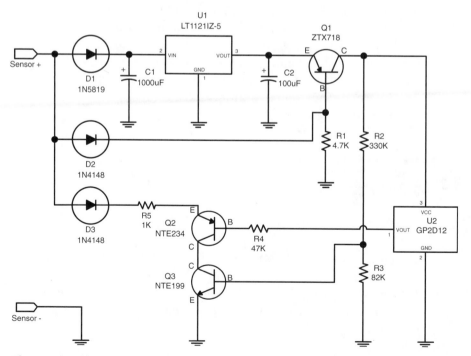

Figure 9-13   The complete distance sensor circuit (designed by Philippe Hurbain).

power the sensor, however, and at three measures per second it should be adequate for the robotic uses we have in mind.

The complete schematic for the circuit we are going to build is shown in Figure 9–13. If you are familiar with electronics you will probably be able to assemble the circuit without even looking at the assembly instructions. The circuit will fit into three 2×4 LEGO bricks when complete, which is tiny. Try taking three bricks right now and stacking them on top of one another. That is how big the final sensor will be, so make sure your 1000 μF capacitor is small enough to fit inside these bricks.

There is also an alternate schematic provided (Figure 9–14). Recall earlier that LEGO sensors can be plugged into the RCX input port in any orientation. The schematic shown in Figure 9–13 only works in two of the four possible orientations. There is a special circuit called *a bridge rectifier* that allows all four orientations to work, but it requires five additional diodes. The preceding schematic easily fits into only three 2×4 bricks, but the circuit shown in Figure 9–14 needs four 2×4 bricks (rather large for a LEGO sensor, which is why it is not recommended).

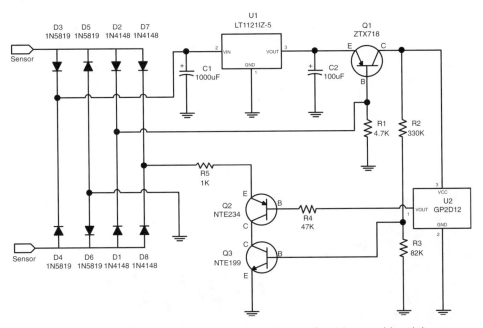

Figure 9–14 An alternate schematic with bridge rectifier (designed by Philippe Hurbain).

Note:

In Figure 9–14, the schematic shows ground (negative) for eight points in the circuit. All this means is the wires should all go to the common point indicated by the connection between D5 and D6 of the bridge rectifier.

Assembly Instructions

To assemble the circuit to breadboard you will need the following:

- Wire cutters
- Wire stripper (optional)
- Soldering iron (optional)
- Utility knife
- Needle-nose pliers (optional)
- Jumpers or wire

Before we begin, it is necessary to prepare a wire so we can plug the RCX into the circuit. I used one of the long 128-cm wire bricks that comes in the RIS set. Cut the wire in half, leaving two 64-cm long wires with bricks on one end (save one half for other projects). With the remaining wire, cut the webbing between the two strands about 4 cm from the end (Figure 9–15). I used a utility knife, but you can also use a wire cutter for this. Strip each end of the wires until about 1 cm (half-inch) of bare wire is showing. Gently twist the strands on each end so they don't fray, then if you have a soldering iron apply a light coating of solder.

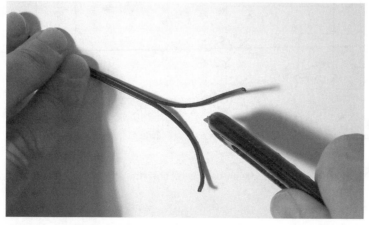

Figure 9–15   Slice the webbing between the two wires.

These wires need to be able to plug into the breadboard, but obviously they are too thick in the present form. I soldered tiny pins to the end of the wires. The pins were simply the leads snipped off from some spare resistors I had. You can also wrap a lead around the wire and squeeze it with pliers to make the connection. This is temporary so don't worry about neatness or permanence—we just need a quick and dirty connection.

Table 9–3 shows where all the components, wires, and jumpers plug into the breadboard. Jumpers are just small, ordinary wires used to bridge gaps in a circuit. I would recommend following along with the photos rather than using the table because some parts, such as the diodes, transistors, and capacitors, must be oriented correctly. Now we can begin plugging parts into the breadboard.

Table 9-3 Distance Sensor Breadboard Assembly

Wire	RCX positive	G1
Wire	RCX negative	D1
Jumper	5 long yellow	A1, ground
Jumper	5 long yellow	J1, positive
C1	1000-µF capacitor	C5, ground
D1	1N5819 Diode	E5, I5
Jumper	4 long orange	J5, positive
Jumper	3 long red	D5, D7
U1	LT1121IZ-5	C7, C8, C9
Jumper	5 long yellow	A8, ground
C2	100-µF capacitor	B9, ground
Q1	ZTX718	D9, D10, D11 (EBC)
R1	4.7K	A10, ground
Jumper	4 long orange	E10, F10
D2	1N4148	H10, positive
R2	330K	E11, E13
R3	82K	B13, ground
Q3	NTE199	D13, D14, D15 (BCE)
Jumper	4 long orange	B14, B17
Jumper	4 long orange	A15, ground

Table 9-3   Distance Sensor Breadboard Assembly (continued)

R5	1K	E16, G16
D3	1N4148	H16, positive
R4	47K	D18, G18
Q2	NTE234	C16, C17, C18
U2 Vo	GP2D12 yellow wire	H18
U2 gnd	GP2D12 black wire	Ground
U2 Vcc	GP2D12 red wire	B11

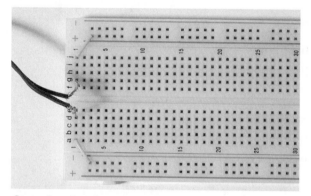

Step 1   Plug the RCX wire ends into D1 and G1. Also, connect jumpers to positive and ground.

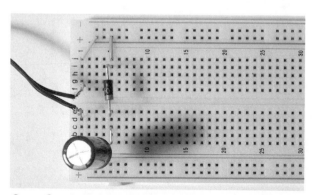

Step 2   Plug the capacitor in, with the negative (shorter) lead going to ground, and the positive (longer) wire going to C5. The 1N5819 Shottky diode will bridge the divide in the breadboard, going from E5 to I5. Make sure the band is facing toward the capacitor. Finally, a jumper connects the diode to the positive power.

Step 3   Insert U1 (LT1121IZ-5) into C7, 8, 9. Make sure the flat portion of the case faces toward ground. Attach a jumper from D5 to D7, and another from A8 to ground.

Step 4   Plug Q1 (ZTX718) into holes D9, 10, 11 (EBC). The white face of the transistor should face toward positive. Insert C2 from ground to B9, making sure the shorter (negative) lead is in ground.

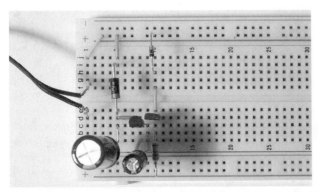

Step 5   Insert R1 (4.7K ohm resistor) from ground to A10. This connects the resistor to pin B of Q1. Insert a jumper across the divide from E10 to F10. Finally, insert D2 from H10 to positive, making sure the band is facing away from positive.

Step 6   Insert R2 (330K resistor) from E11 to E13. Insert R3 (82K resistor) from B13 to ground.

Step 7   Insert Q3 (NTE199) in holes D13, 14, 15 (BCE) with the flat side facing toward positive. Connect pin E to negative by placing a jumper from A15 to ground.

Step 8   Insert D3 (1N4148 diode) from positive to I16. Make sure the black band faces away from positive. Insert R5 (1K resistor) across the divide from G16 to D16. Finally, plug Q2 (NTE234) into pins C16, 17, 18 (ECB). The flat side should face ground.

Step 9   Insert resistor R4 (47K) from D18 to G18. Insert a jumper from B14 to B17 to connect the collectors of Q2 and Q3 together.

Step 10   Before attempting this step, try attaching the three wires (red, yellow, and black) to the GP2D12 as the instructions that come with the sensor indicate. You will need to wrap the ends of the wire to a lead so you can plug the wires into the breadboard. Now you can attach the GP2D12 sensor. Plug the red wire (Vcc) into C11. Plug the yellow wire (Vo) into H18. Finally, plug the black wire (Gnd) into ground.

Note:

Some GP2D12 sensors do not come with colored wires. If this is the case, check the pin out from the sensor (Vcc, Vo, and Gnd) and follow the wires to the circuit.

Test Code

Now that we've got our circuit assembled it's time to test it. The code we use simply changes between the two phases: charging and reading. These phases will alternate using 250 ms for charging and 50 ms for reading. The output will go straight to the LCD to verify our results. Let's examine the code:

```
1. import josx.platform.rcx.*;
2. public class DistanceTest implements SensorConstants {
3.
4.     private Sensor sharpSensor;
5.
6.     public DistanceTest(Sensor sharpPort) {
7.         sharpSensor = sharpPort;
8.         sharpSensor.setTypeAndMode(SENSOR_TYPE_RAW,
                SENSOR_MODE_RAW);
9.         sharpSensor.activate();
10.        // Initial charge:
11.        try{Thread.sleep(1000);}catch(Exception e){}
12.    }
13.
14.    public synchronized int getRaw() {
15.        // Charge capacitor:
16.        sharpSensor.activate();
17.        try{Thread.sleep(250);}catch(Exception e){}
18.
19.        // Read value:
20.        sharpSensor.passivate();
21.        try{Thread.sleep(50);}catch(Exception e){}
22.        int raw = Sensor.S1.readValue();
23.        return raw;
24.    }
25.
26.    public static void main(String [] args) {
27.        DistanceTest dt = new DistanceTest(Sensor.S1);
28.        while(true) {
29.            LCD.showNumber(dt.getRaw());
30.            Sound.beep();
31.        }
32.    }
33. }
```

This code is quite basic. First it sets the sensor to raw mode, and the type of readings as raw. Then a never-ending loop begins switching between the charging and reading phases. Charging is accomplished by using the activate() method. When 250 ms has elapsed the code uses passivate() to stop the current flow from the RCX, which causes the current to flow from the capacitor to the GP2D12 sensor. It waits 50 ms for the sensor to produce a value, then reads it and shows it on the LCD screen. If you get a value in the 300s when nothing is in front of the sensor and in the 700s when something is about 10 cm away, then your circuit is working fine! If not, the next section will help you get things working.

What If It Doesn't Work?

You've assembled the circuit, plugged it in, and uploaded the test code, but it doesn't work. Now what? This section attempts to go over some of the more common problems that can occur, starting with the simple fixes. If it still doesn't work, you could try taking some measurements with a multimeter to target the problem.

Does the LCD show raw readings hovering in the 1,020 range that don't seem to change when an object is close to the sensor? This indicates no readings are getting to the RCX brick, and this can be caused by a few simple problems. Your sensor wire is probably plugged into the wrong sensor port. The code expects it to be plugged into Input S1 so make sure it is plugged into Port 1.

Another problem that could cause this is if the positive and negative wire leads are mixed up. Try switching the two wires from the RCX brick that connect to the circuit. Alternately, you can rotate the connection on the RCX brick 180 degrees.

Are there any leads or wires touching each other in the circuit? Make sure components are not inadvertently contacting each other, causing a short circuit. Are all the components plugged all the way into the breadboard? It is rare for components not to make contact, but it does sometimes occur if they are not pushed in all the way.

The orientation of the components in the circuit is very important. Resistors can be oriented in any direction, so there is no need to check them. The rest of the components must have the correct orientation. Check your diodes against the schematic and make sure the colored band (black, sometimes silver) is facing the direction of the line in the diode symbol. Capacitors also have a positive and a negative lead, the positive lead being longer than the negative (the side of the capacitor also usually indicates which side is negative). Make sure the negative leads are connected to ground (negative). Transistors have three pins: base, collector, and emitter (BCE on the schematic). Check the transistor's packaging to identify these pins. If there is no diagram on the package, try doing a search on the Web for the part number—there are an abundance of specification sheets available online, and these usually have diagrams.

Do you get readings other than 1,020, possibly hovering around 950, that do not change when objects are in front of the sensor? Do they seem to jump around a bit? If this is the case, you probably have the transistors oriented wrong in the circuit. Once again, check the base, emitter, and collector and make sure they match the schematic.

Make sure you have the right components in the circuit. I ordered a package of 1K ohm resistors, but was accidently sent 1 ohm resistors. Luckily I noticed this as the component was going into the circuit, but it's worth double checking. Also, if you have replaced some components with other components not listed here, they are likely the culprits.

Are you getting a reaction from the sensor when objects are in front, but the range does not span the 300s to 700s (e.g., only 760 to 820)? This might be because your circuit is using alternate transistors. Sometimes electronics component sellers will tell you off-hand that any transistor will replace the one you need. This is sometimes true, but not in the case of this low-current circuit. Make sure you are using the proper parts listed for this circuit.

Still not working? Try double checking the position of all of the wires and components. I would suggest using the schematic to follow the entire circuit, starting with the positive sensor, and placing a check mark next to each wire or component to make sure it is properly assembled in the circuit. Also, make sure none of the components have been mixed up, such as a 330K resistor with a 82K resistor. If things are still not working, it might be a good idea to purchase a multimeter.

Multimeter Measurements

If you are reading up to this point then it is obvious the simple procedures listed already did not help. For this section you need a simple multimeter, available at most electronics components dealers for a low cost (Radio Shack sells them). The multimeter is able to read voltages, current, and resistance. These three measurements should be enough to determine where the problem may lie in your circuit. The multimeter contains two probes, usually red and black. The red probe is positive and the black probe is negative. To test the two phases of the circuit we need to use code that allows us to manually switch the circuit between charging and reading mode. The following code accomplishes this:

```
1. import josx.platform.rcx.*;
2. public class DistanceTest implements SensorConstants {
3.
4.     public static void main(String [] args) {
5.
```

```
6.        Sensor sharpSensor = Sensor.S1;
7.        sharpSensor.setTypeAndMode(SENSOR_TYPE_RAW,
                SENSOR_MODE_RAW);
8.        while(true) {
9.            // Charge capacitor:
10.           sharpSensor.activate();
11.           try{
12.               Button.RUN.waitForPressAndRelease();
13.               Sound.beep();
14.           }catch(InterruptedException ie){}
15.
16.           // Read value:
17.           sharpSensor.passivate();
18.           try{Thread.sleep(50);}catch(Exception e){}
19.           int raw = Sensor.S1.readValue();
20.           LCD.showNumber(raw);
21.           try{
22.               Button.RUN.waitForPressAndRelease();
23.               Sound.beepSequence();
24.           }catch(InterruptedException ie){}
25.       }
26.   }
27. }
```

Once this code is uploaded, sit down at a table with the circuit in front of you. To try to isolate the problem, first disconnect GP2D12 pin 3 (Point C on the schematic in Figure 9–16). Set your multimeter mode to voltmeter and the scale to 15 volts. Attach the negative lead to ground on the breadboard. Rather than holding it with your hand, I suggest coiling a wire around the end of the lead and plugging the wire into the ground row. Now both your hands are free and we are ready to start reading some values.

Start the program and the RCX will immediately go into charge mode. While it is in charge mode verify the voltages at Points A, B, and C . You should read 8.5 V at Point A (almost the same voltage as on RCX output), 5 V at Point B (this is the proper output from the voltage regulator), and almost 0 at Point C (transistor Q1 should be blocked so no voltage should register).

If A and B are okay but the voltage at Point C is 5 V instead of 0, check transistor Q1 and resistor R1. If A is okay but the voltage at Point B is not 5V (either 0 or 8.5 V), check the pin out of voltage regulator U1. It might be backward.

If A is too low, try to disconnect at Point B, then A. If it doesn't go up, check voltage at RCX (point H). If it is okay, there's probably a problem with diode D1. It should probably be reversed so the black band points in the

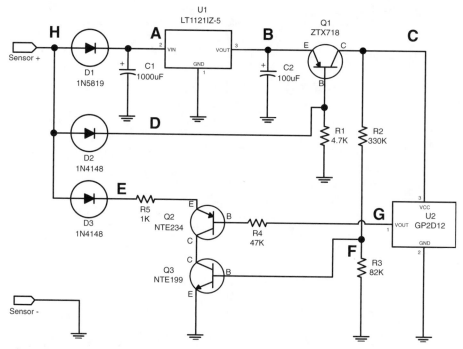

Figure 9-16 Troubleshooting points.

other direction. If not, something is using too much current. Try to disconnect Points D and E.

If all this works, hold the positive lead (red) of the multimeter to Point C and press the Run button on the RCX to switch to read phase. Point C should rise to 5 V then drop slowly as the capacitor loses its power. In case of a problem, check diode D2 and Q1 again.

If all is okay, measure the voltage at Point F in both charge and read modes. It should be 0 V in charge mode and 0.7 V in read mode.

Now, reconnect GP2D12 at Point C. While in charge mode there should be no difference with or without it attached because Q1 is blocked. Now if you switch to read mode, the voltage at Point C should rise to 5 V and decrease very rapidly. This is difficult to observe with a simple voltmeter but you should see the needle jump up, then fall back quite rapidly. You should also see some voltage at Point G (about 2 V without anything in front of the sensor), but again it will disappear very quickly.

Still having problems at this point? You might want to find someone knowledgeable about electronics to explain the situation. If all else fails there is always the option to purchase the complete interface online (see Appendix A).

Permanent Assembly

In this section we assemble the circuit onto a tiny punchboard (available at most electronic component stores). The board is less than one square inch (2.5 × 2.5 cm) so it will help if your hands are the size of a squirrel monkey's! Punchboard has a layout of holes, just like the breadboard and with the same spacing. Components are inserted into the holes and connected underneath the board using thin wire, connected with a wire-wrap tool. The completed layout will take the form of Figure 9–17. The underside of the circuit board is shown in Figure 9–18. Instead of using holes, the figure shows a 10 × 10 grid, with each square representing a hole of the punchboard. You can assemble the entire circuit using this diagram only, but it would probably be better to use the following steps along with the diagram for detail.

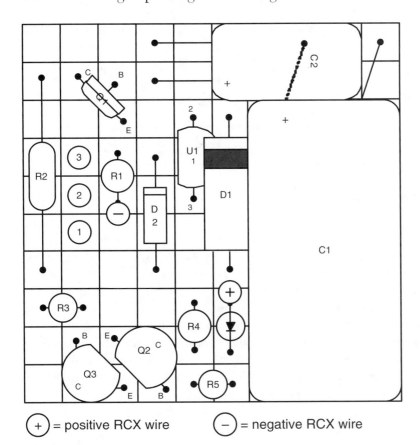

$\left(+\right)$ = positive RCX wire $\left(-\right)$ = negative RCX wire

Figure 9–17   Top side of the circuit board.

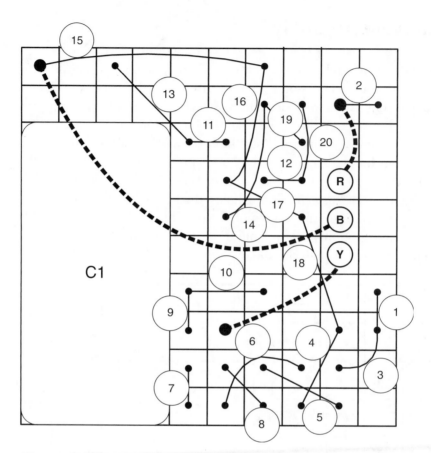

Figure 9-18 Underside of the circuit board.

A wire-wrap tool is excellent for connecting component leads together without making a mess. The wire-wrap tool itself looks a little like a screwdriver (Figure 9–19). It has the benefit of being inexpensive and easy to use. A thin piece of wire is inserted into the end of the tool, and it is placed over the end of the lead. The tool is rotated, which wraps the wire around the component lead (the wire-wrap tool should come with more detailed instructions). The wire-wrap tool can be your best friend when assembling small circuits. It is preferable to use wire-wrapping with square leads, not round ones, but it still works quite well with round leads. To make sure that connections are good and remain so, they can be soldered (optional).

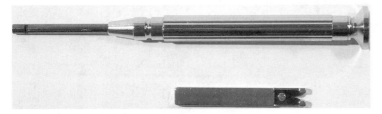

Figure 9–19 Wire-wrap tool.

Note:

Keep the component leads (resistors, transistors, diodes) about 1.5 cm (5/8 inch) long so the wire-wrap tool can spin freely on the lead. All leads should poke through the underside of the punchboard by approximately this distance (there's no need to be exact).

For this portion of the project you will need the following:

- A wire-wrap tool
- A sharp utility knife
- A piece of punchboard
- Needle-nose pliers
- A pencil

Any visions you might have of nice, clean soldered parts like you've seen on factory-assembled circuit boards should be completely tossed out. Unless you are a professional with hundreds of hours of experience, your board is going to look messy when you are done. The good news is that once the circuit is complete we will stuff it into some LEGO bricks so you won't be able to see it anyway!

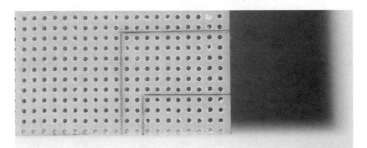

Step 1 Using a pencil, trace out an area of 10 × 10 holes in one corner of the punchboard. This will be the entire surface for the circuit. Within the square trace out an area of 4 × 8 holes. This is where the large capacitor will fit, because it takes up too much space if it rests on the surface.

Step 2   Using the utility knife, score the surface of the punchboard along the pencil outline. Start sliding the knife slowly over the line, and as a groove develops you can press harder. Do this for both sides of the punchboard. When you have scored both sides deep enough, use the needle-nose pliers to snap off the smaller piece.

Step 3   Sand down the rough edges. You may need to use the utility knife to trim away larger edges, but be careful of your fingers! The edges must clear enough room for the large capacitor.

Step 4   Snap off the entire square, first using the needle-nose pliers to bend along each of the scored lines. The edges should be sanded as close as possible to the holes to ensure the board will fit into the LEGO bricks

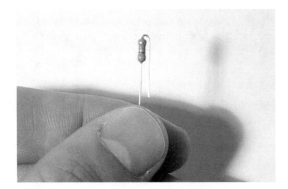

Step 5a   Take an 82K resistor (R3) and bend one lead all the way over (180 degrees). Using the needle-nose pliers can help, and make sure not to put too much pressure on the wire connection to the ceramic shell, or it might crack. The wire must be bent close to the body so it can fit in the LEGO brick.

R2

R3

Step 5b   Insert R3 into the board. Bend the leads of a 330K resistor (R2) 90 degrees and insert it into the board.

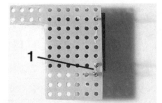

Step 5c   Connect a single wire between the bottom lead of R2 and the lead of R3 (see Figure 9–18 for clearer view).

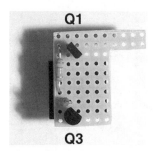

Step 6a   Insert Q3 into the board with the middle leg sticking out backward. Insert Q1 with the middle leg sticking out toward the top. For both of these components, double check Figure 9–17 to make sure the leads are in the correct position.

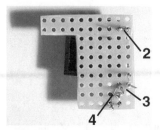

Step 6b   (2) Connect the top lead of R2 to Pin C of Q1. (3) Connect the right lead of R3 to Pin B of Q3. (4) Connect Pin E of Q3 to the other lead of R3.

Step 7a   Bend the middle pin of Q2 backward and insert opposite Q3 (it's a tight squeeze). Bend one lead of a 1K resistor (R5) 180 degrees and insert it into the board.

Step 7b   (5) Connect Pin C of Q2 to Pin C of Q3. (6) Connect Pin E of Q2 to the closest lead of R5 (see Figure 9–18 for better view).

Step 8a   Bend one lead of a 47K resistor (R4) 180 degrees and insert it into the board. With D3, bend the lead farthest from the black band 180 degrees and insert it into the board (check the schematic to make sure it is inserted in the correct direction).

Step 8b   (7) Connect the remaining lead of R5 to the lower lead of D3. (8) Connect lead B of Q2 to the lower lead of R4 (see Figure 9–18 for clearer view).

Step 9a   Insert D1 and D2, making sure the band is closer to the top of the circuit.

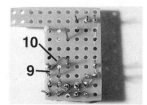

Step 9b   (9) Connect the remaining lead of D3 to the lower lead of D1. (10) Connect the lower lead of D1 to the lower lead of D2.

Step 10a   Bend one lead of a 4.7K resistor (R1) 180 degrees and insert it into the board. Insert U1 (LT1121IZ-5) into the board with the pins lined up (top to bottom) as follows: In (2), Gnd (1), Out (3).

Step 10b   (11) Connect the remaining lead of D1 to Pin 2 of U1 (the top pin). (12) Connect the upper lead of R1 to the remaining lead of D2.

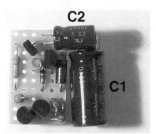

Step 11a   Bend the leads of C1 90 degrees and insert it into the board. The negative lead (shorter) must be to the right of the board. Make sure C1 lies about halfway under the board, otherwise it will not fit into the LEGO bricks. Insert C2 into the board and bend the leads 90 degrees so it rests over C1's leads. The negative lead must be closer to the top of the board.

Step 11b   (13) Connect the positive lead of C1 to D1. (14) Connect the positive lead of C2 to Pin 3 of U1.

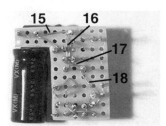

Step 12a   In this step we are going to connect the parts to ground. (15) Connect the negative lead of C1 to the negative lead of C2. (16) Connect the negative lead of C2 to Pin 1 (Gnd—the middle pin) of U1. (17) Connect Pin 1 of U1 to the lower pin of R1. (18) Connect R1 to R3 (see Figure 9–18).

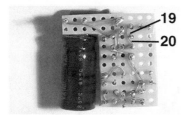

Step 12b   (19) Connect the positive lead of C2 to Pin E of Q1. (20) Connect Pin B of Q1 to R1.

That's it for the interface. The next few steps add the GP2D12 sensor and RCX input wires to the circuit. At this point I would recommend two things. First, lightly hook up the GP2D12 sensor and RCX brick and test out the circuit (Figures 9–17 and 9–18 show where these connections go). Second, look ahead to see how the circuit will fit into the brick. This will help you understand why the board is so small, and how the GP2D12 is hooked up and attached to the front of the brick.

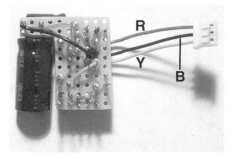

Step 13   Before doing this step you might want to slice off the two appendages on each side of the GP2D12 sensor. Carefully score each side of the appendage close to the sensor, and when it is deep enough try breaking them off. Sand or carve away any plastic edges. Once this is done, insert the red, black, and yellow wires through the holes on the top side of the circuit (see Figure 9–17). Leaving only about 2.25 cm (7/8 inch) of wire to the white clip, tie knots in each of the wires. Estimate the distances to each connection, and clip the wires to the appropriate lengths. Strip the ends of each wire, leaving about 0.5 cm (1/4 inch). Wrap the wires around the appropriate terminal (see Figure 9–18). I used a wire-wrap tool to wrap it, but you can use a soldering iron if you prefer. Now that everything is hooked up you can cut the lengths of the component leads right down to the wires. When doing this, keep in mind the leads must be short enough so the circuit fits into a 2 × 4 brick.

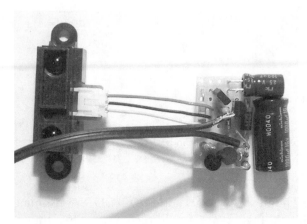

Step 14   Attach the sensor by plugging it into the white connector. Take the RCX wire and cut it down to about 22 cm (8 1/2 inches). Strip the ends of the wire and attach one end to R1 and the other to D3 (see Figure 9–17). Wrap the wire around itself and if you have a soldering iron, solder the wires so they are secure.

Note:

The wires from the RCX wire brick are either positive or negative. It doesn't really matter which end is connected, however, because the connection to the RCX input port can be rotated 180 degrees to get the correct polarity. If you would like the brick wire to face upward, however, you should test the circuit on the RCX before moving on.

Enclosing the Circuit

Now that you have the circuit assembled, it is time to enclose it in LEGO bricks. These bricks will be cut up and glued together, which sometimes makes LEGO owners cringe because the RIS kit will be a few parts short. If you don't want to use these parts, you can order additional parts from LEGO (see Appendix A), which gives you the advantage of choosing the color of the bricks. You might want to stick with blue for the enclosing shell and dark gray for the bottom plate, which is standard for LEGO active sensors. The parts and tools needed are as follows:

- Three 2 × 4 bricks (any color)
- One 2 × 4 plate (any color)
- Molecular bonding agent (such as Krazy Glue)
- Utility knife
- Needle nose pliers

Step 1 With two of the 2 × 4 bricks, score the top of the brick all the way around the edges, going around the studs (Figure 9–20). Flip the brick over and extend the utility knife so it is about 3/4 inch long. Cut the inner appendages so the inner cylinders are not attached to the sides of the brick. With enough scoring, the top should be able to pop out. Use the utility knife to remove any unevenness from the edges of the brick and be careful not to cut your fingers!

Note:

It would be a good idea to try sliding the circuit board through the brick opening at this stage to ensure there is enough clearance.

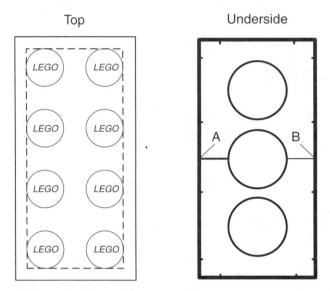

Top   Underside

Figure 9–20   Scoring lines of 2 × 4 brick.

Step 2   For the third brick, make cuts at Point A and Point B of Figure 9–21, and also slice each of the cylinders into quarters. Be very careful not to slice through the top of the brick. Using the needle-nose pliers, pull the debris from the brick. Keep picking at the inside of the brick with the pliers until everything is removed.

Underside

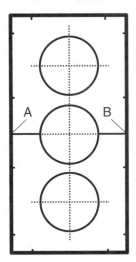

Figure 9–21 Slicing the cylinders into quarters.

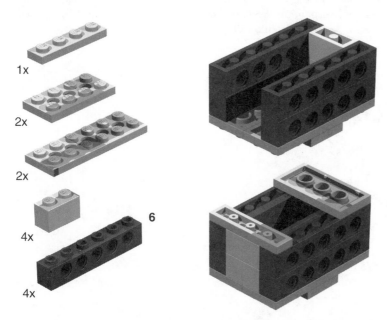

1x

2x

2x

4x

4x

6

Step 3 In this step we glue the bricks together. Start with the top brick (the one with studs on top) and the middle brick (a hollow brick). Create a vise out of LEGO bricks as shown in the diagram, and place the two bricks within it. Apply a drop of glue to all four sides on the inside of the brick so glue drips don't ruin the exterior. Allow to dry and repeat for the bottom brick.

Caution:

The glue is very fluid. Try to use small drops only, and you might want to consider protecting the vise by placing wax paper or thin plastic (from plastic bags) along the inside of the vise.

Step 4   Cut two notches in the bottom brick for the wires. The notches should be just wide enough for the three sensor wires (front) and the RCX wire (back). Carefully squeeze the circuit into the bricks. You may need to adjust some parts or trim leads a little shorter to make it fit.

Step 5   Glue the sensor to the front of the bricks, about halfway between the top brick and the middle brick. Make sure to apply pressure and allow enough time for the glue to bond.

Step 6 The bottom plate will need to have parts of the studs removed to allow the circuit to fit. Using the utility knife, slice the studs in half, as shown in Figure 9–22, and remove the *inner half* of each stud. Test fit the plate before gluing it on. With the sensor complete, we can now move on to some more interesting projects!

Top

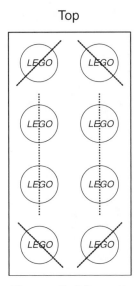

Figure 9-22 Studs must be trimmed to allow the plate to fit.

Programming the Proximity Sensor Driver

In this section we'll program an easy-to-use class to obtain distance readings from the proximity sensor. We could just as easily use raw values but it is more meaningful to retrieve actual distance measurements from the sensor, in millimeters. So how can we calculate distance from the raw values? By using the following equation:

```
distance = 10000/(m * raw + b)
```

For now, ignore the meaning of the equation. It is described in the calibration section for those who want more accurate readings. I previously calculated the *m* and *b* values for my sensor as follows:

```
m = 0.2436
b = -78.016
```

The *raw* variable will of course be supplied by the sensor. Now that we have our calculation figured out, let's see how the previous test code can be adapted to produce distance measurements:

```
1. import josx.platform.rcx.*;
2.
3. public class DistanceSensor implements SensorConstants {
4.
5.     // The following are obtained by graphing distance vs.
            raw:
6.     private static final float M = 0.2436f;
7.     private static final float B = -78.016f;
8.     private static final float OFFSET = 0f;
9.     private static final int CHARGE_TIME = 250;
10.
11.     private Sensor sharpSensor;
12.
13.     public DistanceSensor(Sensor sharpPort) {
14.         sharpSensor = sharpPort;
15.         sharpSensor.setTypeAndMode(SENSOR_TYPE_RAW,
                SENSOR_MODE_RAW);
16.         sharpSensor.activate();
17.         try{Thread.sleep(1000);}catch(Exception e){}
18.     }
19.
20.     public synchronized int getDistance() {
21.         // Charge capacitor:
22.         sharpSensor.activate();
23.         try{Thread.sleep(CHARGE_TIME);}catch(Exception e){}
24.
25.         // Read value:
26.         sharpSensor.passivate();
27.         try{Thread.sleep(50);}catch(Exception e){}
28.         int raw = sharpSensor.readValue();
29.         double dist = 10000/(M*raw+B)+OFFSET;
```

```
30.        return (int)dist;
31.    }
32. }
```

This code is almost identical to our test code except it converts the raw value to a distance. There is no main method because this is just the sensor driver, so we need a small piece of test code to start things off:

```
1. import josx.platform.rcx.*;
2. public class Test {
3.    public static void main(String [] args) {
4.        DistanceSensor ds = new DistanceSensor(Sensor.S1);
5.        while(true) {
6.            LCD.showNumber(ds.getDistance());
7.            Sound.beep();
8.        }
9.    }
10. }
```

Try this code with your sensor to test the accuracy. Use a ruler to measure off distances from objects at several key intervals, such as 100, 200, 400, 600, and 800 mm. In most cases it will be within 20 mm at close distances and within 200 mm at far distances.

The problem is that variations in the electrical components cause the readings to differ from one circuit to another. Resistors and other components have certain tolerances, so a resistor that is 100K ohms ±5% could be 95K ohms or 105K ohms. These differences account for slight changes in the readings. If you are not satisfied with the readings produced by the preceding code, you will have to determine the proper m and b values, which are demonstrated in the next section.

Calibration

To properly calibrate a distance sensor it is necessary to gather data produced by your sensor. Let's examine the raw numbers produced by the sensor from various distances (Table 9–4).

The raw value readings were recorded as an object moved at 5-cm increments from the sensor. No sensor readings will work within 10 cm, as the design of the GP2D12 states, so the closest data point is 10 cm. The data was graphed (Figure 9–23) and as you can see, the relationship between distance and raw values is inverse; that is, as distance increases, the raw value decreases. Also, when the object is far away from the sensor the raw values hardly change. This means readings are much more precise at close distances. As one final characteristic, the curve is nonlinear. If you have a

Table 9-4 Distance vs. Raw Values

Distance	Raw Value
10	727
15	599
20	526
25	486
30	458
35	438
40	423
45	410
50	402
55	395
60	388
65	381
70	377
75	377
80	369
85	372

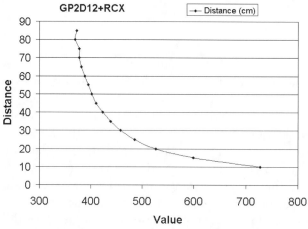

Figure 9–23 Raw value vs. distance.

spreadsheet program such as Microsoft Excel, you will be able to use this data to create a scatter graph that will display the slope and *y*-intercept automatically.

Remember the equation we used earlier? We can modify it slightly by adding an additional variable, offset, as follows:

```
distance = 10000/(m*raw + b) + offset
```

where:

```
m = slope
b = the y axis intercept
offset = subjective adjustment of values
```

This equation is the product of the famous Cartesian equation taught in high school:

```
y = mx + b
```

This equation is used to represent a straight line on a graph, known as a *linear curve*. The GP2D12 sensor produces a nonlinear curve, so we need to linearize the curve by calculating the inverse of the *y* axis numbers. The raw value readings will remain unchanged on the *x* axis, but the distance values will be replaced by using:

```
y = 1000/distance
```

The linearized curve is shown in Figure 9–24.

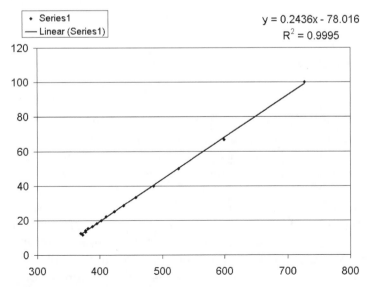

Figure 9–24   Linearized data.

This curve was created by choosing the best fit for a line through the plotted points. Once we have this we can pick out slope (m) and y intercept (b) from the graph. Slope is calculated by taking any two points on the graph, and calculating the change in y value divided by the change in x:

```
m = (y'- y)/(x' - x)
m = (50 - 25)/(526-423)
m = 0.2427
```

Once the slope is calculated it is easy to calculate b, the intercept with the y axis. Take any point on the curve that lies on the line. I'll use the location where y is 50 and x (raw) is 526. We already know m, so substitute all these numbers into our equation to find b:

```
y = mx + b
50 = 0.2427 * 526 + b
b = 50 - 0.2427 * 526
b = -77.6602
```

Offset is the final number in the equation. Try setting it to 0, and plug m and b into the preceding code. Now measure distances, and if the readings appear to be slightly high or low, adjust the offset variable accordingly. Hopefully, once you have performed these calculations your readings will be more accurate.

A Wall Follower

A wall follower is one of the classic robot projects hobbyists like to attempt because it is an interesting way to interact with the environment. The goal of the robot is to stay the same distance from the wall at all times (Figure 9–25). Robots using a differential drive (e.g., Tippy and Trilobot) are not really optimal for this type of exercise because they can only make sharp turns, but don't have much control over gradual turns. Analog steering, on the other hand, can do any range of turns, from sharp to extremely gradual. This ability comes in handy because if the robot wanders only slightly closer to the wall, a slight turn is optimal to straighten out. If it is much too close to the wall, however, then a sharp turn is required. So for this project we use a new robot called Philo that uses analog steering.

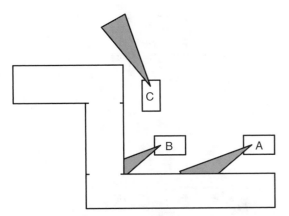

Figure 9–25 Wall following.

Philo Chassis

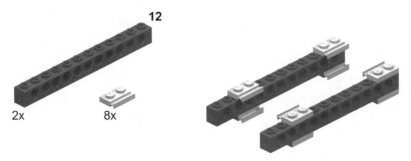

Step 1 The drive motor and the steering motor are both mounted on two 12-unit beams. Attach eight 1 × 2 plates with door rails.

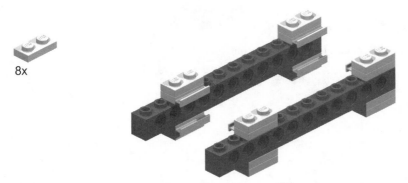

Step 2 Place 1 × 2 plates above and below each pair of door rails.

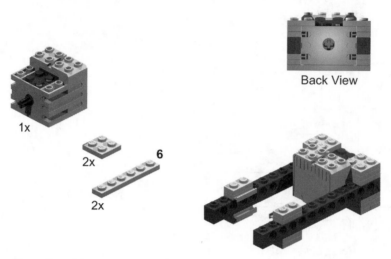

Back View

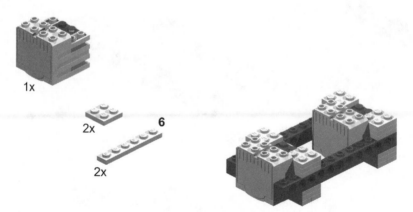

Step 3   Slide a motor onto the door rails, and secure it using square plates on the top, and 6-unit plates on the bottom. (1 × 6 plates are used instead of 2 × 6 plates because the 2 × 6 plates are in limited supply and will be needed later.)

Step 4   Slide the second motor in place and lock it in.

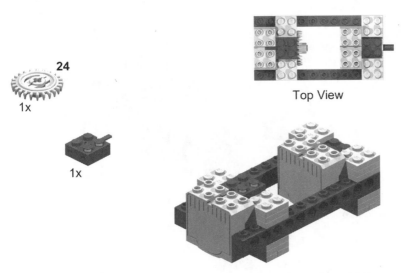

Top View

Step 5   Attach a crown gear to the rear motor and attach an RCX wire to the motor, with the wire facing through the groove in the motor.

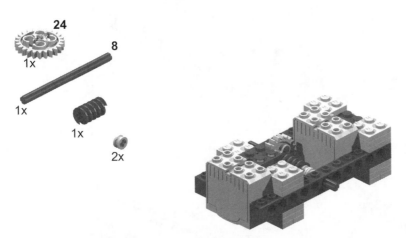

Step 6   The gear train for the steering uses a worm screw. Insert an 8-unit axle and add the following components, from left to right: a 24-tooth gear, a worm screw, and two half bushes. Half bushes were used instead of a Technic bush because there is a slight gap which causes the worm gear to slide a bit, causing the steering to be a little loose. Using two half bushes, a space can be made in the middle to prevent the screw from sliding (it might help to assemble this first to understand the explanation).

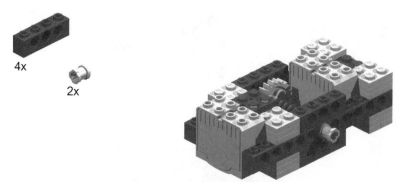

Step 7   Place Technic bushes on the end of the axles. These are used as finger handles to straighten the wheel, not to hold the axle in place. Place 1 × 4 bricks above and below the frame.

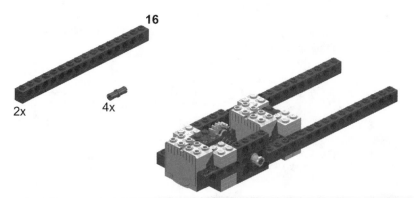

Step 8   Attach two 16-unit beams to the frame. The friction pins are inserted in the first and fourth holes.

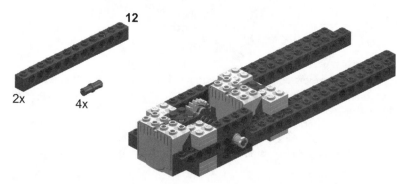

Step 9   Attach two 12-unit beams to the inside of the 16-unit beams. The friction pins go in the second and eleventh holes.

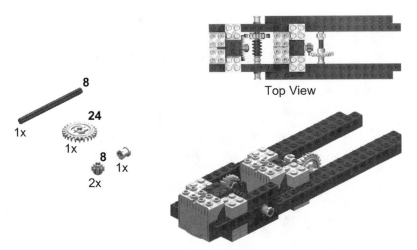

Top View

Step 10   Attach an 8-tooth gear to the second motor. Insert an 8-unit axle into the chassis and attach a Technic bush, a crown gear, and another 8-tooth gear.

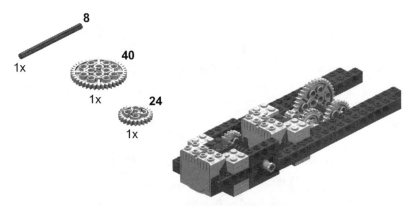

Step 11   The speed of the robot must be slowed down because the distance sensor can only take a reading every 300 ms. To accomplish this the model uses gear reduction. Insert an 8-unit axle into the frame and add a 40-tooth gear to the left and a 24-tooth gear to the right.

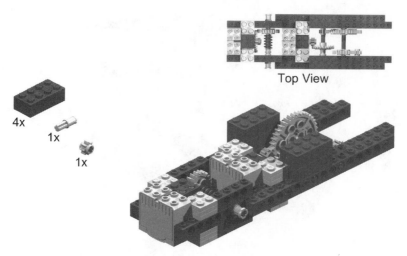

Step 12   Add an 8-tooth idler gear to interlock with the 24-tooth gear. Add four 2 × 4 bricks that will support the RCX brick.

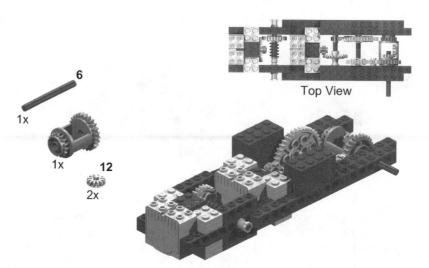

Step 13   This model is front wheel drive and uses a differential drive so it can execute sharp turns. When making a turn, one wheel will turn faster than the other. (Without this differential the tires will skid and the model will jump around when making turns.) Assemble the first half of the differential.

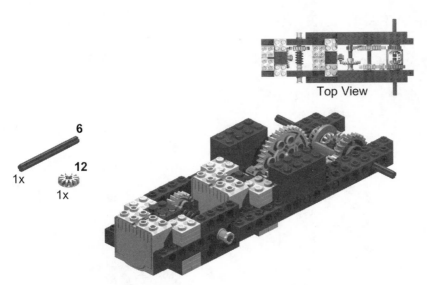

Step 14   Assemble the remainder of the differential drive.

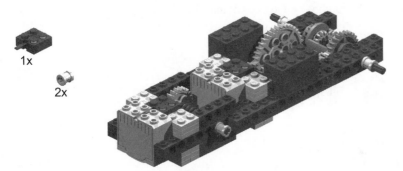

Step 15   Attach Technic bushes to the end of the axles. Wheels will be added to these later. Attach an RCX wire to the motor with the wire going through the groove of the motor.

Rear Wheel

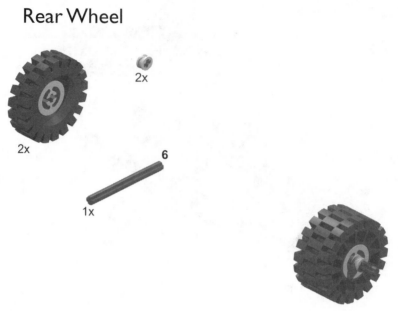

Step 1   Sandwich two large hard plastic wheels together, with the outside of the tires facing inward. Place halfbushes on the ends of the axle.

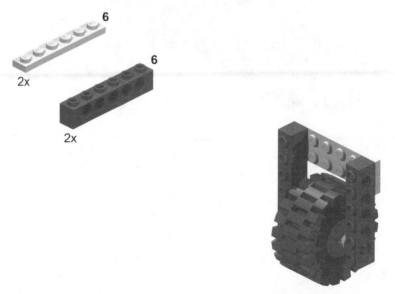

Step 2   The wheel will rotate on two 6-unit beams. Secure them with two 1 × 6 plates.

Green

1x

2x

Step 3   Add a 1 × 2 brick with axle hole to support the steering column, and two 1 × 2 bricks on each side.

8

1x

2x

Step 4   Insert the axle into the axle hole and secure it in place with two halfbushes.

6

2x

Step 5   Cap the assembly with two 1 × 6 plates. This adds enormous strength to the wheel support.

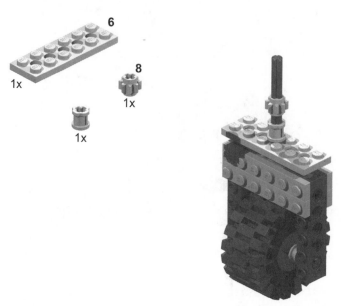

Step 6   Slide the axle through a 2 × 6 plate and secure it with a Technic bush. Make sure the round side of the bush faces down. Slide an 8-tooth gear onto the axle.

Final Assembly

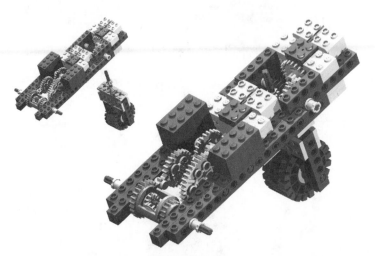

Step 1   Attach the rear wheel to the chassis. The 2 × 6 plate on the wheel should attach to the frame, and the 8-tooth gear should mesh with the worm screw.

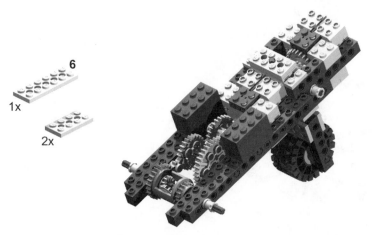

Step 2   Secure the wheel with a single 2 × 6 plate and two 2 × 4 plates. The axle should be just level with the top of the last plate, because the RCX brick will rest on this.

Step 3   Attach motorcycle wheels to the chassis.

Step 4   Attach the RCX brick to the chassis and attach the wires. The rear motor that steers is attached to Port C with the wire facing outward. The drive motor wire should poke out of the space in the middle of the chassis, and attaches to Port A facing outward.

Step 5   Lock down the RCX brick using two lift arms.

Sensor Mount

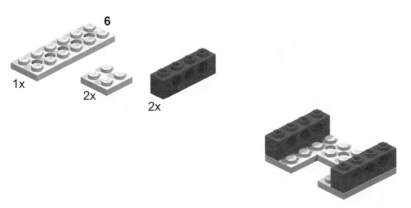

Step 1   The base of the sensor mount will rest right on top of the RCX brick.

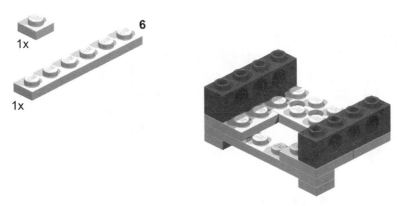

Step 2   Clip on the legs to the bottom of the structure.

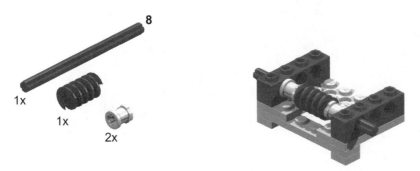

Step 3   Add a worm screw to an 8-unit axle and secure with two Technic bushes on either side.

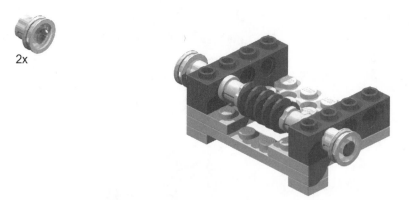

Step 4   Add two pulley wheels as finger handles to adjust the sensor angle.

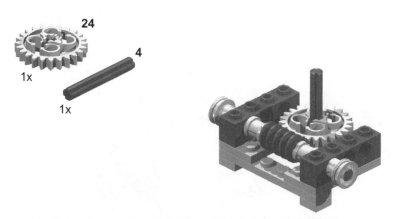

Step 5   Insert a 24-tooth gear onto a 4-unit axle. Insert the axle through the center hole in the 2 × 6 plate. Don't worry if it doesn't turn freely at this point.

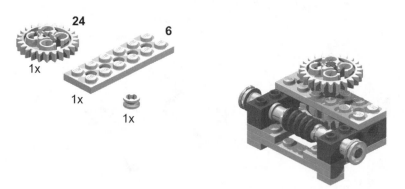

Step 6   Snap a 2 × 6 plate over the axle and place a half bush and a 24-tooth gear on the end of the axle. The axle should not protrude above the top of the gear.

4x

Step 7   Snap four half-pins into the gear. The studs on the end of the pins will serve as attachment points for the sensor.

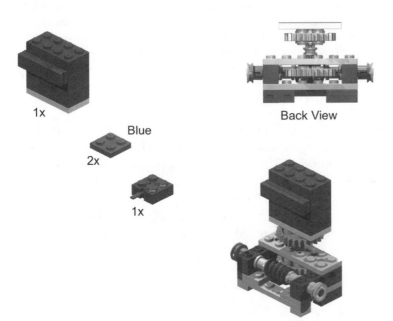

1x

Blue
2x

1x

Back View

Step 8   Attach the wire of the distance sensor to the bottom of the structure. The wire should go out the front under the legs, around the right, and then snap the sensor to the top of the gear. Add two 2 × 2 plates for the other leg.

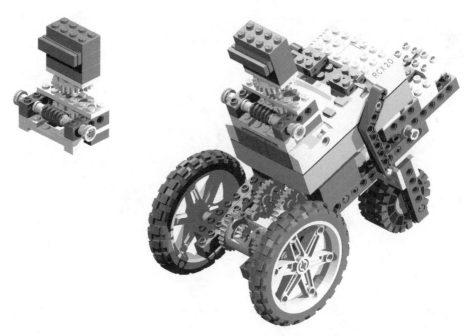

Step 9 Attach the sensor mount to the top of the brick. The sensor wire should attach to input Port 1. Turn the finger knobs on the side of the sensor to rotate the sensor so it is angled 45 degrees to the left. Adjust the finger screws on the rear wheel so it is straight (this will need to be readjusted each time the program is executed).

Programming Philo

Now that we have a robot, Philo, let's program it to follow a wall. The strategy of Philo is to stay a consistent distance from the wall. The constants we'll use are midway between 300 mm and 470 mm. If the robot is a small distance off this track, the wheel will make a shallow turn. If the robot is a large distance off (either too close or too far), it will make a sharp turn. The analog steering works well with this sensor because the sensor reading is essentially analog, too—a constant range of numbers from 100 mm to 800 mm. Let's examine the code for Philo:

```
1. import josx.platform.rcx.*;
2. public class WallFollower {
3.
4.     public static int position = 0;
5.     // Millis it takes to turn steering to extreme:
6.     public static final int FULL_TURN = 300;
7.
```

```
8.    // Range to stay in
9.    public static final int FARTHEST = 470;
10.   public static final int CLOSEST = 300;
11.   public static final int MIDTH = (FARTHEST+CLOSEST)/2;
12.
13.
14.   public static void main(String [] args) {
15.
16.       DistanceSensor ds = new DistanceSensor(Sensor.S1);
17.       Motor.A.forward();
18.       while(true) {
19.           int dist = ds.getDistance();
20.           LCD.showNumber(dist);
21.           float percent = (dist - MIDTH)/((FARTHEST-CLOSEST)/2);
22.           int steering = (int)(percent * FULL_TURN);
23.           turnTo(steering);
24.       }
25.   }
26.
27.   public static void turnTo(int toPos) {
28.
29.       // Make sure steering doesn't over steer
30.       if(toPos > 300)
31.           toPos = 300;
32.       else if(toPos < -300)
33.           toPos = -300;
34.
35.       int delay = toPos - position;
36.       if(delay < 0)
37.           Motor.C.forward();
38.       else
39.       if(delay > 0)
40.           Motor.C.backward();
41.       else
42.           return;
43.       try {
44.           Thread.sleep(Math.abs(delay));
45.       } catch(Exception e) {}
46.       Motor.C.stop();
47.       position = toPos;
48.   }
49. }
```

Through experimentation I determined it takes about 300 ms for the wheel to rotate from center to an extremely sharp left or right turn (Line 7). Lines 20 to 23 determine which position the wheel should be in (0 for center,

–300 for extreme left, +300 for extreme right). The turnTo() method calculates the current position of the steering wheel, then takes the difference from the position it should turn to. It rotates the motor, delays the appropriate time, then stops the motor. It's a pretty simple program. Try placing Philo close to a wall and letting it go.

Note:

The wheel must be straightened out using the finger knobs (Technic bushes) before starting the code.

Warning:

If the sensor readings become erratic when motors are hooked up to the RCX, the batteries are likely a little low. As previously mentioned, the capacitor has no problem charging in 250 ms with no motors hooked up to the RCX. However, when two motors are pulling current from the batteries there is not much left for the sensor. There are two ways to resolve this: recharge or replace the batteries, or increase the capacitor charge time to about 350 ms (or more, depending on battery level) in the DistanceSensor class.

It would be nice for this robot to move more speedily, but due to the delay between readings it sometimes manages to get itself into a bad position where it is on a collision course with the wall. For this reason Philo must move very slowly.

You may find it necessary to adjust the sensor angle if you find the robot crashes into a wall before executing the turn. Try rotating it closer to center if this happens. Also, you can play around with the Farthest and Closest constants to determine the distance it stays from the wall.

That's it for the wall follower, but there are many more projects the distance sensor can be used for, given a clever mind.

NAVIGATION WITH A COMPASS SENSOR

Topics in this Chapter

Chapter 10

The main problem encountered in the navigation strategies used up to this point is the cumulative effect of small errors that occur when estimating position. It only takes a few minutes of travel before the robot has no real idea of where it is. In Chapter 8, "Navigation with Rotation Sensors," we took accuracy one step further by using rotation sensors to estimate travel and keep the robot straight. This was a substantial improvement in accuracy but still susceptible to the cumulative effect from tiny errors, especially when it comes to knowing the direction the robot is facing. It would be ideal if there was a directional sensor available that would still be accurate after traveling for hundreds of meters. There is no such ready-made sensor available for the RCX on the market, but this chapter shows how to build an electronic compass that can be used with the RCX. With this compass, you can even lift up the robot and turn it around and it will be able to recover its current heading, making it much more reliable, especially after several minutes of travel.

The Compass Sensor

At the heart of this project is an electronic analog compass sensor. This sensor is available from two different companies under two different names.

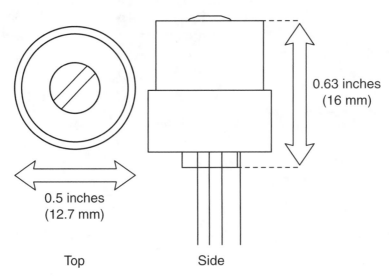

0.63 inches
(16 mm)

0.5 inches
(12.7 mm)

Top   Side

Figure 10–1   The compass sensor.

European readers will be able to obtain the 6100 sensor from Pewatron, and North American readers can obtain the 1655 sensor from Dinsmore (see Appendix B for details). Both of these models are identical in every characteristic, including shape, size, and pin configuration (Figure 10–1), so there is no need to worry about incompatibilities with the interface or code.

According to the documentation for the sensor, it contains a miniature rotor on sapphire bearings holding a compass magnet. For optimal accuracy, the sensor must be kept within two degrees of vertical. The compass sensor is dampened, so there is no overswing when it rotates. Regular magnetic sensors often take a long time to settle down after a rotation, bouncing back and forth until homing in on the proper angle. With damping, a viscous fluid surrounds the needle to negate this effect, but it also makes the compass slower to reach a final angle. When the compass is rotated 90 degrees it can take 2.5 to 3.5 seconds for the compass to reach the proper reading. This factor must be accounted for when programming a driver for the compass sensor. If our robot makes a sudden rotation it is not useful to take a compass reading until about 3 seconds have elapsed—a little slow, but still useful for navigation.

Note:

The sensor is designed to operate in a vertical position with leads down. Pewatron offers a special edition that can operate with leads up, but it must be specified when ordering. Sensors can also be supplied without damping.

Theory of Calculating Direction

The compass sensor produces two separate output signals, in the form of fluctuating voltage levels, depending on which direction the sensor is in. (The RCX interprets voltage levels as raw values between 0 and 1,023, but for now we just examine the voltage levels.) These signals form sine waves, each out of phase from the other by 90 degrees (Figure 10–2). This produces a sine wave and a cosine wave. You might wonder why we can't just use one signal to determine direction. Looking at Figure 10–2, if we have a voltage of 2.5 volts then it indicates the compass is facing 90 degrees (north), but 2.5 volts also indicates 270 degrees (south), so there is some question over which direction the compass is facing. The other sine wave can act as a designator of the correct direction. By looking at the other sine wave it is possible to determine the true direction. If the cosine signal is 2.5 volts, and the sine signal is 1.9 volts, we can immediately tell the true direction is 270 degrees.

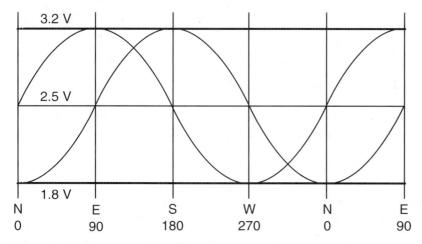

Figure 10–2   Sinusoidal waves produced by the compass sensor.

Building the Compass Interface

The complete schematic for the compass interface is shown in Figure 10–3. At first glance this looks quite complicated, but actually the circuit is composed of two identical circuits. Each half of the circuit has its own separate power supply, and attaches to different pins of the compass sensor.

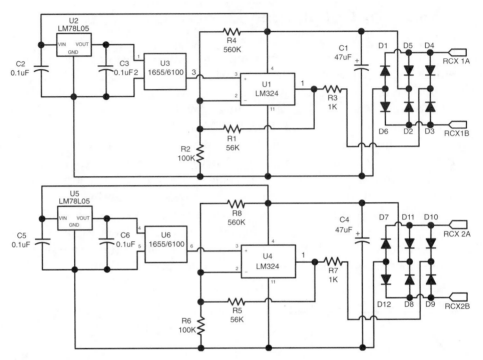

Figure 10–3 Compass sensor schematic. (Circuit designed by Claude Baumann.)

The parts for assembling the compass sensor interface are quite easy to find, especially when ordering online. Most of the parts are industry standard, so they are produced by multiple vendors and availability should not pose a problem. All of these components (except for the compass sensor itself) are extremely inexpensive. Just to be safe, I recommend buying at least double the amount needed in case some parts are damaged or destroyed during assembly. For building the interface you will need the following (see Appendix B for ordering details):

- (1) Pewatron 6100 or Dinsmore 1655 Compass Sensor
- (2) LM78L05 three-terminal positive voltage regulators in TO-92 casing
- (2) LM324 low-power quad operational amplifiers
- (2) 1K resistors, 1/4 watt, 5% tolerance
- (2) 56K resistors, 1/4 watt, 5% tolerance
- (2) 100K resistors, 1/4 watt, 5% tolerance
- (2) 560K resistors, 1/4 watt, 5% tolerance
- (4) 0.1 μF (microfarad) 50-V electrolytic capacitors

- (2) 47 µF 25-V electrolytic capacitors
- (12) 1N4148 diodes

Note:

Both Pewatron and Dinsmore market another analog compass sensor that is almost identical to the 6100/1655 sensors. The Pewatron 6070 or the Dinsmore 1525 will work for this project, but the signal produced by these only swings from about 2.1 volts to 2.9 volts (about 0.75 volts). The 6100/1655 signal, on the other hand, swings from about 1.8 volts to 3.2 volts (about 1.3 volts) so it provides better resolution.

Tools

The basic tools required for this project are as follows:

- Soldering iron
- Wire-wrap tool
- Breadboard
- Jumpers
- Wire cutters
- Wire strippers
- Multimeter (optional)

Circuit Assembly

In this section we assemble the circuit on a breadboard. Table 10–1 and Table 10–2 describe the row and column numbers to plug the components into, but you can also follow along with the assembly instructions (recommended) or assemble it straight from the schematic (Figure 10–3). Once the circuit is confirmed working, you have several options: keep using it on the breadboard, transfer the parts to an experimenter board, reconstruct the circuit on punchboard, or more experienced users can even professionally etch the circuit on PC board (see Appendix B for details). My favorite of these three options is using the punchboard with a wire-wrap tool because it takes up a small amount of space but it is relatively easy to assemble. The completed circuit can be enclosed in LEGO bricks, although it is quite large and ungainly.

Note:

If your breadboard only has a single row for positive and one for negative then you will only be able to assemble half the circuit at a time. You can also buy separate positive–negative modules for the breadboard that plug together.

Table 10-1 Breadboard Components for Circuit A

D1	1N4148	B4, negative
D2	1N4148	J3, positive
D3	1N4148	H2, H3
D4	1N4148	D2, F2
D5	1N4148	J4, positive
D6	1N4148	B3, negative
R3	1K	G2, F5
Jumper	4 long (orange)	E3, F3
Jumper	4 long (orange)	E4, F4
Jumper	3 long (red)	C1, C4
C1	47µF	E6, F6
Jumper	4 long (orange)	J6, positive
Jumper	5 long (yellow)	B6, negative
U1	LM324	F7 TO F13, E7 TO E13
Jumper	4 long (orange)	J10, positive
Jumper	5 long (yellow)	B10, negative
Jumper	9 long (gray)	G5, G13
Jumper	3 long (red)	H12, H14
Jumper	5 long (yellow)	H11, H15
R2	100K	D14, G14

Table 10-1 Breadboard Components for Circuit A (continued)

R4	560K	J14, positive
R1	56K	I13, I14
Jumper	5 long (yellow)	A14, negative
U2	78L05	G17, G18, G19
C2	0.1μF	F17, E17
C2	0.1μF	F19, E19
Jumper	4 long (orange)	J19, positive
Jumper	11 long (brown)	F16, negative
Jumper	5 long (yellow)	B17, negative
Jumper	11 long (brown)	F18, negative
Jumper	5 long (yellow)	B19, negative
U3	Compass sensor (1/2)	J15, J16, J17
Wire	RCX Sensor 1A	D3
Wire	RCX Sensor 1B	G4

Table 10-2 Breadboard Components for Circuit B

D7	1N4148	I36, negative
D8	1N4148	B37, positive
D9	1N4148	C37, C38
D10	1N4148	E38, G38
D11	1N4148	B36, positive
D12	1N4148	I37, negative
R7	1K	D38, E35
Jumper	4 long (orange)	E36, F36
Jumper	4 long (orange)	E37, F37

Table 10-2 Breadboard Components for Circuit B (continued)

Jumper	3 long (red)	H36, H38
C4	47μF	E34, F34
Jumper	5 long (yellow)	A34, positive
Jumper	6 long (green)	I34, negative
U4	LM324	E27 to E33, F27 to F33
Jumper	5 long (yellow)	A30, positive
Jumper	6 long (green)	I30, negative
Jumper	9 long (gray)	D27, D35
Jumper	3 long (red)	C26, C28
Jumper	5 long (yellow)	C25, C29
R6	100K	D26, G26
R8	560K	A26, positive
R5	56K	B26, B27
Jumper	6 long (green)	J26, negative
U5	78L05	D21, D22, D23
C5	0.1μF	E21, F21
C6	0.1μF	E23, F23
Jumper	5 long (yellow)	A21, positive
Jumper	12 long (2 green)	E22, negative
Jumper	5 long (yellow)	J21, negative
Jumper	12 long (2 green)	E24, negative
Jumper	5 long (yellow)	J23, negative
U6	Compass sensor (1/2)	A23, A24, A25
Wire	RCX Sensor 2A	G37
Wire	RCX Sensor 2B	D36

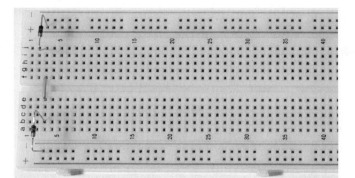

Step 1 Plug a 1N4148 diode into J3 and positive. Make sure the black band of the diode is on the same side as the positive lead. Plug another 1N4148 diode into B3 and negative, with the black band of the diode on the same side as the B3 hole. Insert a jumper from E3-F3 to bridge the gap.

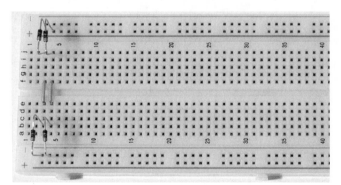

Step 2 Insert a row of components identical to Step 1 in the next column.

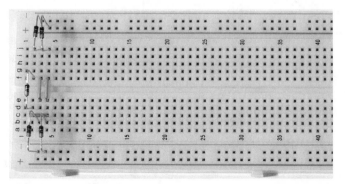

Step 3 Insert a 1N4148 diode across the gap, from D2 to F2. The black band of the diode should be closest to F2. Insert a jumper from C2 to C4.

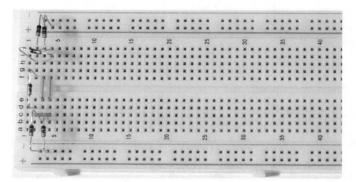

Step 4   Insert a diode from H2 to H3 with the band closest to H2.

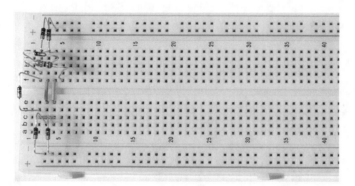

Step 5   Insert a 1K (R3) resistor from G2 to F5.

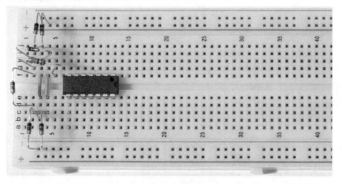

Step 6   Insert LM324 (U1) across the bridge as shown. One end of U1 has a small half-circle indentation that should face right.

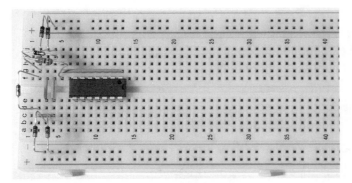

Step 7   Connect a long jumper from G5 to G13.

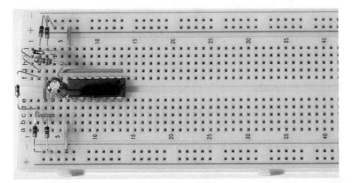

Step 8   Insert a 47 μF capacitor (C1) between E6 and F6. The longer (positive) lead should go in hole F6. Attach jumpers to join ground to B6, and positive to J6.

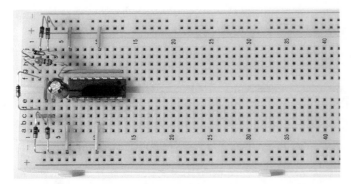

Step 9   Attach additional jumpers from ground to B10 and positive to J10.

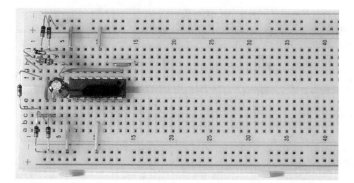

Step 10   Insert a jumper from H12 to H14. *Over top* of this, place a jumper from H11 to H15.

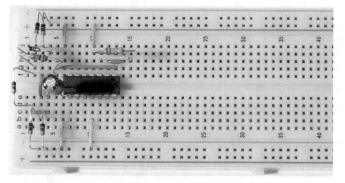

Step 11   Place a 56K resistor (R1) from I13 to I14.

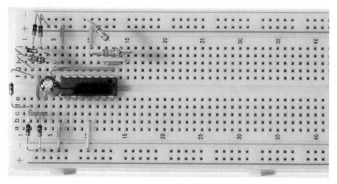

Step 12   Place a 560K resistor from J14 to positive.

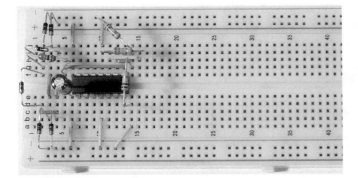

Step 13 Insert a 100K resistor (R2) from D14 to G14. Insert an additional jumper from negative to A14.

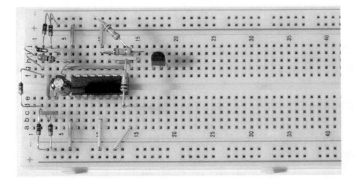

Step 14 Insert 78L05 (U2) into holes G17, 18, 19. Make sure the flat part of the component is facing toward the bottom of the breadboard.

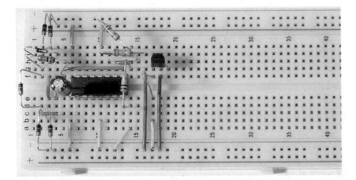

Step 15 Attach a long jumper from ground to F16 and another from ground to F18. Bridge a 0.1 µF capacitor (C2) from E17 to F17. There is no positive or negative lead with ceramic capacitors so it can be inserted in any orientation. Insert another jumper from ground to B17.

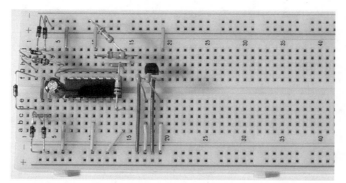

Step 16   Insert another 0.1 μF capacitor (C3) from E19 to F19. Insert jumpers from ground to B19 and from J19 to positive.

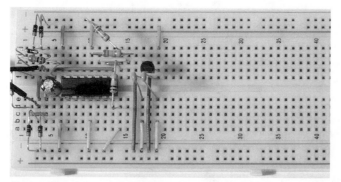

Step 17   Prepare the RCX wires by cutting a long RCX wire in half and slicing the webbing about 2 inches (see Figure 9–15 for details). Insert one wire into D3 and the other into G4 (far left of photo).

Step 18   Prepare the compass sensor by bending Pins 4, 5, and 6 away from the body (see Figure 10–1) so Pins 1, 2, and 3 can be inserted into the board. The pins should be inserted into holes J15, 16, and 17 (3, 2, 1). At this point you can test this first half of the circuit using the test code (see later).

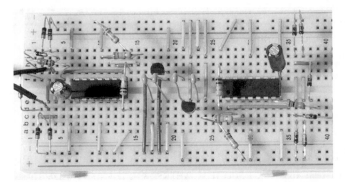

Step 19 Remove the compass sensor and assemble the other half of the circuit. It is easy to do because it is identical to the first half, except rotated 180 degrees (see Table 10–2 for hole numbers).

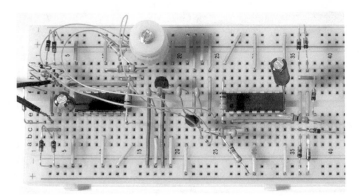

Step 20 Using the wire-wrap tool, attach wires to Pins 4, 5, and 6 of the compass sensor. Attach small leads (I snipped off leads from spare resistors) to the other ends of the wire. Reinsert the compass sensor (Step 18). Connect Pins 4, 5, and 6 to holes A23, A24, and A25, respectively.

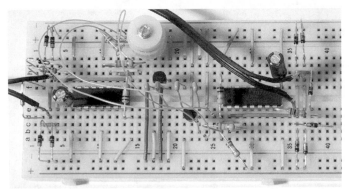

Step 21 Attach one RCX wire to G37 and the other to D36. That's it for construction!

Note:

If you are interested in making this circuit permanent, see Appendix B for instructions. Keep in mind the robot in this chapter uses the breadboard circuit.

Testing the Circuit

Now that the circuit is complete (or half complete if you've jumped here from Step 18), you can test it out to see if it works. We'll start by trying to read some raw values. The following code displays the value to the LCD screen. Pressing the View button changes between readings from Input 1 and Input 3.

```
1.  import josx.platform.rcx.*;
2.
3.  class ReadRaw implements SensorConstants, ButtonListener  {
4.
5.      private Sensor s1;
6.      private Sensor s2;
7.
8.      private int current; // Current value to display
9.
10.     public static void main(String [] args) {
11.         ReadRaw rr = new ReadRaw(Sensor.S1, Sensor.S3);
12.         rr.showRaw();
13.     }
14.
15.     public ReadRaw(Sensor sensor1, Sensor sensor2) {
16.         sensor1.setTypeAndMode(SENSOR_TYPE_LIGHT,
                 SENSOR_MODE_RAW);
17.         sensor1.activate();
18.         s1 = sensor1;
19.
20.         sensor2.setTypeAndMode(SENSOR_TYPE_LIGHT,
                 SENSOR_MODE_RAW);
21.         sensor2.activate();
22.         s2 = sensor2;
23.         current = 1;
24.
25.         Button.VIEW.addButtonListener(this);
26.     }
27.
28.
```

```
29.    public void buttonPressed(Button b) {
30.        ++current;
31.        if (current>2)
32.            current = 1;
33.        Sound.beep();
34.    }
35.
36.    public void buttonReleased(Button b) {}
37.
38.    public void showRaw() {
39.        int val = 0;
40.        while(true) {
41.            if(current == 1)
42.                val = s1.readValue();
43.            else
44.                val = s2.readValue();
45.            LCD.showProgramNumber(current);
46.            LCD.showNumber(val);
47.            try{Thread.sleep(100);}catch(Exception e){}
48.        }
49.    }
50. }
```

If all is well you should see readings anywhere from 500 to 1,000 (the battery level really affects the readings). As you rotate the circuit the values should change as well. If everything seems to be working at this stage, skip ahead to the section "Programming the Compass Sensor." If not, read on.

What If It Doesn't Work?

You've assembled the circuit, plugged it in, and uploaded the test code, but it doesn't work. Now what? The first thing to do is rotate the connection to the RCX by 180 degrees. If it still doesn't work, double check the position of all the components. This is probably the most frequent error in a circuit like this. Make sure the diodes, voltage regulators, and ICs are oriented correctly. It's best to use the schematic and check off parts as you verify the orientation.

Make sure you have the right components. If you have trouble obtaining parts, don't use substitutions. If anything is not working, the culprit might be the substituted part. Make sure none of the components have been mixed up. In a circuit like this, the most likely parts to get mixed up are the resistors.

Hopefully things are working now. You can now move onto the programming portion of this chapter, or, if you wish, you can mount the components to a more permanent setting. I heartily recommend using the breadboard because mounting the circuit permanently takes a lot of time and effort.

Programming the Compass Class

In the previous sections we assembled and performed some rudimentary tests of the compass sensor. If your sensor is working, congratulations! In this section we explore the various ways to program the sensor and get the best results possible from it. The first task is to calibrate the sensor—finding out what the minimum and maximum raw values are for each sinusoidal wave produced by the sensor. Then we examine methods to convert the output from raw values into an angle value. Along the way we learn why battery charge is so critical to the results, and why it is important for the compass values to be calibrated properly at all times. We then program a complete Navigator class that uses the compass to get around, and finally build a robot suitable for carrying the compass. There are some calculations included in this chapter, but if you are not interested in the theory behind the compass programming, feel free to skip them and just use the code as you see fit.

Calibration

An unfortunate part of real-world projects such as sensors is that the real world is not as perfect as the pure logical world of computer programming. There are tiny variations in the resistors, capacitors, transistors, and even in the compass sensor itself that affect the output of the raw values. There are also variations in the overall battery charge. Because of these imperfections, the values produced by my compass sensor will be different from the values produced by your compass sensor. Even between sessions of the same sensor the values can change, depending on the batteries. The peak value produced by my circuit with rechargeable batteries is about 800 raw units, but when using fresh alkaline batteries the peak value is closer to 1,000 raw units. RCXs using lithium batteries may even produce values higher than this. To watch how battery charge affects the raw value output, try outputting the raw data from one of the compass sensors to the LCD screen. Leave the RCX and compass sitting still on a desk, and the value will slowly drop as it sits there. If the batteries are weak and need to be recharged, the value will drop rapidly, but if batteries are fresh the value may not noticeably fall.

There are also differences in the output produced by Pins 1, 2, 3 compared to the output from Pins 4, 5, 6. When my circuit is using alkaline batteries, the maximum output values from Pins 1, 2, 3 (cosine) of the sensor is about 984 raw units but the maximum from Pins 4, 5, 6 (sine) is about 975 raw units (Figure 10–4). The sinusoidal waves must be virtual mirror images

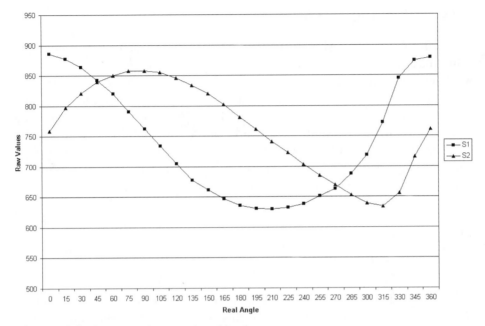

Figure 10–4 Raw values produced by the compass sensor.

of one another for the calculations to work properly, meaning our code must also manipulate the data slightly to make the curves similar. In other words, the values for one curve must be *normalized* so it matches the other curve. Let's examine how we will perform these calibrations.

Finding Min and Max Values

To find the outer values produced by each half of the circuit it is necessary to make the compass rotate a full 360 degrees. For now, try manually rotating the compass in your hands and watching the LCD for each sensor input. Record the max and min values for each. These are used in the compass sensor driver later.

Note:

A driver using automatic calibration (and the AutoCalibration class) is used later in this chapter.

Normalizing the Curves

As mentioned previously, corresponding cosine and sine waves need the same maximum and minimum values to calculate angle properly. Now that we have determined the min and max values, we can adjust the curves so they both peak and bottom out at the same values. A simple equation adjusts Curve 1 (the curve produced from Pins 1, 2, 3, which is Sensor 1) to match Curve 2 (Sensor 2). All values retrieved from Sensor 1 simply go through the equation to convert it. In concept, the equation first stretches (or shrinks) Curve 1, then moves it up or down so the top and bottom of each curve match one another. The equation is as follows:

```
adjustedS1 = a * rawS1 + b
```

where:

```
a = (max S1 - min S1) / (max S2 - min S2)
b = max S1 - (a * max S2)
```

This equation is incorporated into the code to derive an angle from the raw values. Let's now examine how this is calculated within our compass driver.

Compass Driver

If our compass hardware were perfect, and produced two symmetrical sinusoidal waves, our task of calculating the angle would be very easy indeed. The basic equation to calculate the angle from raw values is easy. First, we calculate the *midth* value, which is simply the average between the max and min values. On a sinusoidal graph the midth is represented by zero. Then we calculate the appropriate sine and cosine values from the raw values by subtracting midth from each of them. Finally we use the atan2() method. The entire code to retrieve an angle from raw values is as follows:

```
int s1Raw = s1.readValue();
int s2Raw = s2.readValue();
// Convert raw to usable sine-cosine values
float cosine = s1Raw - midth;
float sine = s2Raw - midth;
// final calculation:
float angle = (float)Math.atan2(sine, cosine);
angle = (float)Math.toDegrees(angle);
```

This produces an angle of between –180 and +180 degrees. As we mentioned in the previous section, however, we must adjust all values from one input curve so they match the second curve. Let's examine code to generate an angle from the compass sensor:

```
1.  import josx.platform.rcx.*;
2.
3.  class CompassSensor implements SensorConstants {
4.
5.      private Sensor s1; // Pins 1-3 = cosine
6.      private Sensor s2; // Pins 4-6 = sine
7.
8.      // Initialize min values with arbitrary high values
9.      // so the low values will be retained.
10.     public int s1_min = 665;
11.     public int s2_min = 684;
12.     // Initialize max values with arbitrary low values
13.     // so the higher values will be retained.
14.     public int s1_max = 984;
15.     public int s2_max = 975;
16.
17.     private float midth;
18.
19.     // Constants used to adjust sensor2 values to same scale
             as sensor1:
20.     private float a;
21.     private float b;
22.
23.     public CompassSensor(Sensor sensor1, Sensor sensor2) {
24.         sensor1.setTypeAndMode(SENSOR_TYPE_LIGHT,
                SENSOR_MODE_RAW);
25.         sensor1.activate();
26.         s1 = sensor1;
27.
28.         sensor2.setTypeAndMode(SENSOR_TYPE_LIGHT,
                SENSOR_MODE_RAW);
29.         sensor2.activate();
30.         s2 = sensor2;
31.
32.         // initialize(); // REM out for error correction
33.     }
34.
35.     public void initialize() {
36.         midth = (s1_max + s1_min) / 2;
37.
38.         // Constants used to adjust sensor2 values to same
                scale as sensor1:
39.         a = (s1_max - s1_min)/(s2_max - s2_min);
40.         b = s2_max - (a * s1_max);
41.     }
```

```
42.
43.    public int getAngle() {
44.        int s1Raw = s1.readValue();
45.        int s2Raw = s2.readValue();
46.
47.        // Adjust s2Raw to same scale as s1Raw
48.        //float adjustedS2Raw = a * s2Raw + b;
49.
50.        // Convert raw to usable sine-cosine values
51.        float cosine = s1Raw - midth;
52.        float sine = s2Raw - midth;
53.        //float sine = adjustedS2Raw - midth;
54.
55.        // final calculation:
56.        float angle = (float)Math.atan2(sine, cosine);
57.        angle = (float)Math.toDegrees(angle);
58.        if(angle < 0)
59.            angle += 360;
60.
61.        return (int)angle;
62.    }
63. }
```

Notice that this code uses the values S1_MIN, S1_MAX, S2_MIN, and S2_MAX, which we found out previously. When this code is run you will see an angle on the LCD. Try rotating the compass to various points and note the result. The first thing you might notice is the reading quivers after each rotation, then settles after about three seconds. This delay is due to the dampening, mentioned earlier. This means we do not get an instantaneous reading of the angle, an obstacle that must be overcome in our programming.

Note:

The angle produced by the compass driver is from 0 to 360, counterclockwise. This is the opposite of reading a real compass, but it is used because it is compatible with the coordinate system.

A second observation you might notice is the angle is not always correct (these errors can be caused by iron objects near the robot, and are discussed later). My sensor produces very asymmetrical sinusoidal curves (Figure 10–5). This asymmetry results in errors in the angle calculated. To accurately assess the errors, place the compass on a piece of paper and then rotate it until the display shows 0 degrees. Draw a line parallel to the compass, and another perpendicular line to form a large cross. Label each end of the cross 0, 90, 180, and 270 degrees, respectively (Figure 10–6). Now rotate the compass by 90 degrees each time, counterclockwise, and record the resulting angle (don't forget to wait until the reading settles down). Table 10–3 shows the results obtained by my compass sensor.

Note:

The angle 0 represents east, and angle increases clockwise, as first mentioned in Chapter 7, "Navigation."

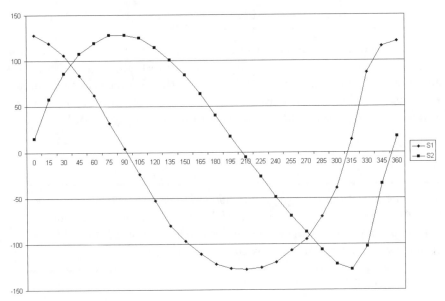

Figure 10–5　Sinusoidal curves produced by my compass indoors.

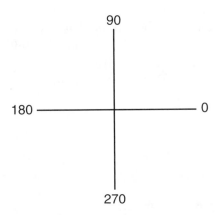

Figure 10–6　Testing compass accuracy.

Table 10-3 Real Angle vs. Compass Sensor Angle

Real Angle	Compass Reading
0	0 (starting point)
90	76
180	151
270	225

As you can see, the results are quite skewed. When it should be reading 270 degrees, it thinks it is at 225 degrees—almost 50 degrees off! This problem could probably be corrected by using the compass away from any metal objects, but because it's always nice to use robots indoors as opposed to the middle of a grassy field, we will try to deal with this problem within the Java code.

Note:

Even if the angles are not right, you should still have a continuous sequence of angles spanning from 0 degrees to 359 degrees. If a full rotation does not produce these values then something is wrong (possibly S1 and S3 have been reversed, or the min and max constants have been reversed).

Previously we stretched out (or shrunk) one curve in the vertical direction to make it match the other curve. Now we will stretch or shrink sections of the curve in a horizontal direction so the overall curve is more symmetrical. For this strategy we divide the circle of rotation into a number of sections—in this example, we use four sections. Section 1 will be 0 to 90 degrees, Section 2 90 to 180 degrees, Section 3 180 to 270 degrees, and Section 4 270 to 360 degrees. For Section 2, we want values between 90 and 180, but according to Table 10–3 we are getting values between 76 and 151. To compensate for this, we use the same equation we used before:

```
adjustedAngle = a * angle + b
```

Where:

```
a = (max real angle - min real angle) / (max sensor angle
- min sensor angle)
b = max real angle - (a * max sensor angle)
```

So for Quadrant 2, the constants are as follows:

```
a = (180 - 90) / (151 - 75)
b = 180 - (a * 151)
```

This information should only be used when calibration is necessary, so we add this as an optional constructor for the Calibration class. The Compass-Sensor class can use the values contained in Calibration. Our new Calibration class is as follows:

```
1. class Calibration {
2.
3.     public short s1_min;
4.     public short s1_max;
5.
6.     public short s2_min;
7.     public short s2_max;
8.
9.     public float midth;
10.
11.     // Constants used to adjust sensor2 values to same scale
            as sensor1:
12.     public float a;
13.     public float b;
14.
15.     // Used for error correcting curves that are not normal
16.     public float [] correction = null;
17.
18.     public void initialize() {
19.         midth = (s1_max + s1_min) / 2;
20.
21.         // Constants used to adjust sensor2 values to same
                scale as sensor1:
22.         a = (s1_max - s1_min)/(s2_max - s2_min);
23.         b = s2_max - (a * s1_max);
24.     }
25. }
```

This object uses no formal constructor in the name of saving memory. All values are public and can be set externally as needed. The correction array consists of the values taken at intervals with your compass (as explained previously). It doesn't always have to contain values at 90-degree values, but the first and last numbers must be 0 and 360. For my compass values (see Table 9–3) I would use the following array:

```
calibration.correction = {0, 76, 151, 225, 360};
```

This code relies on the user manually setting the min and max values of each input. This requires the user to manually rotate the compass, but it would be much more convenient if the robot itself would rotate and record the values itself. There are a few obstacles to overcome in doing this, however. The first problem is the compass reading lags behind the actual angle by about three seconds for each 90 degrees it rotates, so to get a correct reading we have to ensure it takes the robot at least 12 seconds to turn a full 360 degrees. The second problem is determining when the robot has actually turned 360 degrees. We could easily overcome this by asking the user to tell us how long it takes to rotate 360 degrees, but this makes it an extra bother to use the classes. Let's take the harder, more elegant route. It would be nice if we could use the compass sensor readings to indicate a complete rotation during calibration. Each curve goes through an upslope and a downslope for each full 360-degree rotation (see Figure 10–4). All we are interested in, however, are the peaks and valleys, so we can monitor the numbers to determine when each required value has been obtained. When a value is increasing and then begins decreasing, the program will know it has obtained a maximum value. When the value is decreasing and then begins increasing, it will know it has obtained a minimum value. Once all four values are obtained the rotation can stop:

```
1. import josx.platform.rcx.*;
2.
3. class AutoCalibration extends Calibration implements
      SensorConstants {
4.
5.    private Sensor s1;
6.    private Sensor s2;
7.
8.    public AutoCalibration(Sensor sensor1, Sensor sensor2) {
9.        this.s1 = sensor1;
10.       this.s2 = sensor2;
11.
12.       s1.setTypeAndMode(SENSOR_TYPE_LIGHT, SENSOR_MODE_RAW);
13.       s1.activate();
14.
15.       s2.setTypeAndMode(SENSOR_TYPE_LIGHT, SENSOR_MODE_RAW);
16.       s2.activate();
17.
18.       try{Thread.sleep(1000);}catch(Exception e){} // Power
              up time
19.
20.       new Thread() {
21.          public void run() {
```

```
22.            short new1;
23.            short new2;
24.            while(true){
25.                new1 = (short)s1.readValue();
26.                new2 = (short)s2.readValue();
27.
28.                s1_min = (new1<s1_min)?new1:s1_min;
29.                s1_max = (new1>s1_max)?new1:s1_max;
30.
31.                s2_min = (new2<s2_min)?new2:s2_min;
32.                s2_max = (new2>s2_max)?new2:s2_max;
33.                Thread.yield();
34.            }
35.          }
36.        }.start();
37.    }
38.
39.    public AutoCalibration(Sensor sensor1, Sensor sensor2,
            float [] curveCorrection) {
40.        this(sensor1, sensor2);
41.        this.correction = curveCorrection;
42.    }
43.
44.    public void calibrate(Motor leftMotor, Motor rightMotor) {
45.        resetMinMax();
46.        leftMotor.forward();
47.        rightMotor.backward();
48.        int new1 = s1.readValue();
49.        int new2 = s2.readValue();
50.
51.        int peaks = 0;
52.        int oldChange1 = 0;
53.        int oldChange2 = 0;
54.        while(peaks <5) {
55.            int old1 = new1;
56.            int old2 = new2;
57.
58.            try{Thread.sleep(400);}catch(Exception e){}
59.
60.            new1 = s1.readValue();
61.            new2 = s2.readValue();
62.
63.            int newChange1 = new1 - old1;
64.            int newChange2 = new2 - old2;
65.
66.            if(oldChange1<0&&newChange1>0||
```

```
67.              oldChange1>0&&newChange1<0||
68.              oldChange2<0&&newChange2>0||
69.              oldChange2>0&&newChange2<0){
70.              Sound.beep();
71.              leftMotor.stop();
72.              rightMotor.stop();
73.          try {Thread.sleep(3000);} catch (Exception e){}
74.              leftMotor.forward();
75.              rightMotor.backward();
76.              ++peaks;
77.            }
78.            oldChange1 = newChange1;
79.            oldChange2 = newChange2;
80.          }
81.        leftMotor.stop();
82.        rightMotor.stop();
83.        initialize();
84.      }
85.
86.      public void resetMinMax() {
87.        // Initialize min values with arbitrary high values
88.        // so the low values will be retained.
89.        s1_min = 10000;
90.        s2_min = 10000;
91.        // Initialize max values with arbitrary low values
92.        // so the higher values will be retained.
93.        s1_max = -10000;
94.        s2_max = -10000;
95.      }
96.
97.      public void calibrate(int milliSeconds) {
98.        resetMinMax();
99.        try{Thread.sleep(milliSeconds);
100.       }catch(InterruptedException e){}
101.       initialize();
102.     }
103. }
```

As you can see, AutoCalibration extends Calibration, so it can be used as an alternative (although it is more taxing on the memory). AutoCalibration has two constructors. The first accepts an array of float numbers, representing intervals (discussed earlier) to correct magnetic anomalies in the room. The second constructor just requires the sensor constants, and it doesn't correct for magnetic anomalies. To perform the automatic calibration, calibrate() is called giving two motor objects, or alternately calibrate() can be called with a delay (milliseconds) to wait for max and min values to be discovered.

Now we need to rewrite CompassSensor slightly to make use of the new Calibration object:

```
1.  import josx.platform.rcx.*;
2.
3.  class CompassSensor implements SensorConstants {
4.
5.      private Sensor s1; // Pins 1-3 = cosine
6.      private Sensor s2; // Pins 4-6 = sine
7.
8.      public float [] error_a = null;
9.      public float [] error_b = null;
10.
11.     private Calibration cal;
12.
13.     public CompassSensor(Sensor sensor1, Sensor sensor2,
            Calibration cal) {
14.         this.s1 = sensor1;
15.         this.s2 = sensor2;
16.         this.cal = cal;
17.
18.         s1.setTypeAndMode(SENSOR_TYPE_LIGHT, SENSOR_MODE_RAW);
19.         s1.activate();
20.
21.         s2.setTypeAndMode(SENSOR_TYPE_LIGHT, SENSOR_MODE_RAW);
22.         s2.activate();
23.
24.         // Curve compensation constants:
25.         error_a = new float[cal.correction.length];
26.         error_b = new float[cal.correction.length];
27.
28.         // Curve compensation calculations:
29.         for(int i=1;i<(cal.correction.length);++i) {
30.             error_a[i] = (360f/(cal.correction.length - 1))/
                    (cal.correction[i] - cal.correction[i-1]);
31.             error_b[i] = ((360f/(cal.correction.length - 1)*i)
                    - error_a[i] * cal.correction[i]);
32.         }
33.
34.         try{Thread.sleep(1000);}catch(Exception e){} // Power
                up time
35.     }
36.
37.
```

```
38.    public short getAngle() {
39.        int s1Raw = s1.readValue();
40.        int s2Raw = s2.readValue();
41.
42.        // Adjust s2Raw to same scale as s1Raw
43.        float adjustedS2Raw = cal.a * s2Raw + cal.b;
44.
45.        // Convert raw to usable sine-cosine values
46.        float cosine = s1Raw - cal.midth;
47.        float sine = adjustedS2Raw - cal.midth;
48.
49.        // final calculation:
50.        float angle = (float)Math.atan2(sine, cosine);
51.        angle = (float)Math.toDegrees(angle);
52.        if(angle < 0)
53.            angle += 360;
54.
55.        // Error adjustment
56.        if(cal.correction != null)
57.            for(int i=1;i<cal.correction.length;++i) {
58.                if(angle>=cal.correction[i-1]&&angle<cal.correc-
                       tion[i]){
59.                    angle = (error_a[i] * angle) + error_b[i];
60.                    break;
61.                }
62.            }
63.        return (short)angle;
64.    }
65. }
```

This code is almost identical to the previous CompassSensor code, except now it accepts a Calibration object in the constructor. It also performs calculations to make the data a little more normal if the values are skewed.

Programming CompassNavigator

Now that we have a working compass it would be handy to have some sort of Navigator class similar to RotationNavigator and TimingNavigator. The leJOS API contains no such class, but there is the Navigator interface that can be used to create a class in the same family. Because two of the three input ports are tied up by the compass, it seems natural to use timing to measure distances traveled, as a bumper or distance sensor is needed to detect collisions.

This class would be amazingly easy to program if it weren't for the fact that the compass has a delay of several seconds before an accurate reading is possible. This means the robot will overrotate while reading the sensor because most robots rotate faster than 90 degrees every three seconds. So we'll use a strategy of rotating until the sensor thinks it has come to the destination, then stop (allowing the compass to catch up), then rotate back and stop, repeating this until it has homed in close enough to the target angle.

As for programming the class, it is not going to be easy. It will implement Navigator, which means all the Navigator methods must also be implemented (no small task). The class requires a CompassSensor object in the constructor, which is actually quite economical because all the calibrations will be dealt with before being passed to RotationNavigator. This class is the largest in the book by far, because it must implement many complex functions, and it is also the most taxing on memory. There isn't going to be much memory leftover to do other things once this class (and related classes) have been uploaded to the RCX brick:

```java
1. import josx.robotics.Navigator;
2. import josx.platform.rcx.*;
3. import josx.util.*;
4.
5. public class CompassNavigator extends Thread implements
      Navigator {
6.
7.    // Time it takes to go one centimeter (in milliseconds)
8.    private float CENTIMETER; // Calculated in constructor
9.
10.   private int command;
11.   private final int STOP = 0;
12.   private final int FORWARD = 1;
13.   private final int BACKWARD = 2;
14.
15.   // Used to coordinate internal angle with compass angle
16.   private static final short ORIGIN_ANGLE = 0;
17.   short startAngle;
18.
19.   // orientation and co-ordinate data
20.   private float angle;
21.   private float x;
22.   private float y;
23.
24.   // oldTime is used for timing purposes in stop():
25.   private int oldTime;
26.
```

```
27.   private CompassSensor compass;
28.
29.   // Motors for differential steering:
30.   private Motor left;
31.   private Motor right;
32.
33.   private static Thread sleepThread; // Thread used for
          delays
34.  private boolean travel = false; // Used in stop() to know
          when to interrupt
35.
36.   public CompassNavigator(CompassSensor compass, Motor
          right, Motor left, float timeOneMeter) {
37.       this.right = right;
38.       this.left = left;
39.
40.       this.compass = compass;
41.
42.       // Convert seconds into milliseconds per centimeter
43.       CENTIMETER = (timeOneMeter/100)*1000;
44.
45.       // Obtain the starting compass angle so compass sensor
46.       // can be altered to match internal starting angle.
47.       // (delay is to make sure compass is settled down)
48.       try{Thread.sleep(2500);}catch(InterruptedException e){}
49.       startAngle = compass.getAngle();
50.
51.       // Set coordinates and starting angle:
52.       angle = ORIGIN_ANGLE;
53.       x = 0.0f;
54.       y = 0.0f;
55.       this.start();
56.   }
57.
58.   public float getX() {
59.       // !! In future, if RCX is on the move it should
              return the present calculation of x
60.       return x;
61.   }
62.
63.   public float getY() {
64.       return y;
65.   }
66.
67.   public float getAngle() {
68.       return this.angle;
```

```
69.        }
70.
71.        public short getCompassAngle() {
72.            int tempAngle = compass.getAngle();
73.            tempAngle = tempAngle - startAngle + ORIGIN_ANGLE;
74.            if(tempAngle < 0)
75.                tempAngle += 360;
76.            return (short)tempAngle;
77.        }
78.
79.        public short getDifference() {
80.            int diff = getCompassAngle() - (short)getAngle();
81.            if(diff > 180)
82.                diff -= 360;
83.            else if(diff < -180)
84.                diff += 360;
85.            return (short)diff;
86.        }
87.
88.        public void rotate(float angle) {
89.            // keep track of angle
90.
91.            this.angle = this.angle + angle;
92.            this.angle = (int)this.angle % 360; // Must be < 360
                    degrees
93.
94.            if(this.angle < 0)
95.                this.angle += 360;   // Must be > 0
96.
97.            gotoAngle(this.angle);
98.        }
99.
100.       public void gotoAngle(float angle) {
101.           this.angle = angle;
102.           angle = Math.round(angle);
103.
104.           while(getDifference() > 5) {
105.               left.forward();
106.               right.backward();
107.               while(getDifference() > 5) {}
108.               left.stop();
109.               right.stop();
110.               while(getDifference() < -3) {
111.                   right.forward();
112.                   left.backward();
113.                   try{Thread.sleep(10);}catch(Exception e){}
```

```
114.              left.stop();
115.              right.stop();
116.          }
117.      }
118.      try{Thread.sleep(1000);}catch(Exception e){}
119.
120.      while(getDifference() < -5) {
121.          right.forward();
122.          left.backward();
123.          while(getDifference() < -5) {}
124.          left.stop();
125.          right.stop();
126.          while(getDifference() > 3) {
127.              left.forward();
128.              right.backward();
129.              try{Thread.sleep(10);}catch(Exception e){}
130.              left.stop();
131.              right.stop();
132.          }
133.      }
134.      try{Thread.sleep(1000);}catch(Exception e){}
135.  }
136.
137.  public void gotoPoint(float x, float y) {
138.
139.      // Determine relative points
140.      float x1 = x - this.x;
141.      float y1 = y - this.y;
142.
143.      // Calculate angle to go to:
144.      float angle = (float)Math.atan2(y1,x1);
145.
146.      // Calculate distance to travel:
147.      float distance;
148.      if(y1 != 0)
149.          distance = y1/(float)Math.sin(angle);
150.      else
151.          distance = x1/(float)Math.cos(angle);
152.
153.      // Convert angle from rads to degrees:
154.      angle = (float)Math.toDegrees(angle);
155.
156.      // Now convert theory into action:
157.      gotoAngle(angle);
158.      travel(Math.round(distance));
159.  }
```

```
160.
161.   public void travel(int distance) {
162.
163.       if(distance > 0) {
164.           forward();
165.       } else {
166.           backward();
167.       }
168.       travel = true;
169.       int delay = (int)(CENTIMETER * Math.abs(distance));
170.
171.       sleepThread = Thread.currentThread();
172.       try {
173.           sleepThread.sleep(delay);
174.           travel = false;
175.           stop(); // Will not be called if Interrupted
176.       } catch (InterruptedException ie) {
177.           travel = false;
178.       }
179.   }
180.
181.   public void forward() {
182.       // Start timer
183.       oldTime = (int)System.currentTimeMillis();
184.       right.forward();
185.       left.forward();
186.       command = FORWARD;
187.   }
188.
189.   public void backward() {
190.       // Start timer
191.       oldTime = (int)System.currentTimeMillis();
192.       right.backward();
193.       left.backward();
194.       command = BACKWARD;
195.   }
196.
197.   public void run() {
198.       while(true) {
199.           while(command == FORWARD) {
200.               //moving = true;
201.               if(getDifference() < 0) {
202.                   Sound.playTone(400, 20);
203.                   left.setPower(1);
204.                   while(getDifference() < 0) {}
205.                   left.setPower(7);
```

```
206.            }
207.
208.            if(getDifference() > 0) {
209.                Sound.playTone(200, 20);
210.                right.setPower(1);
211.                while(getDifference() > 0) {}
212.                right.setPower(7);
213.            }
214.
215.            //Thread.yield();
216.        }
217.
218.        while(command == BACKWARD) {
219.            //moving = true;
220.            if(getDifference() > 0) {
221.                Sound.playTone(800, 20);
222.                left.setPower(1);
223.                while(getDifference() > 0) {}
224.                left.setPower(7);
225.            }
226.
227.            if(getDifference() < 0) {
228.                Sound.playTone(1600, 20);
229.                right.setPower(1);
230.                while(getDifference() < 0) {}
231.                right.setPower(7);
232.            }
233.            //Thread.yield();
234.        }
235.    }
236. }
237.
238. public void stop() {
239.    // Only call interrupt if traveling
240.    if(travel == true)
241.        sleepThread.interrupt();
242.    left.stop();
243.    right.stop();
244.    command = STOP;
245.    // Recalculate x-y coordinates based on Timer results
246.    if (oldTime != 0) {
247.        int totalTime = (int)System.currentTimeMillis() -
                oldTime;
248.        float centimeters = totalTime / CENTIMETER;
249.        // update x, y coordinates
```

```
250.          x = x + (float)(Math.cos(Math.toRadians(angle)) *
                  centimeters);
251.          y = y + (float)(Math.sin(Math.toRadians(angle)) *
                  centimeters);
252.          oldTime = 0;
253.      }
254.  }
255. }
```

This code was mostly taken from the TimingNavigator class and altered to accommodate the compass sensor. The reason TimingNavigator itself was not extended is because it would use too much memory due to redundant code. Let's forgo any boring explanations of the code and try using this class with an actual robot.

A Robot Using the Compass

The robot for the compass sensor actually needs to be a little special because magnetic disturbances throw off the compass readings. The LEGO motors contain magnets that could really distort readings, and apparently the RCX has some influence over the compass as well. A distance of about six inches is apparently good enough to negate these effects, so the design must place the compass some distance from the motors and RCX. It would also be beneficial to have the compass off the floor a distance so nails and metal heating ducts do not have as profound an effect. The basket is designed to hold the bread-board circuit presented earlier in the chapter. This robot is called Mozer because it's part bulldozer, and because of the way it moseys along, making wobbly movements when turning to a new angle.

Chassis

The chassis for Mozer separates the tank treads far apart to make rotation as slow as possible, giving the compass sensor a better chance to keep up.

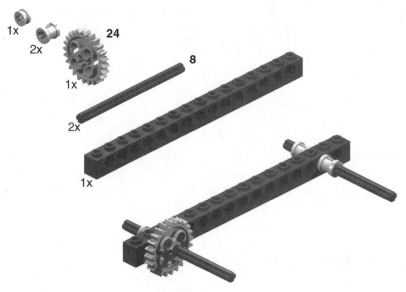

Step 1   We'll start by building the first half of the chassis. Insert an 8-unit axle into the second to last hole of a 1 × 16 beam. Place two Technic bushes on either side of the axle (spacing is shown in diagram). Insert another 8-unit axle on the other end, securing it with a half bush and a 24-tooth gear.

Step 2   Sandwich the gear with another 1 × 16 beam and cap it off with two Technic bushes.

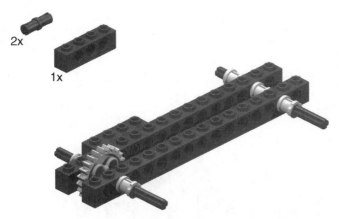

Step 3   Attach a 1 × 4 beam to the side of the chassis with two friction pins.

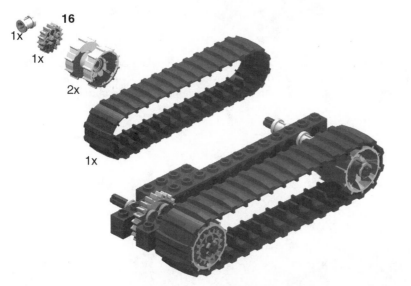

Step 4   Place a rubber tread over two sprocket wheels and slide them onto the axles. Secure the rear sprocket wheel with a Technic bush and the front sprocket wheel with a 16-tooth gear.

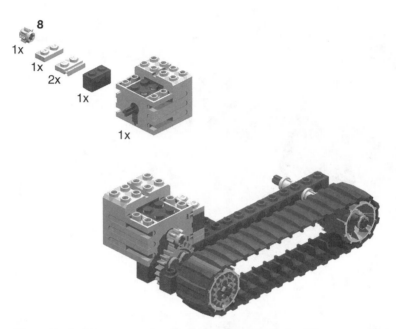

Step 5   Build a support for the motor by stacking the following parts (in order, bottom to top): 1 × 2 plate, door rail, 1 × 2 brick, door rail. Insert the door rails into the side of the motor. Add an 8-tooth gear to the motor and attach the unit to the chassis.

Step 6   Cap the unit with a 1 × 2 plate and a 2 × 2 plate. This completes half of the chassis.

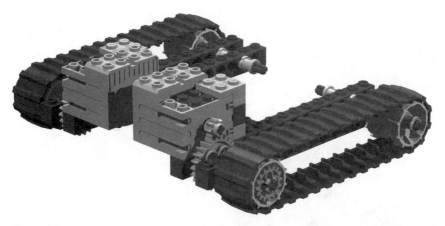

Step 7 Repeat Steps 1 to 6 in mirror image to assemble the second half of the chassis.

Compass Basket

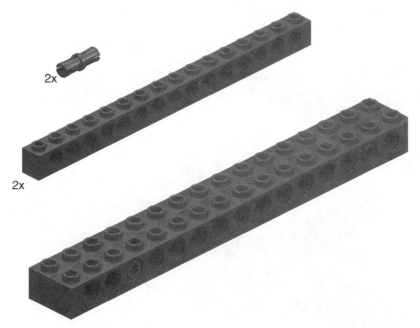

2x

2x

Step 1 Secure two 1 × 16 beams together into one unit using friction pins.

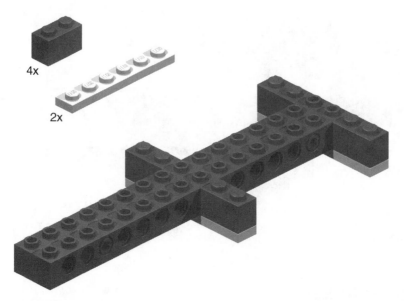

Step 2   Add support for the basket by placing two 1 × 6 plates under the center beam. Add four 1 × 2 bricks to the top of the plates.

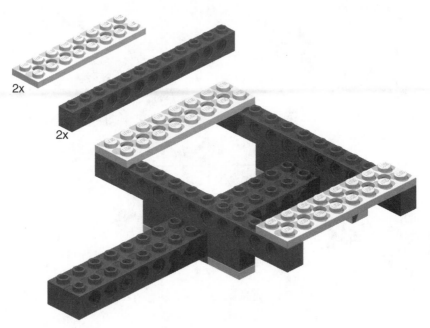

Step 3   Attach two 1 × 12 beams to the top of the supports. Brace them using two 2 × 8 plates.

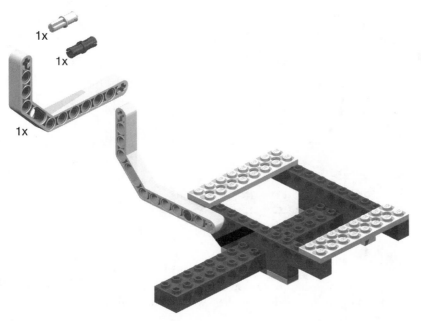

Step 4   Insert an axle pin into the last axle hole of a yellow lift arm. Insert a black friction pin into a hole two spaces from the axle pin. Attach this to the 1 × 12 beam.

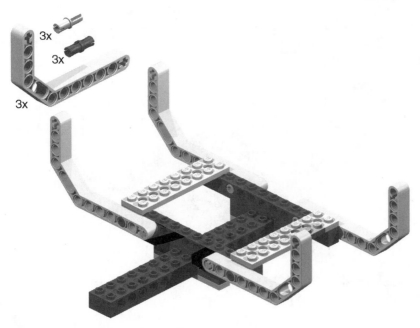

Step 5   Repeat this with the other three lift arms.

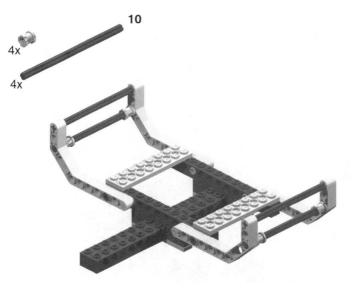

Step 6   Insert two 10-unit axles into the top of the lift arms. Insert two more 10-unit axles just below the previous two and secure them with Technic bushes.

Step 7   Finish the basket off by attaching a 6 × 10 plate and two 1 × 12 beams to act as rails to hold the breadboard in place.

Front Bumper

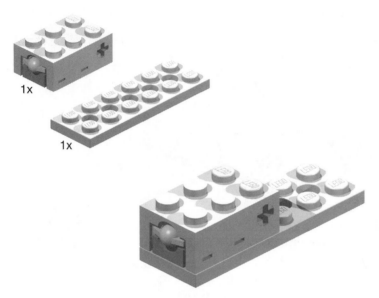

Step 1   Attach a touch sensor to a 2 × 6 plate.

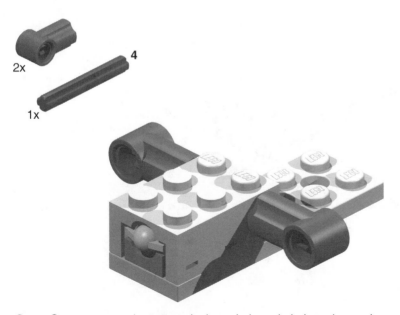

Step 2   Insert a single 4-unit axle through the axle hole in the touch sensor. Attach two blue angle connectors to the axle.

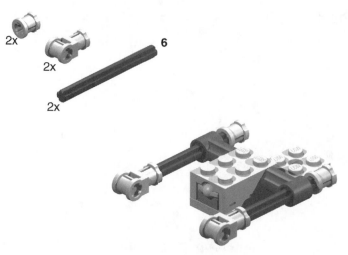

Step 3   Insert two 6-unit axles through the blue angle connectors. Secure the axles with two Technic bushes and two connectors with axle holes.

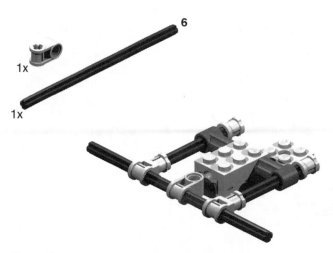

Step 4   Insert a 6-unit axle through the axle holes and attach an axle joiner in the center of the bumper. This should make contact with the touch sensor.

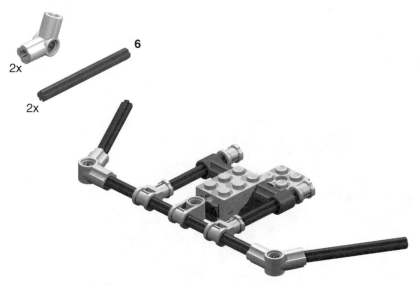

Step 5   Attach two angle connectors to the end of the bumpers and extend the bumper with two 6-unit axles.

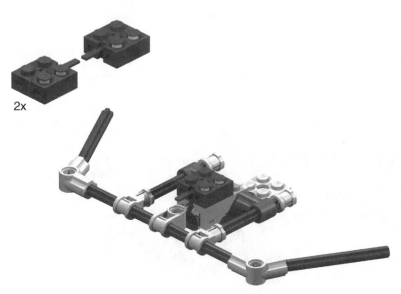

Step 6   Attach a wire brick to the touch sensor, with the wire facing outward.

Final Assembly

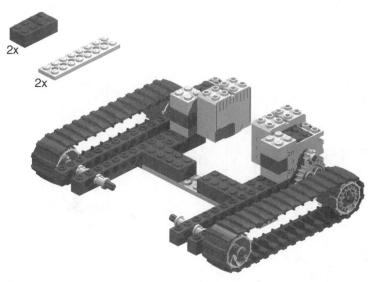

Step 1   Attach two 2 × 8 plates to the bottom of each half chassis. Add 2 × 4 bricks.

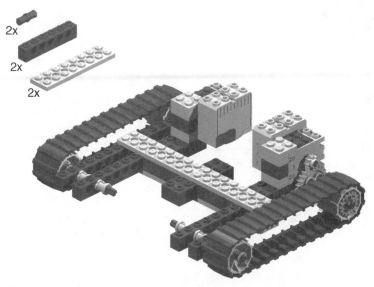

Step 2   Join two 1 × 6 beams together using friction pins in the second and fourth holes. Add to the model as shown and cap with two 2 × 8 plates.

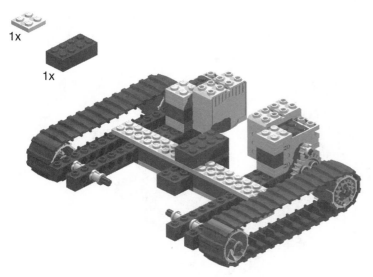

Step 3 Add a 2 × 2 plate and 2 × 4 brick as shown.

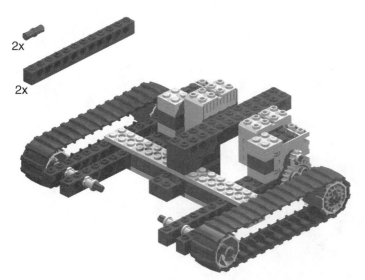

Step 4 Join two 1 × 12 beams together with friction pins in the third and ninth holes.

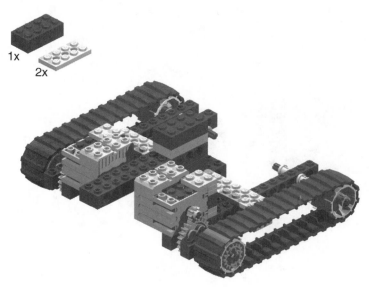

Step 5   Add two 2 × 4 plates and a 2 × 4 brick as shown.

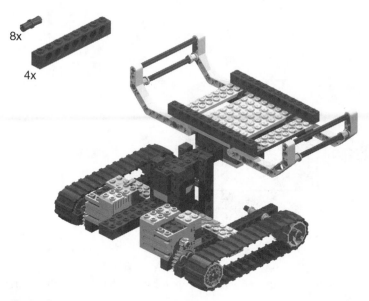

Step 6   Attach the basket as shown. Secure the basket to the chassis using four 1 × 8 beams. Friction pins should be inserted into the highest and lowest beams on the chassis.

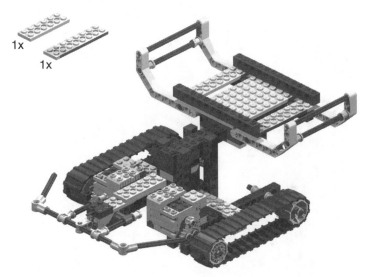

Step 7   Attach the bumper to the front of the chassis. Secure it with a 2 × 8 plate. On top of that, place a 2 × 6 plate to build up height for the RCX brick.

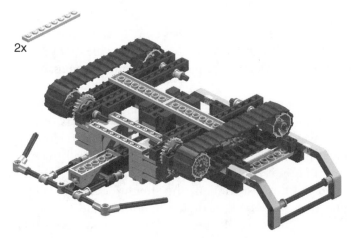

Step 8   Flip the robot over and attach two 1 × 8 plates to the underside of the motors.

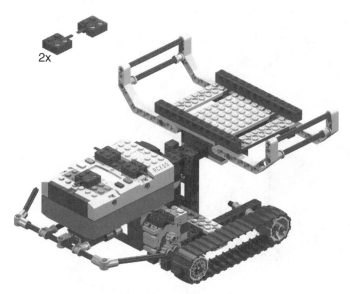

Step 9 Attach the RCX to the chassis, making sure it is securely in place. Attach wire bricks for the motors and touch sensors.

Note:

Mozer is not stable until the breadboard circuit has been placed in the basket to counterbalance the RCX brick. If your breadboard is too light you may have to attach ballast (LEGO bricks) to the basket, or move the basket further back.

Now that we have a robot, we can demonstrate the new powers of compass navigation. The best way to demonstrate this is simply to travel along the edge of a square repeatedly. If navigation is 100% successful it will trace the same square in the floor ad infinitum. As we know, the TimingNavigator and RotationNavigator classes fail this test. Initially they might be able to keep to a square, but over time they lose track of their orientation and the square rotates all over the place (Figure 10–7). After a minute or less, these techniques cause the robot to be helplessly lost. Not so with the CompassNavigator. It might not make every segment at a precise angle, but after several minutes of travel the left segment of the square is still on the left, the top segment is still on the top, and so on. The position of the square may migrate due to lack of accurate distance measurement (a rotation sensor would help with this), but it keeps the directions consistent.

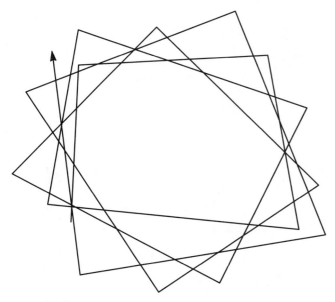

Figure 10–7   Cumulative errors without a compass sensor.

The code for this program is amazingly simple, now that all the functional classes have been written:

```
1. import josx.platform.rcx.*;
2.
3. class SquareTest {
4.     public static void main(String [] args) {
5.         float [] corrections = {0,68,141,198,360};
6.         AutoCalibration cal = new AutoCalibration(Sensor.S1,
                Sensor.S3, corrections);
7.         cal.calibrate(Motor.A, Motor.C);
8.
9.         CompassSensor cs = new CompassSensor(Sensor.S1,
                Sensor.S3, cal);
10.
11.         CompassNavigator cn = new CompassNavigator(cs,
                Motor.C, Motor.A, 9.0f);
12.         while(true) {
13.             cn.gotoPoint(0,100);
14.             cn.gotoPoint(100,100);
15.             cn.gotoPoint(100,0);
16.             cn.gotoPoint(0,0);
17.         }
18.     }
19. }
```

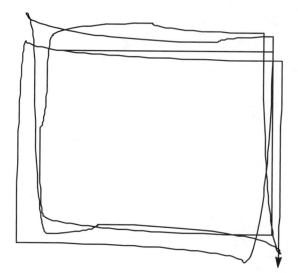

Figure 10–8   Drawing a square using the compass sensor.

When this code is run you should see something similar to Figure 10–8. The robot might not draw exactly straight sides to the square, but the top segment will always be at the top, even after a long period of traveling. The square might migrate around a bit, but it is quite consistent, especially when contrasted with Figure 10–7.

Compass Accuracy

The first problem encountered with the compass sensor is the fluctuation of battery charge. This affects the raw values, with weaker batteries producing lower values. This wouldn't be a problem, except the equations need to use constants for min and max to calculate angle. If the values are changing with time, the constants will become invalid after a while.

Another large problem is magnetic interference. The earth's magnetic field is relatively weak, so almost any iron object can distort those readings if close enough. When testing my robot in the kitchen, as soon as it got near the refrigerator it was almost sucked into it. To observe the effect of magnetic interference, you can try walking around the area with a regular handheld compass.

The overall distortion in my living room is likely caused by an abundance of iron objects at one end of the room. The room has two large metal-framed doors, a heating unit along the baseboard, a fireplace with metal shielding, and just outside there is a heavy iron railing. All of these objects are grouped in the same area, so this is likely the cause of the asymmetrical readings from the compass.

There is also the question of angle resolution. The resolution of the readings can actually be increased using a method described in the Dinsmore compass literature. Notice the tops and bottoms of the peaks are rather shallow (Figure 10–4), due to small voltage change per angle increment. The slopes of the curves, however, have a larger change in voltage versus angle, so the slopes produce better accuracy of the angle. There are two points on the graph where the sine curve meets the cosine curve. The top point makes the upper crossing line, and the lower point makes the lower crossing line. When the sine curve is above the upper crossing line it is at its weakest with respect to indicating accurate angles, so it makes more sense to use the cosine curve to read the voltage and the sine curve to designate the proper quadrant. Then, at 135 degrees, the cosine curve falls below the lower crossing line, so it makes more sense to read the voltage of the sine curve to determine the angle. So cosine is used from 45 degrees to 135 degrees and 225 degrees to 315 degrees. Sine is used from 135 degrees to 225 degrees and 315 degrees to 45 degrees.

Note:

I did not use this method to increase resolution because the magnetic distortions probably overrule any benefits.

This chapter concludes explorations into navigation. If the RCX had more input ports available (and more memory) we could use two rotation sensors to complement the compass sensor. Rotation sensors can more accurately gauge distance than timing methods, so they would improve overall accuracy. They could also be used for helping with turns. Imagine the rotation sensors performing the initial rotation, then a compass sensor reading could be taken and the angle adjusted accordingly. Unfortunately there are some limitations to the RCX that prevent combining several of these strategies together.

RCX
COMMUNICATIONS

Topics in this Chapter

- The Communications API
- Uploading Map Data
- Controlling the RCX Through a Network
- Controlling the RCX from a Web Page
- Alternate Data Transfer Methods
- Alternate Communication Uses

Chapter 11

Communications between the RCX brick and a PC can greatly expand the potential of robotics projects. Memory is quite limited on the RCX but today's PCs contain an abundance. A clever programmer can off load complex code to the PC side, allowing the PC to control the RCX brick. For example, one acclaimed RCX project involves a Rubik's Cube solver that scans the faces of the cube, then rotates the cube until it is solved. This project actually uses an algorithm on the PC to analyze the cube faces and calculate a solution—a very memory-intensive operation. Once the solution is found it uploads the sequence of moves as an array to the RCX brick.

Of course, it is also possible for the RCX to send useful data back to the PC to be analyzed. Projects are often created using the RCX to monitor repetitive events, such as toilet flushes or the number of times a light has been turned on in a room. Light levels are also sometimes measured over long periods of time, especially for experiments in which it is necessary to see how much light a plant is taking in over time. Of course, mapping a location and sending the map coordinates back to the PC is a classic example of data collection, which is shown in this chapter.

There are also possibilities for *telerobotics*, the ability to control a robot from vast distances. Using the java.io package, commands to the RCX can be sent across any network, including the Internet. This opens up the possibility of controlling and monitoring experiments away from the lab. This chapter shows you how to control the RCX from any computer using Java data streams, as well as setting up a simple Web server to control a robot through a Web page using JavaScript.

Finally, it is also possible for two RCX bricks to communicate with each other using infrared signals. Communication between two RCX bricks is often used to make a "super RCX brick" with six inputs, six outputs, and 64 kB of memory. In this architecture, usually one brick is the controller brick, and the other merely takes commands for turning motors on and off or reading sensors. RCX robots can also be built to interact with each other, sending messages to achieve interesting "social" behavior. Communications truly opens up incredible possibilities for robotics.

The Communications API

Data flow is the lifeblood of computers, and leJOS allows communication on many levels: IR tower to RCX, RCX to RCX, and probably even IR tower to IR tower (although there isn't much practical use for this). In fact, leJOS can also receive data from the LEGO MINDSTORMS remote control (see Appendix A)—both to the RCX, or even to the IR tower to control your computer. All of these combinations can be handled with leJOS.

The leJOS Communications API can be found in the java.io, pc.irtower.comm, and josx.platform.rcx.comm packages. The communications classes use streams, just like the standard java.io package, so anyone familiar with streams will find it easy to use. The leJOS java.io package contains only the most basic streams relevant to sending and receiving data: InputStream, OutputStream, DataInputStream, and DataOutputStream. Input/Output Streams are the foundation of Streams, and they are only useful for sending bytes. If you want to send other data types such as characters, integers, and floating-point numbers, you will need to use data streams (see "DataInputStream" and "DataOutputStream" later).

InputStream

InputStream is the superclass of all classes representing an input stream of bytes. It is an abstract class so it cannot be instantiated on its own. The main function of InputStream is to return the next byte of input from a data source. In leJOS an instance of InputStream can be obtained using DataPort.getInputStream() (see "PCDataPort" and "RCXDataPort" later).

`java.io.InputStream`

- `public int read() throws IOException`

  Reads the next byte of data from the input stream. The value byte is returned as an int in the range 0 to 255. This method blocks (waits) until input data is available, the end of the stream is detected, or an exception is thrown.

- `public int read(byte[] b) throws IOException`

  Reads some number of bytes from the input stream and stores them in the buffer array b. The number of bytes actually read is returned as an integer. This method blocks until input data is available, the end of the file is detected, or an exception is thrown.

  Parameters: b   The buffer into which the data is read.

- `public int read(byte[] b, int off, int len) throws IOException`

  Reads up to len bytes of data from the input stream into an array of bytes. An attempt is made to read as many as len bytes, but a smaller number may be read, possibly zero. The number of bytes actually read is returned as an integer.

  Parameters: b   The buffer into which the data is read.

  off   The start offset in array b at which the data is written.

  len   The maximum number of bytes to read.

- `public void close() throws IOException`

  Closes this input stream, calls flush() and releases any system resources associated with the stream.

  Note:

  In standard java.io.InputStream the methods mark() and reset() are used to jump back to a previous point in a stream. There are also methods for skip() and available(). The leJOS java.io.InputStream does not support any of these methods.

OutputStream

OutputStream is the superclass of all classes representing an output stream of bytes. It is an abstract class so it cannot be instantiated on its own. Its main function is to send a byte of data to a destination. Like InputStream, an instance of OutputStream can be obtained using DataPort.getOutput-Stream() (see "PCDataPort" and "RCXDataPort" later).

`java.io.OutputStream`

- `public void write(int b) throws IOException`
  Writes the specified byte to this output stream. The general contract for write is that one byte is written to the output stream. The byte to be written is the eight low-order bits of the argument b. The 24 high-order bits of b are ignored.

- `public void write(byte b[]) throws IOException`
  Writes b.length bytes from the specified byte array to this output stream. The general contract for write(b) is that it should have exactly the same effect as the call write(b, 0, b.length).

  Parameters: b   The data.

- `public void write(byte b[], int off, int len) throws IOException`
  Writes len bytes from the specified byte array starting at offset off to this output stream. The general contract for write(b, off, len) is that some of the bytes in the array b are written to the output stream in order; element b[off] is the first byte written and b[off+len-1] is the last byte written by this operation.

  Parameters: b   The data.

  off   The start offset in the data.

  len   The maximum number of bytes to write.

- `public void flush() throws IOException`
  Flushes this output stream and forces any buffered output bytes to be written out. The general contract of flush() is that calling it is an indication that, if any bytes previously written have been buffered by the implementation of the output stream, such bytes should immediately be written to their intended destination.

Warning:

Flush is one of the most important but often forgotten methods of streams. The nonuse of this method probably accounts for most bugs when using the java.io package. Don't forget to call flush() after sending data, otherwise the data may never be sent to the destination!

- `public void close() throws IOException`

  Closes this output stream and releases any system resources associated with this stream. The general contract of close is that it closes the output stream. A closed stream cannot perform output operations and cannot be reopened. A call to flush() is made in this method as well.

DataInputStream

DataInputStream extends InputStream, so it has all the methods of Input-Stream implemented (discussed earlier). This method allows data types other than bytes to be sent. This includes short, int, float, double, char, and bool-ean. Unlike the standard Sun java.io.DataInputStream class, the leJOS ver-sion does not include methods for receiving strings. If you wish to receive strings you can simply write code to read char values and assemble a new string. Also, to save memory the leJOS DataInputStream class does not extend FilterInputStream nor does it implement a DataInput interface.

Note:

The java.io classes are used on the PC side as well as on the RCX. The PC side uses standard Sun Java classes, but the RCX uses special java.io classes written specifically for the RCX. Both "brands" communicate fine with one another, however (i.e., the leJOS OutputStream can talk to the Sun InputStream and vice versa).

`java.io.DataInputStream`

- `public DataInputStream(InputStream in)`

  Returns an instance of DataInputStream. The constructor requires an InputStream object obtained using RCXDataPort.getInputStream().

  Parameters: `in`   The input stream.

- `public final boolean readBoolean() throws IOException`

  Used to send a Boolean value through a stream. Reads one input byte and returns true if that byte is nonzero, false if that byte is zero.

- `public final byte readByte() throws IOException`

  Reads and returns one input byte. The byte is treated as a signed value in the range –128 through 127, inclusive.

- `public final short readShort() throws IOException`

  Reads two input bytes and returns a short value.

- `public final char readChar() throws IOException`

  Reads an input char and returns the char value (a Unicode char is made up of two bytes).

- `public final int readInt() throws IOException`

  Reads four input bytes and returns an int value.

- `public final float readFloat() throws IOException`

  Reads four input bytes and returns a float value.

- `public final double readDouble() throws IOException`

  Reads eight input bytes and returns a double value.

DataOutputStream

If DataInputStream is the catcher then DataOutputStream is the pitcher. It encodes various data types into byte values and sends them across a data stream. DataOutputStream extends OutputStream, so it has all the methods described in the OutputStream API. Unlike the Sun DataOutputStream, DataOutputStream does not extend FilterOutputStream, nor does it implement DataOutput. It has most methods of the standard java.io.DataOutputStream, but excludes methods dealing with text data transfer.

`java.io.DataOutputStream`

- `public DataOutputStream(OutputStream out)`

  Creates a new data output stream to write data to the specified underlying output stream.

  Parameters: out   The output stream.

- `public final void writeBoolean(boolean v) throws IOException`

  Writes a Boolean value to this output stream.

  Parameters: v   A Boolean value.

- `public final void writeByte(int v) throws IOException`

  Writes to the output stream the eight low-order bits of the argument v.

  Parameters: v   A byte value.

- `public final void writeShort(int v) throws IOException`

  Writes two bytes to the output stream to represent the value of the argument.

  Parameters: v   A short value.

- `public final void writeChar(int v) throws IOException`
  Writes a char value, which is comprised of two bytes, to the output stream.

  Parameters: v   A char value.

- `public final void writeInt(int v) throws IOException`
  Writes an int value, which is comprised of four bytes, to the output stream.

  Parameters: v   An int value.

- `public final void writeFloat(float v) throws IOException`
  Writes a float value, which is comprised of four bytes, to the output stream.

  Parameters: v   A float value.

- `public final void writeDouble(double v) throws IOException`
  Writes a double value, which is comprised of eight bytes, to the output stream.

  Parameters: v   A double value.

DataPort

DataPort is an abstract class at the top of the RCX communications hierarchy. A data port is a pretty general term, and can refer to a USB port, a serial port, or an RCX IR port. The DataPort class functions much like java.net.Socket in standard Java. These classes have in common the ability to hand out InputStream and OutputStream objects, which are absolutely vital for sending and receiving data in Java. Anyone familiar with Sockets should be comfortable using DataPort.

`josx.platform.rcx.comm.DataPort`

- `public InputStream getInputStream()`
  Returns an input stream for this DataPort.

- `public OutputStream getOutputStream()`
  Returns an output stream for this DataPort.

Note:

You might wonder how this receives an InputStream or OutputStream object because these are abstract classes. The underlying returned classes

*are actually called RCXInputStream and RCXOutputStream, which are
protected inner classes of DataPort.*

- `public void close()`

  Closes this DataPort.

- `public void setTimeOut(int timeOut)`

  The timeOut value represents the amount of time the DataPort will keep
  trying to exchange data. If it fails to receive a response from the target it
  will keep trying for this number of milliseconds. (The value is 0 by
  default, meaning it will keep trying forever.)

  Parameters: `timeOut`   The number of milliseconds to keep
                              trying if data communication fails.

- `public int getTimeOut()`

  Returns the current timeout value for this DataPort.

PCDataPort

PCDataPort extends the DataPort abstract class and implements all abstract
methods. The main purpose of this class is to provide an InputStream or OutputStream *on the PC side* to communicate through the IR tower. This class
cannot and should not be used in any code intended for the RCX brick. To
use this code in your regular Java code, simply import the pc.irtower.comm
package (or import just the PCDataPort class).

Communication with the IR tower is complicated by the fact that the IR
tower can only receive data while the green LED is on. If an RCX brick is sitting in front of the IR tower and it starts sending data, the IR tower does not
detect this. It sits there, unpowered, until the PC side sends data. In other
words, the PC must initiate all data transfers. The leJOS API deals with this
problem, however, so it is almost invisible for a programmer:

`pc.irtower.comm.PCDataPort`

- `public PCDataPort(String port) throws IOException`

  Returns an instance of PCDataPort.

  Parameters: `port`   A string describing the port to use.
                          Accepts a value from COM1 to COM4 or
                          USB (case does not matter).

- `public InputStream getInputStream()`

  Returns an input stream for this DataPort.

- `public OutputStream getOutputStream()`

  Returns an output stream for this DataPort.

RCXDataPort

RCXData port allows data to be sent from the RCX IR port to another source and vice versa. This class is very easy to use, and the only methods of importance come from extending DataPort—getInputStream() and getOutputStream():

`josx.platform.rcx.comm.RCXDataPort`

- `public RCXDataPort()`

  Returns an instance of RCXDataPort.

- `public InputStream getInputStream()`

  Returns an input stream for this DataPort.

- `public OutputStream getOutputStream()`

  Returns an output stream for this DataPort.

Note:

There are plans to implement a java.net package for leJOS so the RCX brick could communicate through IP addresses directly to the Internet. (This will require a small server class on the PC side.)

Installation

There is nothing special to do to use the leJOS Communications API with the RCX, but the PC side must have access to special classes to work. Currently the leJOS Communications API depends on the JavaComm API to work. This is needed because different platforms use different forms of communicating with ports, so a platform-independent solution is needed.

Warning:

By the time this book hits the shelves installation of the Javacomm API may be unnecessary. There are plans to include Java Native Interface (JNI) communications within leJOS, eliminating the need for Javacomm installation. Check with the leJOS readme file first for installation notes.

Win32

1. Download the Windows version of JavaComm 2.0 from Sun at *java.sun.com/products/javacomm/.*
2. Extract the zipped file to any directory.
3. Copy Win32comm.dll to the bin directory of your JDK (e.g., C:\jdk1.3.1\bin).
4. Copy comm.jar to the lib directory of your JDK (e.g., C:\jdk1.3.1\lib).
5. Copy javax.comm.properties to the lib directory of your JDK (e.g., C:\jdk1.3.1\lib).
6. Add the comm.jar file to the CLASSPATH system variable (e.g., set CLASSPATH=c:\jdk1.1.6\lib\comm.jar).

Linux

1. Download the Solaris CommAPI release at *java.sun.com/products/javacomm.*
2. Copy comm.jar into your JDK bin directory.
3. Add this JAR file to your CLASSPATH (e.g., export CLASS-PATH=$CLASSPATH:/usr/local/jdk1.1.5/bin/comm.jar).
4. Download and build RXTX at *www.rxtx.org*
5. Add the RXTX directory to your CLASSPATH as instructed in the RXTX documentation.
6. Create a text file in your JDK lib directory. This file must be named `javax.comm.properties`. The contents of this file is a single line that should read:
   `Driver=gnu.io.RXTXCommDriver`
7. You can test your installation by running the BlackBox demo included with CommAPI:
   `java -classpath BlackBox.jar:$CLASSPATH BlackBox`

IDE Setup

If you plan on using an IDE (such as JCreator) to program your PC side programs, then it is necessary to include some settings in the IDE. JCreator automatically overrides the system CLASSPATH settings when compiling and running Java programs (it does not override these settings for the leJOS tools, however). For this reason we must add the settings to JCreator.

1. In JCreator, select Project ➤ Project Settings and click the Required Libraries tab (Figure 11–1).

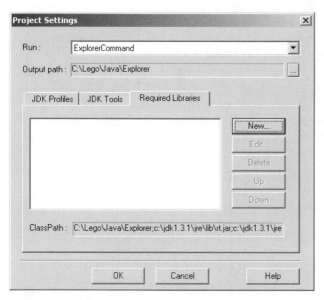

Figure 11–1   Project Settings dialog box.

2. Click New to add a new CLASSPATH setting and a dialog box appears (Figure 11–2). Type in leJOS Comm as the name. Click Add ➤ Add Package, and browse to the leJOS classes.jar file (e.g., C:\lejos\lib\classes.jar). Click OK when done.

Figure 11–2   Adding leJOS to the CLASSPATH.

3. Now add the Javacomm CLASSPATH setting. Click New and type Javacomm as the name (Figure 11–3). Click Add ➤ Add Package, and browse to the comm.jar file (e.g., C:\jdk1.3.1\lib \comm.jar). Click OK when done.

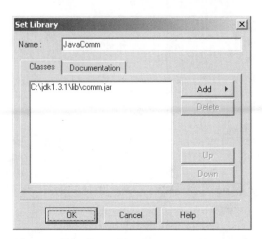

Figure 11–3   Adding Javacomm to the CLASSPATH.

4. Select the check boxes next to the two settings (Figure 11–4). That's it! You can now use the Compile File and Execute File buttons on the toolbar for PC Java programs using leJOS Comm.

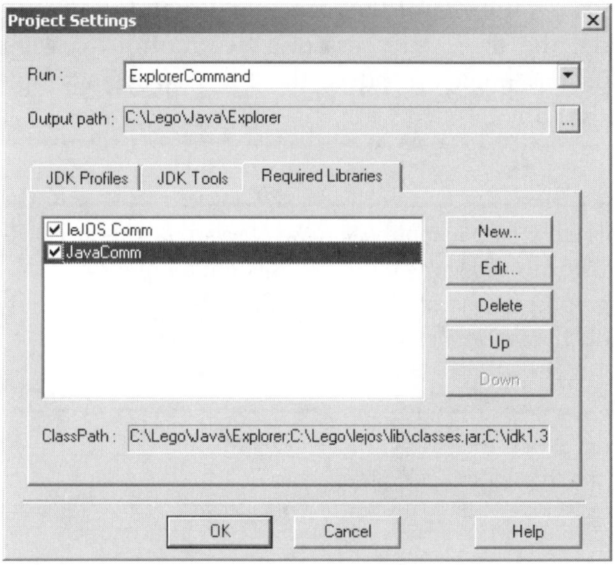

Figure 11–4   Activating the CLASSPATH setting for the project.

Uploading Map Data

The RCX brick is great for collecting real-world data, but it is not so good at displaying and analyzing that data. A PC is the best platform for this, so it's useful to be able to send data results back to the PC. For data transmission to take place there must be a program running on the RCX and a separate program running on the PC (Figure 11–5).

The following project creates a robot that will map the coordinates of objects it bumps into. The strategy of the robot is to store the coordinates in two arrays; one for *x* values and one for *y* values. Once it has encountered 10 objects the robot's movement should be stopped by pressing the Run button,

PC Code

Robot Code

Figure 11–5   Basic communication with an RCX brick.

then the robot should be placed in front of the IR tower. When the PC side program is up and running, the user can press the View button to begin transmission. Once all data has been uploaded, the PC displays a simple approximation of the robot's trail.

Note:

Theoretically this code will work on any robot using the Navigation interface (Trilobot, Tippy Senior, or Mozer). However, this code uses a total of 47 classes (displayed using verbose option of lejos.exe), which pushes the RCX to the limit. I was only able to use TimingNavigator without running out of memory.

```java
1. import josx.platform.rcx.*;
2. import josx.platform.rcx.comm.*;
3. import josx.robotics.*;
4. import java.io.*;
5.
6. class DataSender implements SensorListener {
7.
8.     Navigator robot;
9.     static final byte ARRAY_SIZE = 10;
10.    public short [] xCoords;
11.    public short [] yCoords;
12.    byte count = 0;
13.
14.    public DataSender(Navigator robot) {
15.        this.robot = robot;
16.
17.        xCoords = new short [ARRAY_SIZE];
18.        yCoords = new short [ARRAY_SIZE];
19.
20.        Sensor.S2.addSensorListener(this);
21.    }
22.
23.    public static void main(String [] args) throws IOExcep-
           tion {
24.        TimingNavigator robot = new TimingNavigator(Motor.C,
               Motor.A, 4.475f, 1.61f);
25.        robot.forward();
26.
27.        DataSender ds = new DataSender(robot);
28.        try{
29.            Button.RUN.waitForPressAndRelease();
```

```
30.          robot.stop();
31.          Button.VIEW.waitForPressAndRelease();
32.      }catch(InterruptedException ie){}
33.
34.      // Send data:
35.      RCXDataPort port = new RCXDataPort();
36.      DataOutputStream out = new DataOutput-
              Stream(port.getOutputStream());
37.      out.writeShort(0);
38.      out.writeShort(0);
39.      for(byte i=0;i<ARRAY_SIZE;++i) {
40.          out.writeShort(ds.xCoords[i]);
41.          out.writeShort(ds.yCoords[i]);
42.      }
43.      out.flush();
44.  }
45.
46.  /** Records the x, y position when bumper hits an
          object.*/
47.  public void stateChanged(Sensor bumper, int oldVal, int
          newVal) {
48.      if(bumper.readBooleanValue() == true) {
49.          robot.stop();
50.          if(count < ARRAY_SIZE) {
51.              xCoords[count] = (short)robot.getX();
52.              yCoords[count] = (short)robot.getY();
53.              ++count;
54.          }
55.          robot.travel(-20);
56.          robot.rotate((float)(Math.random() * 180));
57.          robot.forward();
58.      }
59.  }
60. }
```

This code creates a Navigator object called robot and starts moving forward. A listener is added to the bumper sensor, so every time the robot comes into contact with an object it can react accordingly (Lines 49–61). The reaction of the robot is simply to record the coordinates of the collision, back up, and turn a random amount. The main() method contains the code to initialize the object, wait for the user to press the Run button, and wait for the user to press the View button. When the View button is pressed, it sends the data back to the PC.

Now that the robot code is complete we need some code on the PC side to receive the data and display it on the monitor. The code to do this is quite

brief considering it uses the Java Abstract Window Toolkit (AWT). To make
things simple, this code begins waiting for input from the IR tower in the
constructor. Once the data has been received it displays it in a window (Figure 11–6).

```
1. import java.io.*;
2. import pc.irtower.comm.*;
3. import java.awt.*;
4. import java.awt.event.*;
5.
6. public class MapData extends Canvas{
7.    int ARRAY_SIZE = 10;
8.    short [] xCoords;
9.    short [] yCoords;
10.
11.   public MapData() {
12.       xCoords = new short[ARRAY_SIZE];
13.       yCoords = new short[ARRAY_SIZE];
14.       PCDataPort port = null;
15.       try {
16.           port = new PCDataPort("COM2");
17.           DataInputStream in = new DataInputStream(port.get-
                   InputStream());
18.           for(int i=0;i<ARRAY_SIZE;++i) {
19.               xCoords[i] = in.readShort();
20.               System.out.println("x = " + xCoords[i]);
21.               yCoords[i] = in.readShort();
22.               System.out.println("y = " + yCoords[i]);
23.           }
24.       } catch(IOException ioe) {
25.           ioe.printStackTrace();
26.       }
27.   }
28.
29.   public static void main(String [] args) {
30.
31.       Frame mainFrame = new Frame("Explorer Command
               Center");
32.       mainFrame.addWindowListener(new WindowAdapter() {
33.           public void windowClosing(WindowEvent e) {
34.               System.exit(0);
35.           }
36.       });
37.       mainFrame.setSize(400, 300);
38.       mainFrame.add(new MapData());
39.       mainFrame.setVisible(true);
```

```
40.    }
41.
42.    public void paint(Graphics g) {
43.        int height = this.getSize().height;
44.        int width = this.getSize().width;
45.        g.setColor(Color.orange);
46.        g.drawLine(width/2,0,width/2, height);
47.        g.drawLine(0,height/2, width, height/2);
48.        g.setColor(Color.black);
49.        for(int i=0;i<ARRAY_SIZE-1;++i) {
50.            g.drawLine(xCoords[i] + width/2, yCoords[i] +
                  height/2,
51.            xCoords[i+1] + width/2, yCoords[i + 1]+height/2);
52.        }
53.    }
54. }
```

Note:

Line 16 must specify the port to contact your IR tower (e.g., COM1 or USB).

Most of the code is devoted to AWT display, but the interesting code for receiving data is found between Lines 15 and 28.

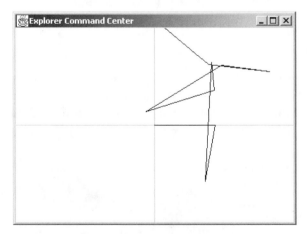

Figure 11-6 PC display of map data.

To test this project out I used Tippy Senior (Chapter 8, "Navigation with Rotation Sensors"). First, let the robot wander around until it has hit at least 10 objects. Once this is done press the Run button to stop the motors and place the robot in front of the IR tower. Execute the PC program and the green light on the IR tower will turn on, indicating you can press View to start sending data. Once all the data has been uploaded it displays a map similar to Figure 11–6.

Controlling the RCX Through a Network

Data communications is great for sending sensor readings back to the PC for analysis, but it can also be used for direct control of the RCX brick. In this project we take it one step further by controlling the RCX from another PC across a network—including the Internet (Figure 11–7). This type of control, where the controller is not present in the same space as the robot, is known as *telerobotics*. The NASA Mars mission controlled Sojourner using telerobotics, as the robot could not be controlled in real time due to the time it takes for radio signals to travel from Earth to Mars. Instead, Sojourner was given a series of instructions to complete on its own, depending on what the NASA controllers chose to do from the pictures they received. It was left up to the internal code of the robot to navigate around obstacles it encountered along the way to its destination.

In this project we have a problem similar to the problem encountered by NASA. We don't have a time delay factor, as a robot could be controlled over a network almost real time, even across the Internet. The problem is that when our rover turns away from the IR tower we lose contact. The best we can do is

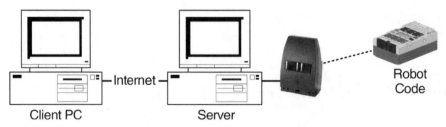

Figure 11-7 Architecture for robot control over the Internet.

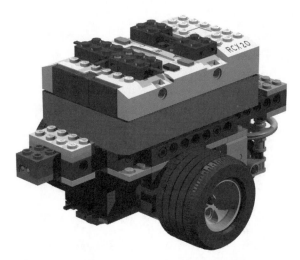

Figure 11-8 Tippy Senior modified with a light sensor.

give the robot a series of instructions, then wait for it to return to the IR tower and report back with some results.

The robot in this project can be any of the Navigator robots we programmed in Chapters 7, 8, and 10. This project is specifically programmed for the rotation sensor robot used in Chapter 8, which has been modified slightly to include a light sensor (Figure 11–8). The robot is given an array of coordinates to move to. Once it reaches the final coordinate it captures a light reading and then uses the coordinates in reverse to make its way back to the IR tower. Once there, it transmits the light reading to the PC. The code for the RCX side is simple, and uses the same concepts introduced in the explanation of leJOS RCX communications.

The architecture for this project is a little more complex than the other projects in this book. It requires code to run on three separate platforms—a client computer, a server, and the RCX brick (Figure 11–7). There are also two separate media used for data transfer—the Internet and IR light. The client application sends user commands from the client to the server. The server acts as a sort of middle man, shuffling commands from the user to the RCX and vice versa. The robot just sits in front of the IR tower waiting for a destination. When it has some coordinates it takes off and records a light reading at the farthest point. Let's examine this code first:

```
1. import josx.platform.rcx.*;
2. import josx.robotics.*;
3. import josx.platform.rcx.comm.*;
4. import java.io.*;
```

```
5.
6. public class RCXExplorer {
7.     DataInputStream in;
8.     DataOutputStream out;
9.     Navigator robot;
10.    final byte ARRAY_SIZE = 4;
11.    short [] xCoords;
12.    short [] yCoords;
13.
14.    public RCXExplorer() {
15.        // TimingNavigator Constructor for Tippy Senior:
16.        robot = new TimingNavigator(Motor.C, Motor.A, 4.475f,
                1.61f);
17.        RCXDataPort dp = new RCXDataPort();
18.        in = new DataInputStream(dp.getInputStream());
19.        out = new DataOutputStream(dp.getOutputStream());
20.        xCoords = new short [ARRAY_SIZE];
21.        yCoords = new short [ARRAY_SIZE];
22.    }
23.
24.    public static void main(String [] args) {
25.        RCXExplorer re = new RCXExplorer();
26.        while(true) {
27.            re.readCoordinates();
28.            short lightValue = re.fetchValue();
29.            re.returnValue(lightValue);
30.        }
31.    }
32.
33.    /** Reads coordinates from PC into arrays.*/
34.    public void readCoordinates() {
35.        try {
36.            for(int i=0;i<ARRAY_SIZE;++i) {
37.                xCoords[i] = in.readShort();
38.                yCoords[i] = in.readShort();
39.            }
40.        } catch(IOException e) {}
41.    }
42.
43.    /** Sends bot to destination to sample light value.*/
44.    public short fetchValue() {
45.        Sensor.S2.activate();
46.        for(int i=0;i<ARRAY_SIZE;++i)
47.            robot.gotoPoint(xCoords[i],yCoords[i]);
48.        short light = (short)Sensor.S2.readRawValue();
49.        Sensor.S2.passivate();
```

```
50.        return light;
51.    }
52.
53.    /** Sends bot back to starting point and sends value to
           PC.*/
54.    public void returnValue(short val) {
55.        for(int i=ARRAY_SIZE-1;i>-1;--i)
56.            robot.gotoPoint(xCoords[i],yCoords[i]);
57.        robot.gotoPoint(0,0);
58.        robot.gotoAngle(0);
59.        try {
60.            out.writeShort(val);
61.            out.flush();
62.        } catch(IOException ioe) {}
63.    }
64. }
```

The next part of our project is the server code. It is responsible for accepting an array of coordinates from a client on another PC and passing those to the RCX. It is also responsible for waiting for the RCX and sending the light reading back to the client computer. Let's examine this code:

```
1. import java.net.*;
2. import java.io.*;
3. import pc.irtower.comm
4.
5. public class ExplorerServer {
6.
7.     ServerSocket server;
8.     Socket client;
9.     DataOutputStream clientOutStream;
10.    DataInputStream clientInStream;
11.    PCDataPort port;
12.    DataInputStream inRCX;
13.    DataOutputStream outRCX;
14.
15.    public ExplorerServer(int portNumber) {
16.        try {
17.            // Internet connection:
18.            server = new ServerSocket(portNumber);
19.
20.            // RCX Connection:
21.            port = new PCDataPort("COM2");
22.            inRCX = new DataInputStream(port.getInputStream());
23.            outRCX = new DataOutputStream(port.getOutput-
                   Stream());
```

```
24.         }
25.      catch (IOException io){
26.          io.printStackTrace();
27.          System.exit(0);
28.      }
29.   }
30.
31.   public static void main(String [] args) {
32.      ExplorerServer host = new ExplorerServer(ExplorerCom-
             mand.PORT);
33.      while(true) {
34.         host.waitForConnection();
35.         while(host.client!=null)
36.            host.waitForCommands();
37.      }
38.   }
39.
40.   /** Wait for a connection from the Client machine */
41.   public void waitForConnection() {
42.      try {
43.         System.out.println("Listening for client.");
44.         client = server.accept();
45.         clientOutStream = new DataOutputStream(client
                .getOutputStream());
46.         clientInStream = new DataInputStream(client.get-
                InputStream());
47.         System.out.println("Client connected.");
48.      } catch(IOException io) {
49.         io.printStackTrace();
50.      }
51.   }
52.
53.   /** Wait for coordinates from the Client machine */
54.   public void waitForCommands() {
55.      int [] x = new int[ExplorerCommand.ARRAY_SIZE];
56.      int [] y = new int[ExplorerCommand.ARRAY_SIZE];
57.      try {
58.         for(int i=0;i<ExplorerCommand.ARRAY_SIZE;++i) {
59.            x[i] = clientInStream.readInt();
60.            y[i] = clientInStream.readInt();
61.         }
62.      } catch(IOException io) {
63.         System.out.println("Client disconnected.");
64.         System.exit(0);
65.      }
66.      sendCommandsToRCX(x, y);
```

```
67.          waitForRCX();
68.      }
69.
70.      /** Send coordinates to the RCX */
71.      public void sendCommandsToRCX(int [] x, int [] y) {
72.          System.out.println("Sending data to rcx: ");
73.          for(int i=0;i<ExplorerCommand.ARRAY_SIZE;++i) {
74.              System.out.println(x[i] + " " + y[i]);
75.              try {
76.                  outRCX.writeShort(x[i]);
77.                  outRCX.writeShort(y[i]);
78.                  outRCX.flush();
79.              } catch (Exception e) {
80.                  e.printStackTrace();
81.                  break;
82.              }
83.          }
84.      }
85.
86.      /** Wait for light reading from the RCX */
87.      public void waitForRCX() {
88.          System.out.println("Waiting for RCX reply.");
89.
90.          try {
91.              short value = inRCX.readShort();
92.              System.out.println("Got value " + value + ".
                     Sending to user.");
93.              clientOutStream.writeInt(value);
94.          } catch(IOException io) {
95.              io.printStackTrace();
96.          }
97.      }
98. }
```

Note:

In Line 21 the string must be the port your RCX tower is attached to (e.g., COM1 or USB).

The final part of the project is the client GUI, which resides somewhere across a network. This GUI includes an area to type in a series of coordinates, and also a series of shortcut buttons to send the robot to predesignated areas (Figure 11–9). Ideally this GUI would also include a map of the area with measurements, or even a live feed of the floor space from a Web cam. For the purposes of keeping this short, however, we omit these features and leave it up to the programmer to implement. Let's examine this program, which is called the Explorer Command Console:

```
1. import java.awt.*;
2. import java.awt.event.*;
3. import java.io.*;
4. import java.net.Socket;
5.
6. public class ExplorerCommand extends Panel {
7.     public static final int PORT = 5067;
8.     public static final int ARRAY_SIZE = 4;
9.
10.     Button btnConnect;
11.     Button btnGo;
12.     Button btnKitchen;
13.     Button btnLivingRoom;
14.     Button btnBedRoom;
15.     TextField txtX;
16.     TextField txtY;
17.     TextField txtIPAddress;
18.     TextArea messages;
19.
20.     private Socket socket;
21.     private DataOutputStream outStream;
22.     private DataInputStream inStream;
23.
24.     public ExplorerCommand(String ip) {
25.         super(new BorderLayout());
26.
27.         ControlListener cl = new ControlListener();
28.
29.         btnConnect = new Button("Connect");
30.         btnConnect.addActionListener(cl);
31.         btnGo = new Button("Go!");
32.         btnGo.addActionListener(cl);
33.         btnKitchen = new Button("Kitchen");
34.         btnKitchen.addActionListener(cl);
35.         btnLivingRoom = new Button("Living Room");
36.         btnLivingRoom.addActionListener(cl);
37.         btnBedRoom = new Button("Bed Room");
38.         btnBedRoom.addActionListener(cl);
39.
40.         txtX = new TextField("",20);
41.         txtY = new TextField("",20);
42.         txtIPAddress = new TextField(ip,16);
```

```
43.
44.        messages = new TextArea("status: DISCONNECTED");
45.
46.        Panel north = new Panel(new FlowLayout(FlowLay-
               out.LEFT));
47.        north.add(btnConnect);
48.        north.add(txtIPAddress);
49.
50.        Panel south = new Panel(new FlowLayout());
51.        south.add(btnKitchen);
52.        south.add(btnLivingRoom);
53.        south.add(btnBedRoom);
54.
55.        Panel center = new Panel(new GridLayout(4,1));
56.        center.add(new Label("Enter coordinates separated by
               commas (e.g. 40,70,10,35)"));
57.
58.        Panel center1 = new Panel(new FlowLayout(FlowLay-
               out.LEFT));
59.        center1.add(new Label("X:"));
60.        center1.add(txtX);
61.
62.        Panel center2 = new Panel(new FlowLayout(FlowLay-
               out.LEFT));
63.        center2.add(new Label("Y:"));
64.        center2.add(txtY);
65.
66.        Panel center3 = new Panel(new FlowLayout(FlowLay-
               out.LEFT));
67.        center3.add(btnGo);
68.        center3.add(messages);
69.
70.        center.add(center1);
71.        center.add(center2);
72.        center.add(center3);
73.
74.        this.add(north, "North");
75.        this.add(south, "South");
76.        this.add(center, "Center");
77.    }
78.
79.    public static void main(String args[]) {
80.        System.out.println("Starting Explorer Command...");
81.        Frame mainFrame = new Frame("Explorer Command
               Console");
82.        mainFrame.addWindowListener(new WindowAdapter() {
```

```
83.          public void windowClosing(WindowEvent e) {
84.              System.exit(0);
85.          }
86.      });
87.      mainFrame.setSize(400, 300);
88.      mainFrame.add(new ExplorerCommand("127.0.0.1"));
89.      mainFrame.setVisible(true);
90.  }
91.
92.  /** Sends coordinates to the server, then waits for
93.   * the server to return a light value. */
94.  private int fetchLightReading(short [] x, short [] y){
95.      // Send coordinates to Server:
96.      messages.setText("status: SENDING Coordinates.");
97.      try {
98.          for(int i=0;i<ARRAY_SIZE;++i){
99.              outStream.writeInt(x[i]);
100.             outStream.writeInt(y[i]);
101.         }
102.     } catch(IOException io) {
103.         messages.setText("status: ERROR Problems occurred
                 sending data.");
104.         return 0;
105.     }
106.
107.     // Wait for server to return light reading:
108.     int light = 0;
109.     try {
110.         messages.setText("status: WAITING for rover to
                 return.");
111.         light = inStream.readInt();
112.     } catch(IOException io) {
113.         messages.setText("status: ERROR Data transfer of
                 light reading failed.");
114.     }
115.     messages.setText("status: COMPLETE The light reading
             was " + light);
116.     return light;
117. }
118.
119. /** A listener class for all the buttons of the GUI. */
120. private class ControlListener implements ActionListener{
121.     public void actionPerformed(ActionEvent e) {
122.         String command = e.getActionCommand();
123.         int light = 0;
124.         if (command.equals("Connect")) {
```

```
125.          try {
126.              socket = new Socket(txtIPAddress.getText(),
                      PORT);
127.              outStream = new DataOutput-
                      Stream(socket.getOutputStream());
128.              inStream = new DataInputStream(socket.get-
                      InputStream());
129.              messages.setText("status: CONNECTED");
130.              btnConnect.setLabel("Disconnect");
131.          } catch (Exception exc) {
132.              messages.setText("status: FAILURE Error
                      establishing connection with server.");
133.              System.out.println("Error: " + exc);
134.          }
135.      }
136.      else if (command.equals("Disconnect")) {
137.          try {
138.              outStream.close();
139.              inStream.close();
140.              socket.close();
141.              btnConnect.setLabel("Connect");
142.              messages.setText("status: DISCONNECTED");
143.          } catch (Exception exc) {
144.              messages.setText("status: FAILURE Error
                      closing connection with server.");
145.              System.out.println("Error: " + exc);
146.          }
147.      }
148.      else if (command.equals("Go!")) {
149.          short [] x = parseArray(txtX.getText());
150.          short [] y = parseArray(txtY.getText());
151.          fetchLightReading(x,y);
152.      }
153.      else if (command.equals("Kitchen")) {
154.          short [] x = {-100,-100,-300,-310};
155.          short [] y = {0,100,100,100};
156.          fetchLightReading(x,y);
157.      }
158.      else if (command.equals("Bed Room")) {
159.          short [] x = {0,200,200,250};
160.          short [] y = {-100,-100,-200,-250};
161.          fetchLightReading(x,y);
162.      }
163.      else if (command.equals("Living Room")) {
164.          short [] x = {-50,-50,-150,-150};
165.          short [] y = {0,-300,-300,-310};
```

```
166.                    fetchLightReading(x,y);
167.               }
168.          }
169.
170.      /** Takes a string of coordinates and parses out
171.       * the short values (using commas) and assembles
172.       * them into an array. */
173.      public short [] parseArray(String coords) {
174.          int order = 0;
175.          short [] ar = new short[ARRAY_SIZE];
176.          for(int i=0;i<coords.length();++i) {
177.              int firstComma = coords.indexOf(",",i);
178.
179.              String leading;
180.              if(firstComma < 0) {
181.                  leading = coords.substring(i);
182.                  i = coords.length();
183.              }
184.              else {
185.                  leading = coords.substring(i,firstComma);
186.                  i = firstComma;
187.              }
188.              ar[order++] = Short.parseShort(leading);
189.          }
190.          return ar;
191.      }
192.    }
193. }
```

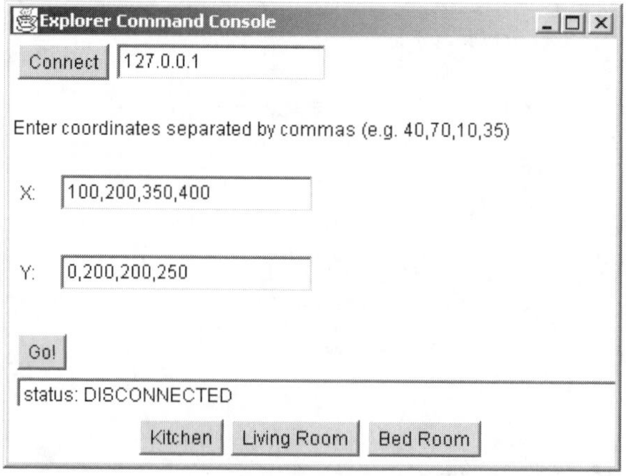

Figure 11–9   The Explorer Command Console.

Note:

In the preceding code, I used several locations in my home for the shortcut buttons, so feel free to customize the locations in Lines 153 to 166 according to your own location.

Now that we have all the code ready, it's time to test it. First, upload the code to the RCX, sit it in front of the IR tower, and press the Run button. The robot waits patiently for a series of coordinates from the PC. Next, run the server code on your PC. It will sit waiting for an Explorer Command Console to connect to it. Finally, run the Command Explorer Console (either on the same machine or on a different machine on the network). Type in the IP address (or leave it as 127.0.0.1 if on the same machine) and click Connect. You can now click one of the shortcut buttons, or alternately enter a series of four coordinates. Once the coordinates have been entered click Go. The robot heads to the location and records a light reading. When the robot returns you are presented with the result. If it fails to return, try using the TimingNavigator.setDelay() method.

Note:

This project really taxes the RCX memory. It uses several large classes, including TimingNavigator, which also uses the Math class. I wasn't even able to use the Sound or LCD class in this project because they pushed memory usage over the limit. This project works with the current release of leJOS, but if leJOS changes in the future and takes up more space, you might see a dreaded exception, which means out of memory. Chapter 12, "Advanced Topics," gives some explanations on how to free up memory in leJOS if you wish to expand this code.

Controlling the RCX from a Web Page

This section describes a very cool way to interact with the RCX brick using a Java Server Page (JSP). In the previous section we accessed the RCX across a network, but the user needed to run the ExplorerCommand class. Now we will create a Web page that allows anyone with a browser to access the RCX. The basic architecture consists of three components: a client Web browser, a Web server, and the RCX brick (Figure 11–10). We will need to create an HTML

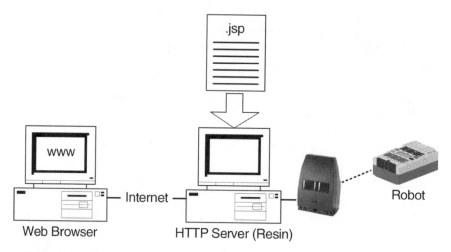

Figure 11-10   Architecture using JSP code and a Web server.

page for the client browser, JSP code for the server, and leJOS Java for the RCX brick. The JSP is actually HTML code and Java code all in one file, so there are actually only two bodies of code we will write for this project.

This setup could be useful for running an experiment with groups of people who might want to monitor (or even interact with) the experiment. Imagine a scenario in which a classroom of psychology students is performing an experiment with a lab rat. The behavior of rats is typically conditioned using a *Skinner box*—a cage containing switches for the rats to push, and food pellets that are dished out to give the animals positive reinforcement. Often the boxes are used to train the animals to perform novel actions, such as play tic-tac-toe or count objects. Using the RCX, it would be very easy for anyone to build a complex Skinner box. A Web cam (or LEGO cam) could even provide a visual presence for viewers. Students could surf to the Web page at any time and look at how the experiment is going, or even interact directly with the animal in the Skinner box. Touch sensors could be used to receive input from the animal, and motors, lights, or sound could be used to interact with the animal. Or, you could turn the tables and have an RCX robot with a neural net run around the Skinner box. There are endless possibilities.

Installing a Web Server

All Web pages are hosted by Web servers, which are just normal computers. The Web server itself must be connected to the IR tower, so you cannot use a third-party Web service to host your Web page. Fortunately there are some free, easy-to-use Web servers available online. Setting up and using the Web server is not going to be a difficult ordeal; in fact, it's about 10 times easier than setting up and using a word processor. You can use any Web server on the market that allows Java Server pages, but in this example we use an excellent server package called Resin by Caucho Technology.

Note:

This server software is free for noncommercial use only.

1. Go to the Resin download site at *www.caucho.com/download*.

2. Download Resin 2.x for the appropriate operating system (Windows or UNIX). The basic Resin package is fine and you do not require Resin-CMP.

3. Extract the files to an appropriate directory, such as Program Files. There is no installation program.

4. We are now going to alter the server configuration slightly. Resin serves pages to port 8080 by default, but the standard for HTML pages is port 80. Open the resin.conf file in the conf directory using a text editor.

5. Scroll down in the file until you see the setting:

```
<http port='8080'/>
```

Modify this to:

```
<http port='80'/>
```

Now save the file and close it.

6. That's it! Resin is now installed and ready to go. Run httpd.exe, located in the bin directory (or standalone.exe if you don't want the Java helper window) and the server will start serving Web pages.

7. To test the server, open your browser and go to the following address: *http://localhost* (alternately, you can try *http:// 127.0.0.1*, or your IP address). A default Web page should come up with Resin information. Any Web pages that are placed in the doc directory will be accessible from your server. Minimize the Resin server window, but leave it running because we will use it for some projects.

Note:

Now that you have a Web server set up you can convert the previous Explorer project into a Java Applet and include it on a Web page. The applet cannot be hosted by a third-party server because network communications would not be allowed by the Java security model, but as long as the Explorer Server is running at the same IP address as the Web page, it will work fine. First, use the following code for the applet:

```
import java.applet.Applet;
import java.awt.*;

public class ExplorerApplet extends Applet {
    public void init() {
        this.add(new ExplorerCommand("209.202.24.208"));
        this.resize(400,300);
        this.setLayout(new BorderLayout());
    }
}
```

Next, type up the following HTML page:

```
<html>
<head>
<title>Explorer Command Center</title>
</head>
<body>
<applet
    code=ExplorerApplet.class
    width=500
    height=800 >
Your browser is not Java-enabled.
</applet>
</body>
</html>
```

Save this file as explorer.html in the doc directory or Resin. Finally, copy ExplorerApplet.class, ExplorerCommand.class, and ExplorerCommand$ControlListener.class to the doc directory. Run Resin and minimize it, then run ExplorerServer.class to start the RCX server (from its normal directory). Upload RCXExplorer.class to the RCX, place it in front of the IR tower, and press the Run button.

Now browse to the following address and you will see this displayed as an applet: http://localhost/explorer.html.

A Simple Project

Now that the server is up and running we can create an RCX project using the Web. This is just a fun example used to demonstrate the ability to read sensors and control motors. This RCX application simulates the game of Russian Roulette, except instead of spinning the bullet chamber the motor spins an arm in front of a light sensor. If the arm stops in front of the light sensor then the player will lose. For this project, code will need to be running on the RCX brick as well as on a JSP page, which will be executed every time a user interacts with the JSP page. The code on the RCX side contains no concepts that haven't been covered already:

```
1.  import java.io.*;
2.  import josx.platform.rcx.comm.*;
3.  import josx.platform.rcx.*;
4.
5.  public class Roulette implements SensorConstants {
6.
7.      private DataOutputStream out;
8.      private InputStream in;
9.
10.     public Roulette() {
11.         RCXDataPort port = new RCXDataPort();
12.         out = new DataOutputStream(port.getOutputStream());
13.         // No Data Stream needed b/c only byte values read:
14.         in = port.getInputStream();
15.         Sensor.S1.setTypeAndMode(SENSOR_TYPE_LIGHT,
                    SENSOR_MODE_RAW);
16.         Sensor.S1.activate();
17.     }
18.
19.     public static void main(String args[]) {
20.         Roulette roulette = new Roulette();
21.         while(true)
22.             roulette.play();
23.     }
24.
25.     /** This method reads a value from the IR tower, rotates
26.      * the arm for the specified time, then returns the light
27.      * reading to the IR tower. */
28.     public void play() {
29.         try {
30.             int spinTime = in.read();
31.
32.             spinArm(spinTime);
```

```
33.              int sensorValue = sensorValue = Sensor.S1.read-
                     Value();
34.              LCD.showNumber(sensorValue);
35.              out.writeInt(sensorValue);
36.              out.flush();
37.          } catch (IOException e) {
38.              LCD.showNumber(1111);
39.          }
40.      }
41.      /** Spins the arm the desired time. */
42.      public static void spinArm(int seconds) {
43.          Motor.A.forward();
44.          try {
45.              Thread.sleep(seconds * 1000);
46.          } catch (InterruptedException e) { }
47.          Motor.A.stop();
48.          try { //Delay to make sure arm is fully stopped:
49.              Thread.sleep(100);
50.          } catch (InterruptedException e) { }
51.      }
52. }
```

As you can see, this code simply reads a value from the IR port, spins the motor for a period of time, then reads the light sensor value and returns it to the IR port. The JSP portion of the code interacts with the RCX bean, so let's explore this API.

RCX Bean

Now we need to create a JSP to interact with the bean. Don't worry if you are not familiar with JSP technology. In a nutshell, a JSP contains code that is executed on the server machine. The JSP code determines what the HTML code that is eventually sent to the client's browser looks like. JSP code can access Java classes on the server, just like regular Java, as long as it can access them somewhere in the CLASSPATH. In our example, we will be using the RCXBean class for communications with the RCX.

The bean uses no constructor, so all properties are set using methods. This includes the COM port the bean will use. If this method is not called before the bean is used, then the bean throws an exception from the JSP code (and the users see an exception on their Web page).

pc.irtower.comm.RCXBean

• `public String getComPort()`

Returns a String representing the name of the COM port used by the bean.

- `public void setComPort(String value) throws IOException`

  Change or set which COM port should be used for communication with the RCX.

  Parameters: `value`   A String representing the COM port (e.g., COM1, /dev/ttyS0, or USB.

- `public void sendInt(int v) throws IOException`

  Sends an int value as four bytes.

  Parameters: `v`   The data.

- `public void send(byte b) throws IOException`

  Sends a single byte value.

  Parameters: `v`   The data.

- `public void send(byte[] b) throws IOException`

  Sends an array of byte values.

  Parameters: `v`   The data in the form of an array of bytes.

- `public byte receive() throws IOException`

  Receives a single byte of data, will wait until one appears in the buffer.

- `public int receiveInt() throws IOException`

  Receives an int value composed of four bytes.

- `public byte[] receive(int n) throws IOException`

  Receive *n* bytes from the RCX.

  Parameters: `n`   The number of bytes to receive, also determines the size of the array.

- `public synchronized void lock(Object o) throws IOException`

  The lock() method creates a lock on the RCX bean. The RCX bean cannot be locked by another object before the free() method has been run. If lock() is called while it is already locked then the bean throws an IOException.

  Parameters: `o`   The lock is bound to this object. It should therefore be unique for the thread.

Note:

The lock() method does not prevent other threads from using the RCX bean!

- `public synchronized void free(Object o)`
  Make the RCX bean available for other threads.

  Parameters: o   The object that has the lock.

- `public void close()`
  Close this RCX bean.

Warning:

For RCXBean to work with a JSP page, the CLASSPATH setting for leJOS must be accessible to the environment the Web server is running in. If you have set up CLASSPATH as a system variable, this is probably already working.

Because a Web page can be accessed simultaneously by many people on the Web, it is necessary to restrict access to the IR tower so only one person will access it at a time. The RCXBean uses two methods for restricting the use of the RCX bean: lock() and free(). The lock() method blocks other users from accessing the bean until free() is called. The rest of the JSP page is pretty standard, and is used for displaying an HTML page for the user to interact with (Figure 11–11). The following code can be entered in a simple text editor, or even in an IDE like JCreator. Keep in mind you should not attempt to compile it. Let's have a look at the code:

```
1. <%@ page contentType="text/html" language='java'
      import='pc.irtower.comm.*'%>
2. <jsp:useBean id='rcx' class='pc.irtower.comm.RCXBean'
      scope='application'>
3.   <jsp:setProperty name='rcx' property='comPort'
        value='COM2'/>
4. </jsp:useBean>
5. <HTML>
6. <HEAD><TITLE>Russian Roulette</TITLE></HEAD>
7. <BODY>
8. Select the amount of time to spin the wheel.
9. Less than 800 means you are safe,
10. greater than 800 means you have lost.
11. <FORM>
12.   <SELECT name='SpinTime'>
13.     <OPTION value='1'>1 second
14.     <OPTION value='3'>3 seconds
15.     <OPTION value='5'>5 seconds
16.   </SELECT>
17.   <INPUT type='SUBMIT'>
```

```
18. </FORM><BR>
19. <%
20.   try {
21.     String sensorIDString = request.getParameter("Spin-
          Time");
22.     if (sensorIDString != null) {
23.       int time = Integer.decode(sensorIDString).intValue();
24.       rcx.lock(request);
25.       rcx.send((byte)time);
26.       int value = rcx.receiveInt();
27.       if(value < 800)
28.       out.println("<b>"+value+"</b>"+"...click.");
29.       else
30.         out.println("<b>"+value+"... BANG!</b>");
31.     }
32.   } catch (NumberFormatException e) {
33.     out.println("The value of <code>time</code> is
          invalid.");
34.   } finally {
35.     rcx.free(request);
36.   }
37. %>
38. </body>
39. </html>
```

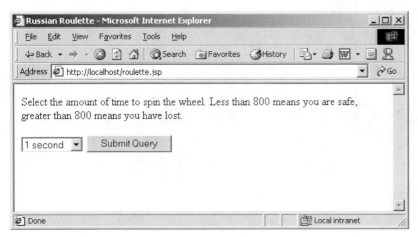

Figure 11–11   The JSP page displayed in a browser.

Save this file with the name roulette.jsp. The file should be saved to the Resin doc directory, which is used to store the Web pages on the server. The very first line of code imports the packages used by the code—in this case pc.irtower.comm. The second and third lines define the JavaBean being used by the JSP, which is RCXBean. The bean is designated with a variable of *rcx* in the code. This is the variable name it is referred to by the JSP code. Because this is a bean, various parameters can be set, including the communications port (make sure this is set to the COM port your computer is using). The body of the HTML page contains a drop-down menu to select one of three options (Figure 11–11). Next comes the Java code, enclosed in the <% %> braces. As you can see, this is just regular Java code so it should be easy to understand what is happening in it. Now we just need one final component to run the project—a LEGO model.

Note:

The root HTML directory for Resin can be changed in the resin.conf file located in the conf directory. The default setting is <app-dir>doc</app-dir>.

Roulette Wheel

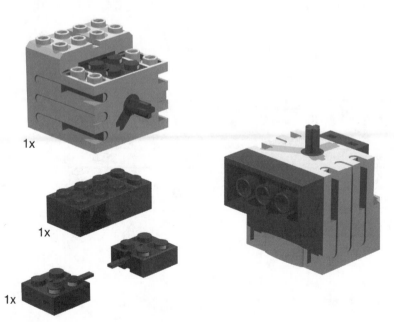

1x

1x

1x

Step 1   The motor must be mounted on its back. Attach a wire brick to the motor with the wire facing downward. Attach a 2 × 4 brick to the bottom of the motor.

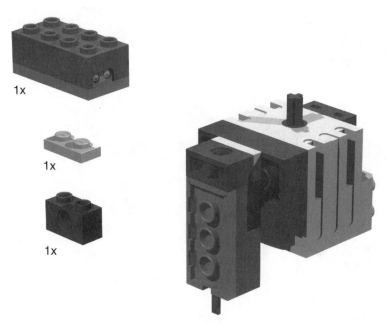

1x

1x

1x

Step 2   Attach the light sensor to the 2 × 4 brick and add a 1 × 2 brick with a hole to shield the sensor.

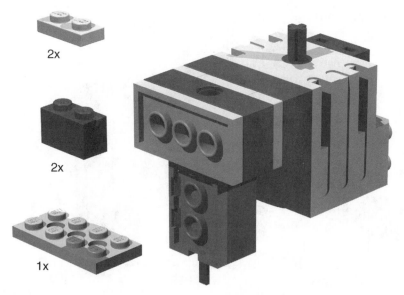

2x

2x

1x

Step 3   Secure the sensor in place by placing two 1 × 2 plates and 1 × 2 bricks on each side of the sensor, then cap it off with a gray 2 × 4 plate.

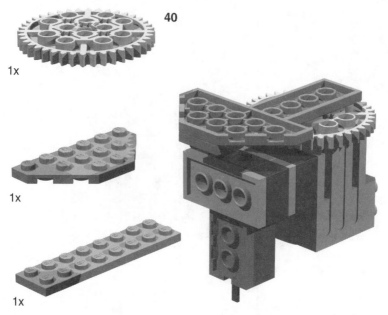

1x

1x

1x

Step 4   Attach the green 3 × 6 plate without corners to a green 2 × 8 plate as shown in the diagram. Attach the 2 × 8 plate to a 40-tooth gear by placing the plate studs into the holes on the gear. Attach the gear to the motor axle.

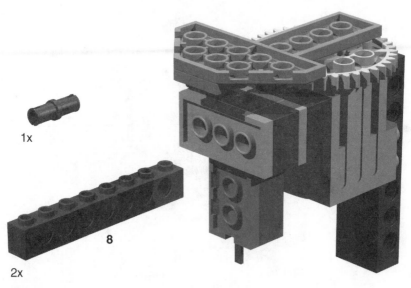

1x

8

2x

Step 5   Place a black friction pin in the center hole of a 1 × 8 beam and attach it to another 1 × 8 beam. Attach the double beam to the back of the motor.

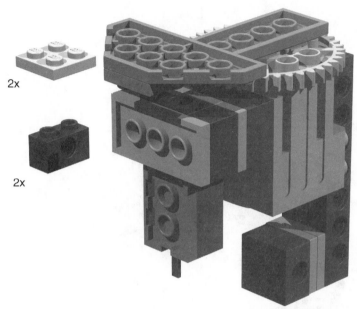

Step 6   Attach two gray 2 × 2 plates to the double beam and attach two 1 × 2 bricks with holes to the plate as shown.

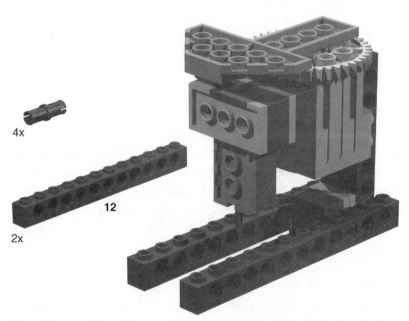

Step 7   Insert black friction pins into the bottom holes of the double beam. Attach two more black friction pins in the 1 × 2 brick holes. Now attach the two 1 × 12 beams by clipping them onto friction pins.

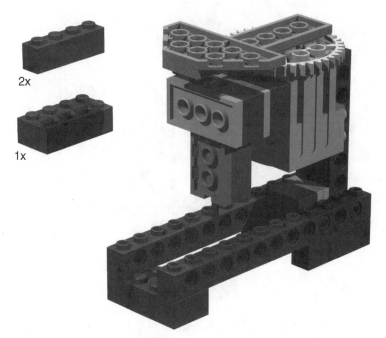

Step 8   Attach support legs to the base as shown.

We're all ready to test out the project now. First, upload the Roulette class to the RCX brick and press the Run button. The brick should be in front of the IR tower, with the IR port facing the tower. Next, make sure the Resin Server is running and go to the following Web address in your browser: *http:// localhost /roulette.jsp*.

You should be presented with a Web page displaying an option to choose the delay time (Figure 11–11). Choose one and click Submit Query. At this point the green light should appear on the IR tower, and the arm will begin spinning. When the arm stops a sensor reading is sent back to the computer, and the Web page displays the sensor value as well as a win–lose message.

Note:

If the Web page seems to freeze when you submit the value and the green light does not go on, this is almost a sure sign the COM port is not properly set. Edit the third line in the roulette.jsp file so the value is equal to the correct port.

Note:

If the Web page returns an error message, it might indicate it was not able to access certain classes. Make sure your CLASSPATH environment variable is set to include jdk1.3.1\lib\comm.jar and lejos\lib\classes.jar.

Now that we know the Web page is working locally, why not try to get others to browse to it? First you'll need to connect to the Internet and find your IP address. Windows users can find this by going to a command prompt and typing

```
ipconfig
```

Linux users can use a similar program in the super-user directory:

```
/sbin/ifconfig
```

These commands bring up data that includes the IP Address. Record this number and call a friend. Have your friend go to your IP address and make sure he or she types the prefix *http://* in the address line; for example:

```
http://255.255.255.255/roulette.jsp
```

Note:

If your computer is behind a firewall there may be problems contacting it. Also, some Internet connections use nonroutable or dynamic IPs that can cause connection problems.

Note:

Not all code in the JSP file Roulette.jsp is sent to the client's Web browser. Only the HTML code (including scripting languages like JavaScript) makes it to the client. The JSP-related code is executed by the server, and it produces an HTML document to return to the client. Any code enclosed in <% %> braces, or using the JSP tag <jsp: .. /jsp: ..> will never be seen by a client. To view this, try going to View ➤ Source in your browser.

Alternate Data Transfer Methods

At first glance it might appear that the IR port on the RCX is the only way to transfer data, but actually the RCX is capable of sending and receiving data

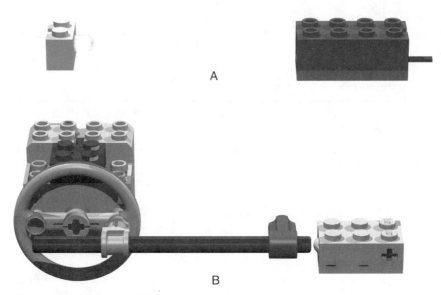

Figure 11–12 Alternate data media.

using other media. Using a Morse code setup with a combination of light sensor and light actuator, it is also possible to receive and send data across distances (Figure 11–12a). Data transmission isn't just limited to the light spectrum; a motor and a touch sensor could also interpret physical movement as data (Figure 11–12b). In fact, any compatible actuator–sensor combination can transmit data. For example, a heating coil and a temperature sensor could conceivably transmit and receive data using the differences in temperature as the data medium (although this would be very inefficient). We could even eliminate the need for actuators and sensors completely and connect an output port from one RCX directly to a sensor port on another RCX, with the sensor port interpreting changes in the voltage as a signal.

To accomplish any data transfer we must first be able to encode the signals into numbers. As most programmers are familiar with, a byte is made up of eight bits (binary digits). A bit has two states represented by an on–off signal (usually described as 0 or 1). These eight bits create binary numbers, which can in turn be converted to decimal numbers. A sequence of bits are ordered, with the first bit having a value of 1, the next as 2, then 4, then 8, and so on (Table 11–1). Thus the sequence 00000001 has a value of 1, the sequence 10000001 has a value of 129, and the sequence 11010110 has a value of 214 (2 + 4 + 16 + 64 + 128). Using these eight values, any number between 0 and 255 can be represented. The key to the whole encoding scheme is to be able to transmit light signals (or others) by representing 0 or 1.

Table 11-1 Bit Values							
Bit	8	7	6	5	4	3	2	1
Value	128	64	32	16	8	4	2	1

Now that we know how to encode bits we just need to figure out how to send a bit. As we know, a bit is just a signal, either on or off. Transmission of bits is generally done by synchronizing the clocks on the sender and receiver. They agree on a transmission speed, and one single bit is sent for each time interval. Given the preceding mechanical example using a touch sensor, if a transmission speed of one bit per second is agreed on, then for each second during transmission the touch sensor is either pressed or released. If you recall modem speeds, a typical phone modem can handle 33,600 bits per second. In our touch sensor example the baud rate is 1 bit per second—not very fast.

The IR port does a fine job of transmitting data, and visible light data transmission takes up additional ports on the RCX, so obviously if someone attempts this on the RCX they are doing it for a learning experience. For this reason I'm not going to include code examples of this in action because it would take away from the experience of learning data transmission. But it is interesting to note how this could fit into the Java API. Assuming a programmer has figured out how to transmit and receive a single byte, it's possible to take this up a notch and incorporate it into streams.

First an InputStream and OutputStream need to be created. This is simple: Just extend the abstract InputStream and OutputStream classes in the java.io package. InputStream has a simple abstract method called read() that reads the next byte of data from the stream. Conversely, OutputStream has an abstract method called write() that writes a byte to the stream. Using the visible light example previously described, the classes might be called Light-InputStream and LightOutputStream. Once these are created, it's as easy as using these classes in the constructor for DataInputStream and DataOutput-Stream to transmit integers, floating-point numbers, and other data types.

Note:

Both read() and write() use int data types to transmit a byte because a byte is a signed value, meaning it can only store numbers with a range of −128 to +127. However, the methods read() and write() need unsigned byte values of 0 to 255, hence an int value is used instead.

Alternate Communication Uses

We've created some basic communications projects, but really we have only scratched the surface of what can be done. For example, we could have tried to make social robots that interact with each other. This can be achieved by having RCX robots send data to one another through the serial port, which is not at all different from communications between the IR tower and RCX. There are also ways to improve navigation using the IR tower that we have not explored yet. The following section describes some of these possibilities, but I leave it up to you to implement your own vision.

So far in this book we have tried navigation using three types of technology: timing, rotation sensors, and an electronic compass. All of these methods use dead reckoning to navigate, with compass navigation being the most advanced. According to author Marc D. Hauser in his book *Wild Minds* (Henry Holt & Company, 2000), all navigating animals use dead reckoning, without exception. It is impressive that an animal as small and simple as an ant can so accurately navigate across large areas of terrain searching for food. The Tunisian desert ant has an amazing ability to navigate large distances from its burrow, a small hole in the sand. It forages around the desert looking for any food source it can find, but the catch is it can only stay outside its burrow for about two hours, otherwise it will die from exposure to the sun. If it can't find its way home after that amount of time, it will fry. The desert sand has no physical features to navigate by, so the ant uses the angle of the sun relative to itself to determine the orientation it is facing (similar to the function of a compass). It even takes into account the fact that the sun slowly migrates across the sky. The ant wanders around in a zig-zagging, criss-crossing pattern until it locates a food source. Once it does, the ant makes a straight line back for home—which can be up to 500 m away—quite a distance when you are only a few millimeters long.

Let's contrast this with the RCX robots we have developed in this book. Each of them also uses dead reckoning to navigate with computer precision, but the accuracy of the coordinates deteriorates with time traveled. Even the compass robot accumulates errors in the distances traveled. Even though the compass angle does not deteriorate, small errors in the angle will add up. Given the same task as the Tunisian desert ant, our RCX counterpart would fail miserably. So how can an ant get such accurate results, finding a small dime-sized hole after so much travel? Apparently within a few meters of the hole it switches from dead reckoning to positional navigation—using fixed points on the surface to navigate by. In the case of the ant, these landmarks can be semipermanent features such as rocks, pebbles, or even scent markers. Once it gets to an area of the terrain it is familiar with, it can close in on the hole. Ironically, if you pick up the desert ant and transpose it by several meters, it will not be able to find its way home. So how can we use this type of impressive navigation with our robot?

With the limited sensors and internal memory of MINDSTORMS robots, it is difficult to recognize external objects in the real world. Even with sophisticated video cameras, algorithms, and tons of memory, visual recognition is not yet perfected. Objects just look so different depending on the direction of the viewer, and changes in lighting also throw off recognition. However, there is one object the RCX has no problem recognizing: the IR tower. With the position of the IR tower known and the serial port set to short range, the robot should be able to recalibrate position by detecting the IR tower. I won't go into details on how to implement this, but if you find this topic interesting it could be good project to tackle.

ADVANCED
LeJOS TOPICS

Topics in this Chapter

- Memory Issues
- Performance Tips
- Alternate Languages on the JVM
- leJOS Architecture Overview

Chapter 12

This chapter deals with topics for those who would like to go a step beyond conventional leJOS use. The first topic demonstrates how to save memory, something important to all RCX users because memory is in such limited supply. No matter how big your program is, there always seems to be a way to squeeze just a little more code onto the RCX. This chapter starts with basic memory-saving methods and delves into hacking leJOS to reduce code size. The second part of this chapter describes a fun, relatively unknown feature of all JVMs: the ability to run other languages. Only leJOS has a stable of alternate programming languages ready to be tested on the RCX. Finally, the last part of this chapter discusses the architecture of leJOS and how to modify it at a low level. This section was written by Jose Solorzano, who knows a thing or two about leJOS, as he designed it from scratch.

Memory Issues

With only 32 kB of RAM at its disposal, memory usage is a key issue with the RCX brick, especially when writing complex programs. This section shows you how to check memory use, including the differences between program upload size and memory usage during program execution. We then examine ways to increase available memory. This includes limiting memory through clever programming, as well as hacking leJOS classes to decrease the size of the API itself.

Monitoring Memory Use

As mentioned before, leJOS takes up about 16 kB of memory on the RCX brick. Of the remaining memory, 4 kB is unusable by the JVM, which leaves 12 kB of free memory space for programs. It would be a good idea to maximize the use of that memory when writing programs, but to do this you first need to understand what eats up memory. There are several tools at our disposal to monitor memory usage, and these can give us clues as to how low the memory is and where the memory is actually going.

The first tool that is often useful in tracking down memory usage is lejos.exe with the -verbose option. This option displays the classes and methods being used by a program just before it is uploaded to the RCX brick. Let's first take at a minimal program with almost no code to see which classes will be uploaded:

```
class MemTest {
    public static void main(String [] args) {}
}
```

As you can see, this is a tiny piece of nonfunctional code. Would you be surprised to learn that 23 classes are uploaded to the RCX brick to run this program? On the surface this program appears negligible, but system-specific classes must be uploaded to the RCX. These classes are as follows (as output by lejos.exe -verbose):

```
Class 0:  java/lang/Object
Class 1:  java/lang/Thread
Class 2:  java/lang/String
Class 3:  java/lang/Runtime
Class 4:  java/lang/Throwable
Class 5:  java/lang/Error
Class 6:  java/lang/OutOfMemoryError
Class 7:  java/lang/NoSuchMethodError
Class 8:  java/lang/StackOverflowError
Class 9:  java/lang/NullPointerException
Class 10: java/lang/ClassCastException
Class 11: java/lang/ArithmeticException
Class 12: java/lang/ArrayIndexOutOfBoundsException
Class 13: java/lang/IllegalArgumentException
Class 14: java/lang/InterruptedException
Class 15: java/lang/IllegalStateException
```

```
Class 16: java/lang/IllegalMonitorStateException
Class 17: java/lang/ThreadDeath
Class 18: josx/util/Test
Class 19: MemTest
Class 20: java/lang/System
Class 21: java/lang/RuntimeException
Class 22: java/lang/Exception
```

The first four classes in the list are absolutely essential. Object is the root class of all classes, so it is needed no matter what. Thread controls program execution, including the main thread, so it is necessary. String is needed to implement one of the opcodes used by the JVM for string literal loading). Runtime is required because a Runtime object is always present in the system to check on memory usage. System is also necessary to keep track of the system time, as well as providing a means to exit the JVM and terminate all program execution. The rest of these classes are basically errors and exceptions, part of the Java error-handling model.

Note:

You may notice that the linker includes code for all methods in classes, including methods that are unused in the code. For example, if the code uses just the Math.tan() method, all the other Math methods such as sin() and cos() are also uploaded to the RCX brick. This is a little wasteful, and there's a possibility the leJOS uploader will exclude unused methods from being uploaded in future releases.

The second tool you can use to estimate memory use and program size is watching the RCX display as a program uploads. This number tells you roughly how big your code is in its inactive state before program execution begins. If the upload size of the program exceeds the available memory on the RCX, there is no chance your program will run, because there must be some leftover memory to be used for variables and program execution. Each incremental unit on the RCX display represents 100 bytes of memory, so if your program starts to get around the 100 mark when uploading, you know it is pushing the limits of the RCX memory even before the program starts running.

A third tool for estimating memory is creating a binary dump of the program. You can dump the program to a file and check its size, using the -o option, as follows:

```
lejos -o MyProgram.bin MyClass
```

This will produce a file in the current directory called MyProgram.bin. The size of this file indicates the size of the code uploaded to the RCX brick.

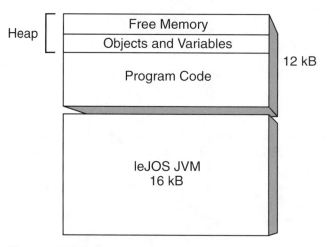

Figure 12–1   The memory heap.

The fourth and final tool for evaluating memory use is the Runtime class. It contains two useful methods to understand how much memory is being used: totalMemory() and freeMemory(). The totalMemory() method returns the size of the memory the program has available to it, called the *heap* (Figure 12–1). The freeMemory() method, of course, returns the unused portion of memory in the heap. When this number reaches 0 the program is unable to run and you see an out of memory error displayed on the LCD.

Let's use the Runtime class in some code to test the before and after effects when creating objects. The following code displays the memory state at two different times during program execution:

```
1. import josx.platform.rcx.*;
2.
3. class MemTest {
4.    public static void main(String [] args) {
5.       outputTotalMemory();
6.       outputFreeMemory();
7.       for(int i=0;i<5;++i){
8.          String s ="Hello";
9.       }
10.      outputFreeMemory();
11.   }
12.
13.   public static void outputTotalMemory() {
14.      int total = (int)System.getRuntime().totalMemory();
15.      LCD.showNumber(total);
16.      try {
```

```
17.          Button.RUN.waitForPressAndRelease();
18.       }catch(InterruptedException e){}
19.    }
20.
21.    public static void outputFreeMemory() {
22.       int free = (int)System.getRuntime().freeMemory();
23.       LCD.showNumber(free);
24.       try {
25.          Button.RUN.waitForPressAndRelease();
26.       }catch(InterruptedException e){}
27.    }
28. }
```

Running this program with leJOS 1.0.3 (other versions vary) will output the numbers 8,888, 8,202, and 8,086 to the LCD. This demonstrates the program has a total heap size of 8,888 bytes (it's a coincidence the figures are all 8), but at Line 6 there are only 8,202 bytes free, so it has already used 686 bytes to get the program up and running. After creating five String objects, there is a total of 8,086 bytes free, meaning 116 bytes have gone into creating five String objects. As you can see, object creation increases the memory used. What can we do to keep this to a minimum? The next section attempts to answer this question.

Programming Efficient Code

The leJOS API contains a lot of classes, but only a fraction of these will actually be uploaded to the RCX brick on the condition that they are used somewhere in the code. Even if you use the import statement on an entire package, only the classes in that package that are used in code are uploaded. So a statement like

```
import josx.platform.rcx.*;
```

does not necessarily mean any classes in the josx.platform.rcx package will be uploaded to the RCX. Only classes that are used in code end up being uploaded. Once a class is uploaded to the RCX, making method calls on the class hardly uses any memory at all. For example, each method call you add to your code for Motor.forward() only takes six bytes of memory in the program space. Examine the following code:

```
1. import josx.platform.rcx.*;
2.
3. class MemTest {
4.    public static void main(String [] args) {
5.       Motor.A.forward();
```

```
6.        //Motor.A.forward();
7.        outputFreeMemory();
8.     }
9.     public static void outputFreeMemory() {
10.        int free = (int)System.getRuntime().freeMemory();
11.        LCD.showNumber(free);
12.        LCD.refresh();
13.        try {Button.RUN.waitForPressAn-
dRelease();}catch(InterruptedException e){}
14.     }
15. }
```

Try compiling and running this program twice, once with Line 6 as is and once without it commented out. You will notice a difference of six bytes of free memory, indicating the method call is using only six bytes of program space. If you use totalMemory() instead of freeMemory() you will also only notice a difference of six bytes for each run. What can we learn from this? Once you have the main classes defined, additional method calls don't constitute a large memory drain. Programs tend to start at a certain size and grow very slowly as more code is added.

You should also keep in mind that adding methods is expensive, and adding classes is even more expensive. As described earlier, if a body of code is used repeatedly it makes sense to create a method for it. However, it does not make sense to break up a long method into many shorter methods just so your code looks neat. If possible, keep methods as one large block of code.

Every time an object is created—that is, every time the new statement is used—the JVM allocates memory space for the object to use. In a standard JVM, when an object is no longer needed it is removed from memory, freeing up memory space. Objects are ready for collection when they are no longer running in any thread, or when they are set to null and no other variables refer to them. The leJOS JVM, however, has no garbage collector. Once an object is created it is never erased from memory, even when it is of no use to the program anymore. Although this may sound dire, it really doesn't affect Java programming very much. The nature of the RCX programming environment means that static methods are usually being called, so there just doesn't seem to be a need to make and dispose of very many objects. As you can see, we got through the entire book without the lack of garbage collection even becoming an issue, and there was some quite complex code.

Note:

As this book goes to press the leJOS team is considering implementing a garbage collector, but this would add to the size of the JVM, so some programmers are understandably against this. A compromise has been put forth of only using the garbage collector if a command-line option is used when uploading code to the RCX.

You should still keep the lack of a garbage collector in the back of your mind when programming, however. Try to think of the *new* keyword as a necessary evil. Examine the following code:

```
1. import josx.platform.rcx.*;
2.
3. class MemTest {
4.    public static void main(String [] args) {
5.        for(int i=0;i<5;++i) {
6.            showWord();
7.        }
8.        try {
9.            Button.RUN.waitForPressAndRelease();
10.       }catch(InterruptedException e){}
11.   }
12.
13.   public static void showWord() {
14.       String word = "WORD";
15.       TextLCD.print(word);
16.       LCD.refresh();
17.   }
18. }
```

This program uses a method called showWord() to output a string to the LCD. Line 14 creates a String object, which is just a shorthand way of saying:

```
String word = new String("WORD");
```

The problem with this code is that presumably the showWord() method will be called repeatedly. Every time it is created, it will create a brand new String object. In a standard JVM the object would be garbage collected, but in the leJOS JVM each new object lingers, clogging up memory unnecessarily. The solution to this is to reuse a single String object, as the following revised code demonstrates:

```
1. import josx.platform.rcx.*;
2.
3. class MemTest {
4.    static String word = "WORD";
5.    public static void main(String [] args) {
6.        for(int i=0;i<5;++i) {
7.            showWord();
8.        }
```

```
9.        try {
10.           Button.RUN.waitForPressAndRelease();
11.        }catch(InterruptedException e){}
12.    }
13.
14.    public static void showWord() {
15.        TextLCD.print(word);
16.        LCD.refresh();
17.    }
18. }
```

This way the same String object is used each time the showWord() method is called. Other methods in the code could also reference this object, as follows:

```
String other = word;
```

Notice the *new* keyword is not used anywhere in this statement. Assigning objects to other variables doesn't use much memory, because it is only a reference to an existing object. No new heap space is being used to define a new object, so sharing objects is a good way to save memory.

Primitive variables don't permanently take up memory. Once a method is finished executing, a primitive variable declared locally no longer takes up memory space. In the following method, temp only exists for the lifetime of the method call. When the method exits, the program reclaims the memory from temp:

```
1. public static void mult(int x) {
2.     int temp = x * 2;
3.     }
```

Another memory-saving idea is to use smaller primitive types wherever possible. Programmers using PCs generally use integers all over the place, even if the numbers being manipulated are small. Keep in mind a byte only takes up one byte. A short takes up two bytes, and a long takes up four bytes (in leJOS). By using the byte primitive where possible, your program could save four times the memory.

What about arrays of primitive values? It is always stated that an array is an object in Java, but is it really an object in all regards? Let's find out. The following code creates a local array each time the button is pressed. If the array is treated as an object, the memory should gradually decrease:

```
1. import josx.platform.rcx.*;
2.
3. class MemTest {
4.     public static void main(String [] args) {
```

```
5.        while(true) {
6.            int [] array = {10,11,12,13,14,15};
7.            outputFreeMemory();
8.        }
9.    }
10.   public static void outputFreeMemory() {
11.        int free = (int)System.getRuntime().freeMemory();
12.        LCD.showNumber(free);
13.        LCD.refresh();
14.        try {
15.            Button.RUN.waitForPressAndRelease();
16.        }catch(InterruptedException e){}
17.    }
18. }
```

The results from this program indicate the free memory decreases by 34 bytes each time the run button is pressed (four bytes per int, 10 bytes for the object) so the array is in fact treated as a real object in Java, and is not garbage collected under leJOS.

There are also some classes with methods that create new objects. For example, some Vector and Hashtable methods allocate memory. For example, setSize() causes the collection to create a new array object of a larger size. Also, if you add an object to one of these collections and it is full, it resizes itself, which in effect creates a new array object. These sorts of methods should be treated like the *new* keyword. In the case of Vector, the capacity can be set beforehand and checked with each addition.

Note:

The josx.util package contains classes for manual object recycling. Refer to the API docs for more details.

Hacking leJOS to Save Memory

It's actually quite easy to modify the leJOS API, either adding or removing methods or variables from classes. Many of the classes in the API are quite full featured—perhaps even too full featured given the small amount of memory on board the RCX. If you find the RCX is running out of memory you can take the next step and remove unused methods from the leJOS API. Let's use the Math class as an example. It contains almost every method in the standard Math class, but usually a leJOS program only needs a few of these. It just makes sense to obliterate the unused one, and it's quite easy:

1. To be safe, make a copy of the Math.java source file located in the directory lejos\classes\java\lang.

2. Open Math.java in an editor and delete all of the following methods: floor(), ceil(), abs(), max(), min(), and round(). Save the file.

3. Copy the file lejos\lib\classes.jar to the lejos\classes directory.

4. Go to a command prompt and change to the lejos\classes directory.

5. If you aren't sure if the environment variable is correct, type the following:
   set classpath = C:\lejos\lib\classes.jar; (assuming leJOS is in your root directory).

6. Compile the Math.java file:
   lejosc .\java\lang\Math.java
   (If you receive an error, make sure PATH is set by typing
   set path=C:\lejos\bin [enter].)

7. Add the new Math class to the classes.jar file as follows:
   Jar uf classes.jar java\lang\Math.class

8. Now replace the C:\lejos\lib\classes.jar file with the new one. It's probably a good idea to keep the old one around in case you want to revert to the original.

That's it! Now you can use the Math class without uploading unwanted methods to the RCX brick.

Warning:

If the compiler starts giving errors, you have likely deleted a method that another method in the leJOS API relies on. To fix this, revert to the original classes.jar file.

Note:

This step is not necessary if leJOS is modified in the future to automatically ignore unused methods.

Performance Tips

Performance hasn't been something I've been especially focused on when programming robots with leJOS. In the applications I've used the RCX brick for, it generally doesn't matter if the robot starts moving 56 ms after a method call or 156 ms. But there are some applications where you would want optimum performance, such as high-speed vehicles, robots that attempt to maintain balance, or even flying robots. This section gives some quick tips to maximize speed from your Java code:

- Declare your methods to be either private, final, or static whenever possible. This prevents the JVM from creating virtual methods while the code is executing.
- The location of nonprivate methods matters: Place nonfinal, nonstatic public or protected methods close to the top of the class declaration. Static methods don't have this problem, except for static initializers and main methods.
- Local variable access is considerably faster than field access. This even applies to constants (but not numeric constants, because the Java compiler optimizes this).
- Accessing array elements of arrays assigned to local variables is faster than field access, but slightly slower than local variable access.
- Synchronized methods are slightly more efficient than synchronized blocks.
- In the leJOS API, some methods are faster than others. There are some low-level methods in Sensor and Motor that are faster than other methods. For example, in the Sensor class, readSensorValue() is faster than calling readValue().
- Using arrays instead of vectors makes the code run faster as well.

Alternate Languages for the JVM

One of the least known features of the JVM is that theoretically any computer programming language can be made to execute on it. The JVM is wide open in this regard, allowing not just Java, but Fortran, LISP, BASIC,

LOGO, Prolog, Eiffel, Rexx, COBOL, Ada, and even C. Typically these languages are implemented to run on the JVM by making their own compilers. These compilers take some specific source code (e.g., LISP) and compile it into regular Java byte code. The byte code can then be executed directly by java.exe. There is even a Web site (see the following note) that catalogs all of the known languages that run on the JVM. This is all very nice, but what does it have to do with the LEGO RCX? Well, leJOS is a JVM so it seems possible that other languages could run on it. The problem is that leJOS does not contain every class that standard Java contains. For example, with standard Java it is possible to display output to the screen using System.out.print(), but leJOS has no such method. If the implementation of a language relies on classes such as these, parts of the language (or even the whole language) will not work. Let's test this theory by installing another language.

Web site:

Languages for the Java VM *is a site maintained by Robert Tolksdorf. The site lists alternate programming languages that run on the JVM. This topic is in a relatively dark corner of the Java world that doesn't get very much coverage in computer media, but the list contains more than 100 entries, so it appears to be quite popular. There are even languages that extend the core Java language, allowing more features than you would normally get with Java. See* http://grunge.cs.tu-berlin.de/~tolk/vmlanguages.html.

Using NetRexx on the RCX

We are going to use a language developed by IBM called NetRexx as our guinea pig. NetRexx is a blend between Rexx and Java, and according to creator Mike Cowlishaw it is a "human-oriented programming language," so presumably the syntax is easier to learn than other languages. For example, instead of using:

```
System.out.print("Hello");
```

to output a String to the display you can merely use:

```
say "Hello"
```

In this section we install and set up the basic NetRexx software, then provide instructions to configure NetRexx under your development environment to make programming in NetRexx a little more user friendly.

Installing NetRexx

1. Download the NetRexx SDK from *www2.hursley.ibm.com/ netrexx/nrdown.html*
2. Extract the file into its own directory (e.g., C:\lego\NetRexx).
3. The *classpath* environment variable must be changed to include the leJOS classes.jar file, the NetRexxC.jar file, and the JDK tools.jar file. These should be added to your existing *classpath* setting. For example, on my system I added the following to my *classpath*, making sure to leave the dot at the end:
   C:\lego\Netrexx\lib\NetRexxC.jar;
   C:\lego\lejos\lib\classes.jar;
   C:\jdk1.3.1\lib\tools.jar;.
4. That's it! We are now ready to test it.

Using NetRexx

To use NetRexx we need a source file with some NetRexx code. This section won't cover the NetRexx language in depth because that would go far beyond the scope of this book. The following example can be saved to any directory (e.g., C:\java\test) as rexxtest.nrx:

```
1. import josx.platform.rcx.
2.
3. class rexxtest
4.
5.   method main(s=String[]) static
6.       Sound.beepSequence()
7.       forward(4000)
8.       rotate(2000)
9.       forward(4000)
10.
11.   method forward(delay=int) static
12.       Motor.A.forward()
13.       Motor.C.forward()
14.
15.       do
16.           Thread.sleep(delay)
17.       catch InterruptedException
18.       end
19.
20.       Motor.A.stop()
21.       Motor.C.stop()
```

```
22.
23.   method rotate(delay=int) static
24.       Motor.A.forward()
25.       Motor.C.backward()
26.
27.       do
28.           Thread.sleep(delay)
29.       catch InterruptedException
30.       end
31.
32.       Motor.A.stop()
33.       Motor.C.stop()
```

As you can see from the preceding example, the syntax of NetRexx is unique but method calls tend to look just like Java method calls. Now let's try compiling the source file. Make sure when you save the file to use the same name as the class name (rexxtest) otherwise the file does not compile. The NetRexx compiler runs under Java, so make sure the JDK1.3.1 bin directory is somewhere in your path. To compile type:

```
java -ms4M COM.ibm.netrexx.process.NetRexxC rexxtest.nrx
```

The argument -ms4M sets the initial Java heap size to four megabytes, which should make it run more efficiently. When the compiler is run, NetRexx converts the .nrx file to a .java file, then compiles it using the standard Java compiler. Once everything has finished you should be left with a file in your directory called rexxtest.class. Now we can upload this file to the RCX brick using lejos.exe (which should also be somewhere in your path):

```
lejos rexxtest
```

Once the code has been uploaded it should run just like any other leJOS program. Make sure you have motors hooked up to Ports A and C; otherwise it will be difficult to tell if anything is happening.

Setting Up NetRexx in an IDE

Those of you who are used to using an IDE might prefer to code NetRexx within your IDE. This is very simple to set up. In this example we use JCreator because it is the IDE used earlier in this book, but the general information applies to other IDEs as well.

1. In JCreator, select the Configure menu and choose Options...
2. Select the Tools option to bring up the list of tools.

3. Click New and select Program. A directory window opens. Choose the java.exe file located in the jdk1.3.1\bin directory. Click Open and a new entry appears in the list of tools called java.

4. Click New and select Program again. Browse to the lejos.exe file located in the lejos\bin directory. Click Open and a new entry appears in the list of tools called lejos.

5. Rename the tools NetRexxC and NetRexx by selecting the name in the list, then clicking again (Figure 12–2).

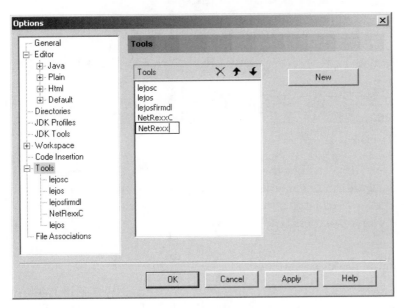

Figure 12–2 Changing the name of the tools.

6. Select NetRexxC to view the options (Figure 12–3). For arguments type:

```
-ms4M COM.ibm.netrexx.process.NetRexxC $[FileName]
```

The initial directory should be:

```
$[FileDir]
```

Under Tool Options make sure the Save All Documents First and Capture Output check boxes are cleared.

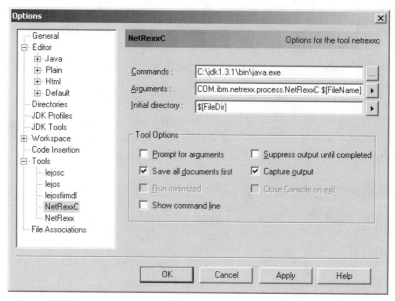

Figure 12–3   NetRexxC options.

7. Select NetRexx to view the options (Figure 12–4). It's not possible to use the class name variable because the IDE does not know how to extract this from an .nrx file, so we use the file base name. For arguments type:

    `$[FileBase]`

    The initial directory should be:

    `$[FileDir]`

    Under Tool Options, make sure all of the check boxes are cleared.

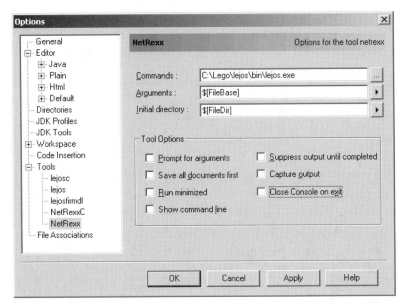

Figure 12–4   NetRexx upload options.

8.   That's all! Load the file rexxtest.nrx, and click the NetRexxC tool to compile it, then the NetRexx tool to upload it to the RCX brick.

Unsupported Features of NetRexx

The sample program we just used is very basic, but not by choice. Many of the keywords in NetRexx don't work with leJOS. As mentioned previously, the *say* keyword just won't work because there is no standard System.out in the leJOS API (more specifically, NetRexx uses netrexx.lang.RexxIO.Say() for output). In fact, all NetRexx functions that rely on classes that are not present in the leJOS API do not work. Examine the following code:

```
1. import josx.platform.rcx.
2.
3. class greets
4.   method main(s=String[]) static
5.
6.     say "hello"
7.     do
8.         josx.platform.rcx.Button.RUN.waitForPressAnd-
              Release()
9.     catch InterruptedException
10.    end
```

This code will actually compile fine, even though the *say* keyword should not be acceptable, because the NetRexx compiler is using the official Sun Java API to compile classes, so it has no problem finding a Print-Stream.print() method to use. It would be nice if we could hide the official Sun Java packages from the NetRexx compiler so it would warn us when a class is missing, but the NetRexx compiler was programmed in Java so it must have access to the entire Java API. How will we be warned that there is a class required by the code that the leJOS API does not have? When we attempt to upload the code using lejos.exe, the linker determines what is missing:

```
Fatal: Class java.io.BufferedReader (file
java/io/BufferedReader.class) not found in CLASSPATH
```

As you can see, the lejos.exe program is capable of detecting if any classes are missing before it even tries to upload it to the RCX. You can try using the -verbose option with lejos.exe (as demonstrated earlier in the chapter) but it will stop as soon as it gets to a missing class, so you cannot tell if there are other classes the code also requires. From the preceding error message we can tell the *say* operation requires the leJOS JVM to have a BufferedReader class. Why BufferedReader? Probably because it is one of many classes used by the netrexx.lang.RexxIO class, which contains the Say() method.

If we wanted to have a fully functioning *say* operation in NetRexx we would have to import several classes to the leJOS API. Although this would take some work, it would be possible. All you would have to do is add the missing classes to the lejos\lib\classes.jar file. Once these classes are present, the lejos.exe uploader is able to find the correct classes to upload to the RCX brick.

There are also some surprising rudimentary operations in NetRexx that fail to work. Examine the following piece of code:

```
1. import josx.platform.rcx.
2.
3. class tones
4.
5.   method main(s=String[]) static
6.
7.     loop i=50 to 2000 by +50
8.         Sound.playTone(i, 50)
9.         do
10.            Thread.sleep(500)
11.         catch InterruptedException
12.         end
13.      end
```

This code should play a series of tones on the RCX, increasing in frequency. As before, it compiles fine under NetRexxC, but when we attempt to upload it to the RCX brick we are hit with the following error:

```
Fatal: Class java.lang.Character (file
java/lang/Character.class) not found in CLASSPATH
```

This error is a little more difficult to explain without knowing more about how NetRexx operates. Apparently the *loop* construct requires the use of the Character class to function, which seems odd because the *loop* construct looks like it should be a one-to-one translation with the *for* keyword in Java. To get the *loop* construct to work (as well as *if*) a Character class must be added to lejos\lib\classes.jar. This might be something you are willing to do if you really want to gain the full functionality of an alternate language. If you are prepared to do a little hacking, you might want to refer to the previous section, "Hacking leJOS to Save Memory," on how to modify, add, or remove classes from the leJOS API.

Note:

If you would like to try alternate programming languages on the RCX it might be a good idea to check the leJOS Web page first to see which programming languages have been tested so far. This could save you the trouble of reinventing the wheel. On the flip side, the leJOS project would definitely like to hear from you if you have tested an alternate language. Even if it didn't work, we would still like to know the results so we can update our list. Go to http://lejos.sourceforge.net.

leJOS Architecture Overview

It can be difficult to understand an open source project with as large a scope as leJOS. This section attempts to explain the architecture from a high level, and also delve into specific issues with developing code for leJOS. If you would like to improve the leJOS code, feel free to hack it as much as you would like. You can even port leJOS to other processors, not just the RCX brick. The leJOS API starts with josx.platform, and any packages under this hierarchy contain platform-specific code. At one time leJOS was even compiling into a Nintendo Gameboy ROM (josx.platform.gameboy). It was never clear if actual code could be uploaded to the Gameboy, and this part of leJOS appears to be abandoned. If any of these concepts sound fun to you then read on! Feel free to join the leJOS development team if you would like to add code to the project.

Warning:

This section contains highly technical information written by Jose Solorzano. To understand this information, the reader should have a knowledge of C programming, low-level programming, advanced software design, and Linux.

Perhaps the main goal in the TinyVM/leJOS project was to keep the firmware footprint as compact as possible, but still end up with a system that is a fairly strict—although small—subset of Java. The first hurdle to this goal was the size of class files. Even though Java class files are widely considered to be relatively compact, they are not compact enough for the RCX. Even the smallest Java source files are compiled into class files of several kilobytes. This is mostly due to class names, method signatures, and line number mappings kept in class files.

Obfuscators, which rearrange Java source code and eliminate unused variables, were considered as a way to reduce class file size; but even with the help of obfuscators, the firmware would still have to decode and resolve class files, which would increase the footprint of the system by several kilobytes.

A better alternative, and the one ultimately implemented in TinyVM and leJOS, was to write a linker that would resolve class files before sending them to the RCX. The byte code contained in class files remains mostly as it was, except that class, method, and field references are resolved in advance so the virtual machine (VM) no longer needs to resolve them. This solution, of course, prevented us from implementing dynamic class loading, but this is probably a necessary price to pay in a system with such memory constraints. So in essence, leJOS consists of three parts:

1. The firmware
2. The core Java APIs
3. The linker or loader

The Firmware

The firmware contains a VM that performs thread scheduling, memory management, exception propagation, and so forth. The main component of the VM is an interpreter that executes resolved byte code. The firmware also contains native method implementations, which in the case of RCX-specific

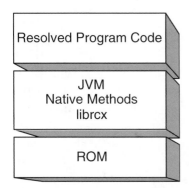

Figure 12–5   leJOS firmware architecture.

routines, rely on Kekoa Proudfoot's *librcx* library to access the ROM. This is illustrated in Figure 12–5.

The VM interpreter is nothing more than an opcode processing loop. Almost everything in leJOS executes within this loop. Unlike conventional VM implementations, the interpreter loop in leJOS is never invoked recursively for a couple of reasons. First, it would be complicated to deal with issues relating to overflowing the native stack. Second, leJOS does not sit on top of a conventional operating system, so it implements it own threading model.

A straightforward threading model completely controlled by leJOS simplifies the task of ensuring that certain operations (e.g., object allocation) are atomic. However, it also requires each thread to create and maintain its own stacks. leJOS creates two stacks per thread: the operand stack and the stack-frame stack.

Essentially, whenever a method is invoked, parameters are pushed onto the operand stack, and a new stack-frame is pushed into the stack-frame stack. On return, a popped stack-frame tells leJOS how to go back to the caller. The top stack-frame also saves information useful during context (thread) switching. Two threads are used instead of one because this allows the parameters pushed by the caller to become locals in the callee without having to copy data.

The API

The core Java API class files are stored in a jar file (lib\classes.jar) that is available to be linked with user programs. leJOS includes a compilation program (lejosc) but this is simply a script that invokes javac after including classes.jar in the CLASSPATH or BOOTCLASSPATH.

The Linker

The linker is simply a Java program that reads class files, starting with an entry (main) class, and links them into a single binary file that is sent to the RCX. Only those classes that have direct or indirect static dependencies from the entry class are linked. There is still room for more memory optimization by excluding unused methods, and so forth.

The linker and the VM agree in advance about certain special classes, such as java/lang/Object and special (native) method signatures, such as long currentTimeMillis(). Special classes are listed in the file common\Classes.db and special method signatures in common\Signatures.db. This tells the linker how it should identify certain classes and signatures so the VM can find them. For example, the class java.lang.Object might always be identified by the number zero, whereas user classes are given variable identities.

Modifying and Recompiling the Firmware

As leJOS is an open source project, users can (and are encouraged to) modify the firmware and APIs to improve the system or shape it to their particular needs. One of the hurdles many users encounter while attempting to recompile leJOS has to do with installing a C cross-compiler for the RCX, especially under Windows.

The recommended approach for setting up a Gnu C compiler (GCC) cross-compilation environment for the Hitachi H8300 processor is to visit *http://h8300-hms.sourceforge.net/* and follow the instructions outlined there.

Savvy UNIX users might want to install the cross-compiler on their own. You can do so by downloading binutils-2.9.1 and gcc-2.8.1 from *www.gnu.org /software/software.html*. Installation of binutils and GCC is typical of other Gnu software:

```
./configure --target=h8300-hitachi-hms --prefix=/usr/local
make
su
make install
```

Additional information can be found in the documentation included with leJOS (docs\hacking\H8300_X_COMPILER).

leJOS also needs to be set up to find GCC. This is achieved by creating or modifying a file named Makefile.config in the root directory of your leJOS installation. You can also copy the Makefile.config.renameme file into Makefile.config. The defaults provided there may or may not work for you. Assuming that your GCC and binutils configuration target and prefix are those given previously, your Makefile.config file should contain:

```
BINDIR=/usr/local/bin
BINPREFIX=h8300-hitachi-hms-
```

You also need to download a small C development environment, librcx. This can be found at Kekoa Proudfoot's home page at *http://graphics.stanford.edu/~kekoa/rcx/tools.html.*

Follow the instructions outlined in the readme file of librcx. Then, set the LIBRCX_HOME environment variable so that it contains the path to the directory where librcx was installed.

At this point, you are ready to build an image of the firmware. One way to do this is to go to the leJOS installation directory and run:

```
make clean; make all
```

Another is to go into the rcx_impl directory, and run:

```
make clean; make
```

In either case, you should end up with a new copy of the file bin/tinyvm.srec or bin/lejos.srec. This file can be downloaded to the RCX using lejosfirmdl or any other publicly available RCX firmware downloader.

Adding Native Methods

leJOS supports native methods, as long as there is only one implementation of a particular native method signature. For example, consider the method System.currentTimeMillis(). Its existence restricts other classes from having their own native currentTimeMillis() method. Other classes may declare such a method, but it will behave exactly as System.currentTimeMillis(). That is, leJOS only considers the signature of native methods, but not the classes where they are declared.

Note:

Overloading of native methods was not allowed in version 1.0.0beta3, but this capability has since been added.

To define a new native method in leJOS, you should follow these steps:

1. Declare your native method.
2. Add a method entry to common\Signatures.db

3. Add the native method implementation to Rcx_impl\Native.c, unix_impl\Nativeemul.c, and so on.
4. Recompile the VM and the linker.

Method signatures listed in common\Signatures.db closely follow Java class file convention. Each entry is a method name followed by argument types in parentheses and a return type. Types are coded, as indicated in Table 12–1.

Table 12-1 Codes for Data Types

Code	Type
B	byte
S	short
I	int
J	long
Z	boolean
V	void
Float	float
D	double
L<className>;	reference
[<type>	array

For example, the entry:

```
assertEQ(Ljava/lang/String;II)V
```

has the following signature in Java:

```
void assertEQ (String[], int, int);
```

To write the native method implementation in C, it's probably best to look at how other methods are implemented. The file rcx_impl/native.c has a function named dispatch_native, which is given, among its arguments, a method signature and a pointer to the parameter stack for the native method invocation. The method signature is a number that can be compared against constants automatically generated at build time into vmsrc/specialsignatures.h. You will find that the names of these constants match the signatures defined in Common\Signatures.db. (The linker also takes advantage of a similarly generated Java file, and that is how byte code is resolved to refer to native methods.)

Return values are pushed into the stack using the push_word or push_ref macros. Note that stack operations need to be executed precisely or the RCX may crash or hang.

The implementation of Thread.currentThread, for example, is given here:

```
void dispatch_native (TWOBYTES signature, STACKWORD
*paramBase) {
  switch (signature) {
    ...
    case currentThread_4_5Ljava_3lang_3Thread_2:
      push_ref(ptr2ref(currentThread));
      return;
    ...
  }
}
```

Note:

These guidelines may change in future versions of leJOS, so to emphasize, check the source code of the version you are using.

Portability of leJOS

Even though leJOS was written specifically as an RCX firmware replacement, the possibility that it could be ported to other small devices was always a design consideration. leJOS is portable in as much as its C source is portable (given that its Java code is inherently portable in theory). Even though leJOS is better compiled with GCC, it should be possible to compile it with other C compilers after a few tweaks here and there.

leJOS has already been ported to other devices to some extent. The emulation environment (lejos-emul) is essentially leJOS running on a UNIX platform. This is why there is a Unix_impl directory similar to the Rcx_impl directory, with its own set of native method implementations. Additionally, there is a Gameboy_impl directory, which at one point was compiling under the Gameboy Development Kit (GBDK). Further linker additions, APIs, and other tweaks are needed to get leJOS to run real programs on a Gameboy, however.

To port leJOS to other devices, the following steps are recommended:

1. Create a directory named <deviceName>_impl, much like Rcx_impl or Gameboy_impl.
2. In your new device directory, create a file named platform_config.h containing macros and constants required by leJOS.
3. Write implementations for all functions defined in Vmsrc\Platform_hooks.h. Note that one of those functions is dispatch_native. (See the section on adding native methods.)
4. Create a main.c file that contains the VM initialization sequence for your platform (which is explained later).
5. Write a Makefile for your device similar to those found in Rcx_impl, Unix_impl, and so on.
6. Make device-specific additions to the linker, as needed.

The platform_config.h file requires typedefs for JBYTE, JSHORT, JINT, TWOBYTES and FOURBYTES. It also requires macros for converting pointers into the STACKWORD type, and vice versa, plus a macro to obtain the system time in milliseconds. It's very important to define the LITTLE_ENDIAN variable as 0 or 1 based on the byte order of the platform. There isn't any formal documentation listing these macros, but it's a safe bet that you will find all the required ones in Unix_impl\Dump _configuration.c, (a program that automatically generates Unix_impl \Platform_config.h to support various UNIX systems).

Your main.c file is another critical part of the port. It should contain the VM initialization sequence, which is roughly as follows:

```
// Tell leJOS where the linked binary image is
install_binary (linkedBinaryPointer);
// (Re)initialize binary
initialize_binary();
// Initialize memory for object allocation
init_memory (startPointer, sizeIn2ByteWords);
// Initialize special exceptions
init_exceptions();
// Create the boot thread (bootThread is a special global
variable)
bootThread = (Thread *) new_object_for_class
(JAVA_LANG_THREAD);
// Initialize the threading module.
init_threads();
// Start/prepare boot thread. Sets thread state to
STARTED,
```

```
// which in the case of bootThread, means main will be
scheduled.
if (!init_thread (bootThread))
{
   // Failure message here
}
// Execute the bytecode interpreter (loops indefinitely)
engine();
```

Again, variations are required if, say, you can rerun a program before the VM exits. Check Rcx_impl\Main.c and Unix_impl\Tvmemul.c for variations on this pattern and the latest implementation requirements.

Regarding additions to the linker, they are normally device specific. Start by looking at jtools\js\tinyvm\TinyVM.java and go from there. In the case of the RCX, the linker creates a binary file and then invokes another program in charge of downloading the binary file to the RCX. To run a linked binary under UNIX, on the other hand, you can simply dump the binary into a file, as the following example demonstrates:

```
lejos -o linkage.bin MyClass
```

Use lejosrun to run it.

To summarize, in the simplest loading scenario (e.g., UNIX), it's feasible to pass the binary file path as a parameter to the VM before it starts. In a more complicated scenario (e.g., RCX), the binary file should be sent via IR link to the firmware while it's running and should override previously downloaded binaries. In what is perhaps the most complicated scenario (e.g., Gameboy), both the VM and the binary need to be linked into a single (ROM) program. In this last scenario, you could modify the linker code to generate a C file declaring an array with every single byte of the linked binary file. It would then compile the generated C file and link it with the rest of the VM. The full linkage would basically be the Java program plus its own private VM.

PARTS AND KITS

Appendix A

The purpose of this appendix is to list parts that might be of interest to LEGO MINDSTORMS hobbyists. Most of these parts are not carried by local toy stores, so you will probably have a better chance of obtaining these by ordering direct. For those parts that are no longer available, try eBay or Brinklink (Appendix D). LUGNet is another great resource for obtaining sets. you can use the Set Reference to find sets using the reference number, then view a list of people who own the kit and would like to sell it.

LEGO Shop At Home

- Telephone: 800-453-4652
- Internet: *http://shop.lego.com*

Ultimate Accessory Set (3801) $49.99

Ultimate Builders Set (3800) $59.99

Remote Control (9738) $19.99

The LEGO IR remote control is used for interacting with the RCX brick (and even possibly the IR tower using leJOS). The remote can control robot functions directly with the LEGO RCX firmware, or it can be custom programmed using leJOS. This remote control is also included in the Ultimate Accessory Set.

Micromotor (5119) $9.99

The Micromotor is a very small motor, approximately 4 × 4 × 4 studs in size. For such a tiny motor it is amazingly powerful. The shaft of the motor rotates very slowly, at about one rotation every 2.5 seconds. The electric brick connects to the underside of the motor, so the motor shaft generally faces up and down (Figure A–1a). There are also two adapter pieces that clip onto the motor, allowing it to attach to a brick sideways (Figure A–1b).

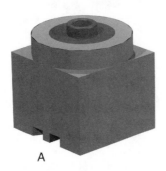

A

B

Figure A–1   Micromotor.

Tip:

You can place the Micromotor on top of a wire brick attached to another motor, allowing two motors to rotate from one output port. It might be a good idea to adjust the power of the output to full, however, and decrease power to other motors to keep the motors balanced.

Solar Cell (9912) $35.00

This is useful if you want to experiment with solar energy.

Capacitor (9916) $15.00

This is normally used with the solar cell to store power and then release it in a strong burst, much like a rechargable battery.

RCX Brick (9709) $119.99

It's possible to order a single RCX brick; however it's probably a better value to order the entire RIS 2.0 kit for approximately $80 more.

1.5 Upgrade Kit (3803) $24.99

Use this kit to upgrade your Robotics Invention System 1.0 kit (#9719). It includes a new Constructopedia with step-by-step instructions to build three inventions, the 1.5 version of the software, and additional elements.

2.0 Upgrade Kit (3805) $19.99

This is an upgrade to the new Robotics Invention System 2.0 software that is compatible with the RIS 1.5 kit.

The Barcode Multiset (8479)

This kit includes the Code Pilot, as described in Chapter 1, "Meet MIND-STORMS." It allows a monster truck to be built, which integrates the code pilot (not available from the Web site as of this writing).

Chassis Pack (5222) $16.99

This kit contains 137 parts for building a steerable chassis.

CyberMaster (8482)

CyberMaster is no longer available for order on LEGO Shop at Home, however if you want to obtain a set you can try using Bricklink, LUGNet or an online auction such as eBay.

Droid Developer Kit (9748) $39.99

Dark Side Developer Kit (9754) $99.99

Exploration Mars (9736) $49.99

Extreme Creatures (9732) $50

RoboSports (9730) $50

Vision Command (9731) $49.99

Robotics Discovery Set (9735) $150

Pitsco LEGO Dacta

- Telephone: 800-362-4308
- Online shopping: *www.pldstore.com*
- Information: *www.pitsco.com*

Pitsco sells educational LEGO kits, which they distribute under the LEGO Dacta line of toys. LEGO Dacta is meant to be marketed to schools, but there is nothing preventing home LEGO users from purchasing their kits online.

IR Tower Cable for Macintosh (W4119830) $15.00

This cable allows a serial (non-USB) IR tower to connect to a Macintosh computer.

Sound Element (W779885) $10.95

A buzzer, somewhat redundant because of the RCX speaker.

Lamp (W970005) $10

A small light that connects to a wire brick.

Lamps and Fittings (W779848) $25

Three lamps, three reflectors, and three enclosures.

RCX 1.0 Adapter (W979833) $20.00

The adapter for the RCX 1.0 brick allows it to run from household electricity rather than from batteries.

Touch Switch (W779888) $18.50

A touch sensor switch with two positions (on–off).

Touch Sensor (W779911) $11.95

Standard RIS sensor.

Temperature Sensor (W979889) $27.50

The LEGO temperature sensor reads temperatures from –20° C to +50° C.

Angle Sensor (W979891) $16.50

The name is a bit of a misnomer, because it counts rotations, not angles. This sensor is also included in the Ultimate Accessory Pack.

Light Sensor (W779758) $22.00

Robolab Starter Set (W979780) $330.00

Team Challenge USB Pack (W990655) $230.00

Cities and Transportation Set (W979723) $115.00

Amusement Park Set (W979725) $115.00

Intelligent House Building Set (W979795) $105.00

Pneumatics I Kit (W979617) $32.00

Pneumatics is the use of air pressure to create a controlled force. This kit is a low-cost introduction to pneumatics. The kit includes a two-way pneumatic cylinder, a pneumatic valve, a hand pump, and tubing (75 parts).

Pneumatics II Kit (W979633) $100.00

This is a slightly more expensive kit that works much better with LEGO MINDSTORMS. The kit includes two large cylinders, a small cylinder, two small pumps, three pneumatic valves, an air tank, and parts for a motorized air compressor and a motorized pneumatic switch (208 parts).

Technology Resource Set (W979609) $230.00

This massive kit contains a wealth of parts including two large pneumatic cylinders, two large hand pumps, two pneumatic valves, T-tubes, and flexible pneumatic tubing. It also includes parts for rack and pinion gears (1,733 parts).

Control Lab Serial Interface (W979751) $270

Allows eight actuators, four active sensors, and four passive sensors to connect to a PC.

LogIT Sensors

- Ordering: *www.pldstore.com*
- Information: *www.dcpmicro.com*

LogIT sensors can be ordered from Pitsco LEGO Dacta. To view all the sensors, go to the online store (*www.pldstore.com*) and select ROBOLAB ➤ LEGO MINDSTORMS ➤ ROBOLAB Components ➤ DCP Sensors.

LEGO-DCP Sensor Adapter (W779917) $55.00

This adapter allows DCP sensors to connect to an RCX input port.

Voltage Sensor (W990252) $55.00

This sensor measures ±25 volts DC; resistance over probes: 410 ohms.

Protemp Sensor (W990249) $55.00

This sensor measures –30° C to +130° C.

Humidity Sensor (W990250) $195.00

This sensor measures 0 to 100% relative humidity over a temperature range of –20° C to +80° C.

Motion Sensor (W990248) $105.00

This sensor measures 360-degree rotation; 340 degrees measured.

Air Pressure Sensor (W990253) $145.00

This sensor measures 0–200 kPa (approx. 0–30 psi)

Sound Sensor (W990247) $80.00

This sensor measures 50–100 dB; frequency response is nominal A-weighted.

pH Sensor Adapter (W990251) $80.00

This adapter works with pH electrodes with an output of 59.1 mV per unit of pH at 25°.

DCP Sensor Pack (W990254) $675.00

This pack includes all six sensors just listed and the pH sensor adapter.

Note:

Additional sensors can be found at DCP Micro that do not work with ROBOLAB 2.5. None of these sensors have drivers for leJOS, but it should not pose much of a problem to write them. All sensors require the RCX adapter to connect (see DCP Web site above).

Mindsensors

- *www.geocities.com/mindsensors*

Mindsensors is a small company that sells custom MINDSTORMS sensors and actuators. Despite the small size of the company, some of the products are quite unique and don't seem to be offered anywhere else on the MINDSTORMS market.

Warning:

This company is in no way affiliated with LEGO, and being a small company there are no guarantees about the product availability or quality. However, it does look authentic and the reason it is mentioned is to give users a chance to obtain the distance sensor from Chapter 9, "Proximity Detection," without assembling it.

Distance Sensor (Complete) $41.00

Distance Sensor (Interface Only) $29.00

(Shipping $4.00 United States, $6.00 Canada, $20.00 International)

This distance sensor is almost identical to the sensor from Chapter 8, "Navigation with Rotation Sensors," except it appears to use miniature surface mount technology (SMT) assembly, so it is only one brick tall!

Infra Red Reflection Based Obstacle Detector $14.00

(Shipping $2.00 United States, $4.00 Canada $13.00 International)

This sensor is based on the same principle of the obstacle detector described early in Chapter 9. It uses IR light to detect an object within 20 to 30 cm of the sensor.

Active Sensor Multiplexer $29.00

(Shipping $4.00 United States, $7.00 Canada, $20.00 International)

Most sophisticated robot designs need more than three sensor inputs, so it would be useful to overcome the limits of the RCX brick. The Active Sensor Multiplexer lets you connect an extra three actively powered sensors to a single input port. In theory, three multiplexers could give a total of nine sensor inputs for a single RCX. Apparently it will work with light sensors, touch sensors, and rotation sensors. I somehow doubt it would work with rotation sensors because the RCX must continually monitor the rotation sensor to count the increments. It would probably lose count while another sensor was active. The compass sensor definitely works with the multiplexer because it works just like a light sensor. The distance sensor should also work, although the program would need to leave it powered for enough time to charge the capacitor.

Passive Sensor Multiplexer $9.00

(Shipping $4.00 United States, $6.00 Canada, $20.00 International)

This simple multiplexer allows three passive sensors (e.g., touch sensors) to be connected to a single sensor port.

Servo Motor Controller $36 plus shipping

Servo motors are special motors that move to a specific position rather than just rotating around and around. They are frequently used in remote control airplanes because they are ideal for controlling wing flaps and ailerons. The servo motor controller offered by Mindsensors allows one or two servo motors to be controlled by a single controller. The actual commands are sent from the RCX brick to the controller via IR. Power to the controller may be supplied by the RCX brick or a separate battery pack.

ELECTRONICS PROJECTS

Topics in this Appendix

- Electronics Sources
- Distance Sensor Parts
- Compass Sensor Parts
- Compass Sensor Circuit Building

Appendix B

Electronics Sources

The following companies can be contacted to obtain the generic parts for your electronics (i.e., everything but the GP2D12 sensor and the 6100/1655 compass sensor). Unfortunately, I wasn't able to find all the electronics parts from one distributor, so you will probably need to use at least two of these suppliers, which are listed by region.

Europe

Farnell
- *www.farnell.com*

RS Components International
- *www.rs-components.com*

Conrad Electronics
- *www.conrad.com*

North America

Digikey
- Telephone: 800-344-4539
- *www.digikey.com*

Digikey is by far the best North American distributor for obtaining the parts required in these projects. They are the only place I could find that carried the ZTX718 transistor for the distance sensor. The service department was friendly and helpful. Their Web site allows you to search the entire inventory of parts and pull-up data sheets. The speed of delivery was amazing—I ordered my parts one afternoon and received them before noon the next day!

Note:

A $5 handling fee is added to orders under $25 U.S., so it pays to consolidate your orders.

Electro Sonic
- Telephone: 800-56-SONIC
- *www.e-sonic.com*

Mouser
- Telephone: 800-346-6873
- *www.mouser.com*

International

Farnell
- *www.farnell.com*

RS Components International
- *www.rs-components.com*

Note:

Transistors and ICs are enclosed in a shell, which the industry calls a package or case (the package is superficial and does not affect the internal circuitry). When ordering, try to get the TO-92 package for transistors when possible. TO-92 is good for breadboard work because the leads are long enough to go into the breadboard holes.

Complex ICs are often contained in a dual in-line package (looks kind of like a beetle), such as the LM324 used in Chapter 10, "Navigation with a Compass Sensor." The TC55RP5002 voltage regulator comes in either the SOT-23A, SOT-89 or TO-92 package. The SOT packages are very tiny and hard to work with, and they don't contain leads long enough to plug into the breadboard. If they are the only components you can find, however, then you can solder wires to them instead. Once again, your best bet is the TO-92 package.

Distance Sensor Parts

The following companies carry the GP2D12 sensor. Table B–1 lists all the standard electronics components for the interface of the circuit, which can be ordered from the companies listed earlier.

Europe

Conrad

- *www.conrad.com*

The GP2D12 distance sensor can be ordered from Conrad using part number 0185309.

North America

Acroname

- *www.acroname.com*

The GP2D12 distance sensor can be ordered from Acroname using part number R48-IR12. Acroname also ships internationally.

Table B-1 Distance Sensor Parts List		
Schematic ID	*Primary Part*	*Alternates*
D1	1N5819	
D2	1N4148	

Table B-1 Distance Sensor Parts List (continued)		
D3	1N4148	
U1	LT1121IZ-5	TC55RP5002
U2	GP2D12	
Q1	ZTX718	NTE383
Q2	NTE234	BC558B or NTE17
Q3	NTE199	BC548B or NTE16
C1	1000µF	
C2	100µF	
R1	4.7K	
R2	330K	
R3	82K	
R4	47K	
R5	1K	

Note:

The tolerance for resistors should be ±5% or lower. The capacitors can be any voltage (e.g., 16, 25, or 50 volts).

Note:

Keep in mind if you use the alternates listed above the pins will be different, so they must be inserted into the circuit differently from the diagrams in Chapter 9.

Compass Sensor Parts

The following companies sell a compass sensor that can be connected to the compass interface described in Chapter 10. Table B–2 lists all the standard electronics components for the interface of the circuit, which can be ordered from the companies listed earlier.

Europe

Pewatron
- Telephone: 00 41-01-8 30 29 44
- *www.pewatron.com*

When ordering from Pewatron, make sure to specify the damped version of the 6100 sensor, otherwise the compass bearing will bounce around too much when the robot turns. The 6070 will also work but it does not provide as great a resolution of angles.

North America

Dinsmore Instrument Company
- Telephone: 810-744-1330
- *www.dinsmoresensors.com*

The 1655 Analog Compass sensor is identical in design to the Pewatron 6100 compass, however the construction doesn't appear to be as precise as the Pewatron. The 1525 will also work in this interface but it does not provide as great a resolution of angles as the 1655 sensor.

Table B-2 Compass Sensor Parts

Schematic ID	Quantity	Primary Part	Alternates
U1	2	LM324	LM358
U2	2	LM78L05	
C1	2	47uF	
C2	2	0.1uF	
C3	2	0.1uF	
R1	2	56K	
R2	2	100K	

Table B-2 Compass Sensor Parts (continued)

R3	2	1K
R4	2	560K
D1–D6	12	1N4148

Note:

The LM324 quad amplifier can be replaced by a LM358 dual amplifier. The advantage of the LM358 is that it is almost half as large as the LM324, but it is a little harder to find. The LM358 pin out is different from the LM324, so use the schematic shown in Figure B–1 as a replacement.

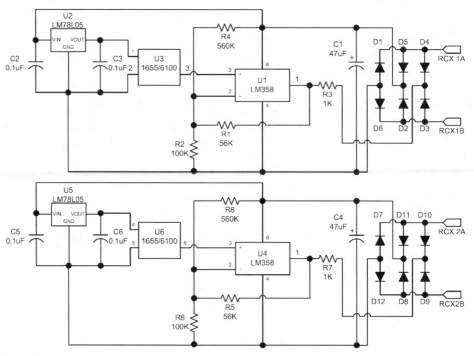

Figure B–1   Alternate schematic for LM358.

Compass Sensor Circuit Building

This section describes several alternatives for permanently mounting the compass sensor circuit.

Experimentor Board

The easiest way to transfer your circuit from a breadboard to a permanent setting is to use an experimentor board. The experimentor 300 PC board is a low-cost, copper contact board used to permanently solder a circuit (available at most electronics stores). The layout is identical to a breadboard so you can transfer the parts over by using the row and column numbers shared by both (Figure B–2a). Components are individually soldered to the underside of the board (Figure B–2b) so you will need a soldering iron for this solution. One of the disadvantages of this method is the large footprint of the finished circuit.

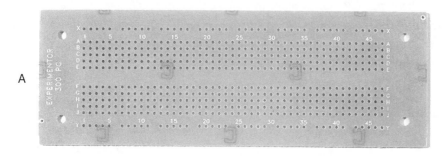

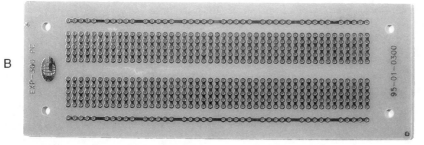

Figure B–2   The PC experimentor board.

Note:

The experimentor 300 PC board does not contain two separate positive/negative rows; therefore you will need to sever these rows in half so the two

halves of the circuit remain separated. This can be done with a utility knife by scratching away the copper surface.

Punchboard

Another alternative for mounting the compass circuit is using Punchboard (the same method described in Chapter 9, "Proximity Detection," for the distance sensor). This method requires a wire-wrap tool to connect the electronic components underneath the board. Figures B–3 and B–4 show the top and bottom plan for the compass circuit. A completed picture of the circuit can be seen assembled in Figure B–5.

Note:

This schematic only shows half of the circuit; the other half is identical, only rotated 180 degrees. Also, the wires to Pins 1, 2, 3 on the compass sensor connect to Pins 4, 5, 6 instead for the second half of the interface circuit.

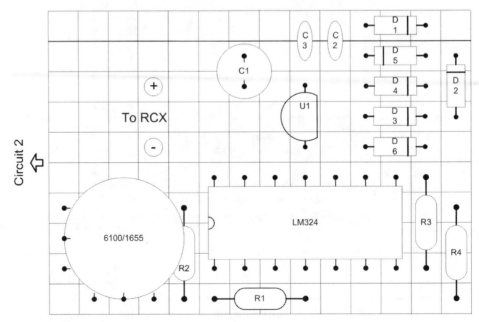

Figure B–3   Top view of component placement.

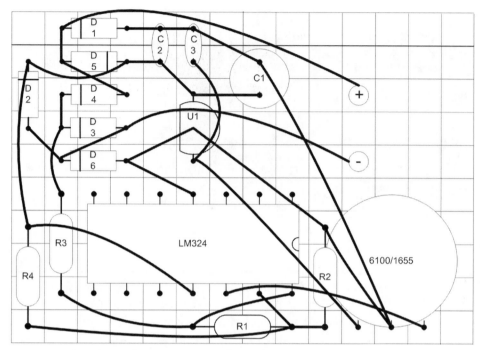

Figure B–4 Connecting the components underneath.

Figure B–5 Assembled half circuit.

When the circuit is complete it can be housed in a simple LEGO structure (Figure B–6). I used the 6 × 10 gray plate as a base and surrounded it with black beams. This can be capped off with more plates to hold it in place.

Figure B–6   Using LEGO bricks to enclose the circuit.

Note:

If you want to reduce the footprint of this circuit you can optionally use two levels for the circuit. Simply assemble the two halves of the circuit on separate 11 × 12 circuit boards and stack them on top of each other.

Etched PC Board

For those who want perfection, it is possible to etch the circuit into a PC board. This requires some specialized tools, including an acid bath, as well as some specialized knowledge. Figure B–7 shows the mask used for etching the circuit.

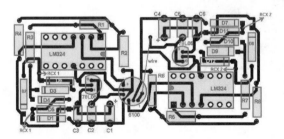

Figure B–7   PC-board. (Circuit designed by Claude Baumann.)

Note:

This circuit can be found in color at: www.convict.lu/Jeunes/ CompassSensor2.htm.

UTILITIES

Topics in this Appendix

- leJOS Binaries
- leJOS Utilities
- LEGO Utilities

Appendix C

leJOS Binaries

So far in this book we have only dealt with three binaries included with leJOS: lejosc, lejos, and lejosfirmdl. However, there are currently nine command-line programs that can provide additional information about your leJOS program. The following sections describe these files and their usage.

lejosc.exe

The file is used to compile Java code into a binary file, as follows:

```
javac -verbose MyClass.java
```

Its options are listed in Table C–1.

Table C-1 lejosc Options

Switch	Description
-g	Generate all debugging info
-g:none	Generate no debugging info

Table C-1 lejosc Options (continued)	
-g:{lines,vars,source}	Generate only some debugging info, depending on what is chosen, (e.g., -g:lines)
-O	Optimize; may hinder debugging or enlarge class file
-nowarn	Generate no warnings
-verbose	Output messages about what the compiler is doing
-deprecation	Output source locations where deprecated APIs are used
-classpath <path>	Specify where to find user class files
-sourcepath <path>	Specify where to find input source files
-bootclasspath <path>	Override location of bootstrap class files
-extdirs <dirs>	Override location of installed extensions
-d <directory>	Specify where to place generated class files
-encoding <encoding>	Specify character encoding used by source files
-target <version>	Generate class files for specific VM version

lejos.exe

lejos.exe (called the *linker*) reads the class files and converts them into a single binary file for the Hitachi processor. It then uploads the resulting file to the RCX brick through the IR tower.

To dump the resulting file to disk (and not upload it to the RCX), use the -o switch with a filename, as follows (see Table C–2):

```
lejos -o MyFile.bin MyClass
```

Table C-2 lejos.exe Options	
Switch	*Description*
-o <path>	Create a binary and dump it to a path (without downloading)
-verbose[=<n>]	Print class and signature information

lejosfirmdl.exe

This file is used to download the leJOS firmware to the RCX brick, as follows (see Table C–3):

```
lejosfirmdl -f
```

Table C-3 lejosfirmdl Options

Switch	Detail
-f	Fast download mode (for serial only).

lejosrun.exe

Any binary file (e.g., a file created using lejos -o) can be uploaded to the RCX using lejosrun (see Table C–4).

Table C-4 lejosrun.exe Options

Switch	Detail
--debug	Show debug output, mostly raw bytes
-f --fast	Use fast 4× downloading
-s --slow	Use slow 1× downloading (default)
--tty=TTY	Assume tower connected to TTY
--tty=usb	Assume tower connected to USB
-h --help	Display help and exit

emu-lejos.exe

The leJOS Java code can be executed on processors other than the RCX! Emu-lejos is the equivalent of lejos, except emu-lejos creates a linked binary file that is compatible with running on your PC processor (likely an Intel) rather than the Hitachi processor of the RCX. Its options are listed in Table C–5.

Creating a linked binary file from a class file is similar to lejos:

```
emu-lejos -o MyProg.bin MyClass
```

Table C-5 emu-lejos.exe Options

Switch	Detail
-o <path>	Create a binary and dump it to a path (without downloading)
-verbose[=<n>]	Print class and signature information

emu-lejosrun.exe

This program is used for executing the linked binary file on your PC (as opposed to executing it on the RCX). Instead of activating motors and reading sensors, however, you will just see the opcodes that are called to the Hitachi processor. You can also use the -v option to get a more detailed explanation of the ROM calls (see Table C–6).

```
emu-lejosrun -v MyProg.bin
```

Table C-6 emu-lejosrun.exe Options

Switch	Detail
-v	Print descriptions of opcode calls

lejosp.exe

This class is similar to javap.exe—the Java Class File Disassembler. It outputs all the members of a class (methods, variables, and inner classes). By default it only outputs public, package, and protected members. Its options are listed in Table C–7.

Table C-7 lejosp Options	
Switch	*Detail*
-c	Disassemble the code
-classpath <pathlist>	Specify where to find user class files
-extdirs <dirs>	Override location of installed extensions
-help	Print help message containing list of switches
-J<flag>	Pass <flag> directly to the runtime system
-l	Print line number and local variable tables
-public	Show only public classes and members
-protected	Show protected and public classes and members
-package	Show package, protected, and public classes and members (default)
-private	Show all classes and members
-s	Print internal type signatures
-bootclasspath <pathlist>	Override location of class files loaded by the bootstrap class loader
-verbose	Print stack size, number of locals, and args for methods. If verifying, print reasons for failure
-b	Backward compatibility with javap in JDK 1.1

lejosp1.exe

This is a special version of lejosp for the JDK 1.1 (see "lejosp").

lejosc1.exe

This is a special version of lejosc made specifically for the JDK 1.1 (see "lejosc").

emu-dump.exe

This program outputs information about a lejos binary file (created using lejos -o). This is primarily useful for leJOS developers for debugging purposes.

leJOS Utilities

The leJOS community has contributed many helpful tools to aid with leJOS development. Some of these are listed here.

RCX Direct-Mode

- *http://rcxtools.sourceforge.net*

RCXDirectMode is an excellent program for controlling an RCX brick. This program is useful when building a robot because it allows testing of the movement of parts without writing and compiling code along the way. The excellent GUI can control all aspects of the RCX, including motor speed, checking sensors, speaker, and confirming the level of remaining battery power.

RCX Download

- *http://rcxtools.sourceforge.net*

RCXDownload automatically sets the JDK and leJOS CLASSPATHS, compiles the chosen Java source, shows the compiler messages, and is able to link and upload compiled classes and the leJOS firmware. However, if you have a good IDE installed, like the one in this book, this software is largely unnecessary.

Bricks Music Studio

- *www.aga.it/~guy/lego.htm*

This is an excellent little program that converts .midi or even .wav files into leJOS code, ready to upload to the RCX (Windows only).

Text to LCD Display

- *http://rcxtools.sourceforge.net*

This tool displays words as they will appear on the LCD window of the RCX. It's actually a small Java applet on the title screen of the Web page, but still very cool.

leJOS Visual Interface

- *http://lvi.sourceforge.net*

This is a nice GUI developed in Java. It's not as full featured as JCreator but it may be useful for non-Windows users.

leJOS Emulators

- *http://sourceforge.net/projects/rcxemul*
- *http://simlink.sourceforge.net*

These are currently two projects in development to create RCX emulators. The first, RCX Emulator, uses a low-level strategy that simulates the RCX ROM. Simlink, on the other hand, is leJOS only and intercepts motor and sensor calls at the API level. Both plan to use the Rossum simulator to simulate a robot environment.

LEGO Utilities

Several programs have been developed by the LEGO community in general, independent from the MINDSTORMS scene. Among them are several useful computer-aided design (CAD) programs.

LDraw

- *www.ldraw.org*

The very concept of LDraw is revolutionary. LEGO is great, but designs created with LEGO are sadly not permanent. There eventually comes a time when you must recycle LEGO parts from a model, which can be a painful thing to do, especially if it is a good robot. This program allows you to build a three-dimensional model of your robot and save it to disk. You can then tear your model apart and feel good about it, then rebuild it months later. The sharing power of this program is also amazing, given the popularity of LEGO MINDSTORMS with Internet users. This program allows you to immortalize your LEGO creations and spread the plans around the globe.

MLCAD

- *http://www.lm-software.com/mlcad/*

This provides an excellent front end for LDraw.

L3P

- *http://home16.inet.tele.dk/hassing/l3p.html*

This program converts an LDraw file into a ready-to-render POV-Ray file.

LEO Cad

- *http://leocad.gerf.org*

This is another LEGO CAD program that uses the same parts library as LDraw.

INTERNET RESOURCES

Topics in this Appendix

- leJOS Resources

- Java Resources

- LEGO Resources

- RCX Resources

- Sensors

- RCX Projects

- Robot Navigation

- Other Hardware

Appendix D

This appendix is for those who are curious about what's out there for leJOS and the RCX—and there's a lot! As is typical of the Internet, each site will link you to several other sites that are of equal interest. Some of these sites have already been mentioned in the book, and others are helpful if you want to go deeper into certain topics.

leJOS Resources

leJOS Home Page

- *http://lejos.sourceforge.net*

This is the main headquarters for all things leJOS. It even includes a section containing plans of robots that users have programmed with leJOS.

leJOS Project Development Home Page

- *http://sourceforge.net/projects/lejos*

Sourceforge is where the programmers and developers of leJOS meet.

Java Resources

Sun's Official Java Site

- *http://java.sun.com*

If you aren't very familiar with Java, the official Java site is a great starting point to seek out more information.

LEGO Resources

LEGO Users Group (LUGNet)

- *www.lugnet.com*

LUGNet is the central point on the Internet for all things LEGO. The newsgroups are the focal point of this site, which contain topics on everything from CAD modeling to programming robotics with Java.

Bricklink

- *www.bricklink.com*

Bricklink is a useful online store for buying and selling LEGO kits.

RCX Resources

RCX Internals

- *http://graphics.stanford.edu/~kekoa/rcx*

This site includes a complete description of the internals of the RCX and the IR tower. Without this information there would be no third-party platforms such as leJOS.

Analysis of the RCX

- *www.rcx.ic24.net/analysis.htm*

This is another analysis of the RCX that is more hardware oriented.

Sensors and Actuators

Distance Sensor

- *www.philohome.com*

This site is the source of the Distance Sensor project described in Chapter 9. It also contains plans for many other interesting MINDSTORMS projects.

Compass Sensor

- *www.convict.lu/Jeunes/RoboticsIntro.htm*

This is one of the better sites on the Internet for people interested in taking the RCX to the next level. It contains many sensor plans, as well as interesting project descriptions. (By the way, it is not run by convicts! Convict roughly means community in French.)

Homebrew RCX Sensors

- *www.plazaearth.com/usr/gasperi/lego.htm*

This is one of the largest central hubs for homemade sensors available on the Internet. If you are looking for a unique type of sensor, look here first.

Resistor Color Bands

- *www.micro-ohm.com/colorcode/rescolor.html*

This is an excellent online utility for reading the color bands of resistors.

Lasers

- *www.blueneptune.com/~maznliz/marius/rcxlaser.shtml*
- *www.inchlab.com/laser_brick.htm*

A couple of plans for RCX-controlled laser actuators. great for allowing your robots to hunt each other!

RCX Projects

Rubik's Cube Solver (and More)

- *http://jpbrown.i8.com*

This site contains some first-rate RCX project descriptions. Here you can find anything from a rowboat to a glider RCX project to the famous cube solver.

LEGO Robotics Network

- *www.lego.com/robotics*

This is the official LEGO Robotics Network. It contains some interesting news on the RCX scene.

Robot Navigation

Mobile Robot Positioning

- *www-personal.engin.umich.edu/~johannb/position.htm*

This site contains an Adobe Acrobat document that details the latest achievements in dead reckoning (up until about 1995). This is probably one of the most detailed documents on dead reckoning and robot navigation around.

Dead Reckoning Contest

- *www.seattlerobotics.org/encoder/200108/using_a_pid.html*

This site is of interest because the winner of this contest was an RCX robot that used standard rotation sensors.

Other Hardware

Tower Hobbies

- *www.towerhobbies.com*

This site markets remote control devices, but some of the products (primarily the airplanes) could conceivably be controlled by the RCX brick.

Draganfly

- *www.draganfly.com*

Draganfly sells some interesting flying machines, including remote control airships.

Index

Special Characters

^, 112
||, 112
&&, 112
!=, 112
==, 112

Numbers

1525 Compass Sensor, 365
1655 Compass Sensor, 362
360-Degree Bumper, 186
6070 Compass Sensor, 365
6100 Compass Sensor, 362
64-bit numbers, 105
9-volt Battery, 14

A

AA Batteries, 14
Abstract Class, 89

Abstract Window Toolkit, 432
AC Adapter Port, 7, 496
Accessing ROM Routines, 142
Accordion Arm (*see* Extending Arm)
Accuracy
   Nonsystematic Error, 246
   Systematic Error, 245
   TimingNavigator, 244
Acidity Sensor (*see* pH Sensor)
Actions, 198
Activating Sensors, 143
Active Sensors, 43
Actuators, 10
Adjacent, 221
Alan Turing, 216
Alkaline Batteries, 14
Alternate Data Transfer, 459–461
Alternate Programming Environments, 78–81
Alternate Programming Languages, 475–483
Alternate Compass Schematic, 506
Amusement Park Set, 33
AND, 112
Angle Measurement, 259–265
Ants (*see* Tunisian Desert Ant)
Antennae, 186